# Developing Thinking and Understanding in Young

*Developing Thinking and Understanding in Young Children* presents a comprehensive and accessible overview of contemporary theory and research about young children's developing thinking and understanding. Throughout this second edition, the ideas and theories presented are enlivened by transcripts of children's activities and conversations taken from practice and contemporary research, helping readers to make links between theory, research and practice. Each chapter also includes ideas for further reading and suggested activities.

Aimed at all those interested in how young children develop through their thoughts and actions, Sue Robson explores:

- theories of cognitive development;
- the social, emotional and cultural contexts of children's thinking;
- children's conceptual development;
- visual thinking;
- approaches to supporting the development of young children's thinking and understanding;
- latest developments in brain science and young children;
- the central roles of play and language in young children's developing thinking.

Including a new chapter on young children's musical thinking, expanded sections on self-regulation, metacognition and creative thinking and the use of video to observe and describe young children's thinking, this book will be an essential read for all students undertaking Early Childhood, Primary PGCE and EYPS courses. Those studying for a Foundation degree in Early Years and Childcare will also find this book to be of interest.

**Sue Robson** is Principal Lecturer in Education, Early Childhood Studies, Froebel College at the University of Roehampton.

# Developing Thinking and Understanding in Young Children

An introduction for students

Second Edition

Sue Robson

 Routledge
Taylor & Francis Group

LONDON AND NEW YORK

First published 2006
by Routledge
2 Park Square, Milton Park, Abingdon, Oxon OX14 4RN

This second edition published 2012

Simultaneously published in the USA and Canada
by Routledge
711 Third Avenue, New York, NY 10017

Routledge is an imprint of the Taylor & Francis Group, an informa business

British Library Cataloguing in Publication Data
A catalogue record for this book is available from the British Library

Library of Congress Cataloging in Publication Data
Robson, Sue.
Developing thinking and understanding in young children : an introduction for
students / Sue Robson. – 2nd ed.
    p. cm.
  Includes bibliographical references and index.
  1. Early childhood education. 2. Thought and thinking–Study and teaching (Early
childhood) 3. Cognition in children. I. Title.
  LB1139.23.R63 2012
  155.4'13–dc23                                            2011031831

ISBN: 978-0-415-60969-2 (hbk)
ISBN: 978-0-415-60971-5 (pbk)
ISBN: 978-0-203-13335-4 (ebk)

Typeset in Galliard
by HWA Text and Data Management, London

MIX
Paper from
responsible sources
FSC
www.fsc.org     FSC® C004839

Printed and bound in Great Britain by the MPG Books Group

# Contents

# List of boxes

# List of figures

# Preface and acknowledgements

The field of early childhood is a vibrant, and dynamic area, cross-disciplinary in outlook and multi-professional in practice. In writing this book I have tried to reflect this richness and diversity, drawing on a variety of disciplines, including early childhood education and care, ethnography, health and psychology, for the contributions they each make to the study of young children's thinking and understanding. I have found myself exploring just about every aspect of young children's development. As a consequence, one of my greatest challenges has been trying to draw some boundaries around the subject. The chief joy of writing has undoubtedly continued to be the opportunity to look more deeply at the thoughts and actions of young children.

In this new edition, every chapter has been completely updated, with the addition of new material, including fifteen additional boxes featuring examples to illustrate ideas. I have tried to reflect some of the developments in policy, practice, theory and research in the five years since the original publication. Some of the changes here reflect the depth of research interest in aspects of cognition, particularly with regard to young children. This is particularly so in the case of Chapter 4, where developments in research in neuroscience continue to enhance our understanding and influence policy and practice. The relationship of biology, cognitive science and education, and the identification of 'mirror neurons' are both considered. Similarly, the very lively research interest in young children's understanding of the mind is evident in Chapters 3 and 5, where executive function, social understanding, theory of mind, self-regulation and metacognition are all considered in greater detail. In particular, the implications of much of this research for how young children's understanding in these areas can be both identified and developed, and the social contexts in which it can be fostered, are explored.

The past five years has seen greater emphasis on eliciting young children's perspectives on their lives, often through innovative methods, and this is explored in Chapter 6, in particular. In Chapter 3, ideas about young children's well-being are considered, again reflecting the growth of interest in this area, for both policy-makers and practitioners. The current emphasis on young children's talk in nurseries and schools is a theme of discussion in Chapter 7, with more extended exploration of the roles of adults in supporting young children's thinking through talk. Approaches to 'teaching' thinking, in particular the part played by creative thinking, is a focus in Chapter 11.

Throughout this new edition, I have tried to reflect developments in our understanding of how children think and learn, including underpinning psychological and sociological perspectives on cognition. The development of ideas about Vygotsky, including activity theory and current ideas about the ZPD, as explored in neo- and post-Vygotskian thinking, and links between Piagetian and information processing ideas on cognition are discussed. In Chapter 8 recent thinking about the role of teaching and telling in young children's concept formation, and young children's understanding of central conceptual ideas about space, number and the Earth are more fully explored than in the first edition. Finally, this second edition has also given me the opportunity to look in more depth at some areas that I had not given sufficient attention to in the original. Inclusion of a new chapter on musical thinking in young children reflects the view that 'music might be one of the most important subjects for general cognitive development' (Geake 2009: 163). There is also more extended exploration of a number of other areas, including ideas about intelligence, magical thinking, memory and metamemory, for example, along with too many others to name here. In every case, the revisions and additions reflect what I hope is my own deeper knowledge and understanding of the topics under discussion.

Throughout this book I make reference to the Froebel Research Fellowship Project 'The Voice of the Child: Ownership and Autonomy in Early Learning'. This project looks at how the thinking of young children aged 3–5 years is supported and developed in early childhood settings, and at the ideas and practices of practitioners working with them. The colleagues with whom I have been privileged to work on the project have forced me, in the most positive way, to try to think as clearly as I can about the area, and I thank them all: Kevin Brehony, Hiroko Fumoto, Sue Greenfield and David Hargreaves, and, most recently, Victoria Rowe. I particularly wish to extend my thanks to Victoria for her enthusiastic response to my suggestion that she write about music and young children in this new edition: her knowledge, understanding and enjoyment shines through, and helps to make this a better book. I am also indebted to all of the practitioners and children who have been involved at different times during the life of this hugely enjoyable project, and I am particularly grateful for their enthusiasm and commitment. I should also like to thank the Froebel Research Committee for their funding of the research project.

The original idea for this book arose out of work on the BA Early Childhood Studies programme at the University of Roehampton. In developing this, I had invaluable help from Deborah Albon and John Griffiths, practitioners and researchers whose own research and experience has taught me a great deal. In addition, I should like to thank Pat Gura and Ann Bridges, and the staff, children and parents of Vanessa Nursery School in the London Borough of Hammersmith and Fulham, for their permission to reproduce material which formed part of the Final Report of the School Improvement Project 'Thinking and Learning Skills', Hammersmith and Fulham, 1997–8.

I should particularly like to thank all of the students whom I have taught, who have helped me to think about children's thinking, especially those whose work is reproduced or referred to here: Lynn Bartlett, Katie Brendon, Philippa Cooper, Jo Dabir-Alai, Sarah Duggan, Lisa Frank, Romina Gor, Lisa Guy, Yvonne Hatton, Joanna Johnson, Samantha McGinley, Kirsty McLelland, Lucy Parker, Frances Pearmain, Nikki Reid, Janet Roberts, Meg Roberts, Sam Segar, Jo Short, Rebecca Shuttleworth, Lynn Skinner, Rachel Spencer, Angela Streek, Kathryn Torres and Esther Whalley. I am also extremely grateful to the children who feature in the observations throughout the book, and for their consent to their ideas, words and actions being recorded. In most cases their names have been changed, apart from where they asked for the observation to keep their own name.

Finally, I want, as always, to give my greatest thanks to my husband, Ken Robson, for his constructive comments on the manuscript, his unfailing encouragement, patience, and timely reminders to back my work up, and to my daughters, Charlotte and Isabella, great thinkers all.

# Chapter 1

# How can we think about young children's thinking?

> Where do the days of the week come from? Do they come from the sun or from the clocks? (Isabella, aged 3.7)

Who would not be intrigued by Isabella's thinking? The puzzling mind of a young child comes through loud and clear in her question, as she tries to understand an everyday (literally!) event. It makes a fitting opening for a book which is about young children as active, persistent thinkers, driven by a desire to make sense and meaning in their lives, to connect what they know and understand to what they do not yet understand. In this first chapter some fundamental, underpinning ideas about thinking are considered, posed as questions which set a context for the book as a whole. What do we mean when we talk about 'thinking' and 'understanding'? What activities might we describe as thinking, and is it different to learning? Do children and adults think in different ways? What parts are played by the environment, and our genetic inheritance, in developing our thinking and understanding? What is the role of memory? In considering these questions links are also made to many other parts of the book, emphasizing a model of thinking as an activity which connects every part of young children's experience.

## What is thinking?

Thinking is a fundamentally human characteristic, an activity in which we all engage, from the moment we are born, and even before. As a child in Fisher (2005: 1) says: 'If we didn't think there'd be no us.' What, though, do we mean when we use the language of thinking, for example, when we say 'I'm thinking about it'? How do we feel when we get a card that says 'thinking of you'? Wilson identifies three different meanings of the word 'think'. First, she suggests, there is an everyday meaning, where think is effectively a synonym for 'believe' or 'suppose'. Second, she suggests we use it as a way of suggesting we are paying attention to something: 'I'm thinking about it...'. The final meaning is the main, though not exclusive, focus here: the special sense of thinking as an 'intellectual/high level process' (Wilson 2000: 6).

White sets out four characteristics of thinking. First, he says, thinking is intentional, it is always '*of* or *about* something, or thinking *that* something is the case' (2002: 101; emphasis in original), which suggests the important role of knowledge and experience for thinking. Second, he says, it is an activity. We engage in it deliberately, it does not happen to us. Sometimes thinking is directed towards an end, and at other times it may be an end in itself. White's third proposal is that thinking employs concepts, whatever the context or activity in which the thinking is happening. His final suggestion is that thinking is a skill. As we shall see later, however, particularly in Chapter 11, and as White himself emphasizes, it is not just a skill, important though this is. Equally important is the development of the disposition to make use of this skill, to want to be a thinker and to enjoy thinking.

What does thinking mean to you? How would you describe it, and what kinds of activities would you include? Practitioners in one nursery identified words such as predicting, representing, recalling, considering, wondering, planning, deciding, modelling and evaluating as useful words related to the practice of thinking. They also suggested other, perhaps initially less likely words, including pretending, playing, picturing and dreaming (Ann Bridges and Pat Gura, in collaboration with the staff, children and parents of Vanessa Nursery School). All of these are important in the context of extending young children's thinking). Let us take three possible words that often come up in discussions about thinking, and consider them in a little more depth: 'intelligence', 'knowing' and 'learning'.

## Intelligence

The idea that thinking is related to intelligence is a very pervasive one. It finds its expression in approaches to intelligence testing and IQ scores, an aspect of measuring individual difference that is considered in more detail in Chapter 6. For the general public 'intelligence' has often assumed the role of a badge of social approval (White 2002).

Defining what we mean by intelligence is, however, tremendously difficult, although this has not stopped people from trying. Francis Galton, developing mental testing in the nineteenth century, saw intelligence as fixed, inherited and underlying all cognitive activity. Those who came after him, including Eysenck and Burt, thus defined it as 'innate, general cognitive ability' (Burt in White 2002:78). This looks very different to Claxton's definition of intelligence as 'knowing what to do when you don't know what to do' (1999a: 4). Claxton's definition has much in common with Perkins *et al.*'s (2000) ideas of 'intelligence in the wild', which focuses on thinking dispositions which may be involved in intelligent behaviour, and how to think in our daily lives. They believe that 'to define intelligence as a matter of ability without honouring the other elements that enliven it is to fail to capture its human spark' (2000: 272). In Chapter 2 a range of theorists is looked at, all of whom have ideas about intelligence. For Piaget, for example, intelligence is about logical reasoning. Sternberg's triarchic theory (1985) proposes three types of intelligence: analytical, creative and practical. Gardner (1983), as we shall see, argues for the existence of multiple intelligences (MI), identifying eight (or even eight and a half) forms of 'intelligence', not just one. These ideas also raise a fundamental question about whether we believe intelligence to be a single ability, or a number of separate abilities.

How we view intelligence will have implications for what we value. Nunes (2005), for example, records the teachers in her studies assessing and defining the children's intelligence almost exclusively in relation to their verbal and literacy ability. In Chapter 6 some of the theoretical perspectives on intelligence are looked at in the context of intelligence testing. Thornton suggests that intelligence is 'the capacity to solve problems and interact with the world in adaptive ways' (2002: 179), a wide-ranging definition that, as she says, views intelligence as the product of all of an individual's knowledge, strategies and 'mental tools'.

## Knowing

Knowing is often seen as a prerequisite to thinking, in that we need to have something to think about, but Duckworth suggests:

> of all the virtues related to intellectual functioning, the most passive is the virtue of knowing the right answer. Knowing the right answer requires no decisions, carries no risks, and makes no demands. It is automatic. It is thoughtless.
>
> (Duckworth 1987: 64)

Gopnik *et al.* (1999) suggest that young children behave in much the same way that adult scientists do, constructing their knowledge about the world, and developing theories such as the children in Box 1.1 have about weight. They often persist in ignoring counterevidence to those theories for some time, as do the children here. This leads Paley to conclude: 'I can't seem to teach the children that which they don't already know' (1986: 126). However, eventually, it becomes impossible to ignore or reinterpret the new experiences, and children's knowledge, and theories, change as a result. Gopnik *et al.* (1999) suggest that this has an impact on children's understanding of more than just the particular element of knowledge and experience in question. This idea is also looked at in more detail in Chapter 8, in particular in relation to young children's scientific understanding.

## Learning

In thinking about thinking, it can be difficult to steer a clear path between it and learning, and the two are sometimes used interchangeably, as if they were one and the same. In addition, there is disagreement about how learning occurs and where (for example, is it solely in the mind, or is learning embodied?), what influences learning and how we can know if learning has occurred (McGregor 2007). It is, nevertheless, important to try to retain a clear distinction between the two. Perkins (1992), for example, suggests that learning is a consequence of thinking.

Claxton (1999a) argues for an approach which he calls learnacy, or learning to learn. This, essentially, is what he means when he says that, for him, intelligence is knowing what to do when you don't know what to do. Crucially, for Claxton, this learning is not confined to 'the articulate, the numerate, the explicit and the measurable' (1999a: 11). Rather, it is about taking a broad view of learning, which includes the use of the imagination, a playful disposition, persistence and the ability to learn with and from others.

Much attention has been focused in recent years on the idea of learning styles, and the view that we all have preferred ways of learning. In particular, approaches such as VAK (Visual, Auditory and Kinaesthetic) have gained popularity in early childhood settings (Bayley 2002; Dowling 2002). Bayley (2002), for example, suggests that the extent to which an individual learns through each style will differ from person to person,

Box 1.1 Ben, aged 3.7, Oliver, aged 4.1, and Jasmine, aged 3.8, at nursery school, sitting at a table with a teacher

TEACHER: We are thinking about which objects are heavy and which are light. We have a sponge and a brush. (The children are shown a large sponge and a brush.) Can you think about which one will be heavier?

BEN: The sponge.

TEACHER: Why do you think that?

BEN: Because it's big.

TEACHER: Oliver, which one do you think will be heavier?

OLIVER: The sponge.

TEACHER: What about you, Jasmine?

JASMINE: That one (points to the sponge).

TEACHER: Ok, so we are going to feel them now and see if we can feel which one is heavier. Can you all hold out both of your hands like this (shows them both hands, palms up). Oliver, here's the sponge (places it in his hand) and here is the brush (places in other hand). Which one do you think is heavier?

OLIVER: The sponge, because the brush is going down. (His hand holding the brush is lowering down and the hand holding the sponge remains in the same place.)

TEACHER: Why is the brush going down?

OLIVER: Because the sponge is going up.

(Jasmine is given both objects to hold.)

TEACHER: Jasmine, which one feels heavier?

JASMINE: This one. (Nods to the sponge.)

TEACHER: (Both objects are now placed in Ben's hands.) Which one do you think is heavier, Ben?

BEN: The sponge, because the brush is down. (His hand holding the brush is lowered below the sponge.)

TEACHER: If your hand has dropped down, it means you are carrying something heavy. The brush is heavy and the sponge is so light because it is full of air. Let's see if the balance scales show the brush is heavier. If it is heavier, the scales will go down on that side. (The objects are placed on the scales and the side with the brush on it goes down.) Has the brush gone down?

ALL CHILDREN: Yes, yes, yes.

TEACHER: So which one is heavier?

ALL CHILDREN: The sponge, sponge, the sponge.

*By estimating through sight alone which object will be heavier, the children must rely on their own concepts of weight to come to a conclusion. In this case, it appears that their schema (Piaget 1962) of weight depends on their experiences of big objects being heavy. The children remain convinced that the sponge is heavier, even after first-hand experience. In an attempt to develop their understanding the children are told the brush is heavier, and shown both objects on the scales. In this case, telling them seems less than effective, as questioning reveals that the children still believe the sponge to be heavier at the end of the episode. As Paley says, 'I can't seem to teach the children that which they don't already know' (1986: 126)*

Abridged and reproduced with permission of Frances Pearmain

but that at least a part of a child's thinking may be lost if their opportunities to learn do not take account of their preferred learning style. These ideas have also sometimes been linked to Gardner's multiple intelligences (MI) theories.

What is the evidence for the claims of those who advocate learning styles approaches? The Learning and Skills Research Centre (LSRC) identify 71 different approaches. Much of the evaluation of these is small-scale, often conducted by the programme developers themselves (LSRC 2004), and tends to refer to older children and adults. Nevertheless, the LSRC do suggest that there is considerable variability between the different learning styles approaches, and that it is difficult to be clear about the impact of any of them. With regard to VAK, Howard-Jones (2007) cites evidence suggesting that presenting material in three different styles, targeted at the supposed learning styles of children, was a wasted effort, of no benefit to the children. The LSRC suggest that, rather than it being a model for learning, VAK is a tool for instruction, in that teaching is directed at identified learning styles. In addition, they quote one student describing herself thus: 'I learned that I was a low auditory, kinaesthetic learner. So there's no point in me reading a book or listening to anyone for more than a few minutes' (LSRC 2004: 56). There are potential dangers in children (and adults) labelling themselves in this way. In support of VAK, the report suggests that it is a user-friendly model.

Claxton (cited in Revell 2005) suggests that there are dangers in uncritical recommendation of learning styles approaches, stressing the need for further research in the area. As Howard-Jones (2007) points out, the popularity of ideas about learning styles, coupled with a lack of scientific research in the area, lends weight to the importance of more dialogue and collaboration between neuroscience and education, to support practice. These ideas are looked at in more detail in Chapter 4. Gardner has also emphasized that his multiple intelligences theory 'begins from a different point and ends up at a different place from most schemes that emphasize stylistic approaches' (1993: 44). He suggests that learning styles are not generic, but context- or subject-specific. Overall, the LSRC report (2004) emphasizes the value of approaches which target metacognition, considered in Chapter 5 here.

## Are there different kinds of thinking?

The short answer to such a question is yes, but a fuller answer would be that there may be different ways of looking at differences in thinking. White (2002) draws distinctions between undirected thinking, or daydreaming, and directed thinking, which he further elaborates into theoretical and practical thinking, and a category he calls contemplation, or thinking done for its own sake.

Gardner (1983), in particular, has been responsible for suggesting that we think in different, domain-specific, ways. He outlines a number of 'intelligences', which differentiate between linguistic, logical-mathematical, musical, spatial, bodily-kinaesthetic, interpersonal, intrapersonal, naturalist and existential domains of thinking (Gardner 1983, 1999). These are looked at in more detail in Chapter 2.

Claxton (1998) differentiates thinking from the perspective of speed of thought. He suggests that the mind has three different processing speeds, which are responsible for different kinds of thinking:

- faster than thought – unselfconscious, instantaneous reaction;

- thought itself – the 'intellect', or deliberate, 'd-mode'– what he calls the 'hare brain';
- less immediately purposeful, more leisurely, playful and contemplative ways of knowing – the 'tortoise mind', or 'undermind' (analogous to White's undirected thinking and contemplation).

Western culture, in particular, he suggests, has tended to focus largely on the *d-mode* or *deliberate-mode*, at the expense of what he calls the undermind, or 'intelligent unconscious' (1998: 7). The blame for this emphasis he lays partly at the door of Piaget. The undermind is, Claxton suggests, about implicit know-how, or learning by osmosis, and is analogous to Piaget's first stage of development (see Chapter 2), which is overtaken by other, more powerful, abstract, and increasingly intellectual forms of thinking. The influence of Piaget's stage theory, Claxton suggests, carries with it an assumption that these later forms of thinking are the highest forms of development. Consequently, parents and adults working with young children may see their role as moving children on from the more intuitive forms of thinking, and encouraging them to become deliberators and explainers as fast as possible. Claxton warns against the narrowness of over-reliance on d-mode, and suggests a range of benefits of what he regards as intuitive thinking. This idea is looked at in more detail in Chapter 11. Perhaps the most important message he stresses is one of knowing how to think, of having a range of ways of thinking available to us, for use in the most appropriate ways possible, whatever the context.

One well-known approach to thinking about thinking is Bloom's taxonomy of cognitive goals (Bloom *et al.* 1956). His hierarchical approach starts with knowledge, and is followed by comprehension, application, analysis, synthesis and evaluation, in order of cognitive challenge. Evaluation, in particular, is linked with so-called 'higher order' thinking. Resnick (here as adapted from Meadows 2006: 410) suggests that the key features of higher order thinking are that it

- is nonalgorithmic: the path of action is not fully specified in advance;
- is complex;
- often yields multiple solutions;
- involves nuanced judgement and interpretation;
- involves the application of multiple, and sometimes conflicting, criteria;
- often involves uncertainty;
- involves self-regulation of the thinking process;
- involves imposing meaning and finding structure;
- is effortful.

As Meadows points out, this includes knowing whether it will soon be tea-time just as much as it is about more complex situations and ideas. It certainly characterizes, in my view, the kinds of thinking that young children engage in every day of their lives.

## Do children think differently to adults?

Implicit in any kind of developmental theory, and many of the theories about children's thinking are developmental, is the idea of change over time. The stage theory developed by Piaget, discussed in Chapter 2, suggests that children's thinking changes in qualitative ways as they develop (this leads to the Piagetian idea that we develop in order to learn). Thus, the thinking of a 2 year old is qualitatively different to that of a 10 year old, and, importantly, the thinking of children is different in kind to that of adults. The major characteristics of this difference are ones of logic and abstraction. In the past 35 years, however, much evidence has been offered to suggest that children's thinking may not be as qualitatively different as Piaget believed. The work of Donaldson (1978), Tizard and Hughes (2002) and many others, suggests that differences between children's and adults' thinking are more attributable to lack of knowledge and experience than to qualitative change. In situations where children have relevant knowledge and experience, whether it is playing chess, caring for goldfish or knowing about dinosaurs, they behave more expertly, and display more mature thinking, than many adults who are novices in the same area (Thornton 2002). As Siegler and Alibali suggest: 'Differences between age groups tend to be ones of degree rather than kind. Not only are young children more cognitively competent than they appear, but older children are less competent than we might think (2005: 24). As Spinney (2010) points out, too, differences in ways of thinking may have much to do with cultural variation and experience, affecting adults and children alike.

Paley suggests that one characteristic form of young children's thinking is 'magical'. For young children, she suggests, it is 'the common footpath from which new trails are explored' (1981: 4), as in Box 1.2.

Young children tend to believe in magic, and act on that conviction, with belief in imaginary companions and fantasy figures peaking in the years between 3 and 8 (Woolley 1997). However, at a similar age, they are also very competent in distinguishing between reality and pretence in their play and in discussion (Woolley 1997). Why, then, should there be this seeming anomaly, and why does magical thinking seem to be such a characteristic phenomenon in young children? Woolley (1997) believes that the fact that young children use magic in their thinking does not indicate that they are unable to distinguish between fantasy and reality. Siegler *et al.* (2011) suggest that it is important to recognize that young children may believe a range of contradictory things

---

Box 1.2  Magical thinking in *A Child's Work*

On this day, Kostos is shouting out directions to anyone who will accept the premises of his plot. Even Vijay is drawn into the drama. 'Don't go there, Vijay! It's a poison river.'

'Did my feet get poisoned?' Vijay asks.

'Don't worry, I'm making you invisible. Touch this paper. Now I got you unpoisoned. It's invisible writing.'

'What does it say?'

'That you're invisible. No one can see you except me.'

'That's good. I was almost dead.'

'You mean poisoned. Now you're unpoisoned.'

(Paley 2004: 60)

at the same time. In so doing, their family and community experiences are important elements. For example, children brought up to believe that Santa Claus is unreal may also assume that other fantasy figures are unreal when they are introduced to them (Woolley 1997). The converse may also be the case, with family encouragement of belief in fantasy figures influencing children's attitudes. Change comes about largely as a result of experiences, as children learn more about the real causes of events, and as they experience more contexts in which fantasy characters are seen not to be 'real' (Siegler et al. 2011). However, as Woolley points out, there is certainly evidence of adult belief in magic and fantasy, suggesting that here, as in other aspects of young children's thinking, there is no qualitative difference between adults' and children's thinking.

## Is thinking a solitary or a collective activity?

A search on the internet for images related to 'thought' and 'thinking' produces large numbers of a very similar image of a solitary figure resting his chin in his hand, invariably in a pose similar to Rodin's *Thinker* (although the image predates Rodin by a considerable period). Is thinking like this, however? The answer to such a question will depend very much on the kind of models of cognition (see Chapter 2) to which you subscribe. For Piaget (1950, 1959), thought is internalized action, and the child is a 'lone scientist', constructing understanding as a result of individual discovery. In so doing, children are viewed as self-regulating, learning when they are ready. Attempts to 'teach', show or explain things to children before they are ready will result in the learning of empty procedures, with little impact on thinking. For Vygotsky (1978), however, children learn as they engage with others, as part of a culture. Vygotsky's perspective has been hugely influential, and current perspectives would accord with Fisher's view that 'The thinking child is a social child' (2005:3). These two very different viewpoints about the process of thinking are discussed, along with others, in Chapter 2.

## Nature or nurture, biology or experience?

The extent to which human growth and development is a matter of genetic inheritance or the result of experience, sometimes referred to as 'nature versus nurture', has long been, and continues to be, a major theme in all areas of child development research (Siegler et al. 2011). Cohen neatly summarizes the dilemma when he poses the following questions:

> Do parents who read more to their children improve IQ by providing a better environment? Or do children whose genes make them brighter insist their parents read to them more?
>
> (Cohen 2002: 158)

The philosopher John Locke, writing in the seventeenth century, was responsible for the idea that children are 'blank slates' at birth, waiting to be written on by their experiences. A similar view is characteristic of a behaviourist approach to learning (see Chapter 2), which rests upon control of the environment as a determinant in children's development. However, this idea is no longer seen as credible. If babies truly were 'blank slates' at birth they would have no basis for making sense of the kaleidoscope of experiences they encounter, and no ability to progress beyond their empty state.

Research in genetics in recent years has tended to emphasize the predetermined nature of our development. As Thornton (2002) points out, every aspect of human beings must have a genetic basis, starting from the fact that we grow into baby humans rather than ducklings! Pinker has emphasized the role of innate systems for development: 'Intelligent behavior is learned successfully because we have innate systems that do the learning' (2002: 41). These innate systems form a 'universal complex human nature' (2002: 73), which allow humans to behave flexibly in response to their experiences precisely because they are programmed with 'combinatorial software that can generate an unlimited set of thoughts and behaviours' (2002: 41). Critics of Pinker's ideas suggest that he relies too strongly on particular 'sciences of the mind', notably cognitive science, behavioural genetics and evolutionary psychology (Midgley 2002), and makes controversial use of other evidence from psychology and neuroscience (Blackburn 2003).

The most widely accepted position is that it cannot be the case that all cognitive ability is inherited. At the same time, it is clear that development is not solely a matter of the actions of the environment on young children. What does seem to be the case is that genes and the environment constantly interact in complex ways in steering children's development (Meadows 2010). Some genetic influences are common to us all as human beings, for example, our long and slow period of maturity in comparison to other mammals. Others are more individual, and part of our inheritance, for example, body shape, inherited diseases and so forth. These differences are encoded in our DNA, and cannot be changed as a result of experience. However, as Meadows points out, 'the individual's experience does affect whether the individual's DNA is advantageous to their well-being or not' (2010: 28), and the environments within which children live influence all aspects of their development. For example, we know that higher levels of nutrition enhance growth. Looking at cognition, higher levels of atmospheric lead pollution have been shown to have a negative effect on children's cognitive development (Cohen 2002), a 'cognitively stimulating' environment can influence children's achievement (Meadows 2010), and research by Cutting and Dunn (1999) suggests a relationship between social class and the development of theory of mind, discussed in Chapter 5. The existence of interventions such as High Scope and Head Start in the United States and SureStart in the United Kingdom are evidence of the assumption that environment can influence young children's development. LeDoux puts it neatly when he says that 'Learning involves the nurturing of nature' (2003: 9).

Rogoff suggests that it is 'a false dichotomy to focus on "nature" and "nurture" as separable influences on human development' (2003: 65). For Rogoff, human biological development works together with cultural institutions and practices, in mutually influential ways. For example, she suggests that the growth in the rate of births by caesarean section for mothers whose babies' heads are too large for the birth canal is a cultural practice which may lead, over a long period of time, to the evolution of larger heads in those populations. To sum up, thinking of this area as an argument for 'either/ or' is misleading, and it is better to think of nature *with* nurture, interdependently supporting our development, rather than nature *versus* nurture.

## What is the relationship of memory to thinking?

The 'remarkable facility' (Goswami 2008: 251) of memory plays a vital role in all aspects of life, throughout life. Memories are central ingredients in our definitions of ourselves, helping to 'make us what we are' (Cohen 2002: 110), and supporting an 'enduring and developing sense of self' (White 2002: 189). Whilst thinking is clearly not merely a matter of recalling memory, it is, as Meadows (2006) suggests, difficult to think of an aspect of human cognitive activity which does not involve memory in some way, even if it is to conclude 'I've never met this situation before'.

Kuhn (2000) stresses the importance of situating the study of memory, and memory strategies, in the broader context of general cognitive development. For example, it is intimately linked with both learning and knowledge (Bauer and Souci 2010; Kuhn 2000). It is useful to very briefly highlight a number of other aspects of children's thinking linked to memory which are looked at in in more detail in the following chapters, particularly Chapters 2 and 5. All of the models of cognition outlined in Chapter 2 include memory processes. Memory is central to information processing theories, as well as having implications for Vygotskian (1978) ideas about the joint construction of meaning and collective memory making, and the modular theories of Gardner (1983), amongst others. Kuhn emphasizes the ways in which memories arise out of social and cultural contexts, and children's 'everyday activities' (Kuhn 2000: 23), the subject of Chapter 3. Memory development is also related to the physiological development of the brain, the subject of Chapter 4. Metamemory, the aspect of memory which is concerned with the ability to think about one's own memory processes, is inextricably linked with the development of metacognition, looked at in Chapter 5. Kuhn (2000) suggests that memories are often represented in narrative form, an aspect of children's thinking which is discussed in both Chapters 7 and 8. In Chapter 8 the development of children's concepts is seen to be dependent, in part, upon their memories of past experience. Finally, in Chapter 11 memory is suggested as an element in the development of problem-solving in children. Whilst this list is not exhaustive, it nevertheless highlights the central role of memory in the development of thinking and understanding.

### Storing memories

A common way of thinking about memory is to see it as being structured according to how long we hold onto particular memories. The classic model used to describe this identifies three components: sensory register/memory, working or short-term memory and long-term memory. Information is initially taken in through the sensory register, and much never passes beyond that. If it does, it becomes a memory. Some memories are short-term, that is, we do not remember them for very long periods of time – exactly how long is short-term is disputed, some psychologists suggest a matter of seconds, others that short-term memory can be measured in minutes (Cohen 2002). When you stop someone in the street and ask them directions to a restaurant, your interest is in remembering these for long enough to get you to the restaurant. Such memories are usually short-term, but may be retained for longer, and thus become part of long-term memory, if necessary. In addition, the information here may also have been retrieved from long-term memory, as needed. Thus, short-term memory is much more than just a form of temporary storage, and plays a vital role in processing information, deciding what to let in and what to keep out. This emphasis on processing capacity has led to the more common use of the term 'working memory' to describe this aspect (Smith *et al.* 2011) although Woolfolk *et al.* (2008) suggest that working memory is a distinct category, which sits between both short-term and long-term memory. For Geake, working memory is 'the central cognitive construct underpinning academic success' (2009: 66). The basic organization of working memory does not change over time. However, what may change are its capacity and speed of operation during childhood and adolescence (Siegler *et al.* 2011), although Meadows (2006) questions whether it is more that our repertoire of processes and strategies increases, leading to more efficient use of the same capacity.

There are also a great many things that we need or want to remember for an indefinite period, for example, the kinds of memories that, at the start of this section, I suggested were what make you what you are. This is referred to as long-term memory. Whilst sensory and working memory systems have limited capacity, long-term memory seems to have no such limits, at least until extreme old age (Meadows 2006). Within the brain, both types of memory arise from the connections between neurons, known as synapses. In short-term memories the effect of this connection is temporary, for longer term memories the connection is permanent. Of interest are the ways in which short-term or working memory is transferred to long-term memory, some aspects of which are looked at below. Box 1.3 describes an episode that seems to draw on J's long-term and working memory, and also, in J's confident statement 'I know this one' links memory with knowledge.

### Memories and memorizing

Kuhn (2000) suggests that, in studying memory, it is necessary to draw a distinction between two aspects of memory: *memories*, which she describes as knowledge structures that are the product of our efforts to understand and know, and *memorizing*, which she suggests is 'a socially situated activity undertaken in the service of individual or social goals' (Kuhn 2000: 21). In relation to the first aspect, that of memories, there is evidence to suggest that foetuses have some capacity for memory (Cohen 2002), and that, from birth, babies can recognize something, or someone, familiar (Thornton 2002). Without this recognition memory every situation would be novel and unique, and it would be impossible to learn from experience (Thornton 2002). An important developmental step forward, however, is the ability not just to recognize events, but to recall them, necessitating the retrieval and reconstruction of a memory stored somewhere. This is essentially a process of reconstruction (Geake 2009), and begins very early in life. Babies as young as three weeks old show learning and memory for simple objects, and by six months have working memories and can form event memories that, given reminders, can be retrieved two years later (Goswami 2008), with clear evidence that children's ability to recall things develops over time. Peterson (2011) looked at the recall of a stressful event in young children between the ages of 12 and 13 years, and found that children became proportionately more accurate in their narrative recall with age. This pattern persisted over time, with similar differences shown when the children were reinterviewed one year and then two years later. Interestingly, though, what her study also showed was that the deterioration in even the youngest children's recall over time was quite modest, with a decline in accuracy of recall rather than in the amount of detail they could remember of the event.

---

*Box 1.3:* Memory in Girl J aged 4.3, reception class of a primary school

J is in the role play area, set up with boxes containing props for retelling stories. After looking along the boxes J starts to unpack the box with props for 'Goldilocks and the Three Bears'.

J:    I'll do this one Mrs C, I know this one (to practitioner).

J lays out the bowls in size order with the largest first. She then collects the three bears and sits them in a row next to the bowls, again in the order of largest first. She repeats this ordering with the pictures of the bears' chairs. Finally J places the three bed pictures on the floor at her feet. The largest bed is first in the line with the others following, again in size order. Once the box is empty J picks up the Goldilocks puppet and begins to retell the story.

J:    Goldilocks went to their house and she ate the porridge. Daddy's big porridge was too hot (places Goldilocks on largest bowl). Mummy's middle porridge was too cold (places Goldilocks on middle sized bowl). And Baby's little porridge was just right so she finished it (places Goldilocks on the smallest bowl).
      Then her sits on the chairs. Daddy's big chair is too hard. (Goldilocks is placed on largest chair in a row of three that are already in the area.)
      Then her sits on Mummy's soft chair but it is too soft. (Goldilocks is placed on middle chair.) Then her sits on Baby's little chair and it is just right but then her breaks it, Oh no! (Goldilocks falls to the floor from little chair.)
      Look Mrs C, her broke it. (J looks to practitioner P and pauses.)
P:    Yes she broke the chair, poor baby bear.
J:    Goldilocks is tired so she goes to bed. Daddy's big bed is too hard. (Goldilocks is placed on picture of big bed.)
      Mummy's middle bed is too soft. (Goldilocks is placed on middle sized picture.) Baby's little bed is just right and she sleeps. (Goldilocks is laid on little bed picture.)
      Bears come home and Goldilocks is still sleeping and Daddy bear says 'Whose been sleeping in my bed?', and Mummy bear says 'Whose been sleeping in my bed?', and Baby bear shouts 'Her's in my bed'. (J grabs Goldilocks and screams as she cuddles her in her arms.)

*The patterning which took place in sequencing the story called for learnt knowledge to be recalled and delivered in an ordered fashion. This action involved the skill of memory recall which required J to bring to mind previous experiences of sharing this story (Goswami 2008). It would appear that this knowledge was stored in J's long-term memory and recalled to her short-term, or working memory.*

Abridged and reproduced with permission of Lynn Skinner

A major factor in this development is the amount of knowledge we all have, both about the world in general, and also about the specific topic or domain in question (Kuhn 2000; Thornton 2002). This domain-specific knowledge seems to be particularly important for memory, enabling us to make connections and see links and relationships that we might not otherwise notice. In young children, a lot of the knowledge they acquire is about everyday events, and they develop what are known as 'scripts' for experiences such as going shopping, or going to a birthday party. This script knowledge helps them to remember and recall the likely sequence of events for such experiences. Other knowledge may be less script-like, for example, learning about the world, or the rules of a game. Both cases, Kuhn (2000) suggests, account for the development of domain-specific knowledge structures that support memory. As we shall see in forthcoming chapters, knowledge and experience are key factors in the development of thinking and understanding.

In these everyday contexts, children's memories are formed as part of the meaningful, social context of the situation. Kuhn (2000) believes that it is in these situations that the best evidence for children's competence in memorizing, the second aspect of memory, is to be found. Claxton suggests that:

> Anything which improves comprehension also improves memory. Trying to remember things that don't make much sense is a thankless task, and the effort of searching for some kind of meaningful 'glue' is usually well repaid.
>
> (Claxton 1999b:143)

There is considerable evidence that children's use of deliberate memory strategies shows marked change over time (Meadows 2006). For example, at age 4, children rarely make spontaneous use of the simplest strategies to aid recall, by the age of 7 the majority of children do, although they may tend to overestimate their capabilities (Thornton 2002). Specific strategies that aid memory performance are the encoding, storage or retrieval of information, and young children may perform relatively poorly in all three areas. Encoding as a strategy includes three further strategies of rehearsal, which refers to the mental repetition of information; organization, which involves structuring and grouping information in some way helpful to memory; and elaboration, which involves making associations between items in order to help recall. Claxton (1999b) and Goswami (2008) emphasize how important language is in this process.

Smith et al. (2011) suggest that older children's greater general knowledge may be an important factor in their enhanced memory strategy use, because it can help them to think of useful associations between ideas. Thornton (2002) believes that one reason that young children do not perform as well as older ones is that they may not understand the point of such memory tasks. In addition, she suggests that they do not yet have sufficient knowledge about how their memories work, part of what is referred to as metamemory, and metacognition (see Chapter 5) in order for them to recognize the value of strategies. Here it is worth looking very briefly at this important aspect of metacognition, known as metamemory, or knowledge about memory. Grammer et al. (2011) cite a range of studies that provide evidence for linkages between metamemory and memory development, with their own work indicating that metamemory is predictive of subsequent memory strategy use. Children's metamemory knowledge is evident in the early years, for example, young children know that a long list is harder to remember than a shorter one (Meadows 2006), but it will show marked development over the school years, as they gain more experience of memorizing. Box 1.4 illustrates metamemory in one young girl, in the context of pretence.

Box 1.4    *Metamemory. Helen, aged 4.5 and Lisa, aged 5.0, role play in 'the doctor's surgery'*

HELEN:    Do you have a 'pointment?
LISA:    Yeah, my mummy rang to tell the doctor I not well.
HELEN:    OK wait there ... OK ready now. Lie on the bed. What's wrong?
LISA:    I got ear ache.
HELEN:    OK I'll look. (Uses an instrument to look in Lisa's ear.) Is it sore?
LISA:    Yeah. Can I have medicine? I had medicine last time?
HELEN:    OK here you go.

*Meadows defines metamemory as: 'one's knowledge of memory, that is one's awareness of what memory behaviour is happening at the moment, and one's knowledge about task difficulties, one's own skills, abilities and deficits, and strategies that will enable one to perform a task satisfactorily' (Meadows 2006: 93). This example seems to complement Meadows's definition as Lisa has identified that she is ill and needs to go to the doctor. This seems to relate to 'awareness of what memory behaviour is happening'. Stating that mummy had rung the doctor suggests that Lisa understands her own abilities and skills. The use of instruments to look inside Lisa's ear implies that Helen is able to use 'strategies ... to perform the task satisfactorily'. Lisa seems to demonstrate that she has knowledge about memory when stating 'I had medicine last time' as she has obviously had this experience in the past.*

Abridged and reproduced with permission of Samantha McGinley

Whilst young children may be less skilled than older children or adults in making use of memory strategies, there is evidence that they can be taught successfully to do so (Kuhn 2000 and Chapter 5), although when they do so they may not recognize their value, and may not apply them outside the specific context in which they have been taught (Kuhn 2000). Interestingly, Claxton also focuses on not trying to remember as an important tool. Letting the unconscious take over, or allowing your mind to 'come at it sideways' (1999b:145), he suggests, is also beneficial to memory. Alongside training in the use of encoding and retrieval strategies, children may benefit from knowing about, and using, other ways of remembering. In Chapter 6 the use of video and still photography is discussed as a way of stimulating recall. Brooks (2004) suggests the use of children's drawings of past events as prompts, which can act as tools for remembering, and as the starting points for discussion which supports shared memory. Lambert (2007) believes that Diagrammatic Representation (DR) as an aid to recall can be a useful metacognitive strategy. One reason for its usefulness, she suggests, is that it relates to visuo-spatial memory, a strong aspect of memory in young children. Looking at a group of 4 and 5 year olds, she shows that the use of DR, along with direct questioning, supported more detailed recall of an event a month after it had occurred. Interestingly, she also found that adults' use of direct, specific questions was more successful in facilitating recall than open-ended questions. It is useful to bear this in mind in Chapters 7 and 8, where adults' use of questions is considered in more depth.

## Further reflection

1  Fisher (2005) suggests that thinking is about orchestrating the 'basic cognitive skills' of perception, memory, concept formation, language and symbolization. Do you agree? How would you define 'thinking'?
2  Look back at Perkins's comment that 'learning is a consequence of thinking'. Do you agree? Is learning always a consequence of thinking?
3  Think about yourself and your family. Are you ever compared to other family members, and told that you are 'just like them'? Do you see yourself as having inherited family traits? In what ways do you think you are unlike others in your family?
4  Do you have strategies for remembering? Do you think that you remember different kinds of things in different ways?

## Further reading

Claxton (1998, 1999a, 1999b)
Cohen (2002: 28–30 and chapters 6 and 8)
Geake (2009: chapters 3 and 4)
Goswami (2008: 4–10, chapter 8, and 295–304)
Kuhn (2000)
Meadows (2006: 84–103)
Paley (1986)
Pinker (2002)
Thornton (2002: chapter 4)
White (2002: chapters 5 and 6)
Woolley (1997)

# Chapter 2

# Theories of cognitive development

## Learning to think and thinking to learn

In this chapter the focus is on theories of cognitive development. What all of them have in common is a desire to establish what develops, and how such development takes place in children. Both constructivism and social constructivism are outlined, along with ideas derived from information processing approaches and modularity. Developmental psychology played a dominant role in early childhood theory and practice in the twentieth century, possibly stemming from a desire to develop a theoretical foundation which could provide an explanatory theory of learning. Piaget's developmental theory, for example, underpins ideas of developmentally appropriate practice (DAP) (Bredekamp 1987). In recent years the work of, amongst others, Dahlberg *et al.* (2007), and James and Prout (1997) has challenged the universalist assumption of some models, emphasizing instead a model of children as social actors, and of childhood as socially constructed, 'always contextualized in relation to time, place and culture' (Dahlberg *et al.* 2007: 49). One of the most significant contributions of postmodernist thinking has been to disrupt 'commonly held "truths"' (Albon 2011: 38) about children's development and learning, and to emphasize that there is no absolute knowledge. Walkerdine (2009) suggests that sociological perspectives have even displaced those of developmental psychology, in seeking to understand childhood. She argues that we should, however, resist simple dualisms of sociology and psychology, and offers instead a view of ways in which psychological aspects such as learning and reasoning are produced as part of social practices. Some of these ideas are looked at in more detail in Chapter 3, but it is important to read this chapter against that backdrop, and to see theories of development as helpful in offering 'signposts to different routes to understanding young children' (Penn 2005: 39).

## Jean Piaget and constructivism

Born in 1896 in Switzerland, Piaget is often seen as the originator of the field of cognitive development (Siegler *et al.* 2011; Thornton 2002). In the 1920s and 1930s, when Piaget's ideas were first becoming known, the prevailing view of children was that they were 'empty vessels', expected to passively receive knowledge from adults. Teaching was largely didactic, and focused on rote learning. His alternative view, of children as active explorers, engaged in discovering things for themselves and constructing their own understanding, was seen as both new and challenging, but also, by some, as a more likely way of accounting for the diversity and creativity of human learning (Whitebread 2000b). By the 1950s his ideas had become known around the world, particularly in the field of early childhood, where they were seen as legitimizing the idea of learning through play, very much part of the nursery school tradition (Penn 2005). They are evident in documents such as the Plowden Report (CACE 1967) in the United Kingdom. The American High/Scope programme is one well-known approach in early childhood which explicitly acknowledges the influence of Piaget on its development (Hohmann and Weikart 1995).

In part, the extent of his influence can be seen as a result of his longevity and his prolixity: he was active for a long time, and researched and published extensively. As we shall see, his work has come under increasing scrutiny and challenge since the 1970s. In hindsight, it is also possible to say that it was probably more talked about than implemented, certainly in mainstream educational practice. Perhaps his most enduring legacies are the ways in which he presented a view of children as active learners, and in the inspiration he provided for many other people to test out his ideas and research. It is important to look at Piaget in the context of his own time and background, which Cohen (2002) suggests may go some way to explaining his emphasis on the importance of logical thought. As a child, he went on expeditions with the curator of the local natural history museum, and studied Latin, Greek and philosophy, including Aristotelian and Socratic logic.

### Piaget and constructivism

Piaget's approach to the development of children's cognition has come to be known as constructivism. Essentially, all of Piaget's work is about the development of thinking and understanding, and he described himself as an epistemologist, that is, someone who is interested in how humans acquire knowledge. For Piaget (1950), thought is internalized action. Actions form the processes of reasoning, and it is actions, and the interplay between the experience of action and thought, that form the basis of the way in which a child constructs a view of the world. Language then serves as a system for representing the world. Duckworth suggests that: 'Through watching the development of sensorimotor intelligence, before the development of language in a small child, he found that the roots of logic are in actions and not in words' (1987: 16).

Piaget saw children as actively constructing their own understanding largely through a process of self-discovery. His image of the child was that of a young scientist, an individual thinker. The role of the adult is to act as a facilitator to the child's development, providing an appropriate environment in which children can hypothesize and ask themselves questions. This raises some important questions for practice, including the extent to which children should be 'left to themselves', and what the role of adult interaction and support is in Piaget's model of cognition.

Piaget's starting point is a biological one: cognition is an example of the adaptation between organism and environment seen throughout the living world. It is 'driven by the need to anticipate events in order to survive' (Thornton 2002: 156). For Piaget, development precedes learning, and we develop in order to learn. His model breaks this adaptation down into a series of procedures, beginning with the idea of scheme or schema (see Athey in Chapter 6). For Piaget, schemas are the mental structures into which we organize our knowledge of the world. That knowledge is based on experience, and can lead us to conclusions which we may later change, in the light of further experience – a classic example of this is the idea that many children hold that heavy things sink, whilst light things float. Much experience will be needed to modify such a schema.

Piaget describes that process of modification through the use of the terms assimilation, accommodation and equilibration, three processes 'that work together from birth to propel development forward' (Siegler *et al.* 2011: 131). Assimilation refers to the way in which we transform incoming information so that it fits in with our existing way of thinking about that schema, for example, a baby will often refer to all men as 'daddies'. Accommodation is what happens when we make adjustments to a schema, and adapt our thinking, in the light of new information – to continue the example, a child's realization that, far from all men being daddies, daddy is part of a group called 'men', might be an example of accommodation, involving a shift in the baby's mental model of the world. Such adjustments can be very different in scale, and may just be a refinement of an existing schema, or may require a rather larger shift in thinking. At what point, however, can we say that accommodation occurs? Meadows suggests that

> the assimilation of new information must lead to some degree of accommodation in the old system of knowledge, if only to the minor degree of 'ah, here's another X: I've seen at least a hundred of those in my time, so now I've seen at least a hundred and one'.
>
> (Meadows 2006: 263)

Anning and Edwards (2006) suggest that problem-solving play is particularly valuable for encouraging accommodation of new information.

The processes of assimilation and accommodation are held together by 'an even more important (and mysterious) process' (Meadows 2006: 266) called equilibration. Siegler and Alibali (2005: 31) describe this as the 'keystone' of developmental change within Piaget's system, whereby the child's model of the world comes increasingly to resemble reality. Essentially, when children encounter new experiences or concepts, their existing frameworks or schema have to adjust. This causes a state of disequilibrium, or cognitive conflict, which acts as motivation to learning until a state of equilibrium is restored. This idea of disequilibrium, or cognitive conflict, highlights that, contrary to much popular belief, Piaget did see a role for interaction in learning. One of the ways in which disequilibrium can occur is through a child's interactions, particularly with peers.

---

*Box 2.1:* Equilibration. Charlie, aged 4.6 and Ella, aged 5.4

CHARLIE:   I live in a house, but it's got no stairs.
ELLA:        So you live in a bungalow.
CHARLIE:   No it looks like a house.
ELLA:        But it has no stairs and bungalows have no stairs. My nanny lives in a bungalow.
CHARLIE:   Oh ... My mummy calls it a house ... but it's not really.

*Charlie appears to have assimilated that all homes are houses. Ella's explanation may enable Charlie to begin to accommodate this new information. However, this new information may cause Charlie to experience disequilibrium as he challenges his previous knowledge in accommodating the new.*

Reproduced with permission of Samantha McGinley

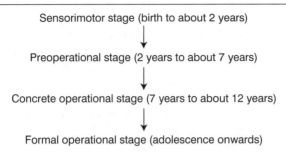

Figure 2.1 Piaget's stages of cognitive development

## Piaget's stages of cognitive development

Piaget suggests that cognitive development is a continuous process through a series of universal, invariant stages in children, in each of which their thinking is qualitatively different both to what has come before, and to what follows. According to Piaget, there are four such stages (Figure 2.1).

Whilst the order of these stages is invariant, their duration is not, and Piaget does not suggest that there is a fixed time span for each stage. He also believes that children may show evidence of elements of more than one stage at a time. He refers to this phenomenon as décalage.

An important element of Piaget's stage theory is the idea of 'readiness' – that is, the idea that children cannot progress to the next stage of their development before they are ready, as a result of having gone through the stage before. Trying to 'teach' children something before they are ready to discover it for themselves, Piaget believes, involves them in learning procedures, and not the development of understanding, with lasting consequences for their development.

The first two of Piaget's stages are within the age focus of this book. The sensorimotor stage is characterized by the ways in which children come to know the world in terms of the physical acts they can perform. At first such acts are inadvertent, but they become increasingly intentional and coordinated. A common characteristic of babies in the sensorimotor stage is their lack of understanding of the permanence of objects. A six-month old baby, Piaget suggests, thinks that, if an object is removed, it ceases to exist. This first sensorimotor stage is followed by the preoperational period which marks the beginning of the means for representing the world symbolically, particularly in thought and language. However, this representational skill is limited to the child's own perspective. Piaget describes this behaviour as egocentric on the part of the child, not in the sense that it is selfish, but meaning that the child is simply unconscious of anything but his own needs. Thus, for Piaget, children under the age of 7 cannot 'de-centre', or see things from another person's point of view, and cannot think about things from a perspective other than their own. This problem of centration is well illustrated by the 'three mountains task'. In this experiment, Piaget asked children to look at a model of three mountains, and to identify what a doll, placed in a position different to themselves, would be able to see. Piaget found that children of 4 and 5 years often chose the view that they could see themselves, rather than that of the doll. As a result, he concluded that young children were egocentric, and could not see something from the perspective of another person.

This egocentricity is linked to young children's difficulties with conservation, that is, an awareness that some things remain the same even if their appearance changes. For example, when water is poured from a tall thin container into a short fat one, young children will tend to say that the amount has changed as a result. For Piaget, this is evidence of an inability to decentre, and to focus, in this case, on both height and width at the same time.

The two following stages, concrete operations and formal operations, are characterized by increasingly systematic, logical thinking, first as rooted in the present, and then later, and increasingly, in abstract, hypothetical terms, although Meadows (2006) suggests that the models given for both of these stages remain controversial.

### Critiques of Piaget

An early critic of Piaget's ideas was Susan Isaacs (see Chapter 6), who, working at the same time as Piaget, suggests a more positive view of young children, emphasizing what they can do rather than what they cannot, and concluding, as a result of her observations, that young children are capable of logical thought, and of taking on the perspective of others. The majority of the critical reappraisal of Piaget's theories has occurred since the 1970s.

A fundamental basis on which Piaget's theories have been criticized is their suggested universality. This is seen as problematic in a number of ways. First, there is considerable scepticism about whether all development subscribes to a single pattern, across time and across cultures, a question which is considered in more depth in Chapter 3. Evidence across cultures suggests different rates of progress through any possible sequence, varying by culture, and amount and level of formality of schooling (Meadows 2006). Bidell and Fischer (1992) suggest that such a singular developmental pathway may tend to disadvantage children who are not from the particular cultural group typified in the model. Gardner (1983), along with others, suggests that development is not even universal within an individual, and, as part of his theory of multiple intelligences (see below) asserts that people have different levels of development in different domains, simultaneously. In recent years, we have also moved away from a view of learning as proceeding in any smooth, orderly direction, and the developmental ladder implied by Piaget's model has been replaced with a view of cognitive development as a much messier business, typified by the metaphor of a spider's web.

Related to these criticisms are others which point to Piaget's lack of acknowledgement of the parts played by social and emotional factors in children's development. Young children are born into a social world, which shapes their development in countless ways (Siegler et al. 2011). As we shall see, this is one of the most fundamental differences between Piaget's model and that of Vygotsky (1978).

Piaget emphasizes the importance of readiness in children's development, suggesting that there is little that an adult, or other person, can do to accelerate children's development. Cohen (2002) and Donaldson (1978) both suggest that, on the contrary, children can effectively be taught skills. Bidell and Fischer point to the difficulties for adults of waiting for just the 'right' moment before they 'pounce' in some way with a child who is deemed to be ready (1992: 16). In this they echo Duckworth's dilemma: 'Either we're too early and they can't learn it, or we're too late and they know it already' (1987: 31). Bidell and Fischer (1992) also highlight readiness as a potential issue for equity and social justice. Readiness, they suggest, may function well for the majority of white middle-class children, in whom mainstream literacy skills, for example, are presumed to develop as part of an unfolding process. Children whose cultural contexts support other kinds of skills may be disadvantaged whilst the adults working with them are waiting for them to become ready for literacy development. MacNaughton (2003) also points to issues around race, gender and culture, and suggests that it may be problematic if adults view negative comments from children about these areas as something they will naturally develop out of, without supportive interventions.

Donaldson (1978), whilst she acknowledges her indebtedness to Piaget, provides a range of evidence which suggests that children are much less egocentric thinkers, capable of disembedded or abstract thinking from a much younger age than Piaget believed. She and many others, including Cohen (2002) and Wood (1998), suggest that, as a result of his methods of gathering data, Piaget may have underestimated children's competence. The problem, Donaldson (1978) suggests, is that Piaget's tests do not make human sense to children, and are couched in ways to which they cannot relate. Wood (1998) suggests that there are three possible main criticisms in this area:

- Piaget may have underestimated the importance of the language used in his tasks;
- children may have had difficulty in making sense of the questions being asked of them, and the questioner's intended meaning;
- the tasks set may be artificial ones, which children could not understand.

Looking at the first of these, Wood (1998) suggests that young children may not understand the adults' use of vocabulary sufficiently to allow them to understand the task, for example, use of an expression like 'as much as'. Wood asks: 'Do children actually *understand* these words and expressions in the way the adult intends?' (1998: 60; emphasis in original). They may have similar confusion with regard to questions, as suggested in the second of Wood's points. Even where they comprehend the wording, children may feel unsure of the questioner's intended meaning. For example, in Piaget's test situations, children were often asked a similar question at least twice, as part of the experimental procedure. In many contexts, this may be a signal that the first answer was wrong. Thus, children may find themselves working very hard trying to infer some alternative meaning to the question, when none is intended. Donaldson (1978) demonstrates how even slight variation in the wording of a question can have a considerable impact on children's understanding of the question, and, as a result, their task performance.

The final point Wood makes may be the most important one for young children's understanding. Piaget's tests on children were carried out in experimental situations, disembedded from meaningful contexts, as in the three mountains test described earlier. Hughes (cited in Donaldson 1978) reframed this perspective-taking test, embedding it in a more familiar and meaningful context for children. In so doing, children aged 3½ had a 90 per cent success rate, much earlier and better than Piaget would suggest. Kate, in Box 2.2, clearly shows this ability to both literally and figuratively take on another's perspective, and to understand how they might feel, at an earlier age than Piaget would have suggested. The meaningful context of everyday life may have had some bearing on her success.

In contexts which make human sense to children, they have been shown to demonstrate object conservation (Fernyhough 2008), the ability to draw inferences (Thornton 2002) and learn by analogy (Whitebread 2000b) at much younger ages than Piaget proposes. Moreover, there is evidence to suggest that Piaget places unnecessary emphasis on logical thinking as a goal of development. Not only have young children demonstrated capability in logical thinking at an earlier age than expected by Piaget, but a reasonable number of adults 'may not attain the holy grail of formal operations' (Cohen 2002: 53). Good examples where adults make exactly the same kinds of errors as children are syllogistic and deductive reasoning, such as Whitebread illustrates (2000b: 146):

---

*Box 2.2:* Kate, aged 4.5, in the nursery

Kate is one of four children seated at a table with their teacher, playing with playdough. Emma (3.3), new to the nursery, approaches the teacher, and points to the nearby easel.

EMMA:      Me want do painting.
TEACHER:   You would like to paint? Well, there's space at the easel, so that's fine.
           Remember that you'll need to wear an apron.

Emma walks past Kate, to where aprons are hanging, takes one from the hook and attempts to put it on. She experiences some difficulty. Kate gets out of her seat and walks towards Emma.

KATE:      Do you want me to help you?

Emma holds out the apron and Kate takes it and holds it in a position that allows Emma to step into it.

KATE:      Now this bit goes over your head. I know how to do it because I'm 4.
           Do you know where to get the paper?
EMMA:      Over there (pointing to paper store).
KATE:      That's right. If you can't peg it up, I can help you.

Kate returns to her seat.

TEACHER:   That was very kind of you to help Emma.
EMMA:      (smiles broadly) I'm 4, so I can do lots of things now.

*According to Piaget, at the age of 4, Kate is right in the middle of the preoperational stage. Piaget argues that, because of a child's essential egocentricity, under the age of 7 there is an inability to view a situation from another's perspective. Throughout the entire episode there are very clear examples of Kate's ability to see a perspective other than her own. She was in no way personally affected by any of Emma's actions, so her only motivation must have been a desire to help. There is clear consideration of Emma's wishes, as she does not simply tell her what she is going to do, but rather enquires if she wants any help. It is also evident when she anticipates the possibility that Emma may have difficulty in pegging the paper to the easel. It would have been several months since she herself had experienced the same difficulty. Even if she can recall herself being in that situation, this is a clear indication of her capacity to decentre. She also shows that she is able to perceive Emma's physical perspective, by positioning the apron so that Emma is able to step into it.*

Reproduced with permission of Yvonne Hutton

There are two kinds of aliens, Blobs and Blips.
Blobs are blue.
I meet an alien. It is blue.
What kind of an alien is it?

Whitebread points out that both adults and children will confidently say it is a Blob, because we have been told that Blobs are blue, and thus infer that it must be a Blob, not a Blip. But a Blip could be blue as well, we just have not been told this.

Piaget has also been criticized on methodological grounds. He seldom reported quantitative information on numbers of children tested, and percentages who passed, and his interview technique is difficult to replicate. He also based much of his study on his own children, and those of other university professors, and it may be important to ask how representative such a sample is.

At the same time, however, Goswami (2008) suggests that there are a number of ways in which Piaget's views and ideas are consistent with current thinking. For example, she suggests that recent neuroimaging data makes Piaget's idea that sensorimotor behaviours become thought more plausible, and that his emphasis on the ways in which babies apply analogy rapidly once a new physical schema is understood is supported by recent experiments.

Box 2.3 illustrates the possibility of multiple interpretations of the same event, drawing particularly on the perspectives of Piaget and Donaldson (1978).

### Some implications for practice of Piaget's theories

- The aim of education is for children to learn how to learn. Children should be encouraged to ask questions, try out experiments and speculate, rather than accepting information unthinkingly (Smith et al. 2011).
- Thinking is a cumulative process and attention to children's different ways of thinking at different ages will need to be considered in making decisions about how they are best educated (Siegler et al. 2011). Children need to be 'ready' in order to learn.
- Learning is a process of active involvement and engagement.
- 'Discovery learning promotes learning by building up schemes and encourages later assimilation and accommodation – children "doing" is better than teachers "telling" (Doherty and Hughes 2009: 267).
- Learning is an individual process of the construction of knowledge by the child, with the process being emphasized over product.
- Emphasis is on child-initiated activity, with the child setting the pace of learning, exploring the world and testing out ideas without external pressure.
- The most important source of motivation is the child, who is intrinsically motivated to engage in activities.
- The social and physical environment is organized to support open-ended problem-solving and self-discovery learning by children.
- The role of the adult is to observe and facilitate children's learning, rather than engage in direct teaching.

---

*Box 2.3:* Charlie, aged 3.8, at the writing table in the nursery

Charlie chooses a stapler to use:

ADULT:      Oh Charlie, that stapler's empty, there's no staples in it.

Charlie chooses a piece of paper and puts it in the stapler's jaws.

ADULT:      Charlie, there's no staples in that.

Charlie is staring hard at the staple and the paper, using both hands and all his concentration. He works the stapler several times but nothing happens.

CHARLIE:    Oh! John! There's no staples in it!

*There is absolutely nothing wrong with Charlie's hearing, so what is the explanation for the above? Piaget might explain it in terms of egocentricity, an inability to decentre and see an immediate situation from another point of view. Donaldson's (1978) interpretation of this would be that Charlie has yet to develop the skill of focusing in on the shared meanings inherent in dialogue.*

Reproduced with permission of John Griffiths

---

## Information processing

There are a range of different accounts of cognitive development which come under the heading of information processing (see Meadows 2006, and Siegler and Alibali 2005, for useful digests). As the name suggests, information processing models are concerned with the impact of information on the processes of cognition. They share with Piaget the view that perception, memory, knowledge and understanding are closely related, and change with development (Wood 1998). Unlike Piaget, they are not so concerned with stages of development. Meadows (2006) suggests that information processing models sit between descriptions of cognition that focus on psychological levels of behaviour and those that describe it in terms of the neurophysiological workings of the brain.

The origins of information processing models lie in computer science and cognitive psychology, and it is easy to see how analogies with computers are used here to try to make sense of the development of thinking in humans. Thus, a common metaphor is that which compares the structural characteristics of cognition (aspects such as the three memory stores of sensory register, working memory and long-term memory, discussed in Chapter 1) to the 'hardware' of a computer, and the processes to 'software'.

### Information processing and memory

Memory has a central role in information processing theories. Woolfolk *et al.* even refer to information processing as a 'model of memory' (2008: 296). One of the first models of information processing was formulated by Atkinson and Shiffrin (1968, cited in Smith *et al.* 2011). They describe cognitive processing in terms of the three memory stores, and the control processes that operate between them (see Chapter 1 for more detail). Short-term memory, in Atkinson and Shiffrin's model, is limited in its capacity to retain units of information. More recently, there has been less emphasis on capacity and greater emphasis on the idea of working memory as the conscious part of information processing, where the constraint arises from the number and variety of the processes being carried out at the same time (Smith *et al.* 2011). Some things we do may be relatively automatic, requiring little active thought and short-term processing. Other, less practised, activities, may make much greater demands on capacity. Information then passes into long-term memory as a result of processes in short-term, or working, memory.

The processes by which these memories are both transferred and retrieved are the fundamental elements of information processing theories. They include strategies such as planning, reasoning, and the kinds of memory strategies touched on in Chapter 1. These memory strategies chiefly involve encoding and recall. Smith *et al.* (2011) suggest that use of encoding strategies such as rehearsal (mentally repeating information to yourself in order to remember it) and organization (grouping information together) become increasingly sophisticated as children get older. A third encoding strategy, elaboration, concerns the ways in which we make associations between items in order to help recall them better. Smith *et al.* note an interesting difference between the ways in which children used this strategy, drawing on the work of Buckhalt *et al.* (cited in Smith *et al.* 2011). Younger children tended to use 'static' elaborations, like 'the lady has a broom', whereas older children's elaborations tended to be more 'active', such as 'the lady flew on her broom to Hallowe'en' (Smith *et al.* 2011). They speculate that the benefit of this may be the creation of more memorable images. Whilst children younger than about 5 years seem not to spontaneously use strategies for recall (Thornton 2002), there is evidence that they can be helped to do so (Kuhn 2000), and that enhanced knowledge will be an important factor in the growth of strategy use (Smith *et al.* 2011).

### Common assumptions of information processing models

All information processing models share some basic assumptions. Siegler and Alibali (2005: 66) summarise these:

- Thinking is information processing – rather than focussing on stages of development, the emphasis is on the information that children represent, the processes they apply to the information and the memory limits that constrain the amount of information they can represent and process.
- The precise analysis of change mechanisms is emphasized – in particular, what are the change mechanisms that contribute most to development, and how do they work together to produce cognitive growth?
- Change is produced by a process of continuous self-modification – the outcomes generated by the child's own activities change the way the child will think in the future, in particular, the strategies that children devise to surmount the challenges posed by the environment and by their own limited processing capacity and knowledge.

Thus, as Meadows (2006: 279) suggests, there is an emphasis on cognition as 'largely a matter of handling information in order to solve problems', with a focus on what mental processes are used to deal with information, how they are organized and how they change during learning or development.

### Processing information: can we get better at it? Do we get better at it?

Information processing views of cognitive development focus on the ways in which children surmount three basic obstacles to their processing capacity: memory capacity, efficiency in basic thought processes and use of helpful strategies and knowledge (Siegler *et al.* 2011). In information processing terms, the three memory stores provide a structure for memory, with a range of processes and strategies operating on the information in those stores. The problem is that both adults and children alike are limited in their capacity to handle information, certainly when it is in a random or unstructured form. Information theorists describe this as having 'limited and relatively fixed channel capacity' (Wood 1998: 34). For example, the largest number of random items that adults can usually hold in working memory is about seven (Woolfolk *et al.* 2008). If presented with a string of random digits, most adults can usually transmit correct information on about seven before they start making errors and forgetting. However, information processing theorists suggest that, with training and experience, and use of strategies such as chunking (organizing individual bits of information into meaningful larger units) and grouping, our accuracy and skill increases considerably. Thus, information processing theorists suggest that the development of thinking is related to our ability to impose meaningful structures on the information we receive, and the ways in which we move that information within our memory systems.

This seems to suggest that the answer to the first part of the question above is yes, we can get better at processing information. What of the second part? Do we also, over time, get better, as part of maturation? Do young children have even less channel capacity than older children and adults? Taking the example of the random string of digits, Wood (1998) records that 3 year olds begin to falter after three items, and 5 year olds after five. It is not until about the age of 8 that mature levels of performance, that is, remembering about seven items, is achieved. He suggests that, because young children are relatively inexperienced, there are bound to be differences between adults and children in their competence in processing information. In essence, children do not have the same amount of experience, and the same levels of expertise, to draw upon which might help them to organize and structure their thinking in the ways that adults do. This idea of expertise may be important, and we shall return to it often throughout the book. Wood (1998) suggests that the benefit of using a word like expertise is that it combines both knowledge and action, and draws attention to them both as two parts of the same process.

Does this combination of action and knowledge, as expertise, have an impact on other aspects of information processing? Siegler *et al.* (2011) suggest that a basic assumption of information processing is that young children are problem-solvers. Problem-solving, and ways in which it may be supported, are discussed in Chapter 11. Here, it is worth looking at two key cognitive processes identified by Siegler *et al.* which link problem-solving and information processing.

### Planning, reasoning and expertise

Children begin to make simple plans before they are a year old (Karmiloff-Smith 1994), a process which requires them to be able to think ahead, and to organize and order their actions, on the basis of the available information. As they grow older, their plans become more elaborate and complex, enabling them to solve more of the problems they encounter (how to get to the biscuit tin, how to climb out of your cot, how to put your shoe on). However, despite the benefits of planning, many children fail to do so in situations where it would be helpful (Siegler *et al.* 2011). Why should this be? Siegler *et al.* (2011) suggest that analysis of the information processing requirements of planning shows that it involves making a sacrifice of immediate attempts to solve the problem in favour of trying to think through which particular strategy might be most effective. Young children often fail to do this for a number of reasons. First, they find it difficult to resist the desire to act immediately. Second, they tend to be overoptimistic about what they can achieve without planning, whereas older children are more realistic about assessing what they can do. Finally, the fact that the plans they make often fail (they still can't get to the biscuit tin) contributes to making planning seem less attractive as an option. Siegler *et al.* (2011) suggest that a combination of brain maturation, along with experiences that demonstrate the value of planning to children, serve to increase the frequency and quality of planning. However, it is knowledge and expertise which are key here, not age. Given appropriate information, younger children can make use of planning strategies as successfully as older children and adults (Thornton 2002). In addition, adults may often not use planning strategies where they would be useful (Siegler *et al.* 2011).

The ability to use reasoning, particularly the kind of analogical reasoning which helps us to understand new situations and problems in relation to familiar ones, also appears by the time children are about a year old. Initially, and for much of early childhood, children's use of analogical reasoning will depend on how closely the two situations resemble one another. Again, as with planning, expertise is key to helping children to progressively see deeper, less superficial similarities between situations and problems, which support the making of analogies between them (Siegler *et al.* 2011).

### Neural networks and overlapping waves

At the beginning of this section I emphasized the plurality of approaches which come under the heading of 'information processing'. Two of the best known which are worth looking at briefly are the neural network (connectionist) approach, and the overlapping waves model.

Traditional information processing approaches emphasize the sequential nature of processing, where thoughts follow one after the other. Neural network, parallel distributed processing or connectionist approaches, on the other hand, emphasize a model of processing in which different types of cognitive activity occur simultaneously, in parallel. In this model, information is not stored in any one place, but exists as a result of stimulation and inhibition: 'thus instead of there being a slot in memory in which information about Piaget is stored, the system has information about Piaget only when particular sets of units are active and stimulating or inhibiting each other in particular connection patterns' (Meadows 2006: 281). Meadows identifies current enthusiasm for connectionist models, and suggests that they have a number of advantages, including compatibility with what is known about the nervous system, and neurone activation and inhibition (this is looked at in more detail in chapter 4). Elman (2005), however, highlights some challenges for connectionist models, principally in capturing social cognition, and in dealing with the fact that children are active, not passive learners.

---

*Box 2.4:* Children aged between 3.1 and 3.11, playing on a chalk-drawn road circuit in the outdoor area of the nursery

Five children have been engaged in road play, with bikes and scooters, for some time. Two sets of zebra crossing markings are drawn across the road and the word STOP is written on both sides of the crossing. The children drive round the circuit, and abide by the road markings. Those on bikes and scooters stop when they see two children standing at the crossing.

TOM :      (To all) We can see your bikes coming so we can go (chants, and uses exaggerated actions). Look left and right and left again.

The driving and safe crossing of the road continues, with all the children joining in the chanting of 'look left and right and left again'.

*Tom extends his learning and helps the children to remember a three-term sequence 'chunking' for safely crossing the road by chanting, which all of the children spontaneously adopt. According to Meadows (2006) the strategy of using verbal rehearsal helps to keep sensory information in the short-term working memory long enough to be transferred permanently to long-term memory.*

Reproduced with permission of Meg Roberts

---

Goswami (2008) draws on Vygotskian ideas, emphasizing his view that part of human development is internal: inner speech (see Chapter 7), imagination and pretending are all internal mediators of cognitive processes, which may not be easily (or even possibly) captured by computational models.

The overlapping waves model of information processing, developed by Siegler (2000; Siegler and Alibali 2005) suggests that thinking is much more variable than both Piaget's theory and traditional information processing models imply (Siegler *et al.* 2011). Three premises underpin Siegler's theory. First, that children typically use a variety of ways of thinking, not just one, in tackling an activity or a problem; second, that these diverse strategies and approaches coexist over long periods of time; and third, that experience results in changes in children's reliance on current strategies, as well as introduction of new, more advanced strategies (Siegler 2000). The model suggests that, at any given time, children may use a number of different strategies for tackling the same activity. Over time, as a result of learning from both successes and failures, they gradually come to rely more upon those that prove most successful for them (Siegler 2000). Thornton (2002) suggests that the overlapping waves model may be particularly helpful in thinking about children's approaches to problem-solving.

### Some implications for practice from information processing models

- Children are seen as active learners and problem-solvers.
- Both adults and children share the same ways of reasoning, but 'what children can think about changes with age as the capacity to construct increasingly complex mental models develops' (Wood 1998: 200).

- The emphasis on task analysis in information processing accounts can be used by adults as a diagnostic tool for identifying and supporting individual children's needs (Siegler *et al.* 2011).
- 'Asking children to explain both why correct answers are correct and why incorrect answers are incorrect produces greater learning than only asking them to explain why correct answers are correct' (Siegler 2000: 33), and can lead to the adoption of new strategies.
- Children can be helped to develop useful memory strategies, with a positive impact on their cognitive activity.
- Children's developing knowledge and expertise supports their use of strategies for planning and reasoning.

## Linking Piagetian and information processing ideas

Meadows (2006) suggests that Piagetian and information processing models of cognition share a common idea that the psychological structures of the mind are invariant across cultures, settings and tasks, and independent of cultural and social context. In the years since Piaget first published his work, many psychologists and educationalists have further developed, and modified, his ideas. Some have combined his ideas about children's construction of knowledge with findings drawn from information processing about aspects such as attention, memory and strategies. The 'neo-Piagetian' theorist Case (1992), like Piaget, rejects the idea of domain-specific structures, but suggests a greater role for adult intervention to support children's development. Case argues that growth in children's information processing capacity is linked to how efficiently they can use memory capacity. He identifies four processes: encoding (speed of processing operations and working memory); strategies that free up mental capacity; automatization of knowledge; and generalization (applying what you know in new contexts) (Doherty and Hughes 2009). Karmiloff-Smith suggests a more modular approach, at least for specific subjects such as language, and also places more emphasis on innate mechanisms than did Piaget (Wood 1998).

## Lev Vygotsky

Born in Russia, in 1896, the same year as Piaget, Vygotsky's work was little known either inside or outside the country until the 1960s. The first translation of *Thought and Language*, with an introduction by Jerome Bruner (see below) appeared in the West in 1961, and it was not until 1978 that *Mind in Society*, a collection of essays, was published. Like Piaget, it is important to look at Vygotsky within the contexts of time and place. A brilliant scholar, he was invited to join the Institute of Psychology in Moscow in 1924. Along with other psychologists in post-revolutionary Russia at that time, he saw human beings as inherently social animals, who could only be understood in the context of their society. His ideas were, however, not well received under Stalin, and much of his work was either suppressed or hidden by colleagues. It was not until the 1950s that, even in Russia, his work began to be more widely available.

Vygotsky died of tuberculosis in 1934, and in the last years of his life worked intensely, producing fragments of writing, half-completed experiments and essays. His early death, coupled with the fact that the vast majority of us are reading his work in translation means that we cannot know how he might have developed his ideas. However, his influence has been widespread, and is felt across the world. His ideas underpin those of the sociocultural theorists looked at in Chapter 3.

Vygotsky differs fundamentally from both Piaget and the majority of approaches in the information processing models looked at above in his emphasis on the social nature of learning. Like Piaget, he views children as actively constructing their understanding as a result of their experiences, and in that sense his ideas can be described as constructivist. However, crucially, for Vygotsky, this construction occurs in the context of children's interactions with those around them. For Vygotsky, the child is more apprentice than lone scientist. As a result, his position is often described as social constructivist. As we saw in Chapter 1, Vygotsky and Piaget differ in their views on the relationship of learning to development. In Chapter 7 the area over which they fundamentally disagree, that of the relationship between language and thought, is explored.

### Social constructivism

Where Piaget emphasizes the role of individual discovery in development, Vygotsky places instruction at the heart of learning, and he argues that the capacity to learn through instruction is an essential feature of intelligence (Wood 1998). For Vygotsky, however, the relationship between instruction and internal learning is highly complex, and this is not a simple transmission model of 'teaching', whereby an adult instructs and a child listens. Instead it is a term which covers a wide range of strategies, including demonstration and discussion. The vehicles for this instruction are principally language and communication. In this, he has more in common with the ideas of Jerome Bruner, and Bruner was one of the people responsible for making Vygotsky's work more widely known in the West.

Thus, for Vygotsky, the social context in which learning takes place is as important as any specific activity the child undertakes. This highlights the different starting points of Piaget and Vygotsky. Whilst both were interested in trying to reconcile psychology and biology in outlining cognition and development (Gopnik et al. 1999), Piaget, as we have seen, starts from a biological model of development. Vygotsky's 'primary concern lay in understanding the nature, evolution and transmission of human culture' (Wood 1998: 11), where 'culture' is used to mean the customs of a particular people at a particular time, and their collective achievements over historical time (hence his perspective is often referred to as sociocultural). This is where language and communication are so important for Vygotsky: language is both the medium through which culture can be transmitted, and it is also a tool of thought.

For Vygotsky, learning is a revolutionary process of continuous quantitative change, where 'each successive layer of understanding transforms the meaning of previous understanding' (Wood and Attfield 2005: 92). He reverses Piaget's idea that development leads learning, and suggests instead that it is learning which fuels development. In Vygotsky's model we first come into contact with knowledge and ideas through experience of how others make sense of things, in our interactions with them. He calls this the interpersonal, or intermental, plane. We gradually come to make this knowledge our own, on the intrapersonal or intramental, plane. In the process of instruction, the knowledge practices and psychological, or cultural, tools of a culture are passed on to children. The idea of cultural tools is an important part of understanding

Vygotsky's thinking. Interacting with cultural tools of all kinds (ranging from physical objects to representational devices such as books and maps, mnemonic devices, and ways of knowing about the world such as science and maths) helps children to better understand the social and physical world. Children's encounters with all of these cultural tools shape the ways in which they think about things. Language is one of the most important tools, allowing high-level cognitive functioning. Meadows describes the role of tools in the following way:

> Individuals 'appropriate' psychological tools from their social and cultural milieu. They do not inherit them as instincts or reflexes, they do not normally reinvent them from scratch, they do not discover them in their independent interactions with the natural world. In particular they learn to use tools through their face to face communication and social interaction with other people who are also using psychological tools. Thus the tools have communication among their functions.
>
> (Meadows 2006: 305)

The process as a whole is referred to as internalization. Trevarthen's (1995) work with babies suggests that this process begins from the very earliest moments of life. Vygotsky

---

*Box 2.5:* Daniel, aged 1.10, in his pushchair

Daniel was sitting strapped in his pushchair holding a small toy car in each hand. He gently attempted to balance each car on the flat metal frame at the end of his seat. Both cars tumbled to the ground. He reached for them but because his safety straps restrained him he could not retrieve them. His childminder, seeing his predicament, picked up and returned the cars to him. This happened several times, and, with Daniel's persistence, both cars eventually balanced. Carefully, so as not to jog the buggy, he arched his head forward and titled it sideways so that he was looking towards the underside of the car on his left. He then turned and in the same way looked at the underside of the car on his right. A smile broke out on his face as he shook his legs and watched both cars fall to the ground. His smile widened and he looked to his childminder. She returned his smile.

*Throughout the observation Daniel is supported by the actions of his carer. I believe she supported his play by returning his cars and by reciprocating a smile. These seemingly insignificant acts are of great importance to social constructivist theory. Vygotsky suggests that 'object orientated movement (Daniel reaching for his cars) becomes movement aimed at another person; a means of establishing relations' (1978: 56). The fundamental proposition of social constructivist theory is that the child's potential for learning is primarily fostered by social interactions, language eventually being the key. In the early pre-language years it is the parent/carer's sensitive responses to the child that get internalized ... Without the interaction of his carer I believe Daniel would not have had this opportunity to develop a reciprocal and trusting relationship within a cultural context.*

Reproduced with permission of Jo Dabir-Alai

describes internalization as 'a series of transformations' (1978: 56), between external social processes and internal psychological ones:

a 'An operation that initially represents an external activity is reconstructed and begins to occur internally': this involves assistance from more capable others, either adult or peer.

b 'An interpersonal process is transformed into an intrapersonal one': the child now provides his own assistance, through talking aloud, or through inner speech.

c 'The transformation of an interpersonal process into an interpersonal one is the result of a long series of developmental events': internalization of knowledge, ideas and concepts is a prolonged developmental process.

(Adapted from Vygotsky 1978:56-7)

Internalization supports the development of 'higher mental processes' (Vygotsky 1978: 57), and leads to more complex understanding, through increased control of external, cultural processes.

Vygotsky (1978) suggests that, for young children, play (essentially role play) is a leading factor in development, and important in preparing the foundations for higher mental functions, particularly symbolic thinking and imagination, and in promoting self-regulated behaviour (Bodrova and Leong 2011). Vygotsky suggests that making one thing stand for another in play, for example, a stick for a horse, creates a 'pivot' (Vygotsky 1978) which detaches meaning from the real object. Increasingly, these representations become more symbolic, supporting the development of more abstract, symbolic ways of thinking. By providing children with opportunities to try out culturally defined roles, using culturally defined artefacts such as toys, play 'acts as a kind of mental support system which allows children to represent their everyday social reality' (Penn 2005: 42). Vygotsky suggests that imaginative play supports children in thinking in more mature ways than they are able to do outside of play, an idea expressed in his assertion that 'In play a child always behaves beyond his average age, above his daily behavior; in play it is as though he were a head taller than himself' (1978: 102). In support of this idea, Rogers and Evans (2008) identify a number of ways in which role play supports the development of young children's thinking and understanding, and role play is highlighted in a number of chapters throughout this book.

## The zone of proximal development

The concept of Vygotsky's which has had the most circulation is the idea of the zone of proximal development or ZPD. This concept refers to the 'gap' that exists for any individual between what he can achieve alone (his level of actual development), and what he can do with the help of another more knowledgeable or skilled person (his level of potential development). The role of this more experienced other person in this process of assisted performance is to guide a child to a more sophisticated solution to a task in order to support the move from regulation by others to self-regulation. This is very clearly a radically different position to that taken by Piaget, for whom such adult intervention represents the teaching of empty procedures to children. Vygotsky defines the ZPD in the following way:

It is the distance between the actual developmental level as determined by independent problem solving and the level of potential development as determined through problem solving under adult guidance or in collaboration with more capable peers ... The zone of proximal development defines those functions that have not yet matured but are in the process of maturation, functions that will mature tomorrow but are currently in an embryonic state ... What a child can do with assistance today she will be able to do by herself tomorrow.

(Vygotsky 1978: 86–7)

This ZPD is not fixed, and will vary both over time, in different areas of experience, and from child to child. Thus, for Vygotsky, two children with similar levels of actual development may have very different zones of proximal development, that is, very different potentials for learning through appropriate instruction. The principle vehicle for actualizing the ZPD is verbal exchange, including mechanisms such as open-ended questioning and the provision of useful prompts, but demonstration, emotional and non-verbal exchanges (Chak 2001), and joint problem-solving (Wood and Attfield 2005) are also valuable. Vygotsky (1978) suggests that play is a particularly important context for creating a ZPD in the early years.

Vygotsky's emphasis on the role of a 'more capable' (1978: 87) other person emphasizes that this support can come from children, as well as adults, as in the example in Box 2.6. What is needed is more knowledge or skill in the particular domain. Thornton (2002) suggests that even quite young children can modify their talk and behaviour in order to support a younger or less experienced child, though the ability to do so develops over time. Parents may do this quite naturally (Cohen 2002; Siegler et al. 2011), in the course of everyday conversation and interactions at home (Tizard and Hughes 2002; Wells 1987). For Vygotsky, this cooperatively achieved success is at the heart of learning, supporting the development of reflection and self-regulation. He suggests that children need to learn in order to be motivated (in contrast to the often held view that motivation is a precondition of learning), and that the creation of a leading edge of development, through the ZPD, helps in this process of supporting motivation.

### Neo- and post-Vygotskian developments

The influence of Vygotsky's theories continues to be strongly felt. Bruner and others such as Karpov (2006), Wells (1987) and Wood and Wood (1996) have further developed the idea of the ZPD, and, as we shall see in Chapter 3, his ideas are fundamental to the thinking of sociocultural theorists such as Rogoff (1990, 2003). Vygotsky's writings about play have been considerably developed by others since his death. Bodrova and Leong (2011) outline the ideas of Karpov and Elkonin, in particular. Elkonin describes play as the 'leading activity' (Bodrova and Leong 2011: 62), which facilitates the development of higher mental functions in four ways. First, he suggests play impacts on the child's motivation; second, it facilitates cognitive decentring; third, it advances the development of mental representations; and fourth, it fosters the development of deliberate physical and mental voluntary behaviours (Bodrova and Leong 2011). Rinaldi, commenting on practice in Reggio Emilia explicitly acknowledges the influence of Vygotsky on their practitioners' thinking, when she says: 'It is our belief that all knowledge emerges in the process of self and social construction' (1998: 115).

---

*Box 2.6:* A group of children aged between 3.9 and 4.4, in the nursery

The previous day the children were spinning saucepan lids on the floor in the home area. In order to follow this interest, a range of spinning artefacts have been planned for. The children have been playing for some time.

CARL:       (using a push down/pull up spinning top) Look I pushed it.
He glances at Amber, who has spent some time attempting to use a dynamo powered spinning top. He takes the toy and speaks to her:
CARL:       I'll show you.
Amber allows Carl to demonstrate the workings of the toy, watching his actions closely. After a short while Carl returns the toy, and says to her:
CARL:       See, like that.
Amber restarts her attempts at making the toy work. Eventually she manages to make the connection and the top spins for a short time on the table. She looks up at Carl and says to him:
AMBER:      See, I doin' it like dis.

*When Carl uses eye gaze (Pellicano and Rhodes 2003) to 'observe' Amber it could be suggested that he was aware of her zone of proximal development, which would imply that Carl displayed second-order intentionality (Bailey 2002). Therefore, it could be argued that Carl was able to use this understanding to scaffold Amber's thinking and understanding.*

Reproduced with permission of Lynn Bartlett

One particular aspect of Vygotsky's thinking which has received attention in recent years is 'the cultural-historical theory of activity', or activity theory, formulated by Vygotsky, Luria and Leontiev in the 1920s (Smidt 2009). Similar to sociocultural theory, it differs in emphasizing the activity itself, rather than then processes of mediation via cultural tools. Smidt (2009) identifies three generations of activity theory, including that developed by Michael Cole, whose work is looked at in Chapter 3.

### Critiques of Vygotsky's theories

An inevitable difficulty in interpreting and analysing Vygotsky's work arises as a result of his early death. In his desire to record as much of his thinking as possible, much is only in outline, and incomplete, with 'brilliant sketches' (Cohen 2002: 59) rather than fully developed research. Wood (1998) suggests that his work is often speculative and self-contradictory. In addition, Cohen (2002) suggests that, methodologically, his studies would not nowadays be seen as models of good empirical practice. In his defence, Cole and Scribner (1978), writing in the introduction to *Mind in Society,* emphasize both the implications of his early death, and the fact that many of the studies were pilots, never, they believe, intended for publication. They also caution against judging the experimental approaches of one culture by those of another – a fitting comment in the context of Vygotsky's emphasis on the role of culture in development.

Smith *et al.* (2011) suggest that there may be some drawbacks to Vygotsky's view of learning as situated in social contexts, pointing out that not all contexts are necessarily conducive to learning, and that some may even inhibit it. Goswami (2008) also expresses doubt about Vygotsky's idea that play will lead to an appetite for school. In addition, whilst Vygotsky accords language a central role in children's cognitive development, the role of perceptual and motor capacities is much less well considered (Doherty and Hughes 2009).

In relation to the ZPD, Bodrova and Leong (2011) draw on Elkonin's definition of mature play as that needed for development to occur, and question whether young children now are capable of this level of play, in which a ZPD can be created. They suggest that an increase in adult-directed activity, more toys and games that limit children's imagination and stronger safety limits set by adults on children have all resulted in a decline in the maturity and complexity of young children's play. Chak (2001) suggests that the ZPD serves more as a metaphor, and may be difficult to operationalize, particularly in the context of nurseries and schools, where one-to-one support and intervention is less likely than at home, for most children. Even where adults are able to do so, questions arise about how and when to intervene in order to provide appropriate support. Wood and Attfield (2005) acknowledge this difficulty, but outline an idea of 'shared zones', with practitioners structuring the environment through resourcing and pedagogical strategies which support high-quality interactions between adults and peers.

### Some implications for practice of Vygotsky's ideas

- Learning is seen as a social process, and collaborative learning with others is prioritized.
- 'Children's learning is maximised when they are regularly working at the upper levels of their competence' (MacNaughton and Williams 2009: 374).
- Instruction is an essential part of learning.
- Imaginative play is a vital source of cognitive development.
- Language is important both as a way in which children develop their thinking and understanding, and as a means for sharing thoughts and understandings with others.
- 'Rather than a "watching and waiting" orientation, skilled practitioners need to know when and how to interact with children, to support learning and development' (Wood and Attfield 2005: 97).
- Adult support is contingent upon children's behaviour: more help is given when children experience difficulty, with this being gradually withdrawn as children succeed in an activity (Wood and Wood 1996). In the early stages the help provided is more elaborate and explicit, later it is less explicit, and less frequent, focusing on hints rather than instructions (Meadows 2006).
- Continuous assessment of children's levels within the ZPD, using verbal and non-verbal cues as indicators, is important, as levels are constantly changing (Chak 2001). Private speech may be significant here: 'if a child is using clear, task-related private speech it is likely that the task being attempted is within the child's ZPD' (MacNaughton and Williams 2009: 374).
- 'The culture (of schools) should be one in which instruction is aimed at deep understanding, in which learning is a cooperative activity, and in which learning a little makes children want to learn more' (Siegler *et al.* 2011: 164).

- Children can learn from each other as well as from adults, provided that one is more knowledgeable about the activity than the other. The gap between their understandings need not be great, however, as then the 'expert' is more likely to understand the problems the 'novice' faces (Smith *et al.* 2011).
- 'The environment needs to be richly stimulating with problems to solve and a wide range of individual, small group, and whole group opportunities' (Raban *et al.* 2003: 72).
- The resources (physical tools) which children use in their play are important supports for their intellectual development (Broadhead 2004).

## Jerome Bruner

Jerome Bruner was, as we have already noted, influential in promoting Vygotsky's ideas in the West. In many ways he sits between Piaget and Vygotsky in his ideas on children's development. Like Piaget, he emphasizes action and problem-solving in children's learning, but, like Vygotsky, he stresses the importance of social interaction, language and instruction in the development of thinking. Wood (1998) suggests that Bruner's thinking owes much to information processing theory, and that Bruner's early work studying adult reasoning had an important impact on his ideas about the development of thinking in young children, emphasizing culture and growth as central factors. Bruner, like both Piaget and Vygotsky, sees play as an important aspect of young children's development. For Bruner 'play provides an excellent opportunity to try combinations of behaviour that would, under functional pressure, never be tried' (Bruner cited in MacNaughton 2003:43). It serves, in his view, both as practice in mastering skills, and as a way of trying out novel ways of thinking and acting in a safe context.

The main focus of disagreement between Piaget and Bruner is over the former's theory of stages of development. Piaget sets out a stage theory based on a gradual move towards more abstract forms of thought. Bruner argues that logical thinking is not the ultimate destination, rather it is one of several special ways of thinking. He is particularly concerned to look at the ways in which young children represent their experiences, and their growing understanding of the world. He suggests (1966) three categories of such representation:

- enactive representation: when children represent through their actions;
- iconic representation: when children represent through looking at or making pictures or images of things;
- symbolic representation: when children use symbolic systems such as written language or mathematical symbols to represent their thinking.

These three categories embody an idea of developing abstraction: clearly, symbolic representation, the ability to represent your thinking in ways which have no perceptual resemblance to the actual event, is a more abstract way of thinking than enacting an event. However, Bruner, unlike Piaget, believes that all three ways of representing are available to young children at any one time, with the adult's role, in scaffolding this process, being vital.

In Bruner's view, children return time and again to ideas and concepts, representing them in these different ways, and deepening their understanding as a result. He characterizes this as a spiral curriculum (Bruner 1960) in which learning is both recursive, that is, repeated in different contexts, and incremental, embodying developing expertise. Children themselves do this without support, for example, the uses to which a baby might put building bricks would be different to the way that same child might use them at the age of 2, or 5. However, Bruner suggests that this principle can also be used by adults to support the development of children's thinking and understanding, as exemplified by his assertion that 'any subject can be taught in some intellectually honest form to any child at any stage' of development' (Bruner 1960: 33).

## Scaffolding

The idea of Bruner's which has received most attention is the metaphor of scaffolding, a term coined in 1976 by Wood, Bruner and Ross to describe the kinds of support children need in order to reach their ZPD. The idea of scaffolding has been progressively elaborated since then, and is particularly important to the sociocultural theories outlined in Chapter 3, although Rogoff (1990, 2003) favours the term 'guided participation' as a more inclusive concept than scaffolding. However, MacNaughton and Williams (2009) also issue a timely warning that we should beware of labelling anything an adult or more expert peer does to support a child's learning as 'scaffolding'.

For Bruner, scaffolding provides the solution to the 'puzzle' of Vygotsky's statement about the ZPD that 'the only "good" learning is that which is in advance of development' (Vygotsky 1978: 89). As Bruner asks: 'how could "good learning" be that which is in advance of development and, as it were, bound initially to be unconscious since unmastered?' (Bruner 1988: 89). He outlines his understanding of this seemingly contradictory idea:

> the tutor or the aiding peer serves the learner as a vicarious form of consciousness until such a time as the learner is able to master his own actions through his own consciousness and control. When the child achieves that conscious control over a new function or conceptual system, it is then that he is able to use it as a tool. Up to that point, the tutor in effect performs the critical function of 'scaffolding' the learning task to make it possible for the child, in Vygotsky's word, to internalise external knowledge and convert it into a tool for conscious control.
>
> (Bruner 1988: 89)

What are the crucial features of this process of scaffolding, and how do adults provide support for children? Their first task is to engage the child's interest, and encourage their involvement. Meadows neatly outlines the adult's role during the activity, once the child is engaged, which she suggests includes the need to:

> highlight critical features and information, buffer the learner's attention against distractions, channel the learner's activities so that there is freedom to succeed and not too much freedom to go wrong. Errors are turned into opportunities to learn, procedures are commented on and explained, efforts are praised, and responsibility for doing the task is gradually transferred to the learner, contingent on his or her having demonstrated an ability to succeed.
>
> (Meadows 2006: 383)

Wood (1998) suggests that, within this general set of practices, some strategies may be more useful than others. Less likely to be successful is the strategy of first showing the child what to do before allowing them to have a go. This may lead both to overloading the child's powers of concentration, and to complaints that they are not able to take a turn themselves. Equally, over-reliance on verbal instructions may also be problematic, as children may not understand them without first being shown the action in practice.

The most effective help may involve what has been termed contingent instruction (Wood and Wood 1996), because it involves changes in the levels of support and control by the adult, depending on the adult's assessment of the child's performance. This features two main ingredients. The first concerns circumstances where a child is in difficulty. Here, the adult immediately offers more specific help or instruction than previously, clarifying ideas, providing fuller explanation and demonstrating actions. The second ingredient is 'fading', or ensuring the minimal help needed to ensure success. For example, where initially a child had needed to be shown what to do, the adult will replace this with verbal hints, then with silence. Put succinctly: 'give more help when the learner gets into difficulty, and offer less help as they gain proficiency' (Wood and Wood 1996: 7).

What remains unclear is the precise nature of what gets internalized during the course of such interactions. Chak (2001) also questions whether, within the restrictions of scaffolding, children's creativity in identifying their own goals, and in using their own strategies for reaching that goal, may perhaps be hindered. The metaphor of scaffolding, with its image of a structure maintained by someone external to the child, has been criticized for its emphasis on the adult's role and power (Jordan 2009). Contemporary interpretations of adult roles have placed more emphasis on intersubjectivity (mutual understanding between people of each other's thoughts and feelings) and co-construction, which recognizes and values the child as a powerful agent in their own learning. Given that sociocultural theorists believe that the foundation of cognitive development is our ability to establish intersubjectivity (Siegler *et al.* 2011), this may be very significant for young children's development. Jordan (2009) describes research which shows young children engaging in more higher order thinking as a result of their experiences of a co-constructive approach than when adults scaffolded their learning. In addition, she suggests that co-construction supports a disposition towards mastery in young children (see Chapters 3 and 6). However, looking at everyday life in settings for young children, adult interactions with large groups and whole classes are may be more likely to be characterized by adult-focused scaffolding, with small groups and one-to-one contexts more easily facilitating co-construction. This suggests the value of trying to find opportunities for small group, pair and individual adult–child interactions.

### Some implications for practice of Bruner's ideas

It is useful to look back at the implications suggested for Vygotsky, as a number of these, in particular those on the role of instruction and adult support, are also appropriate here. In addition:

- High-quality scaffolding involves joint problem-solving, intersubjectivity, warmth and responsiveness, keeping the child in the ZPD, and the promotion of self-regulation (children's control of their own learning) (MacNaughton and Williams 2009).

- In scaffolding children's understanding adults need to decide on the focus of what support is to be offered, how specific that help should be and the timing of any intervention (Wood and Wood 1996).

## Modularity and Howard Gardner

A number of theorists propose that the mind is organized as a collection of mental modules, or organs, each prestructured for processing different kinds of input, for example, perception or language (Chomsky 1957; and Chapter 7). For Pinker, the rationale for such a view is that 'the mind has to be built out of specialized parts because it has to solve specialized problems' (1997: 30). Some advocates of modularity suggest that every domain of knowledge is processed by a separate module. Of these, one of the best known whose work has had an impact on educational thinking is Howard Gardner.

### Howard Gardner and multiple intelligences

Gardner suggests that 'the mind is organized into relatively independent realms of functioning' (1993: 120). He believes (1999) that those who suggest a single form of intelligence look increasingly isolated, particularly in light of recent developments in understanding about the physiological make-up of the brain (see Chapter 4). In his view, we all possess a number of intelligences (Multiple Intelligences or MI), and that, in every individual, the relative strengths of each combine to give a unique overall profile of intelligences (1999).

Gardner defines intelligence as 'the ability to solve problems, or to fashion products, that are valued in one or more cultural or community settings' (1993: 7), a definition that has elements in common with the ideas of both Piaget and Vygotsky. Concerned about what he saw as a narrow conception of intelligence, generally centred on linguistic and logico-mathematical understanding, Gardner originally identified seven intelligences, or types of thinking, in 1983:

- Linguistic – relating to language and words
- Logical-mathematical – abstractions and numbers
- Musical – rhythm and sound
- Spatial – patterning and imagery, knowing the environment
- Bodily kinesthetic – physical skills, reflexes and timing
- Interpersonal – sensitivity to others' emotions and mental states
- Intrapersonal – self-knowledge and inner-focusing

In 1995 he added a further one:

- Naturalist – categorization of natural objects

He has since suggested the existence of a further 'half', which he calls existential intelligence, or 'the proclivity to pose (and ponder) questions about life, death and ultimate realities' (1999: 72). Much conventional practice, Gardner suggests, focuses

Box 2.7: The zone of proximal development and scaffolding. Carrie, aged 3.5, in the nursery

Carrie has been watching the practitioner roll playdough with a rolling pin, and adding dough to the practitioner's pile. Carrie smiles, then gathers all the dough on the table and squashes it onto the practitioners' pile. Carrie stands back, smiles and watches the practitioner roll the dough again. Carrie looks at the table for more dough. She picks up an alphabet cutter that has dough stuck in it. Using her fingers she tries to poke the dough out with little success. She pinches the dough with her right hand and manages to take tiny amounts of it out. Carrie grumbles, frowns and looks at the practitioner. The practitioner picks up a modelling tool on the table and an alphabet cutter of her own, and pushes the dough out using the modelling tool while Carrie watches. Carrie smiles when the dough pops out of the cutter and onto the table. She picks up the piece of dough and adds it to the pile of rolled dough and the practitioner rolls it, smiling.

She moves around the table to another alphabet cutter which has playdough stuck in it, picks up the modelling tool and uses it to poke the dough out. She smiles when the dough falls onto the table, and adds it to the pile and the practitioner rolls it once more. Carrie smiles. She looks around the table and collects all the alphabet cutters. She selects one with dough stuck in it and, using the modelling tool, removes the dough. She smiles as she adds it to the pile of dough. She selects another and repeats the action of removing the dough using the modelling tool and then adding it to the pile of dough for the adult to roll flat.

*It would seem that initially Carrie did not know how to use the modelling tool to remove the playdough. After the adult demonstrated, Carrie was able to carry out this action independently with success. This therefore suggests that with adult support and demonstration Carrie moved through what Vygotsky (1978) refers to as the 'zone of proximal development', where with the assistance of a more knowledgeable other Carrie is enabled to reach a higher thinking process than she would have independently.*

*Bruner's concept of scaffolding children's thinking is similar to Vygotsky's notion of the zone of proximal development in which previous knowledge is built upon and, through guidance by a more experienced person, new skills are developed.*

Abridged and reproduced with permission of Samantha McGinley

on a few of these forms of thinking, often at the expense of the development of the others.

In practice, just about every possible aspect of human activity may involve a blend of Gardner's different intelligences. A child digging in the garden will draw upon naturalist intelligence, as well as using physical intelligence to dig, spatial intelligence to understand the environment, interpersonal intelligence to negotiate a space alongside others, linguistic intelligence to talk about what is happening, and existential intelligence in her awe and wonder about the natural world!

For Gardner, one important implication of his ideas is that, in practice, one of these intelligences will probably act as an entry point to engage others, and that strength in one area may facilitate performance in another (1993). Gardner (1999) suggests that a multiple intelligences perspective can enhance children's understanding in three important ways. First, as a result of the ways in which multiple intelligences provide powerful entry points to a topic; second, by offering analogies that help connect the new to the better known and understood; and finally by providing multiple representations of the core ideas of a topic. He believes that these three elements imply a distinct order for adults working with children. First, begin with entry points, then offer analogies, and finally converge on multiple representations of the same idea.

Gardner stresses that his approach is supported by empirical evidence, and the rigorous application of a set of criteria for the inclusion of each intelligence. These criteria are drawn from psychology, anthropology, biological sciences, cultural studies and case studies of learners. Adapted from Gardner 1983, they are:

- the potential isolation of the area by brain damage;
- the existence in it of prodigies, savants and other exceptional individuals;
- an identifiable core operation or set of operations;
- a distinctive developmental history within an individual, along with a definable nature of expert performance;
- an evolutionary history and evolutionary plausibility;
- support from tests in experimental psychology;
- support from psychometric findings;
- susceptibility to encoding in a symbol system.

Gardner's ideas have been influential worldwide, spawning multiple intelligence programmes, schools, tests and even board games (Gold 2002). He maintains that this was never his intention, and that, ultimately, he developed his theories as a psychologist for other psychologists. He has also been critical of attempts to link his ideas with learning styles, for example (see Chapter 1).There are, however, a number of ways in which his ideas link directly with others in early childhood. The emphasis on children's opportunities to represent their ideas in a wide range of different symbol systems – spoken and written language, dynamically, enactively, graphically – links with the work of Chris Athey discussed in Chapters 6 and 9. In recent years he has worked closely with settings in Reggio Emilia, including on the *Making Learning Visible* project (Project Zero and Reggio Children 2001), looked at in more detail in Chapters 6 and 9. He has also developed an argument that identifies five different 'minds', each of which he believes will be important for the future. These are the 'disciplined mind' (developed through education and supporting expertise in a subject), the synthesizing mind, the creating mind, the respectful mind and the ethical mind (Gardner 2007).

### Critiques of Gardner's ideas

White (2002) provides the most trenchant criticism of Gardner's ideas, asserting that Gardner's criteria for selection, listed earlier, are open to serious criticism. Fundamentally, he suggests that Gardner provides no justification for the particular criteria he includes, and that at least two depend not on empirical evidence, as Gardner stresses, but on 'psychological or philosophical theories whose credentials rest on shaky foundations' (2002: 94). In addition, he questions whether all, or only a number, of the criteria must be fulfilled, saying that Gardner himself has provided contradictory commentary on this point.

Gardner acknowledges that some of his ideas have proved controversial, for example, the use of the word 'intelligence' to describe some of the abilities. Geake (2009) suggests that there are not multiple intelligences so much as multiple applications of general intelligence, whilst Woolfolk *et al.* (2008) point to criticisms that some of his intelligences are really talents (for example, musical intelligence) or personality traits (interpersonal intelligence). Gardner is emphatic in his insistence that either all or none of them should be called intelligences, and that to do otherwise devalues aspects such as musical or bodily kinaesthetic intelligence (1999). He has also been criticized for the basis of his selection, with the suggestion that it overemphasizes the arts, and undervalues practical intelligence (Gold 2002). For White, the eight look 'too close to familiar curricular areas for comfort' (2002: 95). In response to criticism that there is no hard psychological evidence that the different intelligences exist, Gardner says that the work to provide this would be considerable and, whilst it is worth doing, that he does not want to spend his time doing it (Gold 2002).

### Some implications for practice of Gardner's ideas

The following implications are derived from Gardner (1993, 1999).

- A holistic approach that gives children the chance to discover interests and aptitudes.
- The importance of presenting ideas and activities to children that may pick up on their preferred ways of thinking ('entry points'), for example, telling stories to support linguistic understanding; physically active activities that support kinaesthetic understanding; and role play and discussion that support interpersonal understanding.
- The need for resources which evoke the use of a range of intelligences. Materials are not specifically labelled 'mathematical' or 'visual and spatial', for example, but may be used either by themselves, or in combinations, which might support various intelligences.
- The starting point is children's strengths, rather than weaknesses, which involves using what they are good at to support the development of areas of intelligence which are less developed, and presenting material in ways which tap into different children's strengths, to support their understanding of new ideas and concepts.

### What conclusions can we draw?

The preceding models suggest a number of often very different processes, and competences, in young children's thinking and understanding. Is it possible to draw some useful conclusions from the current understandings? Whitebread (2000b: 147–51) suggests some key areas in which there is clear development in childhood:

- More exhaustive information processing: as children grow older they become less impulsive and more reflective, more likely to consider relevant information before acting.

- The ability to comprehend relations of successively higher orders: a progression from only being able to consider the task or object at hand towards being able to consider issues at a more abstract level, and to more easily see relationships between things.
- Flexibility in the use of strategy or information and the development of more sophisticated control strategies: a process of an increasing ability to monitor and evaluate cognitive processes, the building up of metacognitive knowledge (see chapter 5) about tasks and our own intellectual processes, and increasing ability to construct and select ever more appropriate strategies.

## A note about other approaches to learning

There are, of course, other models of cognition. One of the most common models, not discussed here, is the behaviourist approach, also known as operant conditioning. Chiefly, this theory is not discussed here because it is a theory for learning rather than a theory of thinking. It casts the learner in a relatively passive role, placing responsibility for the selection and pacing of learning with the teacher. It stems very much from the work of Skinner, and, before him, of Pavlov, and is characterized by the ideas of stimulus, response and consequence (often referred to as S–R approaches). The influence of behaviourist theory is clearly evident in, for example, the use of positive reinforcement of effort and achievement, and negative sanctions to modify behaviour. The ideas behind these practices are complex, and deserve careful consideration. However, when looking at the development of children's thinking and understanding, they may have a more limited role. As Pinker (1997) suggests, we bring our thoughts to bear on a situation, we do not act merely in response to a behavioural trigger. In response to seeing a burning building, people do not always act on this danger signal by running away. They may, indeed, react in a number of different ways. They may attempt to save someone they can see trapped; they may stand and watch; they may even, if they are suicidal, or motivated by seeking publicity for a cause, run into the flames. All of these alternatives are governed, Pinker (1997) suggests, by thought processes such as belief and desire. Whilst this is a rather crude interpretation of behaviourist theory, it nevertheless draws attention to the complexity of the thought processes which guide people's actions.

## Further reflection

1   For all of the models of cognition discussed here – constructivism, information processing, social constructivism, modular theory – now try to complete the following sentences:

The image of a learner is _____

The image of thinking is_____

Characteristic child activity might be_____

The potential advantages of this theory are_____

The potential drawbacks of this theory are_____

2   Try to think about your own educational experiences: can you trace any particular models in the ways you were taught?

3 Do you agree with Penn's assertion that 'Piaget now belongs to history' (2005: 40)?

4 How would you define scaffolding? How does it relate to the ZPD?

## Further reading

*Piaget*

Cohen (2002: ch. 2)
Donaldson (1978)
Duckworth (1987)
Meadows (2006: ch. 4)
Piaget (1950, 1959, 1962)
Siegler *et al.* (2011: ch. 4)
Smith *et al.* (2011: ch. 13)
Thornton (2002: chs 3, 5 and 7)

*Information processing*

Meadows (2006: ch. 4)
Siegler and Alibali (2005: ch. 3)
Siegler *et al.* (2011: ch. 4)
Thornton (2002: 112–15)
Wood (1998: 12–14, 31–7 and 44–5)

*Vygotsky*

Bodrova and Leong (2011)
Bruner (1988)
Chak (2001)
Meadows (2006: ch. 4)
Thornton (2002: ch. 7)
Vygotsky (1978, 1986)
Wood (1998: introduction and chs 1, 2 and 4)
Wood and Wood (1996)
Wood and Attfield (2005: ch. 4)

*Bruner*

Bruner (1960, 1986, 1988)
Wood (1998: introduction and chs 1, 4 and 8)
Wood and Wood (1996)

*Gardner*

Gardner (1983, 1993, 1999, 2007)
Project Zero and Reggio Children (2001)

# Chapter 3

# The social, cultural and emotional contexts of thinking and understanding

It is this chapter, perhaps more than any other in the book, which demonstrates the interrelationship of thinking and understanding to all aspects of children's experience. Children's thinking and understanding occurs in, and is conditioned by, the social and cultural contexts in which it takes place. Those contexts embody particular constructs of childhood, and what are seen as appropriate ways of inducting children into a culture, and 'bringing them up'. In addition, the ways in which children see themselves as thinkers and learners is dependent upon their self-concept, self-esteem and view of themselves as part of their surrounding social world. It is a reciprocal process, in which the socio-affective domain impacts upon children's cognitive development, and vice versa. Meadows suggests that there is 'good reason to believe that the social and interpersonal context is particularly important in the development of complex cognitive skills' (2006: 446). The importance of this area is reflected in the emphasis placed upon it in policy documents, for example, DfES (2005), DfES (2007), Ministry of Education, New Zealand (1996), and practitioner-focused books such as Dowling (2010) and Roberts (2010). Dunn (1993) outlines the growth of interest in this area:

> Cognitive development was formerly conceptualized chiefly in terms of an individual actively exploring and acting on his or her environment in an autonomous fashion. Now, however, the social interactions and relationships within which children grow up are widely accepted as important in their cognitive development, both in fundamental cognitive advances and influencing cognitive performance.
>
> (Dunn 1993: 2)

In this chapter we shall look at perspectives that have developed since Lev Vygotsky, and which have often been influenced by his work. The influence of children's social and cultural worlds, particularly those of family and friends, are considered, along with the vital part played by emotion in the development of young children's thinking and understanding.

## Urie Bronfenbrenner

Urie Bronfenbrenner provides something of a bridge between the constructivist and social constructivist theories of development outlined in the previous chapter, and the sociocultural perspectives outlined below. The *bio* aspect of his bioecological model recognizes that people bring their biological selves to the process of development (Bronfenbrenner and Ceci 1994). Emphasis in the *ecological* aspect is on layers of influence on a young child's development, identified as a series of concentric circles radiating out from the child 'like a set of Russian dolls' (Bronfenbrenner 1979: 22), with progressively less direct influence as the circles widen. The most immediate layer of influence is the microsystem of immediate experience: the home, family and friends. The next layer, the mesosystem, encompasses the relationships between the different microsystems with which a person is involved: neighbourhood, school and religious settings. After these comes a layer of exosystems, in which children do not directly participate, but which, in Bronfenbrenner's view, are very influential. These include the parent's workplace, local government and health systems, local industry and mass media. The outermost layer, the macrosystem, is the 'overarching patterns of ideology and organization of the social institutions common to a particular culture or subculture' (Bronfenbrenner 1979: 8).

Bronfenbrenner is particularly interested in the interconnectedness between these different systems. He suggests that development can be defined as 'the person's evolving conception of the ecological environment and his relation to it, as well as the person's growing capacity to discover, sustain, or alter its properties' (Bronfenbrenner 1979: 9). The emphasis is less on traditional psychological processes such as perception and motivation, and more on the ways in which a person's interactions with their environment, and the content of that environment, impact upon those psychological processes.

Whilst acknowledging the contribution Bronfenbrenner makes to ideas about cultural aspects of human development, Rogoff suggests that his model of separated, though mutually influential, systems (the nested structures of the Russian doll model), serves to constrain 'ideas of the relations between individual and cultural processes' (Rogoff 2003: 48). As Penn (2005) points out, however, Bronfenbrenner's model attempts to show how the wider political and policy environments of the macrosystem ultimately affect what happens to children at the micro level.

## Sociocultural perspectives

Barbara Rogoff herself is one of a number of psychologists, including Michael Cole (Cole *et al.* 1971) and Jean Lave (Lave and Wenger 1992), whose approach is described variously as sociocultural, sociohistorical, cultural-historical and even synonymously with the cultural-historical activity theory of Vygotsky, Luria and Leontiev, discussed in Chapter 2 (Cole 2005: 1). Building on the ideas of Vygotsky (Rogoff 2003), what sociocultural theorists have in common is a view of the sociocultural context as 'the crucible *for* rather than influence *on* development' (Edwards 2003: 259; emphasis in original). Rogoff defines the overarching concept of a sociocultural-historical process as 'Humans develop through their changing participation in the sociocultural activities of their communities, which also change' (2003: 11). From this perspective, cognitive development is not merely the acquisition of knowledge or skills. As Rogoff sees it:

> Cognitive development consists of individuals changing their ways of understanding, perceiving, noticing, thinking, remembering, classifying, reflecting, problem setting and solving, planning, and so on – in shared endeavors with other people building on the cultural practices and traditions of communities.
>
> (Rogoff 2003: 237)

Learning, she suggests, comes about through a process of guided participation, a term which includes a whole range of ways in which children learn as they participate in activities within their communities, in 'rich configurations of mutual involvement' (Rogoff 1990: 97) with caregivers, friends, neighbours and teachers. It thus includes processes which are intended to be instructional, as well as ones which are incidental, for example when children 'help' their parents, or observe and participate in everyday activities. She suggests that there are some basic processes of guided participation (adapted from Rogoff 2003):

- Mutual Bridging of Meanings: mutual understanding occurs between people in interactions, as participants adjust to communicate their ideas and coordinate their efforts, the new perspectives gained involve greater understanding.
- Mutual Structuring of Participation: 'children and caregivers and other companions together structure the situations in which children are involved' (Rogoff 2003: 287). The structuring occurs through the choice of which activities children observe and engage in, and through shared situations such as conversations, recounting, elaborating and listening to narratives, and in practice and play with routines and roles.

Sociocultural theorists suggest that this process of guided participation, and ideas such as situated learning (Lave and Wenger 1992) are cross-cultural. What changes across cultures is the content, as embodied in the values, skills, symbols systems and artefacts of a society, and these shape children's thinking. A useful example to bear in mind in working with young children may be the place of play across cultures. Very different types of children's play occur across cultures, and the valuing of play, and its linkage with young children's growth and development, may reflect its often privileged position in Western societies, and be inconsistent with views about children and learning in many parts of the world (Grieshaber and McArdle 2010).

## Cultural context

A necessary consequence of this view is that development will, to some extent at least, be determined by cultural context, and reflect what is valued, and what is learned (and therefore thought about), in a particular social context. Children growing up on a farm, for example, may have a better understanding of life and death from a much earlier age than children growing up in the city. There are, then, major differences between societies, and within societies, in expectations about what children will know about, and be able to do, at what age. Thornton suggests that, given some characteristics of development which she sees as universal, 'by and large, children live up to whatever expectations their culture has of them' (2002: 168).

This may have considerable implications for children's success in educational contexts. Heath (1983) describes the experiences of a group of children coming from a small community who, on starting school in the 'mainstream' community of the nearest town, were faced with language and discourse practices with which they were unfamiliar. For the children from Trackton in Heath's study this meant learning about very different uses for questioning, for example. In their home community questions served a range of purposes, important amongst which were questions as rhetorical devices to start oral stories: 'Do you remember Tiggy's dog? Well ...' On entering school they responded to questions as they had done at home, by settling back to hear the story they assumed was to follow. As a consequence, their teachers, when faced with the children's lack of response to common school-type questions (implicit directives, or ones which required answers that demonstrate knowledge, for example, 'what colour is this?') assumed a lack of knowledge and understanding on the part of the children. Success in this new context of school may, as Brooker (2002) suggests, be most likely for the children when the social and cultural capital of the family most closely matches that of the setting, and Hedegaard (2004, cited in Fleer 2006) emphasizes the importance of cultural alignment in the contexts of home practice, school practice and work practice for young children's development.

Heath's work points to the very localized nature of cultural context. It is inappropriate (and inaccurate!) to conceptualize culture on regional, national or ethnic bases. Lave's use of the idea of 'communities of practice' (Lave and Wenger 1992), to describe the cultural practices of particular groups, may be more helpful. In addition, as Hedegaard's ideas (2004 cited in Fleer 2006) and Bronfenbrenner's (1979) bioecological model suggest, children will be interacting with a variety of different groups, all of whom may have particular cultural practices. These cultural practices are not static, but evolve continually. The last 30 years have seen a huge growth in distinctive types of children's popular culture, in the form of television, personal computers and the internet. Whilst it is not my intention to review the research on technology and children, it is worth remembering that the impact is global. Thus, it could be argued that, to some extent, cultural difference is being eroded by globalization. At the same time, as Penn (2005) suggests, those in rich and poor countries alike can now know more about each other's experiences and opportunities, or lack of them.

## Social understanding

'Human beings', Thornton asserts, are 'supremely social creatures' (2002: 159). Such an assertion is supported by the work of Trevarthen who believes that, 'from their very earliest days, babies are highly motivated to learn, and are profoundly influenced in their learning by the interplay or "protoconversations" between themselves and their parents and carers' (Trevarthen 1995: 5). These protoconversations, part of a wider idea referred to as 'intersubjectivity', are driven by babies' needs to co-construct meanings with others about the culture in which they live. Mercer (2000) relates this to his idea of 'interthinking', considered in Chapter 7. Studies of mothers and babies in the first hours after birth reveal the beginnings of these protoconversations, for example reciprocating the gesture of sticking out the tongue. Karmiloff-Smith (1994) suggests that such acts mark the dawning of social cognition, or our 'understanding of our own mental state and other people's mental states to gauge feelings and predict behaviours' (Doherty and Hughes 2009: 348). In order to reciprocate the adult's gesture, the baby must be able to see the adult as a separate person. A growing sense of self runs alongside this sense of others, and supports children in making relationships with others.

Dunn proposes that, in order to live in the social world, children need to develop the following understandings (adapted from Dunn 1988):

- An understanding of the feelings of others: the development of empathy, and the ability to see things from another person's point of view, and to understand how they might feel.
- An understanding of the goals of others: a realization that other people want things as well as us. In children this may come about through conflicts over toy ownership, or when children are playing together, with a common goal – a board game, or shared construction for example.
- An understanding of social rules: the generally unwritten rules and routines that all groups have, both at home and outside of it. For example, the understanding that you do not write on the wall, or that everyone sits down to have their snack.
- An understanding of other minds: the ability to 'read' other people – is she in a bad mood? Is he worried?

In so doing, she suggests, children develop prosocial behaviour, behaving in ways which promote good social relationships. Box 3.1 shows evidence of all four aspects of Dunn's proposed list, mostly in Lizzie, aged 3, but also in Freddie, at the age of 1.

### What develops?

As with other aspects of development, Piagetian theory was a strong influence on people's thinking about social development, and the ages and stages at which young children are able to understand the emotions, perceptions and intentions of other people. However, a wide range of research, in particular naturalistic observational studies, has resulted in much rethinking of views about young children's social understanding. As we saw earlier, Trevarthen suggests that the roots of intersubjectivity, that is, mutual understanding shared between people during communication, are in the earliest days of life (1995). Before they are a year old, babies show capability in what is known as joint attention, or sharing with another person an intentional focus on something in their environment. For Carpendale and Lewis, this is fundamental to social and cognitive development. They propose that 'human forms of cognition are built on the capacity to engage with other people's attention' (2006: 253). It includes behaviours such as gaze monitoring and pointing gestures, in a triadic interaction, between infant, other person and object, one of the functions of which Goswami (2008) believes to be epistemic, whereby babies are directed towards reliable new information about the object concerned. Gaze monitoring (following another person's gaze to identify what is capturing their attention) begins early in infancy, with studies citing its appearance at different times between three and eighteen months (Carpendale and Lewis 2006).

The related behaviour of social referencing, or looking to significant others to gauge how they should themselves react to a situation, may begin by the age of six months (Doherty and Hughes 2009). Other aspects of joint attention relate to children's own actions, particularly pointing. Protodeclarative pointing, that is, an intentional gesture by an infant to draw attention to something and thus initiate joint attention, is thought to be a precursor of theory of mind, in that it implies an understanding on the part of the child that the other person may be thinking about something else. The mean age of its emergence is 12.6 months, with an advantage for girls (Goswami 2008). These skills of social understanding are linked to the development of theory of mind

*Box 3.1:* Lizzie, aged 3, and Freddie, aged 1, in the kitchen at home

Freddie is sitting in a high chair, being fed by his mother, who is chatting to a relative. He is watching his sister, Lizzie, while occasionally opening his mouth for food. Lizzie is sitting on the floor playing with a toy mobile telephone. She hits the buttons, which make different noises, and laughs at the sounds, often holding the toy out to her mother and brother. She then speaks into the toy:

LIZZIE:   Ello? Mummy, it's for you! (She holds the toy out).
MOTHER:   Tell them mummy's busy.
LIZZIE:   Okay, mummy's busy. Freddie, it's for you.

Freddie's attention is drawn to Lizzie at the mention of his name. Lizzie gets up.

LIZZIE:   I'll take it to you 'cos you can't come here. (She holds the toy to Freddie's ear and presses a button. The toy plays a tune and Freddie laughs. Lizzie giggles, presses another button, and Freddie laughs again. Then Lizzie walks back to her original spot. Freddie's face drops, and his expression shows frustration. He pushes his food away, begins to make unhappy noises, and wriggles in his chair, his hand out towards Lizzie. She sees this and pauses.)

LIZZIE:   Oh okay Freddie, you can play. (She walks back to the table, then pauses.) But you're not meant to play when you eat! (She looks at her mother, deep in conversation, then at Freddie's food, and finally at Freddie, who is trying to grasp the toy.)

LIZZIE:   Oh okay Freddie, but don't tell mummy. (She whispers and hands him the toy which he cheerfully accepts. She leaves the room, leaving Freddie happily engaged.)

*In her pretend play, described by Dunn as 'the beginnings of social understanding' (1988: 8), Lizzie explores social roles and norms. She understands that it is normal to greet a caller, and has observed that the majority of calls to her home are for her parents. From early on she shows she wants her mother and brother to experience the joy of her toy, but understands that her mother is busy. She joins Freddie at his highchair, knowing he is not able to leave it, and even holds the toy to his ear. Lizzie understands that Freddie is enjoying the toy noises, and so repeats them to make him laugh more. The two are clearly responding to each other's playful moods.*

*Freddie shows an understanding that he must interact with Lizzie if he is to get back the phone. Lizzie, recognizing Freddie's unhappiness, shows that she has learnt to put others' needs before her own. She empathizes with his feelings, and returns the toy to him, understanding that this will comfort him. However, she recollects that playing at table is not allowed. She acknowledges the social rules that operate within her family, but, realizing that her mother is inattentive, breaks the norm. Her hesitancy suggests that she has considered the consequences of her actions, but her compassion for Freddie overrides this.*

Abridged and reproduced with permission of Philippa Cooper

(Yamaguchi *et al.* 2009), and a deficit in their development is associated with autistic spectrum disorder (Gutstein and Whitney 2002).

The period from around eighteen months onwards sees the emergence of a number of critical features, including a child's recognition of the self, which supports them in their efforts to make sense of others (Siegler *et al.* 2011). In addition, at around this time children show evidence of being able to differentiate between their own desires and those of others (Gopnik *et al.* 1999) and to talk about mental states, in particular about emotion, commenting on their own and other people's feelings, desires and perceptions (Dunn 1993). Around eighteen months also sees the emergence of early prosocial behaviour. By the age of 2, children show sympathy for others (and empathy with them), in the form of attempts to help others, to share and to provide comfort in difficulty or distress. Between the ages of 2 and 3 children talk about why people behave the way they do, and are able to begin to manage conflict (Dunn 2005). Dunn suggests that this early focus on emotion and desires is significant, in that the later understanding of, and ability to talk about, cognitive states such as thinking and believing arises out of children's earlier understanding of emotional states. It may be, though, that children continue to find it easier to talk about feelings than thoughts, for some time after they are able to do both. In our research we asked practitioners working with children aged 3–5 years how they provided opportunities for children to communicate their thoughts, ideas and feelings, a requirements of the curriculum guidance at the time (DfEE 2000) . One practitioner said 'Expressing their ideas and their feeling – yes, but thoughts? They (the children) can talk about their ideas, they talk a lot about their feelings, but it's getting them to verbalize their thoughts in that way, you have to do a bit of delving, I think' (Robson and Hargreaves 2005: 91).

Dunn (2005) suggests that children's talk about emotions supports the idea that they develop a theory of mind at a younger age than was hitherto believed. This is looked at more fully in Chapter 5. There is ample evidence to suggest that children are well able to take on another's perspective, and to see things how others might see them, by the age of 3, when set in contexts which have some meaning for them (Gopnik *et al.* 1999). By the same age they also make reference to social rules, and the expectations of their wider social world (Dunn 1993).

## The importance of relationships

What is it that supports the emergence and development of these social understandings? There now seems to be clear evidence that children's social understanding is associated with social experience, gained through their social relationships and interactions (Carpendale and Lewis 2006). It is within the arena of young children's relationships with parents and carers, siblings and friends that their understanding is both developed and revealed. These relationships are complex and varied, and highly context-bound. Children behave differently depending upon whom they are with, and also at different times with the same people, and these different kinds of relationships 'present very different challenges to children's sociocognitive sophistication' (Dunn 1993: 13). Parents will also differ in their treatment of children within a family, dependent upon factors such as first-born or later sibling, older or younger parent, and just with experience over time (Thornton 2002). Hughes *et al.* (1999) believe that this means it is impossible to identify universal relationships between parenting and children's sociocognitive development, because of variations in factors such as gender and family culture. This, of course, lends support to the views of Vygotsky (1978), Rogoff (2003) and others, discussed earlier, that development is culturally bound, and that models of social development, like those for cognitive development, are subject to as much variation as commonality.

### Family relationships

For young children the social world of the family, in all of its forms, is a central part of their experience. Parental attitudes clearly have an important influence on young children's social development. Explicit parental discussion of emotions, for example, is linked to children's recognition of, and responses to, others' emotions, (Meadows 2010). Family conflict, in the form of disputes between themselves and parents or siblings, teasing and witnessing disputes between other family members, both demonstrates and develops children's understanding of their social world. Children as young as fourteen months may perform acts which seem to reflect some understanding of what will annoy another family member (Dunn 1987). Family life also provides the earliest forum for observation of, and discussion about, feeling states, as outlined above. Other aspects of children's family lives are similarly important: conversations about family events, social rules and routines, stories and television, sharing jokes, and all types of play and collaborative activity, particularly shared pretence (Dunn 2004a) provide valuable opportunities for the development of social understanding. Joint problem-solving, for example, may be valuable not, as Piaget might suggest, because of the exposure to a potential conflict of views, but because of the ways in which children compromise in their sharing of decision-making (Thornton 2002).

Significantly, younger siblings may display such understandings earlier in life than their older brothers or sisters (Dunn 1987, 1993), and develop a theory of mind at an earlier age than their older siblings (Gopnik et al. 1999). What is not clear is exactly what it is about having siblings that facilitates such social development. Gopnik et al. (1999) speculate that it may be the result of a number of factors: parents may provide fewer opportunities to develop social understanding via conflict situations (though speaking as a parent I am not so sure about this!), older siblings may be particularly attractive to younger brothers and sisters and getting them to do what you want may require considerably more expertise than it does with a parent. However, it is not merely having a sibling that matters, and Carpendale and Lewis (2006) point to the importance of the nature of relationships for children's social understanding. Box 3.2 describes an everyday episode in family life which illustrates some aspects of sibling relationships, through an emotionally charged episode involving a boy, his older sister and their mother.

### Friendship

Whilst the family provides a major context for these kinds of interactions, they also occur between friends. Paley (1981) suggests that friendship, along with fairness and fantasy, are the three things that interest a young child most, and that these are the themes which constantly come through in their play and in their conversations with her. Children take pleasure from their social effectiveness in negotiation, conflict and its resolution, sharing jokes and play (Dunn 1988), and it is with friends that this social

*Box 3.2:* Jack, aged 3 and Alice, aged 7, at home after school with their mother

Alice and Jack are playing in Jack's bedroom. Mother hears the children start to shout at one another. By the time she arrives, Alice is going into the bathroom, muttering. Mother asks Jack what has happened. He looks uncertain, and slightly anxious.

JACK:       She hit me. (As he says this he looks away, embarrassed.)

MOTHER:  Jack, are you certain?

JACK:       Yes, very hard, in the tummy! (He starts to cry. Mother takes his hand and takes him into the bathroom. She asks Alice what happened.)

ALICE:      He had my bouncy ball, and he wouldn't give it back when I asked him nicely, so I took it, and he started shouting.

MOTHER:  He said that you hit him.

JACK:       Yes, she did mummy, she hit me.

Alice becomes highly indignant, and starts to cry.

ALICE:      I didn't mummy, I wouldn't hit him.

Jack observes Alice furtively. His body language indicates discomfort.

MOTHER:  Did Alice hit you Jack?

Jack shifts uncomfortably, and looks down.

JACK:       She did mummy, really.

MOTHER:  Jack, this is very important. Alice is very upset, and is crying. She is upset because she says she didn't hit you. It is unfair to get Alice into trouble. You need to tell mummy what really happened.

Jack moves towards Alice, puts his head on her tummy.

JACK:       I didn't mean to Alice, I'm sorry, you didn't really. I'm sorry. (He looks at his mother.) I wanted her ball, but she took it back. I'm sorry, mummy. (Jack takes Alice's hand and looks up at her) I didn't mean it Alice.

Alice smiles and puts her arm around him.

*It is apparent through his body language that Jack is not telling the truth. Dunn suggests that 'often ... acts of denial or blame are made in situations where it is transparently obvious that the child is in fact the culprit' (1988: 30). We see this occur when Jack says 'she did mummy, really'. He insists again that Alice has hit him, because by this stage he realizes he will get into trouble for telling a lie. Dunn suggests that a child may use his 'growing understanding in his family relationships to get his way, to escape blame, to deflect punishment onto his sibling' (1988: 26). Early on it appears that Jack recognizes he has done something wrong. Dunn suggests that a 3 year old has the capability to show an understanding in real-life family dramas. This could, she claims, be 'linked to the emotional significance of those family encounters' (1988: 81). Throughout the episode Jack is uncomfortable. He appears to recognize the stress he is causing Alice, displaying what Dunn calls 'moral intuition' (1988: 27). In addition, Dunn highlights Jack's possibly deeper understanding of the social consequences of his behaviour, as a result of his birth order. By apologizing and admitting what happened, it appears that he understands why Alice is so cross and upset with him. He shows that he knows that he was directly involved in making his sister unhappy, and understands the social rituals involved in making amends.*

Abridged and reproduced with permission of Kathryn Torres

effectiveness is often most needed. As the poet Robert Frost says: 'home is the place where, when you have to go there, they have to take you in' (1915). Families are usually there for life, whether we like it or not. Friendships, on the other hand, are chosen and friendship has to be worked at, to support 'connectedness' of communication, and to understand when and why friends feel as they do, and what will comfort or amuse them (Dunn *et al*. 2002). Practitioners in Reggio Emilia ensure that they model conflict, and its resolution, in front of the children, discussing and negotiating ideas and practice. In so doing, not only are they demonstrating to the children that adults disagree too, but they are also helping children to develop strategies of their own, for use in their own interactions with their friends and peers. If this is to be most effective, however, it will be important for practitioners to have an understanding of just how (and why) conflict arises between children. Licht *et al*. (2008) illustrate how complex the motivations of even very young children are in this respect. Often thought to revolve solely around the idea of object possession ('you have a toy and I want it'), Licht *et al*. (2008) identify a range of different motivations for conflict in the first eighteen months of life, including exploration, actions to ameliorate interruptions to a chosen activity, dominance, contact and sensation-seeking. Recognizing this complexity can help adults to develop young children's social competence, including strategies for regulating their emotions and behaviour associated with both positive peer relationships and later school achievement (Siegler *et al*. 2011).

Dunn (2004a) emphasizes the importance of friendship as marking the beginnings of children's independence from their family. When with a familiar peer, babies less than a year old behave differently to how they behave with an unfamiliar peer (Meadows 2010), and Dunn (2004a) cites evidence for the existence of friendship, as characterized by reciprocity and mutuality of affection, in children under the age of 2 years. At first, what may be most apparent is an interest in doing the same things together, but between about eighteen months and 2½ years of age, behaviours such as turn-taking, coordination of actions and cooperation in order to solve a problem, play a game, or engage in shared pretence, become much more evident. By 3 and 4 years, children's 'passion for playing with other children has taken off in an astonishing trajectory' (Dunn 2004a: 31), and the time they spend with peers has already outstripped that spent with adults (Layard and Dunn 2009).

Dunn suggests a number of ways in which young children's friendships may be significant for both their understanding of others, and the development of their thinking. First, she suggests that, in the context of a close friendship, children make more efforts to conciliate, negotiate and make compromises than they do in their relationships within the family, because they care about their friend, and want to maintain the relationship. Second, the kind of talk about thoughts, feelings and inner states that takes place both in conversation and in pretend play (see below), and which may be particularly significant for later sociocognitive outcomes, is especially likely to happen between friends. Third, she suggests that friendship 'is a context in which moral understanding is demonstrated very early' (Dunn 2004a: 157), and in which children display more evidence of having learned about relationships than in their interactions within the family. Underpinning all of this is the emotional power of young children's friendships. In her view, it is this combination of emotion and understanding which makes friendship such a source of potential influence on children's development.

### Pretend play

A particularly valuable context for the development of young children's social understanding and social self-regulation, and one shared often, though not exclusively, between friends, is shared pretend play, or sociodramatic play (Smilansky and Shefatya 1990). Dunn *et al.* suggest that 'the experiences of sharing and negotiating an imaginary world in pretend play provides a potent context for talking and learning about why other people behave the way they do, and the links between inner states and human action' (2002: 631–2). In the context of the family, she points to longitudinal research which demonstrates the significance of shared pretend play with a friendly older sibling for the development of an understanding of feelings and other minds (Dunn 2004a). Play, particularly shared pretence, is discussed in other places here, notably in Chapters 5 and 7. Looked at in the context of young children's social understanding it is worth noting Broadhead's conclusion that, the more cooperative the children's play was, the more likely it was that children would connect with and understand the knowledge and thinking of the other players (2004). Doherty and Hughes (2009) cite research on 3–5 year olds which shows that children who were 'better' at pretence were also the most socially competent. Wood and Attfield are similarly positive, in their suggestion that play is valuable for developing young children's social cognition: 'Play provides many different opportunities for children to learn about social and cultural norms: appropriate and inappropriate behaviours, society's rules and conventions, roles and relationships, and boundaries' (2005: 82). It is, however, important to bear in mind the findings of Farver and Shin (1997) that culture will be an important influence. In their comparison of pretend play themes and communicative strategies, the Korean-American children focused on everyday activities, whilst the Anglo-American children engaged with fantasy and danger in their play themes.

What all of these contexts have in common is their shared nature, and there seems good reason to conclude that shared experiences are a key part of children's development as thinkers. In Chapters 7 and 8 the role of talk in these experiences is considered. At this point it is important to stress the ways in which shared experiences, which can be referred to by the participants, and reflected upon later, can help a child to develop their thinking about the past, and about the future.

## Emotion and cognition

Along with the closer focus in recent years on social processes in support of children's thinking has come a similar emphasis on the relationship between emotion and cognition. Bell and Wolfe suggest that, whilst acknowledging that the processes are complex, the two are 'dynamically linked and work together to process information and execute action' (2004: 366). Arnold describes the ways in which young children's schematic behaviour (see Chapters 2 and 6) shows their feelings as well as their experiences, and that some schemas may be 'more readily understood as part of children's emotional lives' (Arnold *et al.* 2010: 22). In Dunn's view (cited in Wood 1998) children often display their most advanced reasoning in situations that have the most emotional significance for them.

## Emotional intelligence

The idea that emotion and cognition are connected, and that 'pleasure, desire and emotions are powerful motivators of learning and that they drive our actions and interactions with others' is not new (MacNaughton 2003: 53). It stems, in part at least, from the psychodynamic theories of Sigmund Freud. In recent years, writers such as Goleman (1996), Claxton (1999b) and Roberts (2010) have stressed the need for us to understand the place of emotions in learning, and, on an individual level, develop the ability to contain, manage and tolerate them. This ability, Claxton suggests, 'is one of the core ingredients of emotional intelligence and nowhere is it more crucial than in the domain of learning' (1999b: 41). Emotional intelligence as a term was first coined by American psychologists Salovey and Mayer (1990). It came to international prominence with the publication of Goleman's *Emotional Intelligence: Why it Can Matter More than IQ.* The idea of emotional intelligence is analogous to Gardner's interpersonal and intrapersonal intelligences outlined in Chapter 2.

What is meant by emotional intelligence (or emotional literacy as it is also sometimes known)? Goleman defines it as 'the capacity for recognizing our own feelings and those of others, for motivating ourselves, and for managing emotions well in ourselves and in our relationships' (1999: 317). He suggests it comprises some basic social and emotional competences: self-awareness, self-regulation, motivation, empathy and social skills, some of which are discussed in this chapter and in Chapter 5.

In support of claims for the importance of emotional intelligence Goleman (1996) cites research which points to a physiological basis to the argument for the value of attending to emotion. Part of the brain consists of two almond-shaped structures called the amygdala, located deep within the brain, which direct emotions. For Goleman, 'the workings of the amygdala and its interplay with the neocortex are at the heart of emotional intelligence' (1996: 16). Claxton similarly emphasizes the importance of biology here:

> When we meet a hitch, when our knowledge and know-how let us down, or when our own goals and interests conflict, feeling afraid (or sad or angry or shocked or disgusted) is part and parcel of the way we are built to respond. Emotions accompany the 'ways of knowing' that evolution has designed to help us out in such situations.
>
> (Claxton 1999b: 39)

## Well-being

The concept of well-being, deriving from the field of positive psychology, can be seen as related to ideas of emotional intelligence (Schutte *et al.* 2002). In recent years, well-being has been of increasing interest to practitioners and policy-makers in early childhood. The New Zealand curriculum, *Te Whariki* (Ministry of Education, New Zealand 1996) has well-being as one of its five domains of learning dispositions (see Chapter 6). Statham and Chase (2010) suggest that well-being and learning are positively associated, in ways which persist throughout children's school lives. At the same time, they, along with others such as Mayr and Ulich (2009), Roberts (2010) and Waters (2009), emphasize the complexity of well-being as a concept. Drawing on Rees *et al.*'s (2010) definition of well-being as an over-arching concept to describe the quality of people's lives, Statham and Chase see well-being as dynamic and multidimensional, including physical, mental and social dimensions.

At the level of policy, well-being indicators have tended to focus on objective data such as children living in poverty, particularly for cross-national comparison. However, the recognition that such indicators only tell a part of the story has led to increased emphasis on subjective indicators. In early childhood, Laevers has coupled well-being with 'involvement' (see Chapter 6), to develop a series of indicators that help practitioners to see how children are 'doing in a setting' (2000: 24). Laevers (2000) suggests that well-being is indicated by children's

- openness and receptivity;
- flexibility;
- self-confidence and self-esteem;
- assertiveness;
- vitality;
- relaxation and inner peace;
- enjoyment without restraint;
- being in touch with one's self.

Mayr and Ulich (2009) have gone on to develop an observation and assessment instrument called PERIK (in English: Positive development and resilience in kindergarten), which uses six dimensions of social-emotional well-being: making contact/social performance; self-control/thoughtfulness; self-assertiveness; emotional stability/coping with stress; task orientation; and pleasure in exploration. What is clear in these dimensions is the link between emotion and cognition. For example, 'pleasure in exploring' includes items like 'asks questions, wants to know about things' (Mayr and Ulich 2009: 51).

There is also an increasing awareness of the importance of children's own views about their sense of well-being, as part of these more subjective measures. This arises from both the recognition of children as experts on their own lives, and from a children's rights perspective (Waters 2009) (see also Chapter 6). Much of the evidence here has been drawn from older children (Statham and Chase 2010), but the *Good Childhood* review (Layard and Dunn 2009) includes responses from children from 5 to 17. Their findings reflect other studies, which highlight the importance to children of family, friendship, feeling safe and secure, a positive sense of self, and having autonomy and agency (Statham and Chase 2010).

### Emotional development

The complex interplay between emotion and cognition begins, like most things, in babyhood. Miller (1999) suggests that a baby will need to begin to develop a sense of being separate from her carer as a first step on the road to independent thought:

> There is a lot of emotional work for a baby to do before he or she can reliably call to mind the mother who is not there. Quite a risk is involved. You have to tolerate the concept, no matter how fleeting, that you are alone, before you can conceive of the other person as not there, as not part of you. With this beginning of a sense

of singularity comes the possibility of mental activity and symbolic thought. Being in touch with another person need no longer mean touching them with your body. Mental contact, memory, a space in the mind where things happen, a distinction between mind and body, all start from here.

(Miller 1999: 37)

As we shall see in Chapter 5, these are also crucial in the development of theory of mind.

A number of aspects of the development of children's social understanding outlined earlier, such as joint attention and social referencing, are also central to emotional development and understanding, and the growth of emotional self-regulation, and it is useful to refer back to the earlier sections of this chapter. Mayr and Ulich (2009) identify a link between children's regulative and social competencies, and suggest that both are foundational to learning.

Children's ability to regulate their emotions develops considerably in early childhood. Meadows (2006) describes a familiar developmental course of adult responsibility for emotional self-regulation, followed by adult scaffolding of the child's attempts, adult and child discussion and reflection, and finally child responsibility. In the earliest months, caregivers tend to try to soothe or distract a distressed or frustrated baby (with varying degrees of success!). However, by six months babies show that they can reduce their stress by averting their gaze, and even self-soothe (Siegler *et al.* 2011). In the course of the first few years children acquire the ability to regulate their emotions by an increasing repertoire of means, adding talking to others in order to negotiate ways of meeting their needs, and inhibiting behaviour, for example slowing down when asked, to those already mentioned (Siegler *et al.* 2011). By the time they are around 5 years old children are increasingly able to rely on strategies based in cognition rather than behaviour in order to regulate their emotions. For example, they are able to focus their attention and thoughts away from a desired treat (Siegler *et al.* 2011). Box 3.3 may be an example of this process of emotional self-regulation.

Whilst cultural differences about what emotions are valued and when they should be expressed will influence children's expression of emotion (Siegler *et al.* 2011), recognition of some fundamental facial expressions of emotion, such as fear and disgust, seem to be common across cultures (Spinney 2010).

### Children's understanding of the connection between thought and feeling

Lagattuta *et al.* (1997) demonstrate young children displaying considerable understanding of the relationship between thought and feeling, with this developing markedly over the pre-school years. Flavell *et al.* (2001) outline what they describe as a three-step developmental sequence in children's understanding of the connection between thought and feeling, with much overlap, particularly between the second and third stages. First, they suggest that objective situations and events cause feelings appropriate to those events: 'even young preschoolers are aware that sad external happenings cause sad feelings' (Flavell *et al.* 2001: 432). The second stage is an understanding that a reminder of a previous sad or happy event can trigger a memory of that situation which, in turn, can trigger emotions about it. As they suggest, this is an

*Box 3.3: Ayesha, aged 3.8, arriving at nursery*

Ayesha enters with her mum, finding it a little difficult to separate. A member of staff supports her for a short period. Ayesha walks slowly to the end of the classroom, her face displaying some of the sadness she is feeling, her shoulders slumped. She stops at the carpet area, watches the group for a moment before dropping to her knees and sitting back on her heels, still looking cheerless. Her gaze appears to focus on one of her peers (Shaun) who is cutting through a large sheet of paper. After a while she jumps up, and selects a large sheet of paper, taking it to a space on the carpet. She alternates her gaze between Shaun's face and the cutting action he is making. She selects a small piece of paper from the many on the carpet, and sticks it carefully in position with tape. She sits back and studies her paper, then says to Shaun:

AYESHA:    It's the Handsome Prince from Snow White.
SHAUN:    I doin' a dinosaur, Tyrannosaurus Rex.
AYESHA:    He hasn't got a hat (pause) a crown. I have to do a crown.
SHAUN:    Tyrannosaurus Rex doesn't got no crown.
AYESHA:    No, the Handsome Prince hasn't got a crown.

Ayesha continues to work on her picture, using tape, paper and felt tip pens. She looks up and, noticing a practitioner, smiles and says:

AYESHA:    He's the Handsome Prince from Snow White and he kisses her to wake her up cos the Wicked Queen gives her an apple and she dies.

*It is possible that Ayesha may have been consciously or unconsciously aware that 'merely perceiving a reminder of a previous ... happy situation can trigger a memory of that situation, and that this memory can then trigger a happy feeling' (Flavell et al. 2001: 432). Consequently, Ayesha may have been using a past experience in order to alter her own emotions. The recollection of the Snow White story may have engendered feelings of emotional security with a significant other. Her purposeful jumping up would appear to signal a change in her thinking and feelings, her actions becoming purposeful as she self-initiates a task. Ayesha may have been cognitively able to alter her affective response (Harris 1989) without the need for intervention by others, demonstrating that through thought, understanding and memory recall she has been able to contain and manage her own emotions.*

Abridged and reproduced with permission of Lynn Bartlett

important step because it involves recognition of a causal connection between thoughts and feelings, and Lagattuta *et al.* (1997) record 83 per cent of the 4 year olds and 93 per cent of the 5 and 6 year olds in their study able to do this, unprompted. The third step is children's awareness that spontaneous thoughts can trigger, and accompany, feelings.

Lagattuta *et al.* (1997) highlight what, for them, is a relationship between individual children's understanding of thinking in the context of emotion and their opportunities for talk about the causes and consequences of emotions with others, particularly parents. They cite a range of evidence that shows girls often outperforming boys in this respect. Dowling (2010) suggests a number of possible factors accounting for this, including parents talking about feelings more often with their daughters than with their sons, using more emotion words in stories, and displaying a wider range of emotions in play with girls rather than boys.

### Attachment

Miller's (1999) emphasis on the importance of children's early interactions with their caregivers for their later emotional and cognitive development is reflected in the ideas of attachment theory, first outlined by John Bowlby. Bowlby (1969) suggests that babies need a warm, continuous relationship with a mother figure. This emotional attachment provides them with a sense of safety and security, and a secure base from which they can then go out and explore their worlds. Bowlby's theory is considerably more sophisticated than this brief outline implies, and is best studied by going to his original work, or to texts on developmental psychology. A major shift in thinking about attachment is the current view that suggests that attachment is not solely a function of a mother–child dyad, but can, and does, occur, between babies and a range of people of emotional significance to a child. What seems to matter most is the responsiveness and engagement of the person involved.

What is important to consider here is the possible relationship of these ideas to young children's thinking. A good starting point is an understanding that attachment is not a one-off event, but a developmental process, which occurs as a function of the developing relationships between babies and young children and their caregivers. Babies develop 'internalized working models' (Gopnik et al. 1999: 49) of relationships, which change as a result of experience, and in light of new information they receive about how people relate to one another. Meins (1999) suggests that mothers who are 'mind-minded', focusing on their children's thoughts and feelings in their interactions with them, may be supporting children's understanding of their behaviour, and there is evidence that, even at the age of about twelve months, babies can form abstract mental representations of social interactions as a reflection of their own attachment experiences (Johnson et al. 2007). Accordingly, it is possible to point to a very close relationship between thought and emotion, in that the knowledge gained through these experiences guides emotion. Gopnik et al. suggest that it does so 'more than emotion distorts knowledge' (1999: 48).

What other links, and possible beneficial relationships, have been suggested between secure attachment and cognition? Secure attachment is linked to academic achievement and school success (Bergin and Bergin 2009). It has been associated with curiosity and problem-solving skills at age 2, with empathy and independence at age 5 (Smith et al. 2011), and possibly even with higher grades and more attention and involvement in school at a later stage (Siegler et al. 2011). Meins (1997) points to the importance of secure attachment in supporting the development of self-efficacy, discussed below. For children with a secure attachment history, the positive internal working models they have developed may help them to regulate their own emotions and 'read' the emotional expressions of others. Children with insecure attachment histories may be less self-confident and socially competent (Bergin and Bergin 2009), and less motivated to complete challenges (Cortazar and Herreros 2010). Dunn (2004a) cites the experiences of children who had been kept in extreme deprivation in Romanian orphanages, where close attachments to caregivers were never made. Subsequently adopted by British families, at the age of 4 they tended to engage in less pretend play, less interactive role-play and made fewer references to mental states.

Given the subject of this chapter, it is important to consider whether attachment, as a construct, is culturally specific. As a way of assessing the level of attachment between a child and her caregiver, Mary Ainsworth and colleagues developed the Strange Situation (Ainsworth *et al.* 1978). In this approach the reactions of children to their caregivers leaving, a stranger entering and then the caregiver re-entering the room are observed. Ainsworth classifies children's reactions as securely attached (child shows wariness and upset on separation, but is comforted on caregiver's return), as anxious/avoidant (child does not take much notice of either the stranger, or the caregiver when he/she returns) or anxious/resistant (child is very upset when caregiver leaves, but not easily comforted on return, and simultaneously seeks and resists being close). A fourth category of 'disorganized' attachment has been identified, to describe chaotic family circumstances in which 'so much has gone wrong that there is no coherent defensive posture' (Gerhardt 2004: 27). Rogoff (2003) points to research which suggests that there may be cultural variation in the extent to which children conform to particular patterns, and suggests that these may reflect cultural values and practices. The Bielefeld study of German infants seemed to identify up to two-thirds of the children as insecurely attached. However, culturally derived child-rearing patterns in German families make stronger demands on infants to be self-reliant than do, for example, American approaches (LeVine and Norman 2008). By contrast, the anxious/resistant pattern is more common in studies of Japanese children, and may reflect child-rearing practices which mean that children are relatively unfamiliar with being left with strangers (Rogoff 2003).

### Children's conceptions of the self: positive and negative emotions

The development of a sense of self, or 'self-concept', is an important element of young children's affective development, and indicates their awareness of themselves as distinct from others. Woolfolk *et al.* (2008) describe it as how we explain ourselves to ourselves. They suggest that its developmental trajectory is similar to general cognitive development: at first, very young children base their comments about themselves on immediate behaviours and appearances, describing themselves in concrete physical, active and social terms. Self-concept evolves as children look at themselves in different situations, and begin to evaluate themselves in different situations. What they say about themselves becomes more comparative, and involves more abstract higher order description. By the age of 5, young children's descriptions about themselves and their characters may be similar to their mothers' accounts (Meadows 2010).

Self-concept is closely related to self-esteem, that is, how we evaluate ourselves, and particularly what we see as the difference between our real self, or who we are, and our ideal self, that is, the image of what we would like to be. Discussion of the reciprocal relationship between emotion and cognition is often centred on what are overwhelmingly seen as the beneficial parts played by children's high self-esteem, high self-efficacy (how 'good' they believe they are at something) and sense of personal agency. In Chapter 6 the value attached to the development of what have been termed 'learning dispositions' (Carr 2001), in particular aspects such as a sense of mastery (Dweck 2000), is considered in relation to their usefulness as observational tools. It is worth looking here at some of the possible connections between thought and feeling as expressed by children's views of themselves as learners.

Dweck (2000) suggests that children's sense of self-competence and self-efficacy, what she calls mastery, begins to develop from an early age, and can have a significant impact on their attitudes to learning. When faced with difficulty or potential failure, Dweck says that children tend to react in one of two ways. Some children display a mastery oriented pattern of motivation, characterized by increasing their efforts to succeed, and not blaming themselves for not doing well. Other children seem to respond in a different way, by feeling bad, blaming themselves personally and not persisting with a task. Dweck calls this a helpless pattern. What characteristics does Dweck (2000: 7–10) record in children in these two responses to difficulty?

The mastery-oriented students tended to

- not see themselves as failing;
- engage in self-motivating strategies;
- engage in self-instruction or self-monitoring;
- remain confident that they would succeed;
- have an attitude that they could learn from their failures;
- did not see failure as an indictment of themselves as people.

The helpless students tended to

- quickly denigrate their abilities;
- lose faith in their ability to succeed;
- focus on their failures rather than on their successes;
- lose focus on the task at hand;
- abandon strategies they had previously used successfully;
- give up trying more quickly than the mastery-oriented students.

In Dweck's view, these differences can be accounted for by children's different personal theories about intelligence, and about how one succeeds. Mastery oriented children, she suggests, attribute their possible failure to unstable factors such as that they did not prepare enough, or put in enough effort. Therefore, with more preparation, or more effort, they believe they can succeed, because they have a 'growth mind-set' (Dweck 2007: 35). She suggests that, in challenging situations, the mastery oriented children often seem even happier, and look upon difficulty as something to 'embrace with relish' (Dweck 2000: 10). Baumeister *et al.* (2005) support Dweck's view, and suggest that high self-esteem improves persistence. Children who display an attitude of learned helplessness tend to see the situation as beyond their control, attributing their failure at a task to stable factors such as that they are not clever enough, or do not have a good memory, and believe that there is nothing that they can do to change that. For such children, choosing not to persist ensures that they will protect themselves from further failure (Zentall and Morris 2010). Dweck believes that such responses 'impair(s) students' ability to use their mind effectively' (Dweck 2000: 9).

In effect, they have a 'fixed mind-set' (Dweck 2007: 34). Drawing on Dweck's work, Claxton suggests that the group most vulnerable here may be girls who have been perceived as 'bright', and who may have the least experience of persisting in the face of difficulty. This is further compounded by the responses of their teachers. Claxton suggests that, in such situations, there may be a tendency for teachers to offer girls comfort or an alternative activity, whereas boys in similar situations are exhorted to 'stick with it' (Claxton 1998: 216).

Dweck believes that even very young children exhibit the two types of response. Furthermore, she believes that young children also relate this to a personal sense of 'goodness', and 'badness'. In a study of kindergarten children in the USA, 60 per cent of the children who displayed a helpless pattern said that they felt that they were not 'good kids' (Dweck 2000: 104), whilst less than 10 per cent of the mastery-oriented children said they felt not good or not nice in a role-play scenario where they were criticized about an activity. Whilst she is at pains to stress that 'most young children

---

*Box 3.4:* Boy O aged 4.9, reception class in a primary school, playing with marble run construction materials

O arrives at the construction activity where three children are already working. He picks up two tubes and immediately pushes them together until they click. He looks around the tray and stretches to select a twisted tube from the table. O attempts to connect this to the tubes in his hand. He pushes the pieces together but they do not seem to fit. He takes them apart and turns over the single tube in his hand and attempts to fit it together with the others, this time it clicks into place and he smiles. Again O looks around the tray.

O:          Can I have that red one? (To another child whilst pointing in the direction of the piece he has requested. His peer picks up the selected piece and holds it out to O.) I'm gonna make it really big, really tall up to here. (Raises hand above his head as high as he can whilst standing on tip toes to demonstrate.)

Later:

O:          This is for the middle here (to teacher, whilst using his index finger to travel backwards and forwards between the two poles in his model).

TEACHER:    Wow, that is very good, how will you fix it?

O:          Yeah and it's going to be really cool. I am going to put this here (gestures to the space) and then put more on top so it is really tall, it will be the tallest one here (points around the activity).

*Whilst occupied in solving the problems which the activity presented O displayed controlled emotional behaviour thus exhibiting proficiency for self-regulation. His confident approach to the task suggests he has feelings of self-efficacy and capability. Dweck (2000) describes O's capacity to consider himself competent, his level of involvement and his flow within the activity as mastery.*

Abridged and reproduced with permission of Lynn Skinner

go around feeling good about themselves' (Dweck 2000: 106), the difference for what she describes as vulnerable and hardy children is in how contingent that sense of goodness is, or how much it is affected by events. Hardy children, she suggests, recognize that they are still worthy when things go wrong. Vulnerable young children, by contrast, lose a sense of themselves as worthy at such times. Claxton calls this sense of worthiness 'resilience', a quality that will be needed in order for children to tolerate uncertainty, and the feeling of 'not knowing', without feeling insecure. He says 'Uncertainty invites an ambivalent response. On the one hand, learning promises greater insight and control. On the other, it might blow up in your face' (Claxton 1999b: 40).

When it comes to thinking, problem-solving and tackling challenge, such resilience and willingness to take risks may help us to respond positively to the anxiety, worry or lack of sureness that we feel. Respond positively, with confidence, resilience and perseverance, and the result can be a benign cycle. Gopnik *et al.* (1999: 163–4) describe the 'intense pleasure' of understanding, and the ways in which this feeds back into ever greater desire to keep developing that understanding.

Does all of this translate into performance? Meadows (2010) highlights the dilemma: is self-esteem critical in determining success or failure, or is it a marker for problems elsewhere that lead to poorer life outcomes? A review of literature in the area suggests, at least in relation to older children and adolescents, that self-esteem may only be weakly predictive of later achievement (Baumeister *et al.* 2005). Siegler *et al.* (2011) suggest that, whilst not conclusive, evidence tends to suggest that academic achievement has a stronger effect on children's self-esteem than vice versa. Whilst in both cases the focus is on older children, it does suggest a need for further research in the area.

Goleman (1996) and Meadows (2006) both point to the impact of emotional distress on learning, suggesting that continued emotional distress, of whatever kind, can have a lasting impact on thinking and understanding. The possibly reciprocal nature of this, that cognitive experience can lead to emotional distress, may also be familiar to most of us. I only have to think of the term 'geometric progression' in order to feel anxiety and butterflies in the pit of my stomach just as I did in mathematics classes when I was 14. Broadhead (1997, 2004) provides a good contrast here, however, suggesting the potential long-term impact of positive emotional experience on children, with examples which show the sheer fun, and shared joy, of cooperative and collaborative experiences, like that shown in Box 3.5.

---

*Box 3.5:* Frank and Jamil, aged 4, in the nursery

Frank and Jamil both put dough in the mincer, and then put the mincer into a saucepan, cooking 'dinner' together.

They then move over to the sand and work together to fill a large cardboard box with all the sand toys. They cover the box in sand. They both laugh as everything falls out. They then work together again to fill it. This is done spontaneously without discussion. They then together fill the bag with sand, and both try to lift it together. They both shriek with laughter as the bag breaks and sand falls out.

## Some implications for practice

- Learning occurs as children participate in activities within their communities. Some of this learning will be instructional, at other times learning will be incidental to everyday life (Rogoff 2003).
- The social world of the family supports children in developing their thinking and understanding, through their participation in family activities and routines.
- 'The identities, skills and behaviours an individual develops are related to the social contexts they experience (Browne 2010: 95), and the cultural context in which children live will be an important factor in determining what is seen as important to know 'about'.
- 'Working with families drawn from a diverse range of cultures means that we need to be willing to consider the validity of different ways of caring for young children' (Browne 2010: 90).
- Young children's friendships are significant both for their understanding of other people, and for the development of their thinking and understanding, in particular because of the emotional significance of friendship.
- Pretend play is a valuable context for the development of children's social understanding (Wood and Attfield 2005).
- Children may often display their most advanced reasoning in situations that have the most emotional significance for them (Dunn in Wood 1998).
- Children's sense of self-competence and self-efficacy can have a significant impact on their attitudes to learning (Dweck 2000).
- Whilst low self-esteem may have an effect on poor outcomes for young children, it is only one of a great many factors that co-occur, and interventions that focus only on raising self-esteem may not have a major effect (Meadows 2010).
- Children's self-esteem may be particularly vulnerable at times of change. For example, transition from home to nursery (Dowling 2010).
- Developing young children's resilience, and willingness to take risks, may be important for children's persistence in the face of challenge (Claxton 1999b).
- There are a number of factors which may influence the effectiveness of practitioners' use of praise with young children: contingency (praise follows targeted behaviour); immediacy; consistency; effect on the behaviour (different effects on individual children); proximity; specificity (describing what exactly is being praised); children's opportunities to respond (avoidance of repeated use of same praise statements, etc.) (Hester et al. 2009).
- 'Praising students' intelligence gives them a short burst of pride, followed by a long string of negative consequences' (Dweck 2007: 36).
- 'Subtle differences in the genericness of language can influence children's conceptions of their abilities and their achievement motivation' (Cimpian et al. 2007: 315–16). For example, 4-year-old children told they were 'good drawers' had lower self-evaluations and lower persistence following failure than those told they 'did a good job drawing'.

## Further reflection

1  Try (with their permission) to observe children in group play of some kind. In what ways do they show social understanding?

2 Think about your own friendships and family relationships. How diverse are they? What makes them 'work', where they do, and what makes them unsuccessful, if any of them are?

3 Below are some possible implications for practice in relation to links between emotion and cognition. Do you agree with them? What others might you add?

- The need to create and support an environment in which children feel free to take risks with their thinking, and able to tolerate the anxiety of 'not knowing'.
- The need to make space for feelings (including adult modelling), and to help children develop *metamood* or *self-awareness* (Goleman).
- Adult sensitivity to the rise and fall of children's self-esteem and confidence.

## Further reading

*Culture and sociocultural theories*

Bronfenbrenner (1979)
Fleer (2006)
Rogoff (1990, 2003)
Siegler *et al.* (2011: ch. 9)

*Social understanding*

Carpendale and Lewis (2006: chs 1, 4, 6 and 9)
Dunn (1988, 1993, 2004a)
Gopnik *et al.* (1999: ch. 2)
Goswami (2008: ch. 3)
Meadows (2010: chs 3 and 4; 2006: 191–4, 373–80, 441–7)
Thornton (2002: 158–69, 194–5, 215–16)
Trevarthen (1995)

*Emotion and cognition*

Arnold (2010)
Claxton (1999b: ch. 2)
Dweck (2000)
Goleman (1996)
Gopnik *et al.* (1999: ch. 2)
Layard and Dunn (2009)
Meadows (2010: ch. 2; 2006: 175–80, 435–9)
Siegler *et al.* (2011: ch. 10)
Statham and Chase (2010)

# Chapter 4

# The developing brain

The focus of this chapter is on the physiological development of the brain and nervous system, and their relationship to the development of thinking and understanding in young children. Current understandings of how the brain develops, particularly in early childhood, are explored, and some of the arguments and possible implications of neuroscientific research for early childhood practice and provision are identified. This chapter can, of course, only provide an introduction to this very complex area: the references at the end of the chapter are invaluable in providing more in-depth accounts.

The relationship of the brain to the mind has been the subject of debate for centuries, and includes theories that effectively separate the two, in a material and mental divide. In recent years, however, much more emphasis has been placed upon the idea that such a divide is artificial and unnecessary, and that all mental activity is associated with some corresponding activity in the brain (Meadows 2006). Goswami (2008) suggests that cognitive neuroscience can potentially have an important role in the development of new explanatory frameworks for understanding cognitive development. Thus, any study of young children's cognition must include some exploration of the functioning of the brain, albeit that our knowledge is still partial, and constantly evolving.

When, in July 1989, the then President of the United States, George Bush Senior, pronounced the 1990s the 'Decade of the Brain', he was highlighting a field of study which was already of considerable scientific and public interest, and which has continued to grow considerably since then. For many years developmental psychology held a prominent position in early childhood theory and practice. The growth of theoretical positions which placed more emphasis on children's social and cultural experiences (Bronfenbrenner 1979; Cole *et al.* 1971; Rogoff 1990) marked a decline in this prominence, and its seeming certainties about patterns of child development. It may be that, for some people, neuroscience offers the promise of a new type of reliability and certainty, that of scientific method (Penn 2005).

This makes it even more important that those with an interest in early childhood, and young children's development, examine the research, and claims being made as a result of it, very carefully. Both Fischer (2009) and Geake (2009) assert that a number of 'neuromyths', often fueled by the media and internet, have become part of popular discourse, influencing the actions of parents, policy-makers and practitioners. In a survey of teachers, 90 per cent stated that they believed that knowledge of the brain is important in the design of educational programmes (Pickering and Howard-Jones 2007), and many early childhood educators have sought to incorporate findings from brain research into their practice. Well-known interventions include ALPS (Accelerated Learning in Practice), described as an approach concerned with 'brain-based methods for accelerating movement and achievement' in children (Smith 1998; Smith and Call 1999), and Brain Gym designed 'to enhance students' experience of whole-brain (using both brain hemispheres simultaneously) learning' (Dennison and Dennison 1994: p. vii). However, Geake (2009) asserts that there is no scientific foundation for such ideas, and Goswami points out that children doing something as simple and ordinary as counting on their fingers prior to counting in their heads are activating neural circuitry in the brain (2004), and Brain Gym exercises may be efficacious purely because exercise can improve alertness (Howard-Jones 2007). This suggests that special interventions may perhaps be effective in making more systematic use of the kinds of things people do already.

Samuels (2009) urges teachers to really engage with the field of neuroscience research if they are to have an influence on the development of work in this area. Blakemore and Frith (2005), Geake (2009) and Goswami (2008) all propose an interdisciplinary approach, bringing together neuroscientists, educators and cognitive psychologists, in order to address the relationship between the brain and thinking and learning. In 2004 the International Mind, Brain and Education (MBE) Society, based in the Graduate School of Education at Harvard, was formed, combining the study of biology, cognitive science and education (Fischer 2009). Such an approach is not, however, universal, and others such as Bruer (1997) have argued that neuroscience cannot directly inform educational practice, but instead the two need to be 'bridged' through cognitive science.

## Studying the brain

A major problem in studying the human brain is one of access. Until quite recently, the chief sources of information were animal studies, autopsies utilizing brain tissues of the dead and neuropsychological studies of brain-damaged patients. All three have limitations, certainly in being able to infer more general human brain development and activity. Advances in medical and experimental technology, particularly the development of functional neuroimaging techniques, have become the major investigating tool in cognitive neuroscience (Geake 2009). Underpinning these techniques is the principle of recording metabolic change within the brain as a result of thought and action. Positron Emission Tomography (PET) scans, and functional Magnetic Resonance Imaging (fMRI) are brain imaging techniques which detect changes in blood flow during an activity, and are used both in the diagnosis of specific problems in the brain and in charting changes in brain functioning. However, both have considerable practical and ethical drawbacks where their use with children is concerned. This is because they are either invasive, as in the case of PET scans, where a radioactive substance is injected into the person's bloodstream, or involve procedures which are unpleasant, as in the case of fMRI, where subjects need to be able to remain still and tolerate the noise and confinement of an MRI machine. In addition, the data may be difficult to interpret (Meadows 2006), we do not yet know if there are any possible long-term side-effects of fMRI, and it is not suitable for many groups of people, for practical reasons. Consequently, these techniques tend to be used with children whose brains are being scanned for diagnostic purposes, or who are aged 6 and above (Siegler et al. 2011).

Non-invasive approaches to monitoring brain activity use EEG (electroencephalographic) and MEG (magnetoencephalographic) recordings which measure electrical and magnetic (respectively) activity in the brain, obtained by placing electrodes on a child's, and even very young baby's, skull. These are useful for understanding temporal changes in brain function, but the data are not of as good quality spatially as that derived from fMRI (Geake 2009). One particular EEG approach, the recording of event-related potentials (ERP), measures changes in the brain's electrical activity which may occur in response to presentation of a particular stimulus. Thornton suggests that this approach, in particular, offers a 'way into understanding what the infant mind is like, and how it changes through development' (2002: 23).

A number of other techniques are also being developed. Functional near-infrared spectroscopy (fNIRS), like FMRI, measures changes in blood flow in the brain, but is more portable and suitable for use with young children, and can provide better spatial quality data than EEG and better temporal accuracy data than fMRI (Goswami 2008). It is also now possible to combine ERP and fMRI data by using non-metallic ERP electrodes in an MRI scanner (Geake 2009).

It must, though, be recognized that there are limitations to all of these techniques. First, most neuroimaging results are open to different interpretations (Geake 2009), and crucially, they all show correlations between neural activity and behaviour, not any kind of causation (Goswami 2008).

## The development of the brain

The human brain begins to develop very early in pregnancy and its prenatal growth and development closely resembles that of other primates. Soon after conception, brain development starts, with brain cells being formed very rapidly from about six to eighteen weeks of gestation (Meadows 2006), at rates of up to 10,000 a second (Fernyhough 2008). We are only now beginning to find out just how, and how much, babies learn whilst in the womb, but we do know that foetuses respond to different voices, can distinguish 'happy talk' from other kinds of speech and may even have developed a preference for particular smells and tastes, even though they cannot directly experience them in the womb (Thornton 2002). It is also clear that the foetal nervous system can process and retain information, for example, newborn babies have been shown to respond to music heard in the womb, whilst showing no such response to unfamiliar tunes (Fernyhough 2008).

At birth, however, brain development, especially that of the cerebral cortex, still has a long way to go, and the first year of life will see considerable maturation. In the earliest days of life, a baby's responses are mainly reflex. The part of the brain which controls these reflex actions is the subcortex, the most primitive part of the brain. With experience, the cortex becomes more dominant, and this is the part of the brain which allows for voluntary action, and, crucially, the development of language and thought.

Over the first year of life, the baby's brain will triple in volume, growing to three-quarters of its adult size by the age of one. At birth the brain already has almost all of the (approximately) 100 billion nerve cells, or neurons, that it will need throughout its life, although few of them are, at that point, fixed in specialist functions. Only in two areas of the brain, the hippocampus and the cerebellum, do brain cells increase after birth (Blakemore and Frith 2005). These neurons are responsible for sending

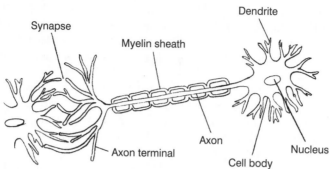

*Figure 4.1* The neuron

and receiving electrical messages both within the brain and between the brain and the body. Although they vary considerably in shape, size and function (for example, sensory neurons transmit information from sensory receptors that detect stimuli in the environment, or within the body, and motor neurons transmit information between the brain and muscles and glands), they all have three main components, as seen in Figure 4.1. At the centre, a cell body contains the nucleus and oversees the basic functioning of the neuron. Dendrites then receive input from other cells and conduct this, in the form of electrical impulses, towards the cell body. An axon then conducts electrical signals away from the cell body, relaying information to other neurons. When a neuron is activated, it sends a brief electrical impulse called an action potential. This leads to the release of chemicals (neurotransmitters) from the axon terminal. These chemicals then cross the microscopic gap between the axon terminal of the original neuron and the dendrites of another.

These microscopic gaps are called synapses, and their total number is 'staggering' (Siegler *et al.* 2011: 103), with some neurons having up to 15,000 synaptic connections with other neurons. The process of synapse formation, called synaptogenesis, begins prenatally, and continues very rapidly both before and after birth. It provides for an 'exuberant explosion' of neuronal connections. (Siegler *et al.* 2011: 108), peaking at the age of two months, when perhaps 1.8 million per second are being formed (Fernyhough 2008).

As well as neurons, the brain contains other types of cells, notably glial cells, which provide vital support for the neurons. In particular, they are responsible for the formation of a myelin sheath around certain axons, which has the effect of insulating the axon and increasing the speed and efficiency of information transmission. This process continues into adulthood (Howard-Jones 2007), and is vitally important in facilitating the ways in which different parts of the brain share information and work together.

This 'exuberant explosion' of neuronal connections is an important feature of infancy and early childhood, entailing considerable overproduction of synapses, such that a 2-year-old child may have 40 per cent more neurons (and hence synapses) than an adult (Geake 2009). In normal patterns of development the synapses develop in response to stimulation, that is, as a result of the baby's experiences. At the same time, they are also selectively pruned, as the brain selects, and preserves (as a result of stimuli), those most useful to the baby's development, and eliminates others. 'Useful', in this context, is defined as level of electrical activity, which essentially stabilizes the synapse in place, cementing the neural pathways which are most useful for that child, in a given environment. Level of activity is itself a function of experience, where the process is as follows: the more frequently the synapse is activated, the more likely it is to be preserved, and thus the greater the strength of connection between the neurons involved. A good example of this is the development of speech. At birth, babies are born with the potential to learn any language, and the capability to make the speech sounds present in any language, but only those that babies hear around them, in their particular environment, will be strengthened. It is often suggested that this leads quite early on in childhood to an inability to vocalize the speech sounds of unfamiliar languages. What may happen, however, is not that the brain loses the ability to detect subtle differences in speech sounds, but it does lose the capacity to treat them as significant (Karmiloff-Smith, cited in Blakemore and Frith 2005). Weikum *et al.* (2007) suggest that this process may be visual as well as aural, with very young babies similarly seemingly able to distinguish speech sounds of different languages by lip reading, until about the age of eight months, when this ability disappears, unless the babies come from bilingual households, where such discrimination remains valuable.

The development of vocalization is what is known as an *experience-expectant* example of synapse production and pruning. That is, it is one of many kinds of experiences that humans as a species generally have, and thus that the brain can 'expect' to shape its development. However, the ability to discriminate between different speech sounds is dependent upon the experiences that a baby has, through hearing the sounds around him. This type of development is described as *experience-dependent*. This capacity of the brain to be affected by experience is known as plasticity, and is, as we shall see below, a key feature of the argument for the importance of brain research to early childhood provision and practice.

It is interesting to speculate why the brain engages in such a seemingly wasteful exercise, of massively overproducing synapses only to destroy them – children lose about 20 billion synapses each day between childhood and adolescence (Fernyhough 2008). Siegler *et al.* (2011) suggest that economy may be a big factor, in that less information initially needs to be encoded in the genes, with experience helping to complete the job of developing the nervous system. This system of 'fine tuning' in relation to environmental experiences may allow for 'a highly ordered and appropriate pattern to emerge from a much less organised one' (Meadows 2006: 342).

Clearly a huge amount of physical development of the brain takes place, both before birth and in the first years of life, with experience playing a key role in that development. As we have seen, and will see, in other chapters of this book, experience also seems to be a central factor in children's cognitive development, pointing to the close relationship between the physiological and psychological development of mind and brain. At the same time, however, it is worth questioning the idea that there is a causal link between 'intelligence' and synaptic density as a result of experience. The clear implication is that more is better, but the relationship of synaptic density to intelligence is not yet (if it ever will be!) proven, and neuroscientists such as Bruer (1999, 1998) urge us to exercise caution in the face of sometimes extravagant claims in this area. As Geake (2009) points out, 2 year olds, whilst they have far more synapses than adults, are not considered to be more 'intelligent', and debate remains over whether overall brain size is predictive of cognitive development (Phillips 2008).

## Mirror neurons

The discovery of a particular type of neuron, 'mirror neurons', may be one of the most important findings in neuroscience in the last decade (Geake 2009). Rizzolatti and Craighero (2004) identify a neurophysiological mechanism, the 'mirror-neuron mechanism', which they believe plays a fundamental part in both understanding and imitating the actions of others. As Goswami (2008) suggests, action is fundamental to cognitive development. Mirror neurons fire when an individual performs a particular action. However, they also fire when an individual observes another person performing a similar action. Interestingly, no such neuronal activity takes place when an individual observes a machine, for example, a robot arm, performing the action; it only occurs as part of observation of a fellow human. As Sylwester suggests, 'mirror neurons connect the subjective worlds of the actor and observer' (2010: 23), with clear implications for children's social and emotional lives (see below). This social and emotional significance is also suggested in the implication of mirror neurons in the kind of protoconversations referred to in Chapter 3, with very young babies imitating and reciprocating the facial expressions of adults. Faces are particularly significant for babies, with studies demonstrating their preference for faces from a very early age (Fernyhough 2008). Goswami (2008) also identifies the possible implications of mirror neurons for a wide range of other aspects of development, for example, theory of mind (Chapter 5), autism (see below and Chapter 5) and communication and language (Chapter 7).

## Individual difference

Our understanding of individual difference in the brain is still very much in development, with few neuroscience investigations of individual differences (Meadows 2006). What we do know, of course, is that the brain functions in very complex ways, that individual differences exist in its anatomy and that we all use slightly different cortical regions to perform the same behaviour (Dietrich 2007).

Whilst such difference is not considered in detail here, it is worth noting that developmental disorders which arise from biological difference, for example, attention deficit/hyperactivity disorder (ADHD), autistic spectrum disorders, dyscalculia and dyslexia, occur in substantial numbers. Dyslexia, for example, affects about 5 per cent of the population (Blakemore and Frith 2005). The effects of such difference are felt in a range of areas related to children's thinking and understanding, for example, in relation to the development of theory of mind in children with autism (see Chapter 5).

This is an area of some controversy, and the idea that developmental disorders can be caused by subtle brain abnormality is not universally accepted (Blakemore and Frith 2005). What does seem clear is that such differences, whilst they may have a biological basis, are not solely attributable to brain difference. Dyslexia is now often viewed as a developmental disorder with its basis in both brain and genes (it often runs in families), and impacted upon by environmental factors. Blakemore and Frith (2005) cite research which demonstrates reduced activity in the major elements of the reading and speech-processing system of the brain. In particular, 'children with developmental dyslexia have not developed well-specified phonological representations of the sound structure of individual words in their mental lexicons' (Goswami 2008: 349). The highly irregular nature of the English language makes this crucial when reading English, but less problematic in the case of a much more regular language such as Italian. By contrast, Geake (2009) looks at the work of John Stein, who asserts that reading is a primarily visual process, in which children with dyslexia experience difficulty because, amongst other things, they cannot accurately encode for the positions of letters in words. These contrasting positions illustrate the difficulties facing educationalists and parents in seeking to interpret the evidence, though, as Geake (2009) points out, interventions that combine phonics, such as language games and rhymes, and whole-language may be valuable.

Autism, and autistic spectrum disorder, is looked at elsewhere (Chapter 5), but recent research suggests that it may be correlated with reduced activity in the mirror neuron system (Geake 2009; Goswami 2008), though what, if any, the causal links are remain unknown. Meadows (2006) suggests that a failure of neurotransmitters to develop properly may contribute to autism. Neuroscientific study of other developmental disorders, such as dyscalculia and ADHD, are likewise beginning to suggest atypicality in the development of areas of the brain (Geake 2009; Howard-Jones 2007). Similarly, Geake (2009) discusses evidence which suggests that, in the brains of adolescent children identified as gifted and talented, the frontal cortices were significantly thicker than average, which, along with other possible factors, might contribute to their high working memory capacity.

## Gender and the brain

This aspect of brain development remains contentious: see, for example, Pinker's (2002) discussion of feminism and gender. Whilst it is accepted that there are differences between male and female brains, there is no general agreement on what these differences mean. Cahill (2005) suggests that there is evidence for anatomical, chemical and functional differences between the brains of men and women, in those areas which affect memory, emotion, vision, hearing and navigation. Geake (2009) describes how female brains (in general) have a more robust corpus callosum, with more fibres projecting into each brain hemisphere, than men. He links this with the female stereotypes of multitasking and emotional literacy. Males, on the other hand, often have denser or thicker parietal lobes, which contributes to working memory and spatial processing. Such spatial understanding is often linked to performance in mathematics, and used as evidence where boys outperform girls in this subject. However, such broad generalizations may obscure differences at different ages, and ignore the roles of social and cultural experiences. For example, as Hutt et al. (1989) demonstrate in relation to the children in their research, girls often seem to be drawn to activities where adults are present. In nurseries and schools these may often be seat-based activities, involving talk. Boys, on the other hand, in Hutt et al's (1989) research, tended to be attracted to activities where adults were not always so evident. These may often be areas such as large block play and gross motor activities, which support spatial and mathematical experience. Thus, not only do boys gain more experience of spatial activities, but also a process of socialization results in the 'gendering' of these activities, such that they may become seen by the children themselves as activities for boys. This may then result in girls having even less motivation to engage with them. The situation may be further exacerbated by the responses that children receive from adults. Wood

(1998) cites research by Dweck which suggested that the teachers in their study gave very different kinds of feedback to girls. In the context of mathematics, for example, negative feedback to boys tended to focus on unstable factors such as inattentiveness, similar feedback to girls tended to reflect on their ability at maths. Positive feedback to boys tended to focus upon, and reinforce, a view that they were 'good' at maths. Nunes (2005) outlines research which suggests that this adult view of boys as inherently better at mathematics than girls can lead to the children themselves taking on this belief. Looked at in this way, differences in achievement may be at least as much to do with experience as biology.

Rogoff (2003) emphasizes that gender differences are based on both biological and cultural heritage. Children develop the distinctive gender roles of their communities as a result of the models they see around them, and the encouragement they receive about gender-related activities. This process of gender role training is often largely taken for granted, and may make changes in gender roles more difficult, because these unconsciously accepted patterns of behaviour are seen as preferable. Baron-Cohen (2004), whilst agreeing that both biology and culture are factors, suggests that there are important psychological differences related to gender, arising more from biological than cultural causes. He contends that 'The female brain is predominantly hard-wired for empathy. The male brain is predominantly hard-wired for understanding and building systems' (Baron-Cohen 2004: 1). In support of his view, Baron-Cohen points to differences between girls and boys in their play preferences, and in their use of verbal or physical skills. He also suggests that girls may develop the ability to infer what other people might be thinking or intending (a central feature of theory of mind – see Chapter 5) earlier than boys. His research demonstrates one-day-old baby boys looking at a mechanical mobile for longer than they looked at a picture of a woman's face. In girls the results were opposite: they looked for longer at the face. At the age of twelve months, boys showed more interest in watching a video of cars, whilst girls showed more preference for a silent video of a 'talking head' (Baron-Cohen 2004). It is interesting to look at Baron-Cohen's assertions in relation to the mapping activity discussed in Chapter 8, where the girls paid more attention to features related to people, and the boys showed more interest in depicting functional features, such as the sewage and electricity systems. As with the examples about mathematics, disentangling the impact of experience from possible physiological difference is tremendously difficult. Baron-Cohen (2004) is at pains to point out, however, that he is talking about statistical averages rather than suggesting that all men can be seen as 'systematizers', and all women as 'empathizers'. Perhaps the most important message, then, is that 'there are brain differences between genders, but even bigger differences between individuals' (Blakemore and Frith 2005: 63), and that the things which make boys and girls similar far outweigh those which might make them different.

## Emotion and the brain

In Chapter 3 some features of the relationship of emotion to cognition were considered. Whilst this relationship has often been downplayed in the past (LeDoux 1998), more emphasis is now placed upon the intimate connection between these two aspects of what makes us who we are. LeDoux believes that 'emotion and cognition are best thought of as separate but interacting mental functions mediated by separate but interacting brain systems' (1998: 69), with the relationship between them being one of bi-directional dependency (Geake 2009). The power of emotional feelings, LeDoux suggests, is that they involve many more brain systems than 'mere thoughts' (1998: 299). Emotions mobilize and synchronize brain activity, enhancing the opportunity for coordinated learning across brain systems. In the face of danger, for example, many different aspects of the brain's resources are focused on one goal, in ways that they may not be in less emotional situations. Immordino-Yang and Damasio (2007) take this further, and emphasize the linkage of cognitive, emotional and social functioning, in ways which support a Vyogtskian view of development. They suggest the term 'Emotional thought' as a way of describing the significant overlap between emotion and thought in learning, memory and decision-making processes.

The biological processes which occur in the brain in relation to emotion, and emotional processing, are complex, and can be read about in detail in LeDoux (1998, 2003). In brief, emotions are significantly involved in learning at a neural level (Geake 2009). This activity is centred on the brain's emotional system, often referred to as the limbic system. LeDoux (2003), however, suggests that, whilst the limbic system remains the predominant explanation for how the brain makes emotions, it is a flawed and inadequate explanation of the specific brain circuits of emotion. For LeDoux, there may be not one emotional system in the brain, but many, all of which have evolved for different reasons. He suggests: 'The system we use to defend against danger is different from the one we use in procreation, and the feelings that result from activating these systems – fear and sexual pleasure – do not have a common origin' (1998: 16). Whilst emotion regulation is related to a range of areas in the brain and connectivity between them (Perlman and Pelphrey 2011), one particular structure does seem to play a central role in some important aspects of the brain's emotional workings. This is the amygdala, two small, almond-shaped structures situated deep inside the brain. In particular, the amygdala is concerned with the automatic processing of emotions, particularly ones associated with fear and distress (Blakemore and Frith 2005). As we saw in Chapter 3, Goleman (1996) places much emphasis on the role of the amygdala in the development of what he calls 'emotional intelligence'.

What happens in the brain when information from the environment (a car speeding towards you or a warm hug from someone you care about, for example) is received and needs processing? LeDoux suggests that 'emotion can be defined as the process by which the brain determines or computes the value of a stimulus' (2003: 206), with the amygdala acting as a 'salience detector' (Perlman and Pelphrey 2011: 608). As a consequence of this process, a number of things may follow. First, emotional reactions occur in response to the information. This is followed by feelings, generated as we become aware of the emotional significance of the information. Finally, we may, but not always, take some kind of action as a result.

The workings of the amygdala illustrate this whole process well. Amygdala cells receive input from the sensory world constantly, but ignore most of them. Once the amygdala does detect a threatening stimulus, it activates a number of other brain networks, with the result that these different systems are coordinated in their response to threat. These networks include sensory ones, others connected with thinking, and, importantly, with memory formation. In stressful situations, the amygdala triggers the release of a number of hormones, including the stress hormone cortisol, the job of which is to mobilize bodily resources to cope with the impact of stress. This is a short-term measure, enabling us to cope until physiological normality is restored. In the longer term, if stress persists, damage, including shrinkage of dendrites and cell death, can occur (LeDoux 2003), and functions like explicit memory are impaired.

These are negative consequences for anyone, but Gerhardt (2004) suggests that the impact may be particularly important for babies. Very young children rely upon adults to manage their stress for them, through the ways in which they care for them, both physically and emotionally. Where adults do not respond appropriately to them, for example by neglecting them, or ignoring their needs, babies become stressed. One consequence of this may be high levels of cortisol production, particularly in the case of newborns. This may have a lasting impact, including on the development of parts of the brain concerned with reading social cues, adapting behaviour to social norms (Gerhardt 2004), attention and working memory (Geake 2009). Gerhardt (2004) links babies' ability to modulate their stress systems to attachment, suggesting that securely attached babies show lower levels of stress hormone production in response to strange or fearful events.

The kind of fear conditioning of the amygdala looked at above is an implicit form of learning, which does not require conscious involvement. At the same time, however, that an implicit memory of an emotional situation is being stored, more explicit memories about the situation are also being created. Let's look at an example of what this means. As a small child I once ran across the road, narrowly missing a particular grey car, speeding towards me. After that, any sight of a similar model and colour car revived an unconscious memory of the incident. At the same time, I also remembered how frightened I was, and often my heart began beating faster, reliving the conscious, explicit memory of the event. LeDoux (1998) suggests that these implicit and explicit systems function in parallel, and, as with my own example, both are likely to be reactivated, as part of one memory function.

Whilst the amygdala is responsible for implicit memory, it is also involved in the formation of explicit memory, along with another region of the brain known as the hippocampus. This idea of separate systems for implicit and explicit memory may be relevant as an explanation for the phenomenon known as infantile amnesia. Most people cannot remember early experiences, usually those that happen before the age of about 3. The hippocampus is an area of the brain which has a relatively prolonged period of maturation, leading to the suggestion that we do not have explicit memories of early childhood because the systems needed for their formation are not yet ready (LeDoux 1998). However, children clearly learn and remember a great deal during this period, which must mean that there are other memory systems in operation, even if they do not have conscious memories of it later.

The examples I have drawn upon here have tended to be about negative emotional states such as fear. Partly this is because this aspect of brain development has been more extensively researched, and partly because there is an innate emotional imbalance which favours negative emotions, particularly fear. This arises from quite natural evolutionary beginnings: experiencing fear, and knowing when to run from a potentially life-threatening predator makes one's survival more likely. However, it is important to emphasize that similar processes govern positive emotional processing. Diamond and Amso (2008) look at the positive benefits of touch for babies, for example, suggesting that the impact may be long-lasting, and include both affective and cognitive dimensions. They cite studies which show lowered cortisol levels and enhanced capacity for attending to subtle environmental cues important for cognitive development in babies who are massaged. Mirror neurons, discussed earlier, may also be important in supporting the development of positive emotional states such as empathy and compassion (Sylwester 2010).

## Neuroscience and early childhood

The scale of neurological development in early childhood has come to be seen as an important reason for focusing on the early years, and three 'big ideas' (Bruer 1998: 14) have come, in particular, to be associated with arguments around interventions in early childhood provision and practice:

- the importance of early synapse formation;
- the idea of critical or sensitive periods in development;
- the impact of enriched environments on brain development.

### Early synapse formation – plasticity and neural connections

As we saw above, synapse formation (synaptogenesis) plays a central role in developing complex neural connections, and at no time does this happen more prolifically than in the early years of life. The plasticity, or adaptability, of the young brain allows, for example, for recovery from injury, in a way that 'would not ordinarily be possible in the later years' (Talay-Ongan 2000: 29). From this, a conclusion has been drawn by some people to the effect that appropriate stimulation will facilitate the fixing of more synaptic connections, and that this, of itself, will be beneficial for children's development.

What, though, is the evidence for such claims? Synaptogenesis was first demonstrated in 1975, following research on cats (Blakemore 2005). Further research on monkeys showed that synaptic densities peak two to four months after birth, after which pruning begins, reaching adult levels at around 3 years. Is this, though, the same in humans? Blakemore (2005) points to the much quicker development of monkeys by comparison to human beings, and suggests that the period of most rapid brain development is likely to be longer in humans than in monkeys.

The timescale for brain development, then, varies between species. It is also true to say that the course of development for different areas in the brain varies. Synapse generation is complete much earlier in the visual cortex than in the frontal cortex, the area of the brain involved in attention, short-term memory and planning (Bruer 1998). In the frontal cortex, neuronal development continues throughout adolescence, suggesting greater plasticity for a far longer period than the early childhood years, at least in some brain areas. In addition, whereas increases in synaptic density may be associated with the initial emergence of some skills and capabilities (for example, visual memory) these same skills continue to improve after synaptic density has begun to decline to adult levels, and adults continue to be able to develop new skills, with brains retaining plasticity throughout the lifespan (Goswami 2008). So, even if synaptogenesis is necessary for the initial emergence of some skills, it cannot account for their continued refinement. In addition, there is also evidence from research to show that, whilst early childhood may be a particularly opportune time for the possibility of neural reorganization following brain injury, it can also happen in later childhood and even in adults (Bailey 2002).

To conclude, Bruer asserts that 'neuroscience suggests that there is no simple, direct relationship between synaptic densities and intelligence' (Bruer 1998: 15). Furthermore, very little is yet known about the ways in which particular forms of learning, for example, learning in nurseries and schools, affects the brain at synaptic level.

### Developmental periods: critical or sensitive?

Extensive research in developmental neurobiology has demonstrated the need for the occurrence of particular kinds of experience at specific times, if some motor, sensory and language skills are to develop normally in human beings (Bruer 1999). For example, babies born with cataracts which are not removed before the age of 2 years may become cortically blind. The work of Hubel and Wiesel (cited in Bailey 2002; Blakemore 2005; Bruer 1999 and 1998) demonstrated that kittens which had one eye temporarily covered early in life did not regain functional use of that eye when it was subsequently uncovered. Moreover, their research demonstrated considerable deterioration of the neuronal connections in the visual area of the brain connected to the covered eye. By comparison, in fully grown cats the same, or longer, periods of sight deprivation had no lasting effect, suggesting that there is a 'critical period', or 'window of opportunity', for sensory experiences such as sight to develop, outside of which achieving that function may be very difficult or even impossible.

Hubel and Wiesel's work has been replicated and further developed, and the results used by some to suggest that a whole range of different learning experiences must occur by a certain age (notably during early childhood) or the brain will never develop properly and achieve function in those areas. Talay-Ongan suggests that these critical periods are evident for 'most domains of development' (2000: 29).

Such a suggestion needs to be examined in two principal ways:

- Are 'critical periods' as rigid as some writers suggest?
- Do such periods exist for a wide range of aspects of development?

With regard to the first question, studies conducted since Hubel and Wiesel's original work have demonstrated that it is not the amount of stimulation which matters in developing the visual cortex, but the balance and relative timing of stimulation. Closing both eyes of an animal for six months during the critical period had no permanent ill-effect on their vision or brain structure, for example (Bruer 1999). In addition, subsequent research suggests that recovery of function may be possible, depending upon the period of deprivation and the use of remedial stimulation and training afterwards (Blakemore 2005). In essence, the 'windows of opportunity' may be open for much longer, and may not even close as firmly as is sometimes suggested, albeit that it may be harder to learn a new skill, or it may not be learned as successfully, later (Bailey 2002). Thompson and Nelson (2001: 10) emphasize that 'although sensitive periods may have a relatively abrupt onset (typically at birth or shortly thereafter), their duration is prolonged, and their offset is gradual'.

Thompson and Nelson's (2001) use of the term 'sensitive' rather than 'critical' periods represents an increasingly strong consensus (Blakemore and Frith 2005; Geake

2009; Goswami 2008; Meadows 2006; Siegler *et al.* 2011). Such periods are neither rigid nor inflexible, and sensory input from the environment does not need to be particularly special for functions to develop normally. Blakemore and Frith suggest the importance of visual and aural stimuli to look at, listen to, touch and manipulate, but conclude: 'what is particularly important in the case of human infants is interaction with other human beings, including language and communication' (2005: 26).

Turning to the second question, research evidence is strongest for the existence of sensitive periods for species-wide, evolution-based (experience-expectant) behaviours. For example, whilst sensory functions such as vision and hearing and learning phonology (learning to speak a language without a perceptible accent) may be subject to stimulation at quite specific times, very little is known about whether sensitive periods exist for more experience-dependent behaviours, such as culturally or socially transmitted knowledge systems like mathematics, reading or music, or of human social and emotional functioning. Even within language acquisition, whilst there may be a sensitive period for the acquisition of phonemic representations (leading to the theory that humans have a predisposition to learn and generalize the rules of language, as suggested by Pinker 1994), acquisition of the semantics and vocabulary of a language can go on throughout life (Blakemore and Frith 2005). Thus, it is possible to conclude that early identification and treatment of sensory problems such as sight and hearing impairment may be very important, and lead to normal (if belated) function. Whether there are sensitive periods for the acquisition of aspects of knowledge such as arithmetic, for example, is less clear.

## Enriched environments and synapse formation

Data on the role of environmental experience in children's neurological development rests, as often in this area, on experimental studies conducted on animals. Greenough (cited in Blakemore 2005; Blakemore and Frith 2005; Bruer 1999, 1998) has conducted a series of studies on rats, with the intention of examining the impact of different environments on brain structure. The results of his studies have often been cited as evidence for the importance of providing so-called 'enriched' environments for young children. Typically, groups of rats are placed in two contrasting environments: one group is separated and rats are raised alone, in laboratory cages with only food and water, the typical laboratory environment for a rat. The other group are raised together, in large group cages that contain tunnels to run through, wheels to spin on and other rats to play with. The rats raised in this enriched laboratory environment had up to 25 per cent more synapses per neuron in the visual areas of their brains, performed learning tasks better and were quicker in navigating their way around mazes (Blakemore 2005: 39). The conclusion reached was that rats living in 'enriched' environments developed better neuronal connections, stronger blood supplies and were cleverer than their counterparts in the isolated or 'deprived' environments. Therefore, provision of enriched environments could lead to similar gains in human beings.

There may, however, be some leaps too far in this. In the first instance, what works for rats may not work for human beings; we just do not know. More elementary, though, is some examination of the two environments. The so-called 'enriched' environment of the socially raised rats is only enriched in laboratory terms. For most rats, living in sewers, running free on the London Underground system, negotiating woodpiles and dustbins, and avoiding rat traps, is not an enriched but a 'normal' environment, with challenges and both social and physical stimulation. By contrast, the laboratory rats living in isolated conditions with little stimulus could be said to be in a 'deprived' environment. Thus, the conclusion that especially enriched environments are advantageous begins to look a little less secure. Bruer (1998) suggests that we should replace the word 'enriched' with 'complex', a word which reflects more realistically the conditions under which most rats (and children) live. Looked at in this way, it is possible to suggest that it may be deprivation which is disadvantageous for brain development, and that what is important for brain development is some level of stimulus. For the vast majority of children, then, their 'normal' environments will provide appropriate conditions for normal brain development, and 'enriched' environments will not, of themselves, necessarily be better. Geake (2009) suggests that the 'natural' environment for most children in Western societies may even be over-stimulating.

Research carried out on children kept in extreme deprivation in Romanian orphanages tends to support both the deleterious effects of such conditions, and the possibility of remediation. Under President Ceauscescu, children were placed in orphanages at only a few weeks old. Studies of their progress after they were adopted by British families showed that, as a result of their poor nutrition, ill health and lack of stimulation, they were likely to have delayed or impaired development in all areas – cognitively, socially, emotionally and physically – with a close association between length of deprivation and severity of impairment. What is remarkable is that 'most babies made a full recovery' (Blakemore 2005: 39), suggesting that remedial stimulation and care can have an important impact. It is important to say, however, that the extent of the recovery of these children was related to the length of time they had spent in the orphanages, and the age at which they were adopted. Those who had been adopted before the age of six months demonstrated levels of development comparable to the control group against whom they were measured at the age of 6 years, those adopted later than that tended to do progressively less well (Siegler *et al.* 2011).

### The three big ideas: some issues of equity and social justice

The three areas looked at above are not, themselves, new: 'Neuroscientists have known about all three big ideas for 20 to 30 years. What we need to be critical of is not the ideas themselves, but how they are interpreted for educators and parents' (Bruer 1998: 14). In outlining some of the research, I have looked at some of the methodological questions that arise from each of them. There are, though, other questions, which revolve around issues of equity and social justice for young children and families. On the one hand, the research evidence about 'enriched' environments can be used to support calls for greater resourcing and funding for early childhood services. On the other hand, it is vital to consider the values implicit in a term like 'enriched'. As Bruer suggests:

> In the popular and education literature, enriched environments tend to be culturally preferred, middle-class environments. These environments tend to include things that the writers value – Mozart, piano lessons, playing chess – and to exclude things that they scorn – video games, MTV, shooting pool.
>
> (Bruer 1998: 18)

The danger is of returning to ideas of providing 'compensatory' care and education for the vast majorities of children who do not conform to this group, replacing their social, cultural and environmental experiences with 'enriched', acceptable ones (Corrie 2000). Using the brain as a way of explaining a child's behaviour or achievement may lead to other possible factors, such as discrimination and disadvantage, being ignored or downplayed (MacNaughton 2003). In addition, locating 'problems' as within a child's brain rather than as part of their whole experience can lead us to a view of children as passive receptors of stimuli rather than as active constructors of meaning (Corrie 2000).

If claims about the vital importance of 'critical' periods are closely adhered to, the potential is there for services, and policy-makers, to give up on children beyond the early years, believing that it would be 'too late' to do anything more, as the critical periods have passed. This could be seen as a danger for all children, but, from the perspective of equity, may unfairly affect those from particular backgrounds. As Corrie (2000) suggests, this position is dangerously close to suggesting that some children may be irredeemable.

## Some tentative implications for practice

Some suggestions from the literature include:

- The importance of diet: the brain uses 20 per cent of all our nutrient energy (Sylwester 2010). A diet rich in fats for babies is important for the production of myelin sheaths around axons in the brain, leading to speedier and more efficient connections between nerves (Fernyhough 2008), whilst caffeine, for example in the form of cola, has a negative impact on children's alertness (Howard-Jones 2007).
- Even small amounts of dehydration can reduce cognitive ability, but drinking water when you are not thirsty can have the same effect: children should be encouraged to drink when they are thirsty (except in unusually hot weather and after exercise, when monitoring systems telling us we are thirsty may be less reliable: Howard-Jones 2007).
- 'Physical exercise may boost brain function, improve mood and increase learning' (Blakemore and Frith 2005: 134).
- 'Regular and sufficient sleep is essential for the brain to learn efficiently' (Howard-Jones 2007: 11).
- Adverse or threatening environments can raise cortisol levels in the body, which can then negatively impact on cognitive functions such as attention and working memory (Geake 2009): we do not learn well when we are fearful.
- The cultural contexts in which children develop have a permanent impact on brain physiology.
- Environments provided for young children should offer them contexts that support their early capacities for responding coherently to, and retaining faithful records of, their sensory world. This means providing appropriate, but not overwhelming, stimuli (physical and interpersonal). In addition, the aim should be to ensure that babies and young children have the opportunity to direct their own sensory exploration of the environment, according to their individual preferences (Catherwood 1999).

- 'Experiences that support children in making connections amongst domains of knowledge … are likely to impact on and enhance the richness of neural networks in the child's brain' (Catherwood 1999: 33).
- Children learn at very different rates, and new learning is heavily influenced by previous experience via stored biases in the neurons (Scoffham 2003).
- 'A spiral curriculum better matches the dynamic nature of memory whereby individual memories change over time with repeated experience and recall' (Geake 2009: 64), thus potentially benefiting learning.
- 'Emotion and cognition, body and mind, work together in students of all ages' (Immordino-Yang 2011: 102).
- Learning and memory are strongly influenced by emotion. 'The stronger the emotion connected with an experience, the stronger the memory associated with it' (Wolfe and Brandt 1998: 13), as chemicals in the brain send out messages about the importance of remembering something, whether it be associated with positive or negative emotions. However, memory and learning may be lessened where the emotion is too strongly negative (LeDoux 2003).
- Memories may be more easily retrieved where the emotional state of the memory matches the state at the time of retrieval; for example, we are more likely to remember happy events when we are feeling happy (LeDoux 2003).
- 'Knowledge and reasoning divorced from emotional implications and learning lack meaning and motivation and are of little use in the real world': emotion is central to supporting children in applying the knowledge and skills gained in educational settings to the rest of their lives (Immordino-Yang and Damasio 2007: 9).

## Further reflection

1 What is your position on the arguments set out above on the implications of brain science for early childhood practice and provision? (The further reading listed below presents differing perspectives.)
2 Do you feel that exercise, food and sleep have a positive impact on your own brain functioning?
3 What impact do you think the environment has on young children's brain development?

## Further reading

Bailey (2002)
Blakemore (2005)
Blakemore and Frith (2005)
Bruer (1999 and 1998)
Cohen (2002: ch 1)
Corrie (2000)
Fernyhough (2008: chs 2, 4 and 7)
Geake (2009)

Gerhardt (2004)
Gopnik *et al.* (1999: 102–10, and ch. 6)
Goswami (2008)
LeDoux (1998, 2003)
Siegler *et al.* (2011: ch. 3)
Sylwester (2010)
Talay-Ongan (2000)

# Chapter 5

# Knowing about the mind

## Theory of mind, self-regulation and metacognition

This chapter focuses on young children's growing awareness, and understanding, of their own, and other people's, minds. Many of the ideas introduced in earlier chapters have a fundamental relationship to this understanding. Children's understanding of other people's minds develops as part of their interactions with others in a social world, and cognitive self-regulation, for example, is part of a bigger picture which also includes social and emotional self-regulation, looked at in Chapter 3. As Astington (1994: 190) suggests:

> The understanding of minds that children acquire in the preschool years underlies their social interactions with family and friends and provides the foundation for their cognitive activities in school. School and family, cognition and affect, work and love – these remain of fundamental importance throughout our lives. It all begins with the child's discovery of the mind.

The importance of the ideas focused on here is reflected in the very lively research interest in the area, particularly in relation to young children. Flavell suggests that the development of metacognition, for example, is 'one of the really central and significant cognitive-developmental hallmarks of the early childhood period' (1977: 64). For Goswami, 'developing an awareness of one's own cognitive functioning is the key to cognitive development once the foundational domains are established' (2008: 412). Interest in this area is also reflected in policy and practice. At the time of writing, the proposals put forward by Dame Claire Tickell (2011) in her review of the English Early Years Foundation Stage (DfES 2007) identify the 'central place of self-regulation in the early years, along with emotional and social aspects of development, as principle determinants of later academic success' (Tickell 2011: 87).

## Executive function

Before looking at children's understanding of other minds (theory of mind) and their own (metacognition), it is worth looking very briefly at some of the relationships between them and the functioning of the brain. In recent years, there has been considerable interest in executive function (EF). Carlson (2011) identifies a fivefold increase in journal articles about EF in childhood over the past ten years. Executive function is intimately related to the development of the brain, particularly the frontal cortex. The systems associated with EF do not begin to develop until about halfway through the first year (Fernyhough 2008), and mature slowly throughout childhood, with a growth spurt between 4 and 7 years (Doherty 2009). Whilst there are some widely differing definitions (Zelazo *et al.* 2003), it can be summed up as a strategic 'cognitive system that controls and manages other cognitive processes, including flexibility of thought, planning, inhibition, and coordination and integration of information' (Drayton *et al.* 2011: 534). Three interrelated sets of cognitive abilities are thought to be involved: cognitive flexibility and the ability to 'set shift' (for example, sorting a set of plastic toys according to colour, then switching to sorting by shape); inhibitory control (for example, delaying gratification); and working memory (particularly the ability to update and monitor working memory representations). Recent neuroimaging studies, showing areas of common activation, tend to support this hypothesis (Monette *et al.* 2011), although it is important to remember that these links are, at present, correlational (Goswami 2008). In recent years, Zelazo and colleagues (see, for example, Zelazo *et al.* 2003) have argued for a distinction between 'cool' and 'hot' executive function, where 'cool' refers to purely cognitive aspects, and 'hot' involves more emotionally significant decision-making.

It is useful to keep ideas of EF in mind throughout this chapter. Executive function has been associated with all of the topics here. Monette *et al.* (2011) view all of the cognitive abilities set out above as 'a cognitive subcomponent of the larger self-regulation construct', and there seems good reason to believe that, as young children's metacognition develops, their EF will improve (Goswami 2008). She describes significant correlations between children's performance on EF tests and theory of mind (ToM) tests, although Henning *et al.* (2011) found this to be strongest in relation to understanding mental states concerning knowledge beliefs, rather than desires and emotions. Doherty (2009) suggests that there are two most likely theories to account for the relationship: EF requires understanding of our own mental processes and ToM requires inhibitory ability. This inhibitory ability is a key element of false belief understanding (see below), and Drayton *et al.* (2011) cite a range of studies indicating that EF is a significant predictor of false belief performance. Like Qu (2011), they also link this with children's social competence, and it is useful to go back to Chapter 3 and some of the evidence discussed there about young children's social understanding. Conversely, EF deficit has been linked to a range of childhood pathologies, including attention deficit hyperactivity disorder (ADHD) and autistic spectrum disorder (see below) (Monette *et al.* 2011).

## Theory of mind

### What is theory of mind?

In 1978 the primatologists Premack and Woodruff posed the question 'Does the chimpanzee have a theory of mind? (Doherty 2009). In so doing, they both coined a term and initiated an 'explosion' of research about theory of mind (ToM) (Carpendale and Lewis 2006). Other writers have used the terms 'mindreading', 'mentalizing', 'adopting the intentional stance', 'social chess' (Bailey 2002: 166), and 'empathizing' (Baron-Cohen 2004). All of them relate to a process which can be defined as 'the ability to impute mental states to the self and to others' (Goswami 2008: 221), which includes an understanding that other people's thoughts, beliefs, feelings and desires may differ to our own, and that these can change over time. Wellman suggests that, along with language, theory of mind is 'a distinctively *human* core capacity' (2004: 2; emphasis in original) that shapes human thought and learning. The capacity to think in this way is closely related to the development of social understanding (Chapter 3), metacognition and self-regulation (see below). Bailey (2002: 163) suggests:

> the ability to infer mental states in ourselves and others lies at the very heart of social interaction, of communication, of co-operation and competition, indeed, of almost every feature of the social life of humans. If you were blind to mental states, what sense would you make of the mosaic of conversations that occur during an average day, some fleeting, others intimate, some involving numerous speakers, others referring to people not even present? What sense would you make of jokes, or innuendoes, or lies?

Astington concurs with this when she says that 'Social interaction is really an interaction of minds, of mental states, but we have to communicate those states to others. We have to let the other person know we want something, or that we want them to believe something' (1994: 43). This implies that ideas (or 'mental states') such as desire and belief underpin the development of theory of mind – we act to fulfil our desires in the light of our beliefs about things, and we infer these same states in the actions of others. She refers to these as 'core concepts' in the theory of mind (see Figure 5.1).

### When do children develop a theory of mind, and what develops?

Precise definitions of what it means to have a theory of mind, and thus at what point children can be said to have such a theory, are contested (Olson and Dweck 2008). The observation discussed in Box 5.1 highlights some of the different interpretations and competing perspectives in this area.

Observations of eighteen month olds recognizing and responding to signs of distress in others, for example, might suggest at least some understanding that others have feelings, but could also just be recognition of an unhappy facial expression, learned more mechanically from noticing an association on previous occasions (Thornton 2002). However, as Thornton (2002) suggests, it seems unlikely that children will have no understanding of mental states one day, and a good understanding the next, making it worthwhile trying to look at what develops, and at what aspects of children's behaviour seem to indicate development of their theory of mind.

The ability to infer mental states in others presupposes an awareness of other people. In Chapter 3 it was suggested that this awareness is present in newborn babies, and

*Figure 5.1* 'Core concepts' in the theory of mind

Box 5.1: Boy I aged 2.10 and Girl D aged 4.1, in a double buggy with their childminder, P.

Boy I was looking at the leaves falling off the trees.

I:          Look, I saw something flying down.

P:          Was it the leaves falling down? They are changing colour now and falling off the trees. Why is that?

D:          Autumn.

P:          The leaves fall down in autumn, don't they?  Then in winter, the trees are bare and in spring the leaves start growing again.

I:          Look, it's melting!

P:          What is melting?

I:          (Not answering but still looking towards the falling leaves) Look it's melting like snowman.

P:          Did you see a leaf falling down off the tree?

I:          Yes, like a snowman, melting.

P:          It fell down to the ground like the snowman when he melts, do you remember when your snowman melted?

I:          Yes.

P:          That's right it melted when the sun made the snow turn to water, didn't it, and then it disappeared. The leaves are falling down too, aren't they, but they are still there, they are on the floor, we can still pick them up, look. (P gives one to I.)

*This conversation involved Boy I and Practitioner P sharing intentions and perspectives, which Vygotsky suggests helps children internalize them and thus aids deeper understanding and the potential for abstract thought (1978). It could be argued that I demonstrated some theory of mind as he seemed to understand that the practitioner did not initially understand what he meant ('Look, it's melting'). I's ability to quickly draw on a previous shared experience to assist the practitioner's understanding might be evidence that he is able to express his viewpoint (Dunn 2004a) or understand what she might be thinking. Conversely, Perner (1991, cited in Doherty 2009: 37) believes that children do not have theory of mind prior to four years of age. Doherty (2009) might agree that I's attempt to explain what he meant by 'melting' was not him drawing on a shared experience. Rather, it is explained by the idea that he thought that she would be holding the same pictures and thoughts in her mind as he did at that moment. Doherty (2009) might also argue that the child's ability to use abstract thinking and to think in past, present and pretend states does not demonstrate evidence of theory of mind. He believes that although a child is able to operate in these different states of mind, they are not aware of it. He believes that he would need to be aware of these states and demonstrate 'metarepresentation' (Pylyshyn 1978, cited in Doherty, 2009: 39) in order to show true theory of mind.*

Abridged and reproduced with permission of Nikki Reid

can be demonstrated by the ways in which they reciprocate the gestures of carers. In the first year of life babies show that they have some understanding that people have intentions (Wellman 2004), albeit that they do not yet recognize that such goal-directed behaviour derives from a mental state (Thornton 2002). A number of aspects of young children's behaviour begin to appear at around the age of eighteen months which do seem to reflect some understanding of the mind. By about this age children are beginning to engage in pretence, which requires them to have an intuitive understanding of the difference between what is real and what is not. Bailey (2002) believes that such play is a precondition for the development of 'mindreading' skills. At some time before their second birthday children begin to comment on feelings and desires (Bartsch and Wellman 1995), and to adapt their speech to suit their audience (Karmiloff-Smith 1994), much as Sean does to his younger sister in Box 7.6 (Chapter 7). By the age of 2 they are talking about emotions in ways which suggest that they understand that these are mental states. They also show some understanding that what one person wants may be different to what someone else wants (Bartsch and Wellman 1995). Box 5.2 shows both this talk about, and understanding of, feeling states in a young boy of 30 months.

The focus in young children's talk on emotion may be highly significant. Young children's talk about desires, and their ability to connect desires with actions, appears at about twelve months (Siegler *et al.* 2011), with talk about beliefs and thoughts not appearing until around the age of 3 (Bartsch and Wellman 1995), as in Box 5.3. Dunn (2005) suggests that Bartsch and Wellman's data demonstrate that young children's understanding of cognitive states such as thinking and believing arises out of their earlier understanding of emotional states. Her research shows a clear association between young children's opportunities to engage in family talk about things such as cooperation amongst siblings, and feelings, and their later emotional understanding and performance in false-belief tasks (see below) (Dunn *et al.* 1991). In addition, the

---

*Box 5.2:* Evidence from Judy Dunn

The older brother Len is crying because his mother scolded him and refused to comfort him after he had bitten his younger brother.
Family J, Child 30 months. Sibling is crying, C attempts to comfort.

C TO SIB:       Len. Don't – stop crying, mate. Stop it crying.
C TO MUM:       Len crying, Mummy! Len crying. Look. Me show you. Len crying.
C TO SIB:       Look, Len. No go on crying (pats sib) … (Sib still sobs.) Ah Len (helps sib with Lego bag). I put it back for Lennie, hey? … (Shows sib a car) There's this man in here. What's this, Len? What's this, Len? Sib sobs.
MUM TO SIB:     Do you want me to smack you?
SIB TO MUM:     No.
MUM:            Then just stop it, please.
SIB TO MUM:     I'm trying to (sobs) …
C TO SIB (STILL CRYING): Stop crying, Len. Smack your bottom.

(Dunn 1988: 94–5)

children's individual experiences of social pretend play with mothers and siblings at the same age (33 months) related to social understanding at 40 months (Dunn *et al.* 1991). As we saw in Chapter 3, the social world of family and friends may be highly significant here. Not only do younger siblings develop a theory of mind earlier than firstborns, but children with two or more older siblings may pass such tasks even earlier (Wood 1998). Astington (1994, 1998) speculates that this may be because of their exposure to more tricks, jokes and teasing, or to more talk about intentions and feelings by parents trying to settle family disputes, but Goswami (2008) also points to the important role of siblings. Just having a sibling seems to be important, because of different kinds of play experiences they offer, and because of the emotional intensity of siblings' interactions with one another. Hughes *et al.* (2005) also highlight the importance of peer influences.

## False Belief

By the age of 3, then, children already know a lot about people. They may have an understanding of the difference between thoughts in the mind and things in the world (Astington 1994). For the majority of them, the following year and a half will be a period of considerable development, notably in their understanding that, just as they themselves have a mind, so do other people, and that the thoughts and feelings in our minds will be different. They will have developed a representational theory of mind: 'By age 4 or 5, children realize that people talk and act on the basis of the way they *think* the world is, even when their thoughts do not reflect reality' (Astington 1998: 47; emphasis in original). What they have come to understand is that thoughts in the mind may not always be true, and that people can hold a false belief, that is, one which contradicts reality. Development of second-order beliefs (for example, A believes that B believes that x ...) may come a little later, around 6–8 years, depending upon the task involved (Filippova and Astington 2008). I recently observed a variant on this in a class session where the teacher was in role, pretending to be the pirate Anne Bonny who, in turn, was pretending to be the pirate Blackbeard. The majority of the 4- and 5-year-olds in the class had considerable difficulty with this context, despite a lot of support from the adults involved.

Investigation of false belief in young children has been one of the most popular research topics over the past few years. Psychologists have developed a battery of experiments designed to explore whether, and at what age, young children appreciate that other people can have false beliefs. Box 5.4 describes a typical false-belief task, the so-called 'Sally-Anne' task.

---

*Box 5.3*: Adam

| | |
|---|---|
| ADULT: | What happened to Tom? |
| ADAM: | I don't know. |
| ADULT: | What happened to him? |
| ADAM: | I don't know. He ran down the street? |

(Bartsch and Wellman 1995:107)

*Box 5.4:* The Sally-Anne false-belief task

In the task, children are shown two dolls, Sally (who has a basket) and Anne (who has a box). Sally has a marble, which she puts in the basket, and then she leaves the room. While Sally is out of the room, Anne removes the marble from the basket and hides it in the box. The children are asked where Sally will look for the marble when she returns.

The typical result from this task is that 3 year olds say that Sally will look in the box, because that is where they know the marble is, and they assume that Sally's thoughts are the same as theirs. By the age of 4, children will typically now understand that, whilst they know where the marble is, Sally will not know that it has been moved.

In a meta-analysis of false belief experiments, Wellman *et al.* (2001) conclude that at the age of 3 the average performance of children in false-belief tasks is significantly wrong. By about 4½ years, children's average performance is significantly correct. However, these statistics belie individual differences not just between the children, but also between both task demand and the type of language used to introduce the task, leading to correct performance at earlier ages in some tasks than in others (Cohen 2002; Siegler *et al.* 2011). Young children's understanding of diverse desires (their own versus someone else about the same object) in false-belief tasks may develop much earlier than, for example, their ability to judge how a person will feel, given a belief that is mistaken (Wellman and Liu 2004). A number of variables seem to affect the age of success in false belief tasks, including temporal marking (use of terms such as 'when' and 'before'); motive (for example, deception and lying); how explicitly the false belief is stated; and children's opportunities to participate in the task (Wellman *et al.* 2001).

By contrast, Fabricus *et al.* (2010) assert that many studies have over-estimated children's understanding of false belief, suggesting that it is not until after 6 years of age that children reason about beliefs. Such contrasting ideas highlight both the differences that exist amongst psychologists about what constitutes false belief, and the difficulties associated with testing it experimentally. The work of some psychologists, notably Judy Dunn and colleagues (1991, 2004a and Cutting and Dunn 1999), suggests that such experimental studies may not be the best way to find out about young children's theories of mind. She emphasizes the value of observation of children in their familiar contexts, in everyday encounters with family and friends, suggesting that in these meaningful, emotionally charged encounters children will tend to display an understanding of other minds earlier than they do in false-belief tasks. Foote and Holmes-Lonergan suggest a positive relationship between false-belief understanding and the use of argument in sibling conflicts, particularly of what they call 'other-oriented argument', such as 'I'll give you all of these … if you give me that one' (2003: 58).

### How universal is theory of mind development?

Opinion differs as to the universality of theory of mind across cultures. Wellman *et al.* (2001) suggest a similar developmental trajectory across different cultural groups, differing only in the ages at which children achieve false-belief understanding (although they do stress that false-belief tasks only measure a narrow aspect of social cognitive development). By contrast, Naito (2004) believes that different cultural practices may contribute to different developmental paths for theory of mind understanding. Cutting and Dunn (1999), Hughes *et al.* (2005) and Sperling *et al.* (2000) also suggest that social class, particularly related to frequency and types of talk (see below) may be a factor. We noted earlier (Chapter 3) that parents may talk about emotions more with girls than with boys. Dunn (2004a) also found that conversations about feeling states were more common in girl friendships than in boys, which may be important for an understanding of other minds. She also cites research in which girls have performed more successfully on theory of mind and emotion understanding tasks (2004a).

Particular groups of children across all cultures seem to experience more difficulty in developing a theory of mind than their peers. Notable amongst these groups are children on the autistic spectrum, who are either autistic, or have Asperger's syndrome. Such children rarely develop theory of mind and, where they do, it is severely delayed. Characteristic of people with autism are difficulties in social interaction (they may have difficulty relating to others, prefer playing with objects rather than people, and be unable to interpret emotions or feelings), social communication (they may have difficulties with language, both speaking and interpreting that of others, and make little physical or eye contact) and imagination (they may have difficulty appreciating other people's perspectives and do not engage in pretend play) (Wall 2004). Gutstein and Whitney (2002) assert that children with autism do not fully understand what it means to share experiences with others, and link this with a failure to initiate joint attention, a key development in early childhood (see Chapter 3). A number of these features seem to be significant for development of theory of mind. Astington (1994: 148) suggests that autistic children are quite different from other children in their lack of awareness of the mind, and their own and others' mental states. Charlotte Moore, writing about her own experiences as the mother of three boys, the first two of whom are autistic, says that she knew, from very early on, that her third son was not:

> I knew, for certain, that Jake wasn't autistic when he was about fifteen months old. He had just learned to walk. He had a biscuit in his hand, and he toddled off into the garden, round the corner, out of my sight. He came back, empty-handed, weeping. 'Want bikkit,' he wailed. He guided me, pointing round the corner, to where the biscuit was, wedged in the spout of a watering-can. He knew he had to tell me where the biscuit was. He knew I didn't know.
>
> (Moore 2004: 74)

As she goes on to say, her other two sons would not have done this. Whilst, as the mother of two autistic children, Charlotte Moore could reasonably be expected to be more 'tuned in' to looking for cues in her son, it nevertheless suggests that it may be possible to see the development of theory of mind from a relatively early age.

The difficulties autistic children have with ToM have been explained in two ways. The first, nativist, neurobiological account suggests that autistic children are 'mind-blind', and that an innate module of the mind is impaired (Baron-Cohen 1995; Pinker 1997). Blakemore and Frith (2005) cite research which suggests that those regions of the brain associated with ToM, or mentalizing, are more weakly connected in people with Asperger's syndrome than in neurotypical people and, as a result, are less active.

The second explanation sees the growth of mental state understanding as a product of social and conversational interaction. Peterson suggests that this latter explanation may also account for the delayed development of ToM in children who are blind, and deaf children who have hearing parents, because 'the child's disability imposes upon the fluent sharing of mentalistic information with family members' (Peterson 2004: 13). The unimpaired development of ToM by deaf children living with deaf parents, it is suggested, is a result of growing up with fluent signing conversational partners, who share a common means of communication and interaction. Further discussion of different attempts to explain autism can be found in Baron-Cohen (1995, 2004) and Doherty (2009) amongst others, but, as Doherty points out, autism continues to resist explanation, and different theories to account for it all have their merits.

### Theories about theory of mind

Three main theoretical positions have been put forward to account for how theory of mind develops. As described earlier, psychologists such as Pinker (1997) and Baron-Cohen (1995) suggest an innate, domain specific modular mechanism, a 'ToMM', or 'Theory of Mind Module'(Leslie 1987), first developed in the context of pretence (see below). A second, domain general, account is usually referred to as 'Theory Theory' because it argues that a child constructs an understanding of the mind that is theory-like (Carpendale and Lewis 2006). It emphasizes the development of children's general cognitive processing power, which enables them to represent two versions of reality: their own, and another person's (Thornton 2002). A third account suggests that children come to understand that others have minds by a process of mental simulation, introspecting on their own subjective experience, and then using this to imagine the thoughts and feelings of another person in a similar situation (Harris 1989). Wellman (2004) believes that these different views reflect wider disputes about general cognitive development, and it is true to say that the relationship between theory of mind and more general cognitive development is an area of considerable current research interest. A generally widespread view is that theory of mind development involves both innate mechanisms and experience (Astington 1998; Bailey 2002; Hatano 2004; Thornton 2002). Doherty (2009) suggests that the way forward may be to see theory of mind as a hybrid of all three theories.

A number of current theorists and psychologists suggest that study of the development of theory of mind needs to take greater account of the sociocultural nature of development. Dunn and Bruner, for example, 'argue for a social constructivist, or "apprenticeship", interpretation of the child's developing competence in theory of mind tasks' (Wood 1998: 166). Astington and Baird (2004, 2005b) draw on Vygotskian ideas on the importance of talk and narrative, and Nelson (2004) believes that it is time to replace 'ToM' with 'CoM', or 'Communities of Minds', with a greater emphasis on the centrality of communication, language and the culture of a community.

### Is having a theory of mind always beneficial?

Are there any negative implications to the development of theory of mind, in particular to its early emergence? Dunn (2004a) speculates that, whilst early sensitivity to others' thoughts and feelings could be advantageous to a child in making and keeping friends, and explaining a point of view, it might also be disadvantageous if it also leads to a similar sensitivity to other people's disparaging comments, including adult criticism. This could be potentially damaging to a child's sense of self, and their feelings of self-competence and self-worth. She suggests the value of further research in this area.

## Language, narrative and pretend play as contexts for developing understanding of the mind

### Language

The relationship between language and theory of mind is complex and multifaceted, and, as yet, still imperfectly understood. The extent to which language is viewed as crucial for the development of ToM may depend on which 'theory' of theory of mind one holds. As Astington and Baird suggest (2004), an innate view of its development suggests a less developmental role for language. There is, however, increasing evidence that language is central to development of young children's social understanding, and hence their theory of mind (Astington and Baird 2005a; Goswami 2008; Milligan *et al.* 2007), and that children's language skills continue to contribute to their abilities to interpret other minds beyond the early childhood years (Filippova and Astington 2008).

What is it that language does so powerfully to support the development of ToM? Astington and Baird (2004) believe that language plays a part in the development of ToM that is independent of social interaction. Social interaction, they suggest, provides opportunities for experiencing mental-state concepts. Language provides for their symbolic encoding, allowing for 'a level of abstraction that can support concepts about unobservable mental states' (Astington and Baird 2004: 8). Through language children are exposed to different points of view, as people talk about what they 'think', 'know' and 'want', for example. This use of mental state terms in metarepresentational contexts may be especially significant (Astington and Baird 2005b), and children's use of mental state terms correlates with false-belief performance in test situations as well as in pretend play with friends (see below) and in conversation (Milligan *et al.* 2007). Conversation is powerful because it highlights different points of view, an understanding of which is crucial to ToM (Harris 2005). Harris suggests that some forms of conversation act as a subtle form of role play. Dunn *et al.* (1991) highlight the significance of family conversation and discourse for aspects such as children's understanding of both the feelings and beliefs of others, as well as false-belief performance.

### Narrative

Are particular aspects of language more important than others for theory of mind development? Whilst pointing out that research has, at different times, suggested just about all aspects, Cutting and Dunn (1999) illustrate a difference between the language abilities of boys and girls in their study. For boys, all aspects of language related to their false-belief understanding. For girls, narrative ability seemed particularly important. Szarkowicz (2000) suggests that narrative contexts may be valuable in studying young children's understanding of the mind, for a number of reasons. First, narrative contexts are often more naturalistic than experimental ones, and so may feel more familiar to young children. Dunn, as we have seen, emphasizes the value of everyday contexts both for developing young children's understanding of mind and for eliciting a more accurate picture of their understanding. Second, narrative is fundamental to how young children make sense of the world (Wells 1987). Finally, narrative 'provides individuals with opportunities to be both in the realm of action and in the characters' minds simultaneously' (Szarkowicz 2000: 73). As she suggests, given that research on theory of mind focuses on an understanding of the interplay between mentalizing and action, narrative may be particularly helpful in exploring this.

Bruner is a powerful advocate of the important role of narrative in the development of theory of mind: 'it is conceivable that our sensitivity to narrative provides the major link between our own sense of self and our sense of others in the world around us' (1987: 94). In support of this, Dunn cites research (Lewis *et al.* cited in Dunn 2004a) which shows children demonstrating more success in their understanding of other minds when they were given the opportunity to link the events involved in a task situation into a coherent narrative. Children's own narratives, in the context of language and thinking, are looked at in Chapter 7, and in the discussion on pretend play below.

Szarkowicz (2000) suggests the value of narrative in the form of children's literature for studying theory of mind. Stories, in picture and story books, are familiar to children in many (though not all) cultural contexts, and form social events, both within the family and in early childhood settings. They are often shared with significant people. Many stories are also multilayered, with parallel narratives of picture and text, providing opportunities for ambiguity and speculation on appearance and reality, for example. Box 5.5 features just such a story, and the children's responses to the practitioner's false-belief questioning.

Szarkowicz's research shows children having a greater chance of demonstrating their understanding of false belief in the narrative activity of sharing a story than in a more traditional task (2000). She suggests that the format of stories, particularly the repetitive and cumulative nature of many texts, may give children better 'markers' of what is important to notice. There are, in her view, some important implications for practice. She emphasizes the role of more experienced others in helping to 'unpack' (2000: 79) the text, particularly in providing support around understanding of mentality in the story. Milligan *et al.* (2007) emphasize the value of stories that embody tricks, surprises and deception.

## Pretend play

Pretend play, especially shared pretence, was first suggested as significantly linked to ToM by Leslie (1987). Since then, it has become one of the most popular areas of research (Carpendale and Lewis 2006). Debate centres on whether pretence is an early, immature expression of some of the skills and concepts necessary for later ToM development, or whether it is an early manifestation of true ToM (Doherty 2009). Either perspective suggests that it may be an important area to consider in looking at the failure of children with autism to develop a theory of mind. As outlined earlier, children on the autistic spectrum rarely engage in pretend play, either alone or with others. For Paley, fantasy play is 'the glue that binds together all other pursuits,

Yvonne, the practitioner here, is reading the picture book Handa's Surprise (Browne 1994) with the children, in order to explore the development of theory of mind through narrative. Set in Ghana, the book tells the story of Handa, who decides to take a surprise to her friend Akeyo, who lives in the neighbouring village. She loads a large basket with different fruits, and sets off with it on her head. On the way, unknown to her, a succession of animals each takes a piece of fruit, until the basket is empty. At this point, a goat, tethered to a tangerine tree, butts the tree as Handa walks past, and fills her basket with tangerines, a fruit not originally in the basket at all. When Handa arrives at Akeyo's village she hands the basket (a 'surprise') to Akeyo – but the biggest surprise is, of course, for Handa herself, and she says: 'Tangerines! That is a surprise!'

YVONNE:     As we read this story, as well as using your ears, to listen to the words, you will have to use your eyes, to look at the pictures carefully. (She reads the story, posing the question 'can you tell me what is happening in this picture?' each time.)

JOE:        The naughty monkey is taking the banana.

DYLAN:      The ostrich is stealing her guava.

LILY:       The elephant is reaching over, with his long trunk, to take Handa's mango.

As the different animals appear in the illustrations, taking fruit from Handa's basket, the children laugh, and appear excited. As I read the last page most of them are smiling broadly.

YVONNE:     What did Handa have in her basket when she arrived in Akeyo's village?

CHILDREN:   Tangerines.

YVONNE:     What did Handa think she had in her basket?

CHILDREN:   Tangerines.

YVONNE:     Okay, listen carefully now. As Handa walked into Akeyo's village, and she had the basket on her head (gesturing to demonstrate) what did she think she had in the basket.

For a few seconds everyone is quiet and looking thoughtful.

ELLA:       Lots of different fruit.

Some of the children look puzzled.

YVONNE:     That's right, Ella. Handa thought she had lots of different fruit in her basket, didn't she? Why did she think that? (Again, several children look uncertain.)

ELLA:       Because she didn't see the animals taking it.

*The children's reactions (laughter and excitement) and their responses to the questions (use of the words 'naughty' and 'stealing') suggest that they understood what was happening in the illustrations. However, they had been prompted at the start to look carefully, and their attention throughout was directed towards the action in the pictures. I deliberately chose not to ask any questions concerning Handa's perspective, so as not to lead them in this area. It is worth considering whether some of the children were not able to answer the final questions because they had lost concentration and so were not sufficiently focused to respond. However, nobody appeared distracted and all of them, except Ella, seemed puzzled by the questions, suggesting lack of understanding rather than attention.*

Reproduced with permission of Yvonne Hatton

including the early teaching of reading and writing skills' (2004: 8). As an activity that often has considerable importance for young children (children in our research often chose as 'their favourite place' areas such as dressing up, role play and construction, all rich in their potential for pretence), pretend play may act both to reflect children's understanding, and promote it.

Several features of pretend play may be especially significant for the development of theory of mind. In pretend play, children step in and out of role, represent situations and transform objects, talk about mental states ('Okay, you be the mum, and you're really cross'), and have to negotiate meanings and actions with others. They have to make the 'leap of imagination into someone else's head' (Baron-Cohen 2004: 26) which characterizes empathy with another person. This act of sharing an imaginative world with friends or siblings, in particular siblings who like each other (Dunn 2004a), involves recognition of their intentions, shared perspectives, and co-ordination of communications about the play, often termed intersubjectivity. This creates the potential for internalization of these perspectives, a process which Vygotsky (1978) suggests supports higher levels of understanding, and the potential for abstract thought. Pretend play seems to embody a complexity of understanding that may not be apparent in other contexts, for example, even 2 and 3 year olds know that they are pretending (Dunn 2004a). In pretend play children can reason and draw causal inferences (Dunn 2004a), and seem able to identify intention as the mental cause of action, and to read intentionality in others (so-called second-order intentionality), at a much earlier age than they can in non-pretend contexts (Bailey 2002; Dunn 2004a). In Box 5.6, Abby clearly shows this second-order intentionality in her comment to her friends, Michaela and Jordan.

A crucial feature of pretend play is its emotional and social significance for young children, as noted in Chapter 3. In the context of ToM, this emotional intensity may affect the development of metarepresentational understanding (Goswami 2008). Dockett suggests that, through their exposure to different perspectives in pretend play, and involvement in negotiations to resolve the kinds of conflicts that arise as a result, 'children may be forced to evaluate and modify their own perspectives and representations of reality, and to realise that their views are not necessarily shared by others' (1998: 112). Higher levels of social understanding are particularly related to experience of engagement in shared pretence, particularly in friendship pairs (Goswami 2008), above other forms of shared play such as rough and tumble play, or shared delight in rule-breaking (Dunn 2004a). The conversations that children share in their pretend play often include reference to thinking and mental states, and children experienced in such talk are more mature in their later ability to 'mind-read' (Dunn 2004a: 59). The

---

*Box 5.6:* Abby, Michaela and Jordan, aged 4, in the role play area

The three have been playing for some time, including shared play with a doll and doll's bed.

MICHAELA:  I'm Cinderella
JORDAN:    Yeah, we're Cinderella
ABBY:      You can't be, you've got a baby.

importance of children's talk in pretend play, and their metaplay behaviours, is looked at in more detail in Chapter 7.

Pretend play, then, may be particularly valuable for the development of theory of mind. However, as with other aspects of development, it cannot be a prerequisite, or children in societies with little pretend play in childhood might not develop theory of mind. Even across societies where children do engage in pretence, the play themes will differ across cultures, and reflect activities important to particular cultures (Garvey 1977). Dunn (2004a) suggests that play themes may also vary with gender, with themes of nurturance and relationships more common in, but certainly not exclusive to, girls' same-gender play than boys. Baron-Cohen (2004) suggests that boys also may be more interested in solitary, rather than cooperative, pretend play, where being empathetic towards co-players will clearly be less of a feature.

## Self-regulation and metacognition – separate and together

The focus of the remainder of this chapter is on self-regulation, particularly cognitive self-regulation, and metacognition. Views differ about the relationship of one to the other, in particular whether self-regulation is subordinate or superordinate to metacognition (Veenman *et al.* 2006). Larkin (2010), for example, sees metacognition as part of the overarching theory of self-regulation. Whatever, the relationship between the two is complex, and intertwined, and it is useful to begin by looking at both separately, for what each might mean, and to then consider how both might develop, and how this development might be facilitated. The close relationship is reflected in some of the research and literature in this area, which occasionally uses the terms interchangeably, including reference to 'metacognitive self-regulation' (Sperling *et al.* 2000), for example. My own feeling is that one possible difference between the two is that self-regulation may be essentially a more unstable concept: one can choose to regulate one's behaviour or not, in many circumstances. Metacognition, on the other hand, may be more stable: it is difficult to *not* know about and have strategies for thinking about one's thinking, once they have been acquired. There are, here, however, two very distinct schools of thought. Some researchers and theorists believe that metacognition must be conscious in order to represent higher order thinking, others include less conscious processing in categorizing behaviour as metacognitive (Veenman *et al.* 2006).

Together, self-regulation and metacognition are recognized as having a 'central role in influencing learning and achievement in school and beyond' (Boekaerts and Cascallar, 2006: 199). This centrality is reflected in their relationship to many other topics throughout this book, including memory and metamemory, information processing, social understanding, goal setting, strategy use, persistence, self-efficacy, feelings and emotions, children's perspectives, language development, dialogic teaching, problem-solving and the idea of private speech. This suggests the importance of a consideration of these ideas for young children's development as thinkers.

## Cognitive self-regulation

Self-regulation is a complex, multifaceted concept, which brings together children's emotional, social, physical and cognitive experiences. There is no single, or simple, definition of self-regulation and like theory of mind it is often referred to in different ways, including as 'impulse control, self-control, self-management, self-direction, independence' (Bronson 2000a: 3). Ideas about the development of self-regulation are often seen as particularly associated with Vygotsky's model of the move from 'other-regulation' to self-regulation, as discussed in Chapter 2. Zimmerman defines self-regulation of learning as 'the degree to which students are metacognitively, motivationally, and behaviourally active participants in their own learning process' (1986, cited in Zimmerman and Schunk 2011b: 4). This highlights that cognitive self-regulation works alongside, and is interrelated with, social and emotional self-regulation.

Bronson's definition of self-regulation as 'the ability to control attention, to direct and monitor thinking and problem solving, and to engage in independent learning activities' (2000a: 3) emphasizes the close relationship of motivation to self-regulation, which she believes are inseparable in most situations, particularly for young children. Perry (2011) believes that it involves attending to key features of the environment, resisting distractions, persisting when tasks are difficult, responding appropriately, adaptively and flexibly, controlling emotions and delaying immediate gratification to meet a more important long-term goal.

### Theoretical perspectives on the development of cognitive self-regulation

Theories to account for the development of cognitive self-regulation in young children feature in all of the models of cognitive development outlined in Chapter 2, as well as in a number of other perspectives, such as psychoanalytic and social learning theory perspectives (Bronson 2000a). They provide useful starting points for thinking about what might develop in relation to cognitive processing, and it is useful to have them in mind when reading here. The characteristics associated with some of these models are set out below (adapted from Bronson 2000a: 113–29):

- Behaviourism: Whilst early behaviourists focused on observable behaviour, more emphasis is now being given to the non-observable behaviour of thinking, with the view that classical and operant conditioning principles of reward and punishment can be used to shape both. Awareness and conscious control of thinking is mediated through language, and children can be taught to regulate their thinking with verbal strategies, self-prompts and rules.
- Piagetian: Awareness and control of thinking come about as a result of cognitive development, with the innate self-regulatory processes of equilibration allowing incorporation of new information into existing structures. This ability to control thinking is universal, and linked to a child's age and stage of development. Neo-Piagetian perspectives hold that this process is domain-specific, and that there are domain-specific strategies for thinking and problem-solving.
- Information processing: 'Awareness and control are mediated by executive processes … which support control of attention and memory, decision making, goal setting, planning, using strategies, monitoring performance, and metacognitive functions' (Bronson 2000a: 129). Children learn to think by developing these functions, in ways that are not always conscious.

- Vygotskian: The pre-eminent tool for gaining mastery over behaviour and cognition is language, serving as the primary vehicle for both cultural transmission, and thought and self-regulation. Cognitive self-regulation is an active process, co-constructed by the child with the assistance of others. Sociocultural theorists such as Cole *et al.* (1971) and Rogoff (2003) suggest that 'people of different cultures may think and solve problems in different ways' (Bronson 2000a: 22).

The most prominent current theoretical position on self-regulation is a Vygotskian one (1978, 1986), in which affective elements such as motivation and social regulation sit alongside cognition as component parts of self-regulation. Pintrich, for example, defines the process of self-regulated learning as the setting of goals by learners who 'then attempt to monitor, regulate and control their cognition, motivation, and behaviour, guided and constrained by their goals and the contextual features in the environment' (2000: 453). Thus, there is an interdependent relationship between the social context and an individual's self-regulation.

Whitebread *et al.* (2005) also point to the increased interest in the part played by the development of the brain in the processes of self-regulation, and you may find it useful to refer back to Chapter 4 in this context.

## Metacognition

Metacognition derives from the ideas of Flavell, who identifies three components: first, the self and others as learners, second, tasks and goals and recognition that different tasks make different types of cognitive demand and, third, strategies to be used to solve identified problems and meet goals (1979). As with self-regulation, there is no universal definition of metacognition. Papaleontiou-Louca defines this 'fuzzy concept' as 'cognition about cognition … thoughts about thoughts, knowledge about knowledge or reflections about actions' (2003: 10). Synthesizing the ideas of, particularly, Flavell (1977, 1979), and Brown (Brown and DeLoache 1983; DeLoache and Brown 1987), a useful working model consists of three closely related elements. These are (Whitebread *et al.* 2005):

- metacognitive knowledge (gradually accumulated knowledge about one's own mental processing, tasks and cognitive strategies);
- metacognitive experience (monitoring one's self-awareness and reflecting upon it);
- 'self-regulation' (control of mental processing, to support appropriate strategy use in a task).

Importantly, a distinction is drawn between knowledge, in particular declarative knowledge, for example about oneself as a learner, and skills, or the procedural knowledge needed for regulating problem-solving. The former can be correct or incorrect (we may have a realistic or unrealistic view about ourselves as learners, for example), whereas the latter embodies an implicit feedback mechanism: if the strategies we employ, or our understanding of the task, fail, then things go wrong (Veenman *et al.* 2006). Thus, metacognition is concerned with both knowledge and regulation of cognition.

---

*Box 5.7:* Metacognition

Joshua, aged 4 years:
Playing at the sand tray, Joshua is using a bottle top as a scoop to empty the tray.
JOSHUA:     This is a good idea. Like this.

Jasmeet, aged 4 years:
Having been asked to tidy up, the children begin to throw the dressing up clothes back into the box, but upon trying to close the box discover that they can't. Jasmeet tells the children that they must fold the clothes neatly in order to make them fit. She solves the problem by drawing on existing knowledge.

Observation of Jasmeet reproduced with permission of Philippa Cooper

*Both Joshua and Jasmeet show metacognitive awareness here, analysing and defining the character of the problem, reflecting upon their own knowledge, and devising a plan for attacking the problem, aspects that Meadows (2006) identifies in her definition of metacognition.*

---

Meadows provides a good map of the territory (2006: 132):

> It involves many basic 'on line' metacognitive processes, including: analysing and defining the character of the problem at hand; reflecting upon one's own knowledge (and lack of knowledge) that may be required to solve the problem; devising a plan for attacking the problem; checking and monitoring how the plan helps in the problem-solving; revising plan (and perhaps the analysis of the problem) in the light of this monitoring; checking any solution reached; and, generally, orchestrating cognitive processes in relation to the cognitive contents and objectives involved, in the service of whatever is one's goal.

As Pramling (1988) suggests, this implies a conscious awareness of one's own learning and thinking, as Joshua and Jasmeet both show, in different ways, in Box 5.7. Look ahead now, too, to Box 7.9 and Abe's comment: 'I don't do thinking, I'm just thinking about my body', and Charlotte in Box 8.2: 'Dad, I've been thinking about it ...'.

There is much debate about whether metacognition is general in nature, or more task- or domain-specific. If it is general, we can expect the processes and strategies that children learn in one context to be available to them in others, and that they will be able to generalize from one context to another. This is a question for all attempts to 'teach' thinking, and is looked at in more detail in Chapter 11. Here it is helpful to note that current research with regard to metacognition is inconclusive (Veenman *et al.* 2006), and that there is research to suggest both that it proceeds from the general to the specific and vice versa (Whitebread 2011).

## The development of cognitive self-regulation and metacognition

At this point, it is most helpful to look at both of these aspects of knowing about the mind together, as many aspects of young children's development are related to them both. In addition, as I have already suggested, it is difficult to say just where self-regulation ends and metacognition begins.

Bronson (2000b) suggests that the capacity to develop self-regulatory functions of all kinds is affected by both innate factors such as temperament, and environmental factors such as interactions with others. Young children's growing physical control gives them opportunities for exploration, and experiences that support their cognitive development. Many of the aspects of development outlined throughout this book are important contributors to young children's control of cognitive processing. The early awareness of, and interest in, patterns in their environments, and of cause and effect, noted in the discussion on children's conceptual development in Chapter 8, for example, both reflects and contributes to babies' increasing ability to organize their ideas and thoughts. Early visual scanning comes increasingly under their control, leading to more organized information (Brown and DeLoache 1983). Their growing ability to anticipate and act in accordance with familiar routines contributes to this cognitive organization. There is evidence that, from about six months onwards, babies are capable of making simple plans in order to attain a goal (Karmiloff-Smith 1994). In the following two years young children's memories and abilities at representing past events improve considerably, allowing for a more deliberate approach to selecting goals, and active problem-solving, albeit that they may not yet be very skilled at planning ahead (Bronson 2004a). Children from as young as eighteen months may spontaneously use error-correction strategies in solving problems (DeLoache *et al.* 1985). The explosion of language competence during these years acts as an important support in young children's abilities in organizing and classifying. Even before the age of 2 children will spontaneously correct errors of grammar and pronunciation in their speech (Bruner 1987).

This kind of implicit metacognitive knowledge and experience is largely unconscious, and something that we all use without realizing. For example, whilst you are reading this book, you may be slowing down sometimes, rereading to clarify your thinking, and skim reading at other times. Karmiloff-Smith (1994: 223) records a mother talking about her son, Kaspar, at 27 months:

> Kaspar started to use both English and German names for the same word and seems to know who to use them with: for example he goes to the 'libree' (library) with my friend Deena and he goes to the 'tek' (Bibliotek) with me.

The period from about the age of 3 onwards is marked by more conscious intentionality in young children's behaviour, and thus can be said to be increasingly self-regulated. They are 'learning how to learn and how to solve the problems presented in their environments' (Bronson 2000a: 134). Children aged 3 have been shown to be capable of monitoring their problem-solving behaviour and, at 4, to use strategies and metacognitive processing in puzzle tasks (Sperling *et al.* 2000). This continues to develop with age. Sperling *et al.* found that, out of two groups of children (aged 3–4 years and 4–5½ years), the older group were better able to both predict how well they would be able to perform in a problem-solving task, and, after performance, to evaluate how well they did perform.

Does all of this, however, constitute evidence of true self-regulation and metacognition in young children? Veenman *et al.* (2006) conclude that the view that metacognition does not begin to emerge until around the age of 8 years is still widely accepted. However, as our research (Robson 2010) and Coltman (2006) and Whitebread *et al.* (2007) show, the metacognitive abilities of younger children may have been severely under-estimated, particularly where this has been based on children's self-report and laboratory-based studies. In contrast, in naturally occurring social contexts which have meaning and purpose for children, they show evidence of self-regulation and metacognition at a much earlier age. Whitebread (2011) also suggests that it depends on how metacognition is defined. If it is seen as conscious and declarative, then Veenman and colleagues' (2006) conclusion may be justified. However, if both conscious *and* unconscious behaviours are included, then there may be good evidence to suggest it starts much earlier, as suggested above. Perry *et al.* conclude that 'young children can and do engage in SRL (self regulated learning) in classrooms where they have opportunities to engage in complex open-ended activities, make choices that have an impact on their learning, control challenge, and evaluate themselves and others' (2002: 14).

### Private speech

One aspect of young children's behaviour which seems to have a strong relationship to self-regulation and metacognition is private speech, the Vygotskian idea of spontaneous self-directed talk in young children, discussed in Chapters 2 and 7. Vygotsky (1934/1987 cited in Elias and Berk 2002) sees private speech as the primary means for transferring regulation of others to the self, with language being used to control complex cognitive processes such as memory, planning and self-reflection. These are fundamental to self-regulation. Private speech peaks in early childhood, between the ages of 3 and 6 (Elias and Berk 2002), but is still evident in much older children (Wigfield *et al.* 2011), particularly in difficult or novel task situations. Open-ended activities, particularly sociodramatic play, and engagement with peers are all associated with more use of private speech, particularly that which is task-relevant and self-guiding, whereas lower rates of private speech may be associated with more direct adult involvement (Krafft and Berk 1998). Bodrova and Leong particularly emphasize pretend play as an optimal context for the development of self-regulation in young children, and it has a central role in the *Tools of the Mind* curriculum (Bodrova and Leong 2011). Elias and Berk (2002) believe that such sociodramatic (not solitary) play may be particularly advantageous for the development of self-regulation in 'high-impulsive' children (those who find it harder to inhibit impulses).

### Memory

An important element in young children's developing self-regulation and metacognition is their ability to use memory strategies. A general tendency which seems to develop over the period of early childhood is of increasingly conscious control over processes which, whilst they may emerge initially quite early in life, function better with the more deliberate use of helpful strategies, in recalling both objects and ideas, as discussed in Chapter 1. Children as young as 2 years old can use rehearsal strategies which help with recall, for example, pointing to, or repeatedly glancing at, the place of an object that they have been asked to find later (Thornton 2002). Over time children will tend to become better at both doing something deliberate at the time of storage to facilitate later retrieval, and in applying more systematic attempts when retrieving (Brown and DeLoache 1983). Three year olds may begin to use deliberate strategies such as looking at, and touching, an object, in order to remember it (Brown and DeLoache 1983), thus demonstrating their understanding of the usefulness of doing something to help them remember. However, even at the age of 7 children will tend to overestimate how well they will be able to remember things, and underestimate the effort needed for memorization (Thornton 2002).

### Knowledge and experience

A number of factors may contribute to young children's less developed skills of self-regulation and metacognition. In Chapter 2 the idea of novicehood was looked at, and young children's relative inexperience may be an important factor here, in not having either sufficient knowledge or strategies for reflecting on their understanding. They may often not know enough about a situation in order to identify its most salient features – an idea looked at in Chapter 8 in relation to young children's conceptual development. They may also not realize that strategies for metacognition and self-regulation are useful in many different situations (Brown and DeLoache 1983), although the extent to which children can usefully transfer strategies across situations is not clearly understood, as we shall see both below and in Chapter 11. Larkin emphasizes the importance of metacognitive experiences for the development of a metacognitive 'knowledge base' (2010: 9).

## Contexts for developing cognitive self-regulation and metacognition

Why is this type of thinking important? As discussed earlier, there is good reason to believe that self-regulation and metacognition play a central role in learning and development. They are associated with higher achievement (Wigfield *et al.* 2011), and there is evidence that self-regulatory and metacognitive behaviour can be taught effectively (Perels *et al.* 2009; Whitebread *et al.* 2007). Brown and DeLoache (1983: 282) suggest these some basic characteristics of thinking can be applied in most situations:

- *predicting* the consequences of an action or event;
- *checking* the results of one's own actions (did it work?);
- *monitoring* one's ongoing activity (how am I doing?);
- *reality testing* (does this make sense?);
- *coordinating* and *controlling* deliberate attempts to learn and solve problems.

Like Brown and DeLoache, Papaleontiou-Louca proposes a range of strategies that can be applied in a wide range of contexts, suggesting that use of these by young children and those working with them will support 'one of the perennial problems of instruction – that of transfer or generalization of what has been learned' (2003: 27–8). Her extensive list includes such strategies as identifying what you know, and what you don't know, generating questions, goal setting, evaluating ways of thinking and acting, role play, keeping thinking journals, inviting 'thinking aloud', and adult modelling.

In recent years, more emphasis has been placed on the importance of social context, and the creation of social environments that support metacognition and self-regulation, with less focus on the direct teaching of skills and strategies (Hadwin and Järvelä 2011; Whitebread *et al.* 2007). Central to this emphasis are the roles of talk and interaction. Pramling, for example, outlines a project with three groups of children aged between 5 and 7 years, working with teachers following the same 'content', but handled in very different ways. Teacher A carried out 'metacognitive dialogues' (1988: 270) with the children, focusing the children's attention on different ways of thinking about their learning in their activities. She asked questions such as 'Did you find out anything that you didn't know before?' and 'How would you go about teaching other people all you have learned? (1988: 271). Teacher B's approach was more 'traditionally' didactic, and Teacher C provided materials for play, and encouraged modelling work with clay, paper and other materials. When asked to think about their learning six months later, eleven of the sixteen children in group A said that they had learned by personal experience, and the remainder went further, believing that they had learned by reflection. All of the children in groups B and C either said that that they did not know what they had learned (30 out of 33), or that it was the result of external influence, not themselves. Pramling suggests that part of the reason for this marked difference lay in the continuous focus on the children's ideas of learning by Teacher A. However, the role of talk *about* learning and thinking here seems central. In our research, we found that opportunities for children and practitioners to talk about and reflect on what they had been doing were especially significant for the children's metacognitive knowledge (Robson 2010). In particular, young children's awareness of talk as a powerful tool for thinking may be important (Mercer 2011). A number of the practitioners in our research also emphasized ideas of thinking and reflection in their interactions with the children, often asking them metacognitive prompts such as 'What did you think might happen?', 'How do you feel about that?' and 'I wonder why that's there?' (Robson and Hargreaves 2005). In Chapter 7 this modelling of speculative talk is looked at in relation to the work of Paley.

Swan and White (1994) suggest that this can also be done through the use of 'thinking books', in which children are encouraged to write about and reflect upon what they have learned (rather than, as is so often the case, what they have done). Swan records her purpose in introducing thinking books with the 8-year-old children she was teaching: 'I had introduced the thinking books to encourage children to see purpose in their learning, so that they would have more control over it and would gain a better understanding of what they learned' (Swan and White 1994: 25). Wall and Higgins (2006) have developed a tool using cartoon-format 'Pupil View' templates of scenarios and situations, which include empty speech and thought bubbles in which children record their ideas. Wall (2008) reports that this has a positive impact on children's awareness of their metacognition.

Wood and Attfield (2005) draw on a Vygotskian model to emphasize the value of appropriate, sensitive and responsive adult intervention, whether in adult- or child-initiated activities, in which adults create both the conditions and time for reflection. Children, they suggest, should not be left just to find out for themselves, but be supported in developing greater awareness of their own learning. Joint problem-solving, and shared regulation (Hadwin and Järvelä 2011), which supports the move from other-regulation to self-regulation, may be an important aspect of the adult's role (Bronson 2000a). Not surprisingly, Frampton *et al.* (2009) found that a positive interaction style by practitioners was a significant predictor of their use of metacognitive language with the 3–5-year-old children in their study. Perhaps more unexpected was their finding that, when they engaged with the children in a more punitive style of interaction, practitioners also stimulated metacognitive thinking through their emphasis on perspective-taking, and seeing things from another child's point of view. However, whether such actions support *self*-regulation, or whether they are more a part of *other*-regulation is a question that must be considered. Bingham and Whitebread (2009) report a project which concentrated on adult–child discussion which supported the children themselves in articulating problems and finding their own strategies and solutions in conflict situations. They suggest that this approach was supportive of children's emotional and social self-regulation.

Whitebread *et al.* (2005) argue that children learn a great deal about becoming self-regulating learners by watching one another, and through peer tutoring. Desautel (2009) concurs, and shows children exhibiting more metacognitive knowledge when they explain a task to another child and talk them through it than when asked only to describe what they did. Children working in pairs, or small groups, in child-initiated collaborative activities, unsupervised by adults, show more evidence of metacognitive monitoring and control (Whitebread *et al.* 2007). In our research with children of a similar age (3–5 years) we found that the metacognitive benefits of playing in a group may differ for participants (Robson 2010). Box 5.8 shows an extract from a pretend play episode between three close friends, who often play together. The extract illustrates the controlling role of Joe in the play, particularly in planning and monitoring its progression. Careful observation by practitioners may be needed to support all children's opportunities to participate in an activity and develop self-regulation and metacognition.

---

*Box 5.8:* Joe, Charlie and Anna, aged 4, in pretend play

Joe, Charlie and Anna have constructed a sleigh from large blocks, and are delivering 'presents'.

JOE:    We have to get back on the train ride. We have to go now (Anna goes back and kneels in front of Joe, Charlie initially follows then runs back to put another block on the structure they have built). We have to get back to Lapland now – come on my creatures, go back to Lapland.

CHARLIE:    Okay (runs back and kneels next to Anna).

ANNA:    (looking at Joe) Going home?

JOE:    Yes, cause Lapland's home. We've given all our presents away. No, we're not here yet.

ANNA:    We're here, we're here.

JOE:    Come on, back to Lapland (A and C go back to the ground).

CHARLIE:    We're ready.

JOE:    Not yet, you have to go.

The roles of adults, and differing perspectives on transferability, are looked at in more detail in Chapter 11, which focuses on approaches to developing young children's thinking through aspects such as problem-solving.

## Some implications for practice: a summary

- The importance of all talk, and particularly talk about emotional states, for supporting theory of mind development (Astington and Baird 2004; Bartsch and Wellman 1995).
- The value of narrative contexts, both personal (Bruner 1987) and in children's literature (Szarkowicz 2000), for the development of theory of mind.
- The value of shared pretence for supporting role taking, symbolic transformations, and talk about mental states (Dunn 2004a; Vygotsky 1978).
- The importance of private speech for early self-regulation.
- The most effective self-regulated learning may be promoted by offering choice to the children, opportunities for them to control the level of challenge in tasks and opportunities for them to evaluate both their own work and that of others (Perry et al. 2002).
- The value of open-ended, child-initiated activities for the development of self-regulation (Elias and Berk 2002; Whitebread et al. 2007).
- The value of adult use and modelling of metacognitive strategies, including identifying what you don't know, generating questions and thinking aloud (Papaleontiou-Louca 2003).
- The importance of dialogue, including 'metacognitive dialogues' with young children, both oral (Pramling 1988; Robson 2010) and written (Swan and White 1994), for their self-regulation and metacognition.
- The value of adult–child joint problem-solving for supporting metacognition (Bronson 2000a).
- When adults get involved children may sometimes be more likely to say that they cannot do something. When working with other children, they may be less likely to question their ability, and often gain confidence through mimicking another child (Whitebread et al. 2005).
- The most effective response from an adult to a child asking for help may be to direct them to another child who has competence or expertise in the area. Often just watching another child supports metacognitive development (Whitebread et al. 2005).

## Further reflection

1   Szarkowicz (2000) has used narrative, in the form of story, as a way of exploring false belief. An author such as John Burningham has made extensive use of parallel narratives which embody false belief in his books. Try to find a children's storybook which could be used in this way, and read it with a child(ren). Discuss the story with them, using questions that focus on an understanding of theory of mind.

2   Looking at the episode in Box 5.9, how, for you, does it show Sunil's awareness of his own knowledge and expertise? Is there evidence of self-regulation and metacognition? What part is being played by the adult?

Box 5.9: Sunil, aged 3.11, in the block area

Sunil sets himself the task of building a tower taller than the teacher. He begins by using large bricks and places 4 on top of each other, in a pattern, one horizontally, one vertically.

SUNIL:    It makes it tall quicker.

He negotiates with Gurpreet to obtain two smaller bricks, but is beginning to get upset. The teacher suggests they operate a swap shop – Gurpreet agrees and Sunil's building continues. He calls the teacher over to stand next to his tower:

SUNIL:    No, it's not tall enough yet, but I can't reach.

The teacher gets a step ladder. On her return he has placed triangular, rounded square small bricks on top of each other, balancing them. He asks her to stand next to the tower again. She does, and it has not got much taller.

SUNIL:    Oh, I need bigger ones again.

(The episode continues.)

## Further reading

*Executive function*

Doherty (2009: ch. 8)
Goswami (2008: ch. 9)
Zelazo *et al.* (2003)

*Theory of mind*

Astington (1994)
Astington and Baird (2005)
Bailey (2002)
Bartsch and Wellman (1995)
Carpendale and Lewis (2006)
Cohen (2002: ch. 5)
Cutting and Dunn (1999)
Doherty (2009)
Dunn (2004a)
Goswami (2008: ch. 7)
Smith *et al.* (2011: ch. 15)
Szarkowicz (2000)
Thornton (2002: 38–40, 63–70)
Wellman *et al.* (2001)

*Self-regulation and metacognition:*

Bronson (2000a)
Brown and DeLoache (1983)

Flavell (1979)
Goswami (2008: 304–22)
Larkin (2010)
Papaleontiou-Louca (2003)
Robson (2010)
Sperling *et al.* (2000)
Veenman *et al.* (2006)
Wood (1998: ch. 4)
Wood and Attfield (2005: 69–76)
Whitebread *et al.* (2007)

# Chapter 6

# Observing, describing and documenting children's thinking and understanding

This chapter looks at some of the ways in which observations of children can be interpreted, and at ways of describing children's attitudes or dispositions to thinking and learning, particularly concepts such as involvement, flow and mastery. Developing on from these, it is useful to consider the relationship between the documenting of observations and children's thinking, and the parts played by the children themselves in informing adults' understanding and actions. In recent years, there has been a valuable, and increasing, emphasis on the importance of the children's own voices, and the gathering of their own perspectives on their lives (Alderson 2005; Clark and Moss 2001; Pramling Samuelson 2004; Harcourt *et al.* 2011).The chapter concludes with a brief consideration of a particular approach to the description and assessment of thinking, the idea of 'intelligence' and 'intelligence testing'.

## Experimental approaches

On first glance, the title of this chapter may appear paradoxical. How can we possibly observe children's thinking and understanding, processes which are essentially occurring inside a person's head? As we saw in Chapter 4, developments in medical techniques allow us the possibility of 'seeing' the brain itself in action, but this, of itself, does not give us a view of young children's thinking and understanding. In addition, these medical and experimental techniques are, of course, not available to practitioners in their daily work with young children, nor would it be appropriate for them to be so.

### Habituation studies

A very widely used experimental approach in attempting to observe the ideas and thinking of young children, particularly babies, is the use of habituation studies. Habituation is one of the simplest and most fundamental forms of human learning (Siegler *et al.* 2011), and involves the way in which we all show a decline of interest in, or response to, repeated or continued experience. For example, a baby may continue to turn his head and look at a rattle being shaken for some time. Over time, however, he will tend to stop turning his head, show signs of boredom and a new stimulus may be required to restart the head turning (this renewed looking is called 'dishabituation'). Such behaviour is taken to imply evidence of learning and memory. The decreased response to a stimulus can be taken to suggest that a child has a memory of what it is:

'oh, I know what that is, I've seen/heard/touched/tasted it before, so I don't need to look at it/listen to it/touch it/taste it now'. Presented with an unfamiliar experience, dishabituation occurs: 'I don't think I know what that is ...' etc. Experimental studies based on this premise can be used to ask a wide range of questions: can babies discriminate between shapes, faces, quantities, for example, and how early in life can they do so? Such studies rely on measurement of observable signals relating to change in a child's behaviour, for example, length of looking at a particular object or display, varying amplitude of sucking on a dummy or pacifier attached to measuring apparatus, or changes in heart rate. It is interesting to note that Siegler *et al.* (2011) suggest that speed of habituation is related to general cognitive ability later in life.

The results of such experimental studies may inform practice, but other ways are needed for use in day-to-day work with children. In seeking to observe something which is, in many ways, unobservable, early childhood professionals, psychologists and epistemologists have developed approaches which rely on applying models of thinking, and the use of outward, observable signals which may indicate thinking and understanding, including what children themselves say about their thoughts and actions.

## Susan Isaacs

Susan Isaacs's influence on the field of early childhood has perhaps been most strongly felt in her emphasis on the value of observation-led records for understanding young children. Her book *Intellectual Growth in Young Children* (1930) provides detailed accounts of episodes at the Malting House School, Cambridge, from 1924 to 1927. The school was initially a small day nursery, for boys aged between 2 and 5, and developed finally into a day- and residential-school for 20 boys and girls, aged up to 8½ years old. Isaacs was particularly interested in children's interest in the physical and human world around them, and what she saw as their enthusiastic curiosity about everyday life, from drains to traffic direction, to the life cycles of plants, animals and human beings. She believed it was important to provide a counterbalance to what she saw as a greater preoccupation at the time with what she describes as 'self-expression' and 'make-believe' in schools for young children. In her view, it is vital to support both children's imaginations and interest in fantasy, and their interest in finding out about the world around them; the two should go hand in hand.

The records of observations in Isaacs's work give an insight into her approach to working with the children, and the importance she placed upon children's active exploration, observation and discovery, in support of their developing thinking and understanding. She emphasized: 'It is the child's understanding that matters, not our pleasure in explaining' (Isaacs 1930: 41). This is well exemplified in the episode described in Box 6.1.

In analysing the observations of children's activities, Isaacs concludes that their efforts at discovery, reasoning and thinking can be categorized under four groups (adapted from Isaacs 1930: 49–52):

1 Applications of knowledge. In particular, the application of acquired knowledge to new situations or problems, including formal or theoretical applications, imaginative and hypothetical application, make-believe and dramatized knowledge, and comparisons and analogies. Application of knowledge is also evident in the children's practical insights and resourcefulness.

2  Increase of knowledge. Gained through experimentation, observation and discovery by the children.

3  Social interchange of knowledge. Characterized by children's use of 'why' and other logical questions, and reasoning, and by discussion.

4  Miscellaneous. Diverse episodes not easily classified.

She emphasizes, however, that no categories are watertight, and that there is considerable overlap, both between the categories themselves, and within any one episode.

Initially influenced by psychoanalysts Anna Freud and Melanie Klein, Susan Isaacs nevertheless was clear in her objectives for teachers at the Malting House School that they should not try to act as analysts for the children. The ideal, she says, is that: '*no interpretations should appear in the records (of observations) ... Only full verbatim records of what was said, and full objective records of what was done should be given*' (Isaacs 1930: 1; emphasis in original). In her view, in any observational situation, adults will always have some impact on the children's behaviour, however involuntary that may be. In addition, any adult selections of observations of children, and their interpretations of children's activities, will always be influenced by their own histories and experiences. Elfer (2006) concurs that all observations will, to some extent, be subjective. Drawing on the Tavistock method (Tavistock Clinic Foundation 2002), Elfer emphasizes the value of acknowledging the subjectivity of the observer, particularly in focusing on very young children's emotional states. For Elfer, the emotional receptivity of the adult observer is what helps them to tune into the emotional states of the child. As we have seen, emotion is intimately linked with young children's thinking and understanding.

Isaacs does acknowledge the practical difficulties of taking such full, verbatim records in the course of working with children, and says that, of necessity, the 'on the spot' records of practitioners working with young children may be more summary and fragmentary. As we saw earlier, she disagreed with Piaget's emphasis on stage theory. She concurs with Piaget that use of such developmental scales may be valuable, but

---

*Box 6.1: The approach of Susan Isaacs*

A rabbit has died during the night at the school.

One child offers his view that: 'My daddy says that if we put it into water, it will get alive again.'

ISAACS:    Shall we do so and see?

The children put the dead rabbit in a bath of water, and hypothesize about it, suggesting that movement means it is alive, and discussing floating and sinking as indicative of life and death: 'If it floats, it's dead, and if it sinks, it's alive'. They then all help to bury the rabbit.

The following day two children talk of digging the rabbit up, and suggest it might not be there because it will have 'gone up to the sky'.

ISAACS:    Shall we see if it's there?

She says, in conclusion:
'They found the rabbit, and the children were very interested to see it still there.'

(Adapted from Isaacs 1930: 41)

stresses that 'it can never be allowed to take the place of a direct examination of the full concrete behaviour of the child' (Isaacs 1930: 6–7).

## Schemas

The work of Chris Athey (first published 1990, now in 2nd edition 2007) has been very influential in its contribution to views on the development of young children's thinking and understanding. Athey's work is underpinned by Piaget's notion of cognitive structures (schemas), and his model of conceptual growth. However, whereas Piaget focuses on the limitations of very young children's preoperational thought, Athey focuses more positively on what children can do and on identifying universal patterns or structures of thought. She argues that repeating patterns and actions (schemas) of children's activity represent forms of thought, which can be nourished by appropriate content, in order to support the coordination of cognitive structures. These patterns of thinking and learning can be accessed through observations of children's representations, language, mark-making and play, all of which provide evidence of the children's persistent interests. In her view:

> The most easily understood meaning of 'schema' is as follows: 'schemas of action (are) co-ordinated systems of movements and perceptions, which constitute any elementary behaviour capable of being repeated and applied to new situations, e.g. grasping, moving, shaking an object' (Piaget 1962, p. 274). Schemas are patterns of repeatable actions that lead to early categories and then to logical classifications ... A schema, therefore, is a pattern of repeatable behaviour into which experiences are assimilated and that are gradually co-ordinated. Co-ordination leads to higher-level and more powerful schemas.
>
> (Athey 2007: 50)

Such patterns of repeatable behaviour are evident from very early babyhood onwards, and are constantly developing and changing, with increasingly complex combinations of schemas as children grow. The coordination of schemas, in particular, is related to the development of concepts (see Chapter 8), and is important because 'as schemas are co-ordinated into more and more complex amalgamations, the environment is comprehended at higher levels by the child' (Athey 2007: 50).

Athey identifies four ways in which children's schemas are expressed: through motor actions; symbolically (graphic representations, action representations and speech representations); functional dependency relationships (children showing understanding of cause and effect) and thought. Whilst all of these coexist, they are each also more closely associated with particular ages. In Athey's research with children aged between 2 and 5 years, motor action schemas were present in largest numbers at age 3.1, symbolic representations at age 4.1, and thought representations at 4.5.

Building on Athey's work, Arnold cites her own research which suggests that some schemas may be more frequently observed than others in young children. In particular, they include (1999: 22):

- Envelopment – wrapping, covering and enclosing objects, space or oneself.
- Trajectory – moving in, or representing, straight lines and arcs, for example, kicking, punching, and graphic representations of straight lines.

- Enclosure – making boundaries around spaces, objects, graphic representations and oneself, for example, painting an enclosing line around a picture.
- Transporting – moving an object or objects from one place to another, or an interest in being moved oneself.
- Connection – joining objects together, or joining oneself to things, for example, tying objects together with string.
- Rotation – spinning and turning oneself around, spinning objects or an interest in things which turn, for example, taps and wheels.
- Going through a boundary – going through a boundary oneself, or making an object go through and come out the other side.
- Oblique trajectory – as with trajectory, but with a focus on the use of oblique lines.
- Containment – putting an object, objects or oneself inside something which can contain them.
- Transformation – showing an interest in things which change state, for example, water and ice or chocolate.

(See also Bartholomew and Bruce 1993; Meade and Cubey 2008; Nutbrown 2011; Arnold and the Pen Green Team 2010; and Chapter 3 here for discussion of schematic representation of children's emotional states.)

In the example in Box 6.2, Michael displays a combination of both a trajectory and a dynamic vertical schema. As Sam, the observer, notes, he shows this both in what he

---

*Box 6.2:* Michael, aged 3.2, at nursery school

Michael is sitting at a table with an old set of wooden bricks of various shapes, sizes and colours – cubes, triangular prisms and rectangular blocks.

Michael builds a tower using the bricks.
'I'm building a tower'
'I put that on there' – placing a brick on top of another one.
'Then I do this' – he knocks the tower over with a sweep of his hand.
5   His facial expression depicts laughter and smiles, whilst looking at the bricks.
He builds another tower immediately afterwards.
This tower falls over by itself.
Again Michael laughs and smiles at the pile of bricks.
He builds the tower again and again. If it does not fall down he pushes it over
10   as before. Each time he laughs and smiles.
He bangs two bricks together: 'I like this'.
He builds another tower. 'You build it very high and go like this' – pushing it over with a sweep of his hand.

*In lines 1, 6, 9 and 12 Michael is displaying a trajectory schema. He is accompanying his speech in line 3 with the action of 'on-top-of' schema (Athey 2007: 131). He is displaying this on a motor and symbolic level when he has named the stack a 'tower' (line 2), and using vertical trajectory symbolism when describing the tower in line 12.*

Reproduced with permission of Sam Segar

does (motor level), and in how he talks about his actions (symbolic representation). If we had observational evidence of Michael, at a later stage, talking about his experience in the absence of the bricks themselves, we would also have evidence of 'thought'.

Athey, and those who have further developed her ideas, such as Nutbrown (2011), place much greater emphasis on the role of other people, particularly adults, in both identifying and nourishing children's schemas, through interaction, and the provision of a supportive environment, than did Piaget. Athey concludes 'Experience is what "feeds" schemas and extends them' (2007: 200). In essence, the role of the adult is to be both proactive with and responsive to children. Clearly, as with any consideration of adult roles, the question of the extent to which adults may themselves 'lead' children's interests is worth putting. In addition, identifying and supporting a child's schemas may require insight and skill on the part of the adult. The example in Box 6.3 highlights the parts played by adults in observing one child's schema, and supporting and extending it.

---

Box 6.3: Joshua, aged 4, at nursery school

Joshua comes into the classroom and goes straight to the woodwork bench. He bangs a couple of nails into a piece of wood. He then comes to the paint table and selects a piece of paper. He takes a brush and makes marks by stabbing the brush down. He then moves the brush in a push pull motion. He moves away from the paint and goes towards the construction area. He picks up two wooden cars and throws them into the home corner. He then gets a pram and takes it outside into the garden where he pushes it around.

*Athey talks of 'fitting not flitting' and this applies to Joshua if one looks closely. He is displaying a trajectory schema and is moving from area to area experiencing this. This continued and so did his delight in throwing objects! His interest was discussed and planned for so that he could be supported and extended in his learning. We provided balls hanging from elastic that could be hit with a bat, and targets he could throw balls at. While using these outside he became interested in the guttering and, with support, set this up so he could roll balls down the pipes. Joshua had not been particularly interested in painting before, except for the occasional fleeting visit. He was offered the chance to paint and shown how he could flick the paint so he could splatter it over the table, he was happy spending time doing this.*

*What would have happened if we had handled Joshua's learning differently? I confess we were sometimes frustrated by his love of throwing things! But we were able to reflect and plan for him drawing upon our knowledge and understanding, what I would consider to be our sound pedagogical notions. Instead of being labelled as a 'naughty' child who would not concentrate, he was viewed as 'strong and capable' and his interest or schema that was at the core of what he was doing was supported.*

Reproduced with permission of Lucy Parker

## Dispositions

The concept of disposition derives from developmental psychology. Learning dispositions have been described as a combination of motivation and 'situated learning strategies' (Carr 2001: 9). Carr suggests that 'situated learning strategies' are knowledge and skills that are being used with a particular purpose in mind, linked to social partners and practices, and tools. She looks at the idea of disposition in the following way:

> In everyday speech we often use it like 'temperament': We comment that someone has a 'cheerful disposition'. It is seen as a quality of an individual, something he or she was born with, or an outcome of facilitating circumstances. When motivation is situated, however, as David Hickey points out, 'context has a fundamental, rather than merely a facilitative role' (1997, p. 177). Lilian Katz made this point when she commented that: 'Dispositions are a very different type of learning from skills and knowledge. They can be thought of as habits of mind, tendencies to respond to situations in certain ways' (1988, p. 30).
>
> (Carr 2001: 21)

It follows from this that not all dispositions are necessarily positive: dispositions to give up, or to be cruel, are as real as dispositions to persist, or to be kind. A useful way of thinking about the idea of disposition is of children being 'ready, willing and able ... a combination of inclination, sensitivity to occasion, and the relevant skill and knowledge' (Carr 2001: 21). To learn successfully, one will need to make use of all three of these aspects. For example, in learning to read, the relevant skill and knowledge about the process of reading will, by themselves, ensure that a child learns to read, in a functional sense. However, the inclination to read, and a willingness to do so, will be needed if a child is to really become 'a reader'. Citing Resnick (1987 in Carr 2001: 9), Carr suggests that much of learning to be a 'good thinker' is dependent upon being ready or willing to identify opportunities to apply one's capabilities. Perkins and Tishman, in their Project Zero research project *Patterns of Thinking*, draw out three similar aspects, describing them as the three components of thinking dispositions: inclination, sensitivity and ability. They suggest that 'it is sensitivity, rather than inclination, that appears to be the chief bottleneck in effective intellectual performance' (http://pzweb. harvard.edu/Research/PatThk.htm). Such sensitivity may be related to the kinds of qualities Dweck (2000) describes in her discussion of mastery orientations (see below).

Carr situates learning dispositions centrally within the approach to observation and assessment developed in New Zealand, called *Learning Stories* (see Carr 1998, 2001), and identifies five domains of learning disposition, which themselves are derived from the New Zealand early childhood curriculum *Te Whariki* (Ministry of Education, New Zealand 1996). The relationship is shown in Box 6.4.

It may be important, though, to think about such learning dispositions not as end states in themselves, but rather as 'dynamic' (Claxton and Carr 2004). Thus, the disposition to persist will not be a once and for all acquisition, but a process that displays itself in different ways at different times, and along three dimensions: robustness, or a tendency to keep responding in a positive way, even under less supportive conditions; breadth, or the ability to apply habits of learning across different domains and in different contexts; and richness, marking increased flexibility and complexity, and the use of a widening repertoire of strategies (Claxton and Carr 2004).

---

*Box 6.4:* Five domains of learning disposition and TeWhariki

| *The strands of the New Zealand Curriculum TeWhariki* | *The domains of learning disposition* (*'The behaviour we look for'*) |
|---|---|
| Belonging | Taking an interest |
| Well-being | Being involved |
| Exploration | Persisting with difficulty, challenge and uncertainty |
| Communication | Expressing a point of view or feeling, communicating with others |
| Contribution | Taking responsibility |

---

Carr describes the *Learning Stories* approach as similar to narrative-style observations, but 'much more structured' (Carr 2001: 96). The strands and domains set out in Box 6.4 provide a framework for recording and analysing observations of children. In settings using this approach, it is evident that many of the learning stories begin with a primary focus on one area of learning disposition, for example, taking an interest. Carr describes how two processes integrate all five areas: *overlapping* and *sequencing*. Overlapping is the process by which different areas often work together, for example, 'Children who have the motivation to tackle and persist with difficulty often express their ideas or feelings in the process' (Carr 2001: 97). Sequencing is the way in which one area may follow on from another, as, for example, in the case of a child whose persistence with challenge followed on from his interest and involvement. Karlsdóttir and Garðarsdóttir (2010) suggest that using a learning stories approach supported a focus on the children's strengths, capabilities and learning processes, and helped to make multiple meanings and adult reflections visible. These aspects are all important supports for children's thinking and understanding.

## Involvement and flow

'Being involved' is identified as one of the five domains of learning disposition described by Carr (2001). The idea of involvement as an indicator of children's understanding and 'intense mental activity' (Laevers 1999) has been developed by Ferre Laevers in Belgium. He links involvement with the idea of flow (Csikszentmihalyi 1979) and suggests:

> Involvement goes along with strong motivation, fascination and total implication; there is no distance between person and activity, no calculation of possible benefits … The crucial point is that the satisfaction that goes along with involvement stems from one source, the exploratory drive, the need to get a better grip on reality, the intrinsic interest in how things and people are, the urge to experience and figure out. Finally, involvement only occurs in the small area in which the activity matches the capabilities of the person, that is in the 'zone of proximal development'. One couldn't imagine any condition more favourable to real development. If we want deep level learning we cannot do without involvement.
>
> (Laevers 2000: 24–5)

Linking involvement with Vygotsky's (1978) idea of the ZPD, Laevers suggests that involvement is a precondition for 'real development'. He identifies a number of observable 'involvement signals' from which children's involvement may be deduced. These include concentration, energy, creativity, facial expression and posture, persistence, precision, reaction time, language and satisfaction (Laevers 2000).

In seeking to measure children's involvement, Laevers (1994) has developed a five-point rating scale, called the *Leuven Involvement Scale* (LIS):

Level 1: No activity, or purely stereotypic repetition of very elementary movements.
Level 2: Frequently interrupted activity (including staring into space, fiddling, dreaming, for approximately half of the time of the observation).
Level 3: More or less continuous activity, but children appear indifferent to the activity, and do not put in much effort. Action ceases whenever an interesting stimulus appears.
Level 4: Activity with intense moments. The activity is of real consequence to the child, and involvement is expressed in the signals for as much as half the observation time.
Level 5: Sustained intense activity. Child's eyes are more or less uninterruptedly focused on the actions and on the material. Surrounding stimuli barely reach the child, and actions are readily performed and require mental effort.

Laevers believes that a key factor of support for the higher levels of involvement is the opportunities children have for choice: 'the more children can choose their own activities, the higher will be their level of involvement' (Laevers 2000: 26). His view is supported by Segar (2004), who found consistently higher levels of involvement when children were able to initiate their own activities rather than when directed by an adult. In Chapter 11 the relationship of choice to children's thinking is considered, including differing perspectives on the balance of adult-led and child-initiated activity in early childhood settings, and its impact on the development of their thinking.

Involvement is one of two dimensions on which Laevers focuses on assessing the quality of children's experiences. The second dimension is the idea of emotional well-being, looked at in more detail in Chapter 3. In his view, this conceptual framework of well-being and involvement 'challenges the assumption that narrowly defined tests of academic achievement are the only means of measuring educational outcomes' (Laevers 2000: 20), a view which can be seen to have elements in common with the ideas of Gardner, in Chapter 2 and below.

Csikszentmihalyi, in describing his work with adults, uses the term 'flow' to describe a similar quality of deep involvement, referring particularly to enjoyment, and a desire to repeat an enjoyable experience (sometimes, for example in the case of rock climbers, even when it is dangerous). In his research, adults often described their experiences of 'flow', that is, times when thing were going well, with activities enjoyed for their own sakes, in very similar ways. It is useful to look at his list of subjective dimensions, as commonly cited by the respondents in his research, in relation to young children, and whether these can be seen as indicators of their thinking (adapted from Csikszentmihalyi 1979: 260–2):

- concentrated involvement in an activity;
- clear goals;
- immediate feedback related to the goals of the activity;

- little sense of time;
- feeling of control;
- loss of ego and self-consciousness;
- no fear of failure;
- merging of action and awareness;
- a balance between challenges and skills, which can vary over time;
- an activity enjoyed for its own sake.

A number of these dimensions are often cited as characteristics of 'play'. Csikszentmihalyi draws a distinction between flow and play, suggesting that a state of flow may occur in a wide range of activities, some of which might be seen as 'play' and others, for example, a surgeon performing an operation, which would generally be described as 'work'. For Csikszentmihalyi, play is a structured form for experiencing flow.

## Mastery

Mastery is looked at in more detail in Chapter 3, but it is useful to look here at this aspect in relation to observation and description. Dweck describes children as having either a 'helpless' or 'mastery oriented' reaction, particularly when they experience difficulty or failure (Dweck 2000). As a tool for the observation and description of children's thinking, the focus is on children's approaches to, and motivation for, tackling an activity, and the kinds of problem-solving strategies they use.

Dweck's ideas are useful in helping to look at how children see themselves, and whether they appear to be engaged in an activity because they are motivated by improving their own competence or understanding, or because they want to gain approbation, or avoid negative judgements of their competence. She summarizes this as having a 'learning goal' on the one hand, and a 'performance goal' on the other. She stresses that both goals are normal and universal. The danger, she believes, arises when performance goals are overemphasized, either by the child, or by the adult. Jo Short, an early childhood practitioner, observes how one boy in her nursery seemed to be oriented towards performance goals. In observing him play with construction apparatus, she records him making comments such as 'Do you like this best of all, this thing that I've made?', 'Is it cool now?' (referring to his model). She also notes that he does not give his construction a name, and speculates 'By failing to give his construction a name, is he protecting himself from criticism? He cannot be judged on the end product if it has no specific identity' (Jo Short, personal communication).

As with involvement, Carr (2001) relates this idea of mastery to one of the five domains of learning disposition (see above): that of persisting with difficulty or uncertainty. However, as Dweck points out, dogged persistence may not always be the best strategy. She suggests that a mastery-oriented response includes 'knowing when to opt out of a task – say, when it is truly beyond someone's current capabilities or when the cost of persisting is too great' (Dweck 2000: 13).

The observation in Box 6.5 includes examples of involvement, flow and mastery.

## Documentation and thinking

The recording of adults' observations of young children has long been a cornerstone of early childhood practice, and many practical books set out a range of approaches to

Box 6.5: Mark, aged 3.2, at nursery school

Mark looks at the equipment in the water tray and selects a scoop and a small plastic bottle. He plunges the bottle deep into the water and pours the water onto the scoop. He watches the water spill over the scoop and repeats this sequence five times. A peer initiates verbal interaction with Mark. He gives no response, visually or verbally. Mark puts the bottle back into the water tray. Still holding the scoop, he walks over to the water play storage containers. He looks in each box before selecting a water wheel. He carries it back and places it in the middle of the water tray. He plunges his scoop deep into the water and pours the water into the hole at the top of the wheel. He watches the wheel spin and repeats this three times. He returns to the storage containers and selects a funnel. He returns to the water tray. Still holding the scoop, he places the funnel in the hole at the top of the water wheel. Using the scoop he pours water into the funnel and lowers his body to watch the wheel spin.  Mark then kneels on the floor, placing his face closer to the wheel. He pours more water into the funnel, and winces as water splashes his face. He places the scoop back into the tray and stands up. He walks back to the storage containers and selects a cylinder, takes it back to the tray and kneels down again. He plunges the cylinder into the water, then lifts it high to pour the water into the funnel. Mark closes his eyes as the wheel splashes water in all directions.

MARK, TO PEER:  It feels like rain.

Mark stands up and walks over to the sink, dries his face with a paper towel, and walks over to the block area.

*Mark's approach can be described in relation to the dispositions of interest, persistence and responsibility for his own actions (Carr 2001). His 'involvement' is what Csikszentmihalyi (1979) describes as the state of flow. Laevers (2000: 24–5) states that 'involvement goes along with strong motivation, fascination and total implication, there is no distance between person and activity'. Mark would score a level 5 on the Leuven Involvement Scale. This is reflected when he does not respond to a peer (however we cannot rule out the question of whether this was a conscious decision, as Mark may not have heard him). He also demonstrated a number of 'involvement signals'. Mark appeared totally absorbed by his work.*

*Mark demonstrated a sense of mastery through his self-competence and self-efficacy. Dweck suggests that this 'mastery orientation' is the result of Mark's engagement in this activity because he is motivated to improve his own competence and understanding.*

Reproduced with permission of Angela Streek

observation and the ways in which they can support planning and provision. In recent years, however, there has been increasing emphasis on the parts played by the acts of observing and documenting children's activities in supporting children's thinking and understanding. (Carr 2001; Edwards *et al.*1998). This approach has come to be closely associated with Reggio Emilia, in Northern Italy, in particular.

For practitioners in Reggio Emilia, children's thinking is made visible through a process of documentation using a range of media, and gathered in a variety of ways, including the children's own representations, and the observations made by adults. This systematically collected documentation of the children's developing ideas, theories and understandings actively shapes thought as children struggle to represent, and reflect upon, their ideas. Young children's thinking is seen as a collective process and, through discussion and 'provocation', their existing theories and ideas can be reflected on, challenged and modified. It is this intersection of documentation and learning, both group and individual, which supports metacognitive activity, and reflection on learning. In collaboration with Howard Gardner and the Project Zero team at Harvard University, they suggest (Project Zero and Reggio Children 2001: 84; emphasis in the original):

> A broad range of documentation (videos, tape recordings, written notes and so on) produced and used *in process* (that is, during the experience) offers the following advantages:
>
> - It makes visible ... the nature of the learning processes and strategies used by each child ...
> - It enables reading, revisiting and assessment in time and in space, and these actions become an integral part of the knowledge-building process ...
> - It seems to be essential for metacognitive processes and for the understanding of children and adults.

Assessment, as 'a precious human measuring tool' (Project Zero and Reggio Children 2001: 202) is viewed as a central part of this process, which, in itself, opens up new possibilities. In the groups in which they have been working, children assess themselves and each other, by revisiting what they have done, and reflecting on this. Documentation relating to their activity is carefully displayed, reflecting the value placed both upon the activity itself, and the records made of it (Edwards *et al.*1998). The intention is to develop attitudes of self-reflection and to deepen children's understanding. They suggest that this process helps children to become more aware of the ways in which their thinking has developed, and view it as analogous to Vygotsky's zone of proximal development. The role of the adult at this point is to highlight to the children the nature of the development in their thinking and understanding.

Whilst they say they are wary of reducing this process to a prescription, they suggest that there may, nevertheless, be some useful indicators that the learning groups are both supporting and demonstrating understanding, and it is useful to look at these (Project Zero and Reggio Children 2001: 247):

a　Children and adults feel they are contributing to a larger, more meaningful whole.
b　The discoveries of individual children become part of the thinking of the learning group.
c　Children express a feeling of continuous growth and awareness that their theories are provisional, and they take pleasure in seeing them modified, developed and advanced.
d　Over time the members of the learning group, alone or as a group, verify, consolidate and apply concepts and competencies acquired in one context to other contexts and domains of knowledge.

e   Children and adults use a language of thinking and emotion.
f   The objective that the group sets for itself is reached by keeping together the procedural and content requirements of the work.
g   Assessment and self-assessment have a strong presence inside the learning group and serve to guide and orient the learning process.
h   Collaboration strategies are an integral part of the group learning process and can determine the quality of learning.

Documentation, then, may have a number of potential benefits if the intention is to support and develop children's thinking and understanding, including deepening children's interest, curiosity and understanding, supporting metacognition, enabling children to revisit and reflect upon their own thinking and learning, and aiding memory and recall.

## Children's perspectives

In recent years there has been considerable growth of interest in approaches to observing children which seek to gain the perspectives of the children themselves. Such approaches reflect a growing concern to ensure that children are active, willing participants in the process, one which arises partly from greater concern for children's rights (Alderson and Morrow 2011; United Nations 1989), but also from a growing acknowledgement of children's agency, and the important part played by the children's own views and ideas, both in shaping practice and in supporting adults' and children's understanding (Harcourt et al. 2011).

In the United Kingdom, the Mosaic Approach to observing and documenting young children's learning developed by Alison Clark and Peter Moss (2001) acknowledges the value of multiple perspectives, including those of the children themselves. The approach uses traditional narrative observations, documentation of parents' views and child conferences, alongside techniques such as giving children cameras to photograph places of importance to them, children taking adults on walking tours of their environment, book making and children's maps of their experiences, as 'tools for reflection' (Clark 2010: 42) by adults and children together. In common with practice in Reggio Emilia, there is an emphasis on hearing the children's voices in a wide range of ways. The product as expressed in words, pictures, song, dance and any of the other 'hundred languages' of children (Edwards et al.1998) acts both as evidence of, and a tool for, children's thinking and understanding. Clark (2010) describes the ways in which the taking of photographs of their 'most important' places by young children involved considerable discussion and reflection, the exercise of choice and judgement, and the exploration of shared and personal meanings by the children. She suggests that approaches such as Mosaic position children as active explorers and meaning makers rather than receivers.

In recent years the field of visual research with young children has developed considerably. The availability of inexpensive digital cameras has helped to make them valuable tools for research and practice, strongly supportive of approaches which foreground children's own perspectives (Robson 2011). Both still and video cameras are helpful for 'bring(ing) into their consciousness the children's own high-level thinking in ordinary moments' (Forman 1999: 3). In our research, the sharing and discussion of video sequences between adults and children supported this kind of

> *Box 6.6:* Rachel, aged 4.7, reflecting on a construction activity as she watches a video of it with an adult in the children's centre
>
> RACHEL:    (looking at screen) Rebecca's spoiling it. That's Yasmin, that's Harry. Jakie's ruining it as well. I'm not. I asked Harry if we needed string, yeah, but Harry said no. I had a good idea. Move them along, yeah, then they can play fine whatever they wanna do with it, and they can break it.
>
> ADULT:     Right, and that was a good idea, was it?
>
> RACHEL:    (nods) Yeah.
>
> ADULT:     So you told other people about building a tunnel, didn't you? It was your idea, was it?
>
> RACHEL:    Yeah, well it was Harry's idea first.
>
> ADULT:     Was it?
>
> RACHEL:    Yeah (looking at screen) That's me trying to do it. They've done it all wrong.
>
> ADULT:     Who's done it all wrong?
>
> RACHEL:    Them two.

metacognitive activity, and often revealed aspects of children's metacognitive knowledge and understanding that were not apparent to adults observing (Robson 2010). Forman (1999) speculates that it may be that the video in effect provides children with a space for the physical memory, allowing them more operating memory with which to think about the activity. A practitioner in our research reflects: 'When I've tried to talk to the children about their own learning ... I've found they would go off the subject really easily, that they actually find it really hard to know what you're getting at ... but a video or photograph can inspire it more' (Robson and Hargreaves 2005: 90) . Box 6.6 shows Rachel's reflections on an activity, with evidence of her ability to consider both her own and other's ideas, intentions and thoughts.

This may be particularly pertinent in relation to younger children. However, as Pramling Samuelson points out, 'toddlers express themselves and communicate with their whole body, and their actions are as trustworthy as spoken language' (2004: 5). A similar view was expressed by one of the teachers in our research. Commenting on Nathan (age 4.3) she suggests that his verbal skills were not yet well enough developed for him to put his thinking into words, instead: 'he was actually just going and doing things, and trying things out by moving bricks, or planks, using different tools. He was actually showing what he was thinking, he was acting out his thought processes' (Robson and Hargreaves 2005: 89). Such statements reaffirm the importance of close observation, and careful listening and watching by adults, if they are to really access children's own perspectives.

## Assessing thinking and understanding: measuring intelligence

So far this chapter has looked at ways of observing and describing children's thinking and understanding that support a detailed picture which reflects the complexity of their understanding. These approaches look at children's development across a range of aspects, including affective as well as cognitive qualities. However, one concept in particular has long been used as a measure of individual difference in cognitive development, and that is the notion of intelligence. As noted in Chapter 1, however, definitions of intelligence vary considerably, making its measurement potentially problematic.

## Intelligence testing

The idea of measuring intelligence goes back to Francis Galton in the nineteenth century. In the 1880s he had an 'anthropometric' laboratory in the Natural History Museum where, for a fee, he offered to measure people on a variety of psychophysical tests (Sternberg 1986), including describing their intelligence in relation to the size of their heads (Cohen 2002). It was not until over 20 years later, however, that the first 'intelligence test' was published, by Alfred Binet, in Paris. Binet had been approached by the Paris authorities to develop a way of identifying those children who might not be capable of succeeding in the normal school system, in order that they could be more effectively catered for. First published in 1905, the Binet-Simon (after his colleague, Theophile Simon) intelligence tests were initially used for this purpose, but soon gained a much wider following in mainstream education and training. The tests were based on the idea of norms of performance for a given age, from which a child's 'mental age' could be derived. This approach was to prove highly influential in a number of ways, not least of which is that it focuses on individual difference within a given age group, rather than on age-related change, the focus of many theories of cognitive development. Test items in Binet's work were chosen to identify the typical performance of children at different ages, which could then be used to determine a total score for each child. This score was relative to the norm for that age group. Thus, measurement of an individual child's intelligence varied along a continuous scale.

In the century since Binet's work was first developed, ideas of intelligence testing have spread across the world, and form the basis for the use of psychometric testing today. Psychologists like Burt and Eysenck suggested that it was possible to measure general intelligence or 'g', a term coined by Charles Spearman (Siegler *et al.* 2011), as a factor which was independent of experience, knowledge or education. As a consequence, it would then be possible to describe people as either 'intelligent' or not. Siegler *et al.* (2011) describe this as a view of intelligence as a single trait, which influences all aspects of cognitive functioning, and is common to all intellectual tasks. Underpinning this general measure is a model of intelligence as 'quickness of mind' (Cohen 2002: 131), or the ability to process information quickly. Thus, in measuring intelligence, tests may look at a subject's reaction time (RT) or inspection time (IT) in response to stimuli (Meadows 2006).

Most familiar is the idea of giving an individual's intelligence a numerical value, the 'intelligence quotient' or 'IQ', developed by the German psychologist William Stern in 1912. This is derived in the following way:

$$IQ = \frac{\text{mental age}}{\text{chronological age}} \times 100$$

Thus, an IQ can be established for any individual at any age, which is relative to the rest of that age cohort. The average IQ is set as 100.

Perhaps the most important questions for practitioners working with young children are: what is the content of the measures being used to establish this 'mental age' and how are they being framed to young children? Donaldson (1978) clearly establishes the centrality of context in supporting young children's understanding. In many instances, intelligence tests comprise disembedded items, which may not allow young children to display the true depth of their thinking and understanding. In addition, the content of the tests may focus on a narrow range of areas, and prioritize convergent thinking, and the 'knowing' of facts. This factual knowledge of the world has been called 'crystallized intelligence' (Cattell 1971; Sternberg 1985) or the 'accumulation of schooling, acculturation and other learning experiences' (Meadows 2006: 217). In acknowledging the drawbacks of such a narrow focus, developers of other intelligence tests have attempted to draw on other aspects of intelligence, such as 'fluid intelligence' (Cattell 1971; Sternberg 1985), or the ability to draw inferences, to think on the spot, to solve problems and to employ inductive reasoning. Examples of this are the Wechsler Intelligence Test for Children (WISC), and the Wechsler Pre-school and Primary Test of Intelligence (WPPSI), for use with children under 5.

Intelligence testing has proved seductive because it was (and still is, in some quarters) seen as a valid, reliable way of comparing cognitive function. As such, it had widespread use in the United Kingdom in the mid-twentieth century in order to select children for secondary education. However, a range of studies have demonstrated that such tests are not objective, or context-free, and are likely to disadvantage children who receive less coaching in the ways of intelligence tests, or who are from cultural backgrounds different to those on whom the tests have been standardized. The heavy verbal and linguistic bias of some tests may disadvantage children who are speakers of English as an additional language (where the test is being taken in English!). In addition, those most favoured by such tests seem to be children whose memory and analytical qualities are strongest, at the expense of those with creative and practical qualities. Significantly, scores in 20 different industrialized countries and in some other cultural contexts have shown a rising curve since IQ tests were first introduced in the early 1900s. This so-called 'Flynn effect' may be the result of a number of things: better nutrition and healthcare, increased parental literacy and smaller families (Woolfolk *et al.* 2008), and the impact upon parts of the brain concerned with working memory and mathematical thinking in young children growing up immersed in a science-based technologically innovative culture (Geake 2009). One outcome of this effect is that the norms used to determine scores have had to be continually revised. As a result, children may appear to be more or less 'intelligent' depending upon the era in which they were tested. As Claxton says, 'IQ begins to look more like a rather arcane ability, at which only rather peculiar people would (and would wish to) excel, than a crucial quality for living' (1999b: 32).

There have been attempts to develop culture- and language-free tests of intelligence, such as the Raven Progressive Matrices, which require individuals to complete the missing piece of a pattern, by choosing from a set of six alternatives. However, as Thornton points out, even a test like this assumes that the person taking it has some knowledge of the conventions of testing, and is aware of the need to balance speed against accuracy (Thornton 2002). Children from particular cultural backgrounds may be more familiar with such conventions, and even the idea of being tested. In addition, children from cultures with no tradition of writing or mark-making may have problems in interpreting such two-dimensional images. The dangers of making cross-cultural comparisons of children based on the same test, or even of using the same test on all children in an average class in much of Europe, North America or Australia, are clear.

## Critics of 'IQ' testing

One of the most influential critics of conventional intelligence testing, suggesting that it rests upon a very narrow view of what it is to be intelligent, is Howard Gardner, whose ideas were looked at in Chapter 2. Essentially, Gardner argues that, rather than one brain, we have a series of semi-autonomous modules, which may sometimes work together, but which may also compete, and which demonstrate a range of different intelligences. If we are to truly measure a person's intelligence, Gardner argues, we must find ways that relate to all of these intelligences, not just the narrowly focused verbal, mathematical and spatial aspects which predominate in conventional intelligence testing. For Gardner, there is no reason why a person should not score highly on some forms of intelligence, and low on others. Pascal and Bertram make a similar point in their discussion of assessment and testing in the early years. They argue for forms of assessment similar to those discussed above, which look at a wide range of indicators, 'not simply focusing on those things that are easily measured' (Pascal and Bertram 2002: 92). In this they are critical of what they see as a narrow focus on literacy and numeracy in some testing regimes. Such a focus may disadvantage some groups of children, particularly those for whom English is an additional language, and boys. In addition, it does not take account of many children's knowledge, skills, understandings and attitudes in very significant areas of their activity.

Sternberg, similarly, suggests that traditional approaches to testing intelligence have severe limitations. In his view, intelligence is a 'mental activity directed towards purposive adaptation to, and selection and shaping of, real-world environments relevant to one's life' (Sternberg 1985: 45). It follows from this that intelligence is situated within sociocultural contexts, and may differ from one culture to another, dependent upon experience, and upon what is valued. His triarchic theory of intelligence comprises three subtheories. The first or 'experiential' subtheory concerns the task itself, and is concerned with how effectively a person learns a new skill, or deals with novel situations. The second, 'contextual' subtheory looks at the ways in which people adapt to, select and shape their environments. Sternberg suggests that this kind of knowledge (much of it tacit, and acquired through everyday experience) may be best measured via tasks which look at social and practical skills. The third subtheory is called the componential subtheory, and considers information processing aspects of tasks, and focuses on the different strategies people might use in solving a task. This third subtheory, which focuses more on metacognitive skills, may be relatively independent of context, but Sternberg concludes that the other two subtheories in his definition of intelligence are, in the case of the 'experiential', more culturally relative, and in the case of the 'contextual', context dependent.

As a consequence, Sternberg argues that behaviour is not intelligent in the abstract, but in context. The person who jumps into a river to save the life of someone he sees drowning is, we would tend to think, behaving more intelligently than the person who stands on the riverbank calculating the specific density of the drowning man as he sinks below the water, however well he is able to perform the calculation.

To return to the idea of intelligence as 'innate, general cognitive ability' (Burt in White 2002: 78), the inevitable consequence of such a viewpoint is that intelligence owes much to our genetic inheritance, that it is a product of our nature, more than it is a result of our experiences. Siegler *et al.* (2011) suggest that no issue in psychology has been responsible for more acrimonious debate than the relationship of heredity and environment to intelligence. In Thornton's (2002) view, the relative importance of nature and nurture will vary according to situation. The area as a whole is probably best summed up by Meadows:

> The only sensible position to take, it seems to me, is that intelligence is affected by one's genes both directly as they work to produce a more or less adequately functioning brain and indirectly through one's kin's behaviour and the environment one seeks out and elicits oneself; but that it is also malleable, affected by the environments to which one becomes adapted.

(2006: 247)

To summarize here, the idea that there are many forms of intelligent behaviour, all of which are influenced by the social and cultural contexts in which they occur, suggests that 'intelligence' as a narrowly understood concept of general ability may not be especially useful in the assessment of young children's thinking and understanding. In addition, the idea that 'individual human minds can be characterized as having a given level of general intelligence' (Thornton 2002: 179) is a theory, and not a fact. Furthermore, knowing a child's score on an IQ test may be of little value in informing practitioners about how they should proceed in order to support that child's further development.

## Some implications for practice

The practical implications of observing, describing and documenting young children's thinking and understanding are implicit throughout the discussion in this chapter. Observation is, of itself, a practical support in informing adults working with young children about all aspects of their behaviour. It plays a valuable part in making children's thinking 'visible' (Project Zero and Reggio Children 2001), in which children's own involvement in the process is critical (Harcourt *et al.* 2011).

## Further reflection

1 With their permission, make a narrative observation of a child or a group of children, or find a recorded example in the references for this chapter. Look at it in the light of the range of approaches discussed in this section, for example using Laevers's involvement signals, or Carr's domains of learning disposition.

- Does each approach add to your understanding in different ways?
- Are the approaches complimentary to one another, or do they conflict?
- Would different approaches be more or less useful in different contexts?

2 How can children's own perspectives on their thinking, learning and understanding be heard? What practical strategies can you think of to support this?

## Further reading

*Schema*

Athey (2007)
Meade and Cubey (2008)
Nutbrown (2011)

*Dispositions*

Carr (1998, 2001)
Claxton and Carr (2004)

*Involvement, flow and mastery*

Carr (2001)
Csikszentmihalyi (1979)
Dweck (2000)
Laevers (1999, 2000)

*Documentation and children's perspectives*

Carr (2001)
Clark (2010)
Clark and Moss (2001)
Clark *et al.* (2005)
Edwards *et al.* (1998)
Harcourt *et al.* (2011)
Project Zero and Reggio Children (2001)

*Intelligence*

Cohen (2002: ch. 7)
Gardner (1983, 1991)
Meadows (2006: ch. 3)
Siegler *et al.* (2011: chs 3 and 8)
Sternberg (1985)

# Chapter 7

# Language, communication and thought

In this chapter the focus is on the role of language, particularly spoken language, and communication, in young children's thinking and understanding. We look at the curious, inquiring minds of young children, and at their efforts to make sense of their world, through talking, questioning, playing and interacting with others, in the contexts of home and early childhood settings. Thornton suggests that the development of language is 'the most striking achievement of infancy' (2002: 42). How this happens, and how children acquire language, remains a contested area, and theories to account for the acquisition of language are very briefly considered below. The main interest here, though, is in the relationship of language to children's thinking, and on the role of language as a tool for thinking (Vygotsky 1978, 1986) which can be used to help children to structure and encode their experiences (Goswami 2008).

## To what purposes do we put language?

The ability to use language to communicate, and to make sense of experience, is a uniquely human attribute. This highly flexible and constantly evolving symbolic system provides a means for humans to represent and communicate their thoughts and ideas. Language enables human beings to reflect on and know about their own thoughts (Goswami 2008) and 'build a mental picture of reality, to make sense of their experience, of what goes on around them and inside them' (Halliday 1985: 101). Whilst, as we shall see, some of this may be a solitary process, the uniqueness of language is in the ways in which it facilitates communication, and the sharing of this sense-making process. As Astington (1994) points out, our thoughts are shared with others in language. Mercer suggests that this is what makes language qualitatively different from other communication systems, in that it 'provides us with a means for thinking together, for jointly creating knowledge and understanding' (2000: 15) and for making better sense of the world together, a process he calls 'interthinking'. We use language to convey our beliefs and desires to others, to make things happen (Astington 1994), to differentiate between ourselves and others, to take advantage of the things that people before us have discovered about the world (Gopnik *et al.* 1999) and, as Wells (1987: 53) says, 'just to remain in contact'. Claxton (1999b: 133) suggests:

> The ability to talk to ourselves supports the development of physical skills. Listening to and telling stories helps people to make sense of challenging and puzzling situations. And language also enables us to develop our powers of memory.

So, while language could be said to be a single system used for two purposes, namely representation and communication (Astington and Baird 2005a), these two purposes interact with one another, with acts of communication serving to support representation, and vice versa. How does this happen? What is the relationship between language and thought?

## The relationship between language and thought

In order to explore this relationship, it is worth looking very briefly at the main theories of how children come to learn to speak in the first place. Flavell's assertion that 'Draconian measures would be needed to *prevent* most children from learning to talk' (Flavell in Thornton 2002: 44; emphasis in original) reflects Trevarthen's (1995) views, considered in Chapters 2 and 3. Theoretical perspectives about how this drive to communicate is built upon fall into approaches which place varying emphases on the role of innate properties, and environmental experience. Behaviourist approaches in the 1950s suggested that language was acquired as a result of conditioning, with children imitating the speech they heard around them. If that were the case, however, we should not expect to see children generating their own grammars and the kinds of expressions with which we are all familiar. Children's comments such as 'my stick breaked', or 'the bath's unfilling' demonstrate the application of grammatical rules which are, in many instances, correct, but which, as here, cause problems in the face of irregular forms, common in English. Partly in response to the behaviourists' ideas, a variety of theorists, of whom Noam Chomsky is best known, suggested that language is too complex to learn from experience alone, so there must be some innate, pre-existing structure that enables young children to acquire it. Chomsky calls this the Language Acquisition Device, or 'LAD', and it relates to the modular ideas of cognition referred to in Chapter 2, as well as to some of the current thinking about brain development looked at in Chapter 4. This perspective, known as a nativist approach, proposes that there is a universal grammar (UG) or set of unconscious rules common to all languages, that humans are preprogrammed with this, and that they are innately predisposed to learn language (Chomsky 1957).

Chomsky's theories have undergone considerable development and reformation since they first appeared (Trott *et al.* 2004), and have been taken forward, most notably by Pinker, in his claim that we all have a 'language instinct' (1994). Thornton, however, refers to a range of studies which may suggest that, whilst predisposed to be social and to interact with others, babies may not be born with an innate predisposition to learn grammar, and that overgeneralizations like 'breaked' are not evidence of a specific focus on grammar rules, but part of 'the very much more general cognitive tendency to extract generalizations from a collection of concrete examples' (Thornton 2002: 58).

A more general criticism of the nativist viewpoint is that it does not take sufficient account of the part played by pre-verbal communication, of the communicative aspect of language, and of the parts played by babies' relationships with the important people around them. This more interactionist viewpoint has much in common with sociocultural perspectives on children's cognition, and positions language learning more within general ideas of cognition. For Meadows (2006), language obeys the same kinds of rules as other aspects of cognitive and social development, and has both biological and social influences.

Three possible relationships between language and thought have been identified:

- Language shapes thought.
- Thought shapes language.
- Language and thought influence each other.

### Language shapes thought

The first of these positions, the so-called Sapir-Whorf hypothesis, after Edward Sapir and Benjamin Lee Whorf, represents an approach known as linguistic determinism. It is based on the idea that language moulds thought so strongly that the 'real world' is to a large extent unconsciously built up by a group's language habits. For young children, then, the language they learn will determine the thoughts that they have, and initiation into the language uses of their community will be a process of socialization into a closely defined worldview (Whitehead 2010). A 'weaker' version of the hypothesis has been used to suggest that language may influence rather than determine thinking. Evidence for the linguistic determinist view derives largely from studies of language acquisition across different communities. Sapir, for example, noted that Native North American Wintu speakers must pay attention to whether the knowledge they are talking about comes from hearsay or direct observation in deciding whether to put a suffix onto verbs. In English such a decision is based upon tense and time of occurrence (Pinker 1994). Motluk (2002) discusses a range of other studies.

The linguistic determinist view has been strongly challenged by psychologists such as Fernyhough (2008) and Pinker (1994, 2007) on several grounds. Methodologically, Pinker suggests that Whorf and Sapir provide circular arguments to make their claim: 'Apaches speak differently, so they must think differently. How do we know they think differently? Just listen to the way they speak!' (Pinker 1994: 61) He also argues that the linguistic practices described by those who assert that language shapes thought may not accurately represent the cultural groups they cite. He outlines a range of recent research by 'neo-Wharfists' (Pinker 2007), but he, along with a majority of psychologists and linguists today (Motluk 2002), rejects the idea that language determines thought. Pinker suggests several reasons, including the inventiveness of human beings: 'when a language isn't up to the conceptual demands of its speakers, they don't scratch their heads dumfounded (at least not for long); they simply change the language' (Pinker 2007: 149). He points out that people think in images as well as words, and in abstract logical propositions, and suggests that people are well able to distinguish in their thinking between different meanings for the same word (spring, hop, key ... ), or even for different strings of words. That being so, 'if there can be two thoughts corresponding to one word, thoughts can't be words' (Pinker 1994: 79). Fernyhough (2008) presents evidence of even very young babies exhibiting a sophisticated ability to distinguish between concepts long before they have the language to express these distinctions in words, and suggests that language may 'fine tune' knowledge, but not create it. In Pinker's view, people do not think in English or any other language, but in a language of thought which he calls mentalese (1994), richer in some ways than any spoken language, and simpler in others. Donaldson seems to be suggesting something similar:

*Box 7.1*: Rachel, aged 4.6, and Rabi, aged 4.3, in the nursery

Sian, Rachel and John (the teacher) were having a discussion about a picnic.

JOHN:     If it's nice we're going to have it outside but if it rains we're going to have it on the carpet.

SIAN:     Yeah if it rains we don't want to have soggy sandwiches.

JOHN:     Or soggy crisps!

SIAN:     Or soggy drink!

RACHEL:   Drinks won't get soggy, they'll … they're … just, they'll more drink.

Rabi, at fruit time in a small group.

RABI:     John, John, the apple … can I have two pieces? (Rabi takes a piece of apple and also a piece of orange. He lingers over eating the orange, sees John looking and grins.)

RABI:     I like orange, it's got (pause), it's got, taste!

*Pinker (1994) maintains that higher order thought processes are independent of language. He says they are conducted by a different process which he calls mentalese. These two observations would seem to support that. Rachel knows that the quality of sogginess doesn't change with the addition of more liquid but, as the hesitation shows, she can't find the right words to explain dilution. In the end she does very well. Rabi is also a victim of the same problem – he knows that oranges have flavour, but can't find that word to describe it.*

Reproduced with permission of John Griffiths

Thinking is an activity in which we engage. We need our representational resources to make the activity effective, but the resources are varied, and they are not the same as the thought they sustain.

(Donaldson 1992: 104)

The children in Box 7.1 would appear to demonstrate this idea, as they struggle to put their thoughts into words. One possible practical implication here must be that if thought does proceed without language, rote verbal approaches to teaching and learning will not be sufficient to develop understanding.

### Thought shapes language

What, then, of the two other propositions, that thought shapes language or that language and thought influence each other? These two represent the most fundamental disagreement between Piaget and Vygotsky, who devotes a considerable part of *Thought and Language* (1986) to arguing against Piaget's position. For Piaget, language is a system for representing thought (see Chapter 2), with the processes of thought having been derived from action. He argues that language is a medium, or way of representing, which 'exerts no formative effects on the structure of thinking' (Wood 1998: 28). As a result, children's language will always be unable to convey what is not already established as a thought. Thus, for Piaget, thought shapes, or leads, children's language. He also argues that early language is egocentric, and only becomes socialized with the advent of concrete operations, that is, at the age of about 7 years. The early conversations of children, he says, are more like monologues than dialogues, and when a child uses egocentric talk 'he does not bother to know to whom he is speaking nor whether he is being listened to' (Piaget 1959: 9). As with Piaget's general view of development, this is 'chiefly because he (the child) does not attempt to place himself at the point of view of his hearer' (Piaget 1959: 9). Only with the development of concrete operations does speech take on a genuinely communicative function, and egocentric speech then die away, to be replaced by socialized speech.

### Language and thought influence each other

Vygotsky asserts that his own 'theoretical position (is) in exactly an opposite direction' to Piaget (Vygotsky1986: 11). For Vygotsky, 'the true direction of the development of thinking is not from the individual to the social, but from the social to the individual' (Vygotsky 1986: 36). Childhood speech, in Vygotsky's model, is not an egocentric matter, but social and communicative from the outset. He argues that children's speech is *intended* to communicate, even if they are not always successful in this aim. A baby's gestures and speech help him to control his world, through the agency of other people. In addition, Vygotsky believes that what Piaget saw as children's egocentric speech is what he would call private speech, acting as an instrument of thought: 'it serves mental orientation, conscious understanding; it helps in overcoming difficulties' (Vygotsky 1986: 228). He points to evidence from his work which shows that egocentric speech is most prolific when children are struggling with symbolic representation. For Vygotsky this speech does not disappear, but eventually becomes internalized, to form inner speech, or verbal thought, and may also resurface in spoken form when older children and adults are thinking through problems. Thus, private speech is a tool for representing the world, and a means of self-regulation, or metacognition. In this way, speech comes to form what Vygotsky terms the higher mental processes. Box 7.2 shows

---

*Box 7.2:* Anna, aged 1.8, in the nursery

Anna is standing at a sand tray, with three other children and a nursery nurse. She tries out different play items before settling on two spades. She quietly transfers sand from the spade in one hand to the spade in the other by pouring, repeating this action over and over again. Every few minutes she spontaneously speaks out loud, seemingly to herself, repeating the words:

Pour, pour, pour
Catch it, catch it
Careful.

*Anna's verbalizations during the task can be defined as egocentric speech. She appears to be ensuring her success by giving herself reminders about how to conduct the activity. This could be seen as 'self-regulatory' utterance.*

Reproduced with permission of Rachel Spencer

a small, but typical, snippet of private or egocentric speech. It is worth taking the time to reflect on whether you see it as a display of thought, entirely for the self, as Piaget suggests, or whether you see it as having a role in helping to shape Anna's thinking, and communicative in intent.

For Vygotsky, then, in 'an inspired compromise between the views of Whorf and Piaget' (Whitehead 2010: 69), language and thought influence each other. Vygotsky outlines what he sees as the developmental path here:

> We consider that the total development runs as follows: The primary function of speech, in both children and adults, is communication, social contact. The earliest speech of the child is therefore essentially social. At first it is global and multifunctional; later its functions become differentiated. At a certain age the social speech of the child is quite sharply divided into egocentric speech and communicative speech … Egocentric speech emerges when the child transfers social, collaborative forms of behaviour to the sphere of inner-personal psychic functions … Egocentric speech as a separate linguistic form is the highly important genetic link in the transition from vocal to inner speech.
>
> (Vygotsky 1986: 34–5)

It is this interactionist perspective which has assumed the most influence in recent years, and the view that the role played by language in children's thinking is both communicative (cultural tool) and sense-making (psychological tool) which allows us to 'work with things that are not there' (Fernyhough 2008: 104) is reflected in the work of, amongst others, Jerome Bruner (see Chapter 2), Tizard and Hughes (2002) and Wells (1987). Wells suggests that children are active seekers of meaning:

> In learning through talk – as in learning to talk – children are active constructors of their own knowledge. What they need is evidence, guidance and support. Parents who treat their children as equal partners in conversation, following their lead and negotiating meanings and purposes, are not only helping their children to talk, they are also enabling them to discover how to learn *through* talk.
>
> (Wells 1987: 65; emphasis in original)

Wells takes Vygotsky's ideas further, suggesting that language is more than just a cultural and psychological tool. Rather, we should conceptualize it as a whole tool-kit, because of the great range of functional varieties it serves, in order to meet our cultural needs (Wells in Mercer 2000).

## Thinking about language: the path to metalinguistic awareness

At the same time as children are, in Wells's (1987) words, learning *through* talk and learning *to* talk, they are also thinking and learning *about* talk. Children's attempts to make sense of spoken language, of its structure, content and functions, reveal much about their thinking. The ability to reflect and talk deliberately, and knowingly, about language, is called metalinguistic awareness. Conclusions about when this occurs in young children vary. Barratt-Pugh and Rohl suggest that many researchers 'agree on somewhere between the ages of three and seven' (2000: 67), whilst Thornton (2002) suggests it occurs at about age 6. She cites evidence of studies from Karmiloff-Smith which suggest that, before this age, children have difficulty in reflecting either upon language as a thing in its own right, or on the structural properties of language.

Whilst this explicit reflection on language may not be available to very young children, there are many ways in which they are both developing and displaying their understanding of language from the very beginnings of life, in ways which show clear evidence of their thinking. Young children's inventions of new words, and new terms, for example 'earsight' and 'nose beard' (Goswami 2008: 175) show their implicit knowledge of word-formation paradigms, such as compounding or combining single words, as in 'earsight' (Goswami 2008). Bilingual children may have a particular advantage. Their experiences of code 'switching' and 'mixing' ('Maman, I've trouved the book', as my bilingual nephew said to his mother), and of manipulating language as a formal system, are just the kinds of characteristics associated with metalinguistic awareness (Romaine 2004; Whitehead 2010).

## Grammar

The way in which young children develop an understanding of grammar provides a good demonstration of their implicit thinking about language. I pointed earlier to ways in which children seem to overgeneralize their understanding, making errors such as 'my stick breaked', which uses a regular past tense ending for an irregular verb, or creating a plural form such as 'childs'. Clearly, in most instances, a child has not heard an adult using these word forms, so it cannot be just imitation. Similarly, children may create one part of speech from another, such as a verb from an adverb: 'Shall I off the lights?' as one 3 year old said to me. In so doing, children are revealing their understanding of aspects of language, such as rules for creating past tenses and plurals. Wood cites Karmiloff-Smith's view that such overgeneralizations serve an important diagnostic role, in that they are important indicators of conceptual change and reorganization (Wood 1998). It is not, as Chukovsky (1963) says, the children's fault that language does not adhere to strict rules of logic. This may have very important practical implications, in that it suggests that children's receptive ability (to listen and understand) may often be in advance of their productive ability (to speak) (Wood 1998). If this is so, then evaluation of a child's understanding and competence based solely on the ways in which they can talk about something may not be entirely reliable.

## Language play

A key way in which young children may be displaying their understanding of language is in how they play with it. Crystal (1998) suggests that language play begins very early in life, and is at the core of babies' interactions with their carers, in the form of motherese (see below), songs and rhymes, all of which are accompanied by non-verbal ways of communicating, including eye contact, and physical interactions such as tickling and cuddling. The message given to babies is that these sorts of interactions, and the verbal exchanges that go along with them, are fun. It is not long before babies are spontaneously engaging with this play with language on their own, at first as a kind of 'vocal play' with noises which may serve a symbolic function (car and telephone

---

*Box 7.3:* Ella and Emily, both aged 2.8, at the playdough table

ELLA:      My mummy says that I am her little princess
EMILY:     My gran says that I'm her carrot top
ELLA:      You can't wear a carrot, you have a stripey top on
EMILY:     No, she calls me carrot top because my hair is red
ELLA:      But your hair isn't red, it's not carrot either
EMILY:     What colour is my hair then?
ELLA:      I know, it's like a penny, isn't it
EMILY:     No, it's like a carrot
ELLA:      OK, penny carrot
EMILY:     OK, Ella bellawella
ELLA:      OK, penny carrot silly billy
EMILY:     Ella bellawellaannabella
ELLA:      Penny carrot silly billy Emily
EMILY:     Ella bellawella silly billy princess annabella

---

sounds, for example), and then, at around the age of 2, more explicit manipulation of language (Crystal 1998). These monologues, of which those recorded by Ruth Weir (in Garvey 1977) are the most famous, reveal children taking language apart and reorganizing it in ways which demonstrate their awareness of language as a system.

In the same way, children then engage in verbal play with others. This social language play necessitates that each player is able to interpret the meaning of the other(s). Telling your friend a joke, at whatever age, is an indication of your awareness of the other person's mental state, which is an important aspect of the development of theory of mind, discussed in Chapter 5. Garvey categorizes children's social play with language in three ways: 'spontaneous rhyming and word play; play with fantasy and nonsense; and play with speech acts and discourse conventions' (Garvey 1977: 69). The first and third of these, rhyming and word play, and play with speech acts and discourse conventions, is illustrated in that of the two girls in Box 7.3. This type of word play is almost inevitably spontaneous, and reveals much about children's understanding of language. It also seems to be significant for children's success in learning to read (Whitehead 2010).

The second of Garvey's categories, play with fantasy and nonsense, requires children to have sophisticated understandings of language and the world. As Whitehead points out, 'jokes and nonsense depend on knowing the right way to do things' (Whitehead 2002: 38–9). Without such an understanding, the humour of the joke is often lost. Gifford gives a lovely example of a 'number joke', which not only illustrates the ways in which nonsense play is apparent in all areas of a child's experience, but also the close links it can have with positive emotion. She records Jermain, a boy in the nursery: 'Jermain pointed to number four on the hundred square carpet, shouted "91!" at me and ran off laughing' (2004a: 88). The best known examples of children's nonsense language play, and their 'topsy turvies', or inversion of reality, are in Chukovsky, who asserts that such topsy turvies 'strengthen (not weaken) the child's awareness of reality' (Chukovsky 1963: 104). The example in Box 7.4 illustrates one kind of topsy turvy, in Jack's play on words and ideas.

---

*Box 7.4:* Jack, aged 3.6, early one morning, at home with his mother

Jack goes into his mother's room. It is still dark outside so she asks him to go back to bed. He says he doesn't want to, and that he wants to play. His mother says that he should go back to bed and daydream. When she later goes to his bedroom door she hears him 'reading' quietly to himself, muttering the lines of the book *Night monkey, day monkey*, by Julia Donaldson, that he has learnt off by heart, under his breath. When she walks in he says:

JACK:      Mummy, I'm daydreaming … and nightdreaming.

They both laugh, and Jack gets out of bed.

*Dunn (1988) maintains that children are building on their knowledge of the world when they play with language. This concurs with the views of Chukovsky (1963) who suggests that humour is a developmental process: 'the more aware the child is of the correct relationship of things … the more comical does this violation appear to him. He has become so sure of truths that he can even play with them (1963: 99). When Jack talks of 'nightdreaming' he knows it is funny, as he laughed after he said it. Chukovsky refers to these word games as 'topsyturvies'. According to him they are not just a diversion, but are a serious mental effort that helps confirm reality.*

*I often propose that the children 'daydream' when they ask what they can do: it may be that Jack was making a joke to check his theory that there is such a thing as 'nightdreaming'.*

Reproduced with permission of Kathryn Torres

---

Children's misconceptions about grammar, their curiosity about language and their play with it reveal both the beginnings of metalinguistic awareness, and their thinking more generally. This kind of play may be very particular to early childhood, helping children to achieve mastery of spoken language, the major need for which will tend to have passed by the age of 8 (Chukovsky 1963). As such, it may be a particularly significant aspect of the relationship between young children's language and thought. For the remainder of this chapter we shall look at some of the contexts in which children's language efforts occur.

## 'Motherese' or infant-directed speech

For the great majority of children, communication and language begin in the home, with other family members. The ways in which those family members attune their own language to the child, providing child-contingent language, is well documented. Characteristics include use of a higher pitch than normal, exaggerated changes of pitch, frequent use of a child's name, restriction of semantic and syntactic content, running commentary on a child's actions, repetition, questions, expansion of the child's utterances and gestures such as lip smacking, although perhaps not all at the same time! Much research has focused, in particular, on the ways in which primary carers, especially mothers, seem to unconsciously do this, using 'motherese' or 'caregiver speech' with their children, as in the example in Box 7.5. This example shows how such interactions

Box 7.5: Leo, aged 3.5 months, at home with his mother, sitting in his swing chair and looking at the toys hanging above him

1    Leo smiles and makes a sound
    MOTHER: Are you talking to me? (high pitch questioning tone and smile).
    Leo smiles and reaches out with hand as if trying to touch mother's mouth.
    Mother moves her face closer to Leo.
5    Leo appears excited, moving arms and legs.
    MOTHER:        (kisses Leo and begins to sing) Twinkle, twinkle, little star
    ... how I wonder what you are?
    Leo stares intently at her face while she is singing then smiles when she stops.
    MOTHER:        Did you like that?  Do you like Twinkle Twinkle?
10    LEO:    Ahwooo (makes and maintains direct eye contact, making 'o' shapes
    with his lips).
    MOTHER:        Ahwooo (imitates his vocalisation and then pauses).
    LEO:    (smiles, and opens his mouth) Aahhhh (then puts his lips together)
    mmmmm.
15    MOTHER:        Mum mummum –
    LEO:    (watches his mother's mouth and frowns briefly) Aaoooo ... aaaoo
    (wriggles excitedly, waving arms and kicking his legs).
    MOTHER:        A bubba bubooo
    LEO:    (kicks his legs and arms, slightly frowns and holds eye contact)
20    Mmmmmmm.
    MOTHER:        You not saying Mum mummum today?  Dad daddad.
    LEO:    (reaches for his mother's mouth) Ayyyyyii ... aaah ... ummm (stares
    intently as he vocalizes).

*Leo's mother's interactions characterize motherese or infant-directed speech. In addition the role of gesture and movement could act as a further sensorial stimulus capturing and enhancing the rhythmical nature of mother-infant proto-conversation, coordinating its nonverbal meaning (Sansone 2004). Leo's mother seems to act as a tool for Leo's thinking and language development as she begins to sing (line 6). Meadows (2006) asserts that because of its rhythm and musical tone 'musical motherese' is preferred by babies and supports them in creating connections between music and vocalization. However, Leo appears to respond with increased vocalizations and body movements to his mother's use of standard motherese (lines 12–23). Powers and Trevarthen offer an alternative view that 'communicative musicality' and the musical tone of these early conversations foster emotional attunement between mother and child as 'Infants and Mothers cooperate in establishing a subtle link between their minds by modulating their voice sounds' (Powers and Trevarthen 2009: 231).*

Abridged and reproduced with permission of Sarah Duggan

involve a number of different aspects of communication, including babies' preference for faces (LeVine and Norman 2008), and the use of gesture, alongside vocalization.

What is clear now is that a baby's siblings, and other young children outside the family, act in the same way. This has led to the phenomenon now often being termed

---

*Box 7.6:* Ciara, aged 1.4, Sean, aged 2.11 and Mark, aged 4.2 (siblings) at the crèche

Ciara, Sean and Mark have been at the crèche for an hour. Ciara is beginning to be distressed, is close to tears, and has a worried expression. Soon Sean and Mark, who have been playing elsewhere in the room, come over to comfort her.

SEAN:          Ok, Ciara, is ok (tickles her tummy quite roughly) Tickle tickle.
CRECHE WORKER:   Sean, gently with Ciara, don't hurt her.
SEAN:          My not hurt her, is ok, Ciara like it (reaches to her again) Tickle tickle.
MARK:          It's okay, Ciara does like it, we always play with Ciara.
Ciara is still sniffling, but seems calmer.
MARK:          Hey, Ciara Ciara, it's okay, Sean and Marky here, mummy coming, back soon.
SEAN:          Yes, Ciara, mummy and daddy come soon.
Ciara has stopped crying. Mark returns to his activity, Sean sits beside Ciara.
SEAN:          Hey CiriCiri, tickle tickle, you like that don't you, yes you do, Ciara. Sean tickle tickle you. All better now, Ciara is all better, you laughing now, tickle tickle make you laugh, my make you laugh, happy Ciara, Ciara happy now, yes you are.

Reproduced with permission of Rebecca Shuttleworth

---

'infant-directed speech' (IDS). The example in Box 7.6 shows one such episode. What is particularly noteworthy here is the young age of the two boys using this type of speech to comfort their sister. Bruner (1988) suggests that 4 year olds use motherese with younger children. In the example here, Sean is not yet 3. As Rebecca, the crèche worker involved, points out, Sean, in particular, seems to have unconsciously picked up this way of comforting babies from the behaviour of others, for example his parents and staff at the crèche. His speech to Ciara is different to the ways in which he talks both to the adult involved and to his brother. What Wells (1987) also shows is that IDS is evoked by the child as well as by the carer or older sibling, suggesting that very young children are able to think about and control such exchanges.

Babies themselves show a preference for infant directed speech (Goswami 2008). In addition, the use of repetition and clear enunciation of speech sounds may support children's acquisition of language (Gopnik *et al.* 1999). Thornton (2002) links infant directed speech with ideas of scaffolding, suggesting that adults' use of it can help children to make connections between events in the world and word meanings. It is important to bear in mind, however, that this form of interaction is not universal. Meadows (2006) suggests that IDS is a cultural phenomenon, most often used in Western middle-class households. Heath (1983) describes the ways in which the black, working-class children in her study grew up amongst adults who used narrative prompts and questions such as 'Did you see Maggie's dog yesterday?', as ways of initiating conversation, and did not engage in motherese at all. In some cultures, children may be ignored conversationally until they are older, or only addressed using correct syntax (Snow *et al.* 2008). The fact that most children rapidly become confident language users suggests that, whilst it may support word identification in babies through the ways in which they attend to cues such as duration and stress (Goswami 2008), IDS is not a prerequisite for language

---

*Box 7.7:* Josh, aged 8 months 3 weeks

Josh is on the train with his mother. He pulls off his hat and drops it on the floor. A woman sitting opposite picks it up and gives it to him. He looks at her and drops it again, she picks it up again and passes it to him. This routine is repeated continuously over the three-minute train ride.

---

development, and does not affect eventual levels of mastery of language that children achieve (Siegler *et al.* 2011). Their description of IDS as 'speech suffused with affection' (2011: 223) may be important here. Use of infant directed speech may be partly about supporting intersubjectivity, and establishing and strengthening relationships. At home, we have a new cat, and every member of the family uses IDS in talking to him. None of us think that, in so doing, he will learn to speak English (at least I don't think so), but we do all seem to see it as a way of connecting with him.

## Conversation and questions, questions, questions ...

Communication begins, as we have seen, in the earliest moments of a child's life. LeVine and Norman (2008) suggest that babies' preference for faces is evidence of their preparedness for communicative interaction from the start of life, with early protoconversations (Trevarthen 1995) with carers laying the foundations of later verbal communication. The intersubjective exchange of gestures, eye contact and sounds is the beginning of turn taking, shared meaning making and inferring what is in your conversational partner's mind. Box 7.7 shows Josh initiating and sustaining an interaction of which he is very clearly in control, whilst he explores the boundaries of what he is doing. Throughout the interaction, not a word is spoken, but Josh has clearly communicated his interest and involvement in the game. By about two to three months of age, babies begin to make their first language-like sounds (Karmiloff-Smith 1994), and the world of spoken language and conversation unfolds.

### Conversation

Wells (1987) suggests that young children's conversation is generally purposeful and goal-directed. That is, in talking to those around them, children are interested in achieving other ends – getting what they want, keeping in contact with others, sharing things of interest – aims that they share with their conversational partners at home. They also share experiences. So, for much of a child's early life, children's conversations in their homes and communities are highly context-bound, and characterized by 'the desire to understand and to be understood' (Vygotsky 1986: 56). They draw upon the shared knowledge and understanding of all participants, and thus are often elliptical and fragmentary. The brief conversation between a mother and her son in Box 7.8 illustrates this shared knowledge and experience between family members.

The success of such a conversation, as an exchange of language and thinking, is dependent upon the shared knowledge and understanding of the participants. However, just as important is the way in which the mother assumes that her son has something important to say, and that he is intent on conveying meaning. She takes what her son says,

---

*Box 7.8:* Boy, aged 2, out with his mother

BOY:         (looking up at a plane flying overhead) That noise?
MOTHER:   That's a plane.
BOY:         Nanny plane.
MOTHER:   Yes, nanny went on a plane.

---

expands it using the shared knowledge they have, and together they jointly construct a meaning which satisfies them both. Wells believes that, in so doing, children gradually come to reflect on action as they speak, and that, eventually, as in Vygotsky's model of language and thought, this dialogue begins to be carried on internally instead. In addition, participation in conversations like these may contribute to an understanding of perspective, and an awareness of mental states, so central to the development of theory of mind (Astington and Baird 2004). They suggest that, whilst the relationship between language and theory of mind is complex and interdependent, there are nevertheless ways in which language plays a role in the development of perspective taking that is independent of social communication *per se*. Cutting and Dunn (1999) speculate on the part played by gender here, suggesting that narrative ability may play a more pivotal role for girls than boys in the development of false-belief understanding (see Chapter 5).

Wells (1987) and Tizard and Hughes (2002) found that the features of conversation noted above were particularly characteristic of conversation at home. The sheer quantity of shared experience gave children and adults much to talk about, and the fact that much of the conversation took place in situations of one adult to one or two children, gave the children many more opportunities to initiate and sustain conversation, and to do so in spontaneous and unplanned ways. Opportunities for conversations between an individual adult and child in early childhood settings will be less plentiful than in the home, and there will be far fewer shared contexts. Katz and Chard (2000) suggest that project work characteristic of the kind found in settings in Reggio Emilia (see Chapter 11) can provide rich contexts for conversations, between adults and children and between the children themselves, and shared experiences of events which can be thought about and discussed. Paley (1986, 2004) reaches similar conclusions about the importance of creating a shared culture in the nursery.

Wells also stresses that the seeming disparity between home and school should not be taken necessarily to be disadvantageous. He suggests that settings need to focus on ways in which they can broaden the range of children's experiences, and 'help them (the children) develop the sustained and deliberate attention to a topic or activity that makes systematic learning possible' (Wells 1987: 67). Above all, he suggests, nurseries and schools can help children to become more reflectively aware of what they already know and still need to know, in ways that enable them to take increasing responsibility for their own learning.

### Questions and the search for understanding

One very characteristic form of young children's interactions is questioning. Ask the parents of young children about the questions they ask and many of them will give you a rueful look which suggests that perhaps there can be such a thing as too many. For the young child, however, there can never be too many questions. Tizard and Hughes (2002) record the 3 and 4 year olds in their research asking an average of 26 questions an hour at home. The mother in Box 7.9 records her son asking seventeen questions in less than fifteen minutes. In Chapter 1 the question of whether children's thinking is qualitatively different from adult thinking was discussed. Challenging Piagetian notions of children's questions as indicators of their intellectual limitations, Tizard and Hughes (2002) suggest that it is children's limited conceptual framework, and comparative ignorance and inexperience, which is the issue, not a fault in their ability to apply logic. One of the ways in which children seek to close the gaps in their experiences is through asking questions. Children's questions reveal a lot about what they do and do not understand, their misconceptions and their interests. Their questions may not,

---

Box 7.9:  Abe, aged 5, at home with his mother

Abe is looking through a 'body' book with his mother. He repeatedly asks questions relating to the pictures in the book. For reasons of space many of her responses to him have not been included. He poses a new question as soon as he gets an answer.

| | |
|---|---|
| ABE: | Is your bones the same shape as your face? |
| | What happens when you spike yourself? (looking at picture of hedgehog). |
| | How do you talk? |
| MUM: | From a thing called your voice box. |
| ABE: | Are there lots of voices? |
| | How do your nose wiggle? (Wiggling his nose.) |
| | How does your teeth make a noise? |
| | Does bones melt inside your tongue, by water going on it? |
| | What's in your blood? |

Mum shows him a picture of a blood vessel and the cells inside it.

| | |
|---|---|
| ABE: | But this is a picture, what does it really look like? |
| | What happens if you eat the same time and you have a ride the same time? (on a fairground ride). |
| | What about if you eat sweets all day? |
| | What gives you energy? |
| | How do you know your arms are going to move? (Looking at a picture of the brain and muscles.) |
| MUM: | Your brain sends a message to your arm muscles. |
| ABE: | How does he stop? |
| MUM: | How does who stop? |
| ABE: | The brain. |
| MUM: | Are you thinking? |
| ABE: | I don't do thinking, I'm just thinking about my body. |
| | What does your heart look like? Do ladies have their heart in their boobies? |
| MUM: | No, under their boobies. |
| ABE: | Will their heart get squashed by their boobies? |

Reproduced with permission of Sam Segar

however, all require an answer. What children may often be doing is using their own questions to help them to shape and clarify their thinking, by thinking aloud in the way that Vygotsky describes.

Children demonstrate considerable persistence in their desires to clarify their thinking. Tizard and Hughes (2002) record that those children who asked the most searching questions were often most likely to have parents who answered them most fully, and, of course, that the parents who were most likely to answer their children's questions were the ones with children most likely to ask. A characteristic form of question for 3 year olds is repeated use of 'why?' questions (Isaacs 1930). Tizard and Hughes record that about a quarter of all of the questions posed by girls in their study were 'why?' questions (their study did not include boys). However, they also point out that it is not just the use of 'why' which is important, rather it is the intention behind the question which matters. Children's intentions in asking questions, they suggest, revolve around seeking new information or explanations, puzzling over something they do not understand, or trying to make sense of apparent anomalies in their limited knowledge of the world. They describe this process in children as engagement in 'passages of intellectual search' (2002). They recount incidences of the 4-year-old children in their research repeatedly returning to a topic, persistently and logically questioning their mothers, often when the conversation has apparently moved on, in their drive to make sense. Paley makes a similar point about the children in her kindergarten: 'confusion – mine or theirs – is as natural a condition as clarity. The natural response to confusion is to keep trying to connect what you already know to what you don't know' (1986: 131).

Characteristic of these passages of intellectual search were children's awareness of, and interest in, other people's viewpoints, including the use of inference, and the application of 'rigorous logic' (Tizard and Hughes 2002: 103). They suggest that such behaviour may be particularly characteristic of children in the age range 3 to 5 years. By the age of 4, they argue, dialogue and exploration with words are as important as physical exploration may be for the younger child:

> The children in this study seemed in some sense aware that their conceptual framework was not yet substantial enough to cope with their experiences, and engaged themselves actively in the process of improving their intellectual scaffolding. The passages of intellectual search seemed particularly useful in this process, and indicated that the children were at some level aware that protracted dialogue with adults was a useful way of developing their conceptual knowledge.
>
> (Tizard and Hughes 2002: 105–6)

Several possible implications for practice arise from Tizard and Hughes's work:

- They found that most of the 'intellectually challenging' conversations at home took place at times of relative leisure, such as mother and daughter sharing a meal, or during a one-to-one story session. The activity orientation of life in early childhood settings may offer fewer opportunities for such times.
- They recommend greater emphasis on feeding children with 'a great deal more general knowledge', which may include 'going beyond the school walls more' (2002: 220), much as Athey (2007) suggests (see Chapter 6).

- They suggest that professionals have much to learn from studying parents and children at home.
- They counsel strongly against underestimating children's abilities and interests.

Siraj-Blatchford *et al.* (2002) and Sylva *et al.* (2010) emphasize the importance of what they term 'sustained shared thinking' (SST) in developing children's thinking skills. This influential idea is looked at in more detail below, in considering the roles of adults, but here it is important to note that they found that episodes of sustained shared thinking happened most often in talk between a child and an adult, or between an adult and a child pair. The larger the group, they conclude, the less likely were such episodes, and the more likely it was that interactions would be monitorial, or involve direct teaching in which children might have fewer opportunities for extending their thinking. Practitioners in our research said similar things, believing that size of group played an important part in supporting children's thinking. One practitioner said that they had focused particularly on pair discussion, because the children worked well together in pairs, and did not feel threatened by each other (Robson and Hargreaves 2005). The National Oracy Project in England (1990) advocates pair discussion, particularly where younger or quieter children are concerned. Another practitioner in our research suggested that groups of about four children were supportive of children's thinking because 'more ideas may be coming through from children in a small group'. Bennett and Dunne, in their study of cooperative grouping, come to a similar conclusion, suggesting that groups of three or four allow for 'lines of communication' (1992: 115) that are not too complex to be manageable.

## Young children's use of narrative

To take up Wells's (1987) point that children are active meaning makers, there is much evidence to suggest that narrative, in the form of children's own storying, or narrative creation, plays an important role in this process, allowing children to represent their experiences, and deepen their understanding, thereby creating 'brain fictions' (Gregory 1977: 394) that support hypotheses about the ways in which the world works. Wells suggests that 'Storying is the most fundamental way of grappling with new experience' (1987: 206), and 'the way in which the mind itself works' (1987: 197). In this, Whitehead (2002) stresses the link between narrative and the organization and function of memory. Narrative is not, however, just an individual act, but intimately bound up with our cultural and communal histories, providing children with 'ways into the shared beliefs and meaning making strategies' (Whitehead 2002: 34) of their culture. Parents may be particularly significant in this, in scaffolding their children's conversations about past family events, and helping them to structure their oral narratives (Siegler *et al.* 2011). These developing oral narrative skills support young children's social communication, their ability to understand and organise event knowledge, and may also be related to later literacy development (Lever and Sénéchal 2011).

The practice of using narrative to make sense of experience begins very early in life. As Wells says, 'Even before they can talk, infants begin to construct a mental model of their world' (1987: 196), in the form of mental stories about perceptual information, and the events of their lives. Children's earliest spoken narratives arise directly out of conversation, as children relate incidents, and hear them related by others: 'My stick breaked', the example used earlier, is a story in miniature. Bruner (1987) describes how children learn to make sense of the world as they develop the ability to tell stories about it. Later on, these stories reflect children's developing understanding of the language of literature. Wally, at 5 years old, is clearly experienced in the language of books, and in thinking about how literary, rather than oral, form sounds:

> Once there was a boy hunter. His little sister didn't like him so he ran away. So he found a baby girl lion.
>
> ('Wally', in Paley 1981: 29)

It is in the work of Paley that some of the richest examples can be found. The contexts for the children's narratives often revolve around real and imagined events in their lives: birthdays, going to stay with a friend, shooting the bad guys. Underpinning many of these contexts, in both their narratives and in pretend play (see below) are the three themes of friendship, fairness and fantasy (1986: 124). These, Paley believes, are the things that really matter to the children, and she recounts how, in the kindergarten when they were up for discussion as part of the children's narratives, 'participation zoomed upwards' (1986: 124). Armstrong believes that this significance is what helps children to be 'masters of make-believe' (2006: 174) in their stories. In paying close attention to the children's narratives, Paley suggests that the connections they make about their knowledge and understanding, their facility with structuring, reinventing and explaining the world, are made more apparent to those listening. Astington (1994) also suggests that one of the things that Paley is doing which is important to the development of children's thinking is her own use of words and expressions *about* thinking, as she comments on the children's narratives: 'oh, I think I know what reminded you of that' or 'are you wondering ... ?', for example. She says: 'In Paley's classroom the talk is not just about things in the world, it is also about the children's thoughts about things in the world' (Astington 1994: 185).

In so doing, Astington suggests, the children's understanding of how they think and learn, a central part of metacognition, is made more consciously explicit to them. Pramling (1988) expresses a similar view, in her suggestion that a focus on the relationship of the child to the world promotes the development of metacognition. In our research, discussions between children and adults about their thinking in activities supported them in both expressing and developing their metacognitive knowledge (Robson 2010). In Chapter 5 the part played by narrative in the development and study of children's theory of mind is also emphasized.

## Young children's talk in pretend play

The role of play, particularly pretend play, is considered throughout this book. Both Piaget (1962) and Vygotsky (1978) outline theoretical frameworks that link pretend play and language, and Goswami (2008) sees them as sharing two essential developmental functions, enabling children to reflect on and regulate their cognitive behaviour, and supporting a deeper understanding of the mind. In the context of language and communication, the role of sociodramatic play, which involves interaction and verbal communication between two or more players, may be highly significant for the development of young children's thinking. Bergen (2002: 2) suggests: 'Pretend play requires the ability to transform objects and actions symbolically, it is furthered by interactive social dialogue and negotiation, and it involves role taking, script knowledge, and improvisation.' What is not clear is the extent to which language, pretence and cognition develop as 'parts of an integrated, reciprocally developing system' (Bergen 2002: 2) or whether it is the experience of pretend play which has a positive impact on children's language and cognition. In her synthesis of research, she concludes that engagement in 'high-quality' (2002: 6) pretence may assist children's linguistic development. As Kenner *et al.* (1996) demonstrate, it may also provide contexts in which children can most confidently display their linguistic competence. Dockett (1998) also points to evidence suggesting that children's involvement in shared pretence, of which communication is an essential part, has a positive impact on cognitive development, particularly theory of mind. This is looked at in more detail in Chapter 5, but children's language use in this context is worth considering. Underpinning such language use is the act of symbolic transformation, which requires the players to define those transformations verbally to each other, in order to establish a shared frame of meaning.

### Pretend communication and metacommunication

Dockett (1998: 113) draws a distinction between two types of language use in sociodramatic pretend play. The first is pretend communication, which describes children's talk when in role. When they do this, children take on another person's ways of speaking, tone of voice, even particular vocabulary. In so doing, what they are demonstrating is their ability to take on another's perspective, and to think about how that person might act, and what they might say. Drawing on Bakhtin, Cohen (2009) describes this as a shift from monologic to dialogic positions.

The second way in which children use language in their play is in order to talk about the play. This is referred to as metacommunication, or 'verbal statements or actions that explain how messages about pretend play should be interpreted' (Farver, cited in Dockett 1998: 113), and, importantly, convey the message 'this is play', signalling that the behaviour it encompasses is symbolic (Giffin 1984). Dockett expands on this idea, and suggests that metacommunications serve several important functions:

> On one level, they serve to separate, in an explicit manner, real from pretend. More importantly, metacommunications are understood by the players on these two different levels. Even when players step outside the play frame, or outside their adopted role, to issue a direction or rebuke, neither they nor the other players seem to experience confusion about the reality or the pretense. On another level, metacommunications frame the play by setting the context and offering guidance and direction as to the ongoing nature of the play. When children add to, or respond to, their partner's ideas and actions in the play, they extend the shared meanings already established.
>
> (Dockett 1998: 113)

Giffin suggests that children's metacommunications will range along a continuum from ones which are very much within-frame ('Mommy, I did something nice for you. I made you a wedding ring cake', Giffin 1984: 81) to out-of frame proposals such as 'let's pretend that ...' In so doing, children are making implicit choices about the extent to which pretence is maintained, and are demonstrating 'evolved skills in human communication' (Giffin 1984: 96)

## Metaplay

Children's metacommunications occur as part of metaplay, a more general term for the act of stepping outside of the play in order to think or communicate about it. Trawick-Smith's typology of metaplay behaviours reveals how complex and varied this act is for young children. He identifies three distinct categories of metaplay behaviour, each of which is further categorized (adapted from Trawick-Smith 1998):

1  Metaplay Initiations: 'behaviors (sic) in which children halted role-playing-in progress to: 1.) initiate a new play activity, or 2.) engage peers in conversations or physical interactions related to play themes' (Trawick-Smith 1998: 436):

   • announcing symbolic transformations;
   • announcing/narrating make believe actions;
   • requests for clarification about make-believe;
   • announcing characters' internal mental states;
   • persuading peers;
   • initiatives concerning object ownership.

2  Metaplay Responses: physical or verbal responses to the play-related behaviours and comments of peers:

   • disagreeing/not complying;
   • agreeing/complying;
   • answering/providing clarification;
   • protecting objects/maintaining ownership.

3  Metaplay Constructions: physical actions, sometimes accompanied by verbalizations, involving constructing a play setting:

   • nonverbal constructions;
   • constructions with verbalizations.

What is clear from this typology is the pivotal role played by language. Only a small number of Trawick-Smith's categorizations have a non-verbal element, and most depend on talk. As with many other aspects of development, children's metaplay seems to increase markedly over time, possibly as a function of children's increased social and cognitive competence. Trawick-Smith records a twentyfold increase between the ages of 2 and 5 years. Metaplay initiations accounted for over half of all interactions, in all three of the age groups Trawick-Smith studied (2 year olds, 3–4 year olds and 5 year olds). Interestingly, it was the youngest children who showed the most incidences of interactions involving persuading peers. Even at the age of 2, children seem to understand that other children have separate minds that need persuading around to their point of view. Box 7.10 illustrates many of the aspects discussed above. Here, Jake and Sam negotiate characters and roles, engage in a range of metaplay interactions and use pretend communication to sustain their play.

---

*Box 7.10:* Jake, aged 4.10 and Sam, aged 4.9, at Nursery School

Jake and Sam are playing outdoors. There are wheeled toys, a changeable traffic light, and a wooden shop with empty crates. They have been playing with the traffic light, when Jake says:

| JAKE: | Hey, Sam, let's do grown-up things. Let's play going to the shops. (They walk over to the shop.) Do you want to be the daddy or the lady? |
|---|---|
| SAM: | I want to be the man in the shop. |
| JAKE: | You can't. You have to be the lady coz there's a lady in my shop and she gives me sweets. |
| SAM: | I want to be the daddy then. |
| JAKE: | OK. (He walks round and positions himself behind the counter, and speaks in a slightly higher voice) Good morning, how may I help you? |
| SAM: | I'd like to buy some carrots please. |
| JAKE: | No, no, you want to buy sweets for your little boy. |
| SAM: | OK, I want to buy some carrots and some sweets please. |

Jake makes a grabbing action into the baskets and holds out a fist to Sam.

| JAKE: | Here we are, lots of carrots. What sweets do you want? |
|---|---|
| SAM: | Nice ones, I don't like the hard ones. Granny has hard sweets, they're not nice. |
| JAKE: | Here we are, these ones are soft. Are they for your boy? |
| SAM: | Yes, he likes soft chewy ones. |
| JAKE: | I bet he's getting very big just like his dad. |

Reproduced with permission of Angela Streek

---

What are the practical implications here? In order to support this form of language use, it may be important for adults to model such usage in play themselves, and to support the creation of shared meanings through play. Trawick-Smith (1998: 450) also speculates that non-realistic objects such as blocks and cardboard pieces may be particularly useful aspects of provision, because their non-representational nature supports speculative talk and discussion about what they might become in the play, with the possibilities this has for developing both metacognition and theory of mind. Umek and Musek (2001) suggest that a certain level of skill at representing ideas in play may be a crucial factor, and demonstrate in their research that younger children (aged 3–4 years) might need more structured, representational, play materials such as dolls, pots and pans, and cutlery. By contrast, Broadhead, in her research on social and cooperative skill development in children aged 4–5 years, found that themed role-play areas which were resourced with structured play materials (home corners, shops, cafes) tended to produce 'social' (some, but limited, reciprocal language and action), but not 'highly social' (increased reciprocity) or cooperative play. She and her co-researchers speculate that this could be because, whilst the themed role play areas related to the children's experiences, they might be more closed in their potential for stimulating play themes and the social interactions required in negotiating roles, talking about the play and announcing symbolic transformations. As a result, they set up areas resourced, as Trawick-Smith (1998) suggests, with items such as pieces of fabric, empty boxes and clothes horses. One child dubbed this area 'the whatever you want it to be place' (Broadhead 2004: 73). What they found when they observed and documented the resultant play was an increase in highly social and cooperative activity, part of which was enhanced language use. Hall and Robinson (2003) also point to the part played by this kind of role play in the development of children's understanding and use of the symbolic language of literacy.

Baron-Cohen (2004) suggests that boys may get involved in more solitary pretence, for example, superhero play, with girls engaging in group play more frequently. Holland (2003) also points out that gun and weapon play, the very type of pretend play which many boys often prefer, is routinely banned in many settings, thus preventing access to a site for meaning making, and consequent language and communication activity, which is most valued, and enjoyed, by them.

## Talk 'in the course of educational activity', and the role of adults in supporting young children's thinking through talk

The quotation above, from Mercer and Littleton (2007: 1) highlights the fundamental significance of considering how practitioners support young children's thinking through talk. Wegerif believes that 'becoming more dialogic is central to learning to think better' (2010: 18). At the same time, adult domination of conversation in schools and nurseries is well documented, alongside the possible reasons for it (Howe and Mercer 2007; Tizard and Hughes 2002; Wells 1987), and there is evidence that classroom talk has the power to inhibit cognition and learning as well as enable it (Alexander 2006). Sylva et al. (2010) record low incidences of sustained shared thinking in talk between adults and children in the settings participating in their research, and approaches to questioning featuring the IRE (adult Initiates, children Respond, adult Evaluates) or IRF (adult Feedback or Follow-up) (Siraj-Blatchford and Manni 2008) format remain common, even with children as young as 2 (Durden and Dangel 2008). In many such exchanges, 'closed' questions, used to elicit and check children's knowledge, are prevalent. Such questions may provoke little more than one-word responses, and not serve as the starting points for rich conversational experiences (although it is valuable to note the conclusions of research discussed in Chapter 8 – Hannust and Kikas 2010; Panagiotaki et al. 2009 – that advocates both telling children facts and the use of very focused, often 'closed' questions in the context of support for children's understanding of the Earth). Siraj-Blatchford et al. emphasize the importance of more open-ended questions for supporting children's thinking, and suggest that adult interventions in the most effective settings in their study 'were most often in the form of questions that provoke speculation and extend the imagination' (2002: 47). Medcalf Davenport (2003) reports more elaborated talk by both girls and boys when they were given greater opportunities for discussion, rather than responding to closed questions. Just allowing children more 'thinking time' before they are expected to respond can result in dramatic improvements in the quality of their responses (Wood 1998).

Adult emphasis on the use of questions as a way of eliciting knowledge may result in children viewing all questions used by them as a form of assessment (Kenner et al.

1996). Wood (1998) asks whether questions are even the best way to find out about a child's thinking. Instead, he suggests that adult speculation and hypothesizing, and closer adult listening, may be more productive. In so doing, adults may be creating more 'space' for the children's own ideas to come out. Hughes and Westgate (1988) noted the greater input of the children, and their use of talk for a wider range of purposes, in classroom contexts where adults, and teachers in particular, were able to create this space, either by being absent physically, and encouraging child–child talk, or 'pedagogically' (i.e. by not taking an instructive role). In this, they differ from the conclusions of Siraj-Blatchford *et al.* that 'when adults manage to find time to talk to children individually or in child pairs, then these interactions are likely to be the most "stretching" interactions' (2002: 59). In our research, practitioners emphasized the value (and difficulty!) of finding time to let children's talk develop.

Questions are, of course, a necessary part of any practitioner's interactions with children. Mercer and Littleton (2007) suggest that what may be most important is to consider the different communicative functions of adults' questions, and see their usefulness as related to the different purposes adults may have for asking them.

### Dialogic teaching and sustained shared thinking

A cluster of different ideas and approaches has developed in recent years, which seek to enhance the quality of talk in educational settings, in particular talk as a mechanism for supporting and extending children's thinking. They share a focus on participation and interaction (Sylva *et al.* 2010). Educators in Reggio Emilia (Project Zero and Reggio Children 2001), for example, suggest that young children's thinking is a collective process, dependent upon discussion and 'provocation' to challenge existing theories and ideas, with adults playing a vital, but equal, part in this discursive process, alongside the children.

Mercer and Littleton (2007) and Wegerif (2010) all emphasize the value of what has been termed 'dialogic teaching': 'in which both teachers and pupils make substantial and significant contributions and through which children's thinking on a given idea or theme is helped to move forward' (Mercer and Littleton 2007: 41). This is essentially a social process of shared enquiry (Wegerif 2010), a principal vehicle is the idea of exploratory talk, which has the following features (Mercer 2011):

- Everyone offers relevant information.
- Everyone's ideas are treated as worthwhile – but are critically evaluated.
- People ask each other what they think.
- People ask for reasons and give them.
- People try to reach agreement.

Mercer and Littleton's approach, *Thinking Together,* was developed for use with older children, aged 8–12, but they have also worked on a version for children aged 6 and 7, called *Talk Box* (Dawes and Sams 2004). However, it is clear that children younger than 6 are capable of such exploratory talk, as both Howe and Mercer (2007) and some of the examples in this book demonstrate. The *Every Child a Talker* initiative in the early years in England advocates a 'dialogic book reading' approach (DCSF 2009). Lever and Sénéchal (2011) show the impact of a similar approach on the oral narratives of 5 and 6 year olds, resulting in use of more expressive vocabulary, improved narrative construction, story comprehension and greater use of decontextualized language.

These ideas of dialogic teaching and exploratory talk have much in common with the concept of Sustained Shared Thinking (SST), and both emphasize Vygotskian ideas of co-construction and participation (Sylva *et al.* 2010). SST is defined as 'any episode in which two or more individuals "worked together" in an intellectual way to solve a problem, clarify a concept, evaluate activities, extend a narrative, etc' (Sylva *et al.* 2010: 157). Siraj-Blatchford *et al.* (2002) identify the types of interaction which may support SST, including:

- *scaffolding* to extend children's knowledge and understanding through the use of strategies such as open ended questioning;
- *extending* by making a suggestion that helps a child to see other possibilities;
- *discussing* which supports the interchange of information or ideas;
- *modelling* which includes the demonstration of activities and verbal commentary from the adult;
- *playing* when the adult uses humour or plays with a child.

As noted earlier, their research showed that episodes of SST were more likely to happen when teachers were working with smaller groups and individual children. Whilst this is not always easy to achieve, it points to the value of trying to provide opportunities for it, and the example in Box 7.11 features a number of these types of interaction between a practitioner and children. Look ahead, too, to Box 11.8 for a missed opportunity to extend the children's thinking through talk. The findings of the EPPE and REPEY studies (Siraj-Blatchford *et al.* 2002; Sylva *et al.* 2010) have been very influential in policy and practice in England, in particular, directly informing the Early Years Foundation Stage (DfES 2007), and practitioner materials such as *Supporting Young Children's Sustained Shared Thinking: An Exploration* (Dowling 2005).

The important role played by adults in supporting the development of children's thinking through talk has been stressed throughout this chapter. In relation to practitioners, Cole (1996: 10) provides a useful summary, in his suggestions that adults working with young children need to have

- sensitivity to the child's current state, and an understanding of the child's level of ability and immediate interests;
- sensitivity to the meanings he or she is trying to communicate; and a desire to help and encourage interaction where both participants have equal space and discourse status;
- the ability to be a sympathetic listener rather than a propensity to dominate the situation and make it adult-led (being 'genuinely curious', Paley 1986);
- skill in responding to the meaning intended – just as a good conversationalist would with people of any age – and to have genuine concern to achieve a mutual understanding (analogous to Mercer's idea of an 'intermental development zone', or IDZ, Mercer 2000: 141).

Box 7.11: Sustained Shared Thinking in a nursery, 6 children aged 3.0–4.6, and Adult A.

The children are looking at a book Boy R has brought in. The book has buttons on the side that, if pressed when the corresponding pictures appear in the book, reproduce some characters' voices and other noises. The adult holds the book, showing the cover.

| | |
|---|---|
| S: | I have a Peppa Pig book and it goes in the bath. |
| M: | Me too, but not a Peppa Pig one! |
| C: | Me too! |
| ADULT: | Can we put this book in the bath? |
| C: | No! |
| ADULT: | Why not? What will happen if the pages get wet? |
| C: | They will, they wil l... you won't be able to read it any more! |
| ADULT: | How come S. is able to put his Peppa Pig book in the bath? |

Children look puzzled. After a few seconds of silence:

| | |
|---|---|
| R: | And the batteries will go flat. |
| ADULT: | Why? |
| S: | The water will go into them and they will run out! |
| C: | Yes, yes, and it will not work again! |
| ADULT: | And what about the pages, what will happen to the pages? |
| M: | They will get ruined! |
| ADULT: | Why? What are they made of? |
| C, M, S: | Paper. |
| ADULT: | So why don't the bath book pages get ruined? Are its pages made of paper? |

Children look at Adult, puzzled.

| | |
|---|---|
| M: | (looks down sideways and after a few seconds says triumphantly) Plastic! |

Almost simultaneously S says:    Soap!

| | |
|---|---|
| C: | (looks at Adult and shakes his head) Noo! |

The rest of the children look in turn at M and S.

| | |
|---|---|
| S: | (almost immediately after saying 'soap', moving fingers as if squashing something) The plastic in my book is a bit ripped, and if I squash it soaps comes out! I can see foam in it; it comes out of the sponge! |
| ADULT: | Do you mean that the book has sponge inside, not soap? |
| S: | Yes, Yes! |
| ADULT: | So where is the plastic? |
| M: | Outside, they covered with plastic outside! |

C shakes his head.

| | |
|---|---|
| ADULT: | What do you think C, do you agree with M? |
| C: | No, mine is not made of plastic. |
| ADULT: | Do you know what it is made of? |
| C: | No. |
| ADULT: | Can you bring it to nursery and show it to us, so we can find out? |

C nods.

Reproduced with permission of Romina Gor

## Some implications for practice: a summary

Along with the discussion of the adult's role above, a wide range of practical implications have been discussed throughout this chapter, and it is useful to briefly summarize some of them here:

- 'Talking out loud helps young children to think better' (Fernyhough 2008: 106).
- The value of 'evidence, guidance and support' (Wells 1987: 65) from adults in talking with children, and an attitude of equal partnership in conversation, for supporting children's thinking and understanding *through* talk (Wells 1987).
- The value of project work characteristic of the kind developed in Reggio Emilia, for providing contexts for conversation, and shared experiences (Katz and Chard 2000).
- The importance of creating a shared culture in the nursery (Paley 1986, 2004).
- 'Children can develop important communicative skills through interaction with their peers' (Howe and Mercer 2007: 18), which they would not learn in taking part in conversations only with adults.
- Settings could focus on ways in which they can broaden the range of children's experiences (Wells 1987: 67). This may include feeding children with 'a great deal more general knowledge', and 'going beyond the school walls more' (Tizard and Hughes 2002: 220).
- Nurseries and schools can help children to become more reflectively aware of what they already know and still need to know, in ways that enable them to take increasing responsibility for their own learning (Wells 1987). Modelling metacognitive strategies (Durden and Dangel 2008) and explicit talk about thinking with young children may help to make them more consciously aware of their thinking (Astington 1994; Pramling 1988).
- The importance of supporting children's questions and 'passages of intellectual search' (Tizard and Hughes 2002).
- The importance of times of relative leisure for intellectually challenging conversations (Tizard and Hughes 2002). Attention to how professionals can find such opportunities in settings may be important.
- Size of group may be important for sustained shared thinking.
- Children's narratives may be particularly important starting points for supporting and developing their thinking (Wells 1987; Paley 1986).
- Pretend play, particularly sociodramatic play, may be valuable in the ways in which it provides opportunities for children to best display their linguistic competence (Kenner *et al.*1996), and in how it supports both pretend communication and metacommunication (Dockett 1998). Adult modelling and involvement, and non-representational resources, may be important supports in pretend play (Broadhead 2004; Trawick-Smith 1998).
- Teachers can support children's achievement by treating learning as a social, communicative process, teaching procedures for solving problems and making sense of experience, and using questions-and-answer sequences to guide the development of understanding (Mercer and Littleton 2007).

# Further reflection

1  What is your response to the following query, from *New Scientist* (6 July 2002):

> I think in English, but my Swedish friend thinks in Swedish. How do deaf people, who have never heard words in any language, think? When I think, I think using words and sentences. Although I can't remember for certain, I don't think I knew any form of language as a baby, so how do babies think?

2  The following observation comes from Athey (2007: 128):

> Gary (4: 2: 16) asked the teacher if he could 'read' to her. After they settled he said, 'Look!' and swivelled a pencil. The teacher expressed interest and said, 'You made that turn round, didn't you? You made it 'rotate'. Much later Gary showed the teacher a picture of a cement mixer in a book. The teacher said, 'That's interesting, you have found something else that goes round, that rotates. Can you think of anything else that rotates?' After a pause Gary replied, 'Yes, a candy-floss maker'.

Do you think that the teacher here is supporting the development of Gary's thinking? If so, in what ways? What could she have said or done next?

3  Marsh (2005) identifies a range of communicative practices: to form social relationships; for identity construction and performance of self; for development of skills, knowledge and understanding in relation to language and literacy; to access or display information and for pleasure and enjoyment. Look for evidence of these practices in young children's engagement with all forms of popular culture and media (for example, all TV, computer games, toys, phones, artefacts and all forms of print including books, comics, catalogues, junk mail and TV guides).

# Further reading

*The relationship between language and thought*

Donaldson (1992: ch. 7)
Fernyhough (2008: ch. 8)
Mercer (2000)
Piaget (1959)
Pinker (1994, 2007)
Thornton (2002: ch. 3)
Vygotsky (1986)
Wood (1998: 27–31)

*Metalinguistic awareness*

Chukovsky (1963)
Crystal (1998)
Garvey (1977)

Goswami (2008: 173–8)
Whitehead (2002, 2010)
Wood (1998: ch. 5)

*Language at home and in early childhood settings*

Bergen (2002)
Dockett (1998)
Gopnik *et al.* (1999: ch. 4)
Heath (1983)
Karmiloff-Smith (1994: ch. 4)
Meadows (2006: 7–30)
Mercer (2000)
Mercer and Littleton (2007)
Paley (1981, 1986)
Tizard and Hughes (2002)
Trawick-Smith (1998)
Wegerif (2010: ch. 2)
Wells (1987)

# Chapter 8

# Knowing about the world

## The development of children's concepts

This chapter looks at the ways in which young children develop their understandings of the world around them. We shall look first at what might be meant by 'conceptual development', and at perspectives on how this occurs in young children, and then consider specific aspects of young children's scientific, mathematical, geographical and historical thinking.

## What are concepts?

Concepts are the ideas and understandings we each have which enable us to group together objects, events and abstractions, in particular relationships. Some of these concepts may be considered universal, whilst others are clearly culturally specific, and involve different ways of categorizing things, according to social practice (Rogoff 2003; Siegler and Alibali 2005). White supports Wittgenstein's claim that concepts are 'public phenomena', and that a key role of adults is to induct children into this 'public heritage' (White 2002: 53). The number of possible concepts is infinite, and they are just as likely to be about the concrete and everyday (pencils, socks and teacups) as they are to be about more abstract ideas such as truth, beauty and speed. In our daily lives we constantly define new concepts, in response to situations. Until we go to visit Granny we have no real need to construct a concept of 'things we must take on our visit to Granny' (Meadows 2006: 154). Concepts, then, are mental models we construct to explain the world around us, which help us to deal with things and events more efficiently. As Siegler and Alibali suggest: 'Concepts allow us to organize our experience into coherent patterns and to draw inferences in situations in which we lack direct experience ... Concepts also save us mental effort by allowing us to apply previous knowledge to new situations' (2005: 269).

Clearly, such a process is extremely useful. It can help us to cope with new and unfamiliar situations, to employ what knowledge and experience we already have, and to use our understanding most effectively. It can tell us how to react emotionally to experiences, as, for example, when my daughter developed a long-term aversion to swans after being bitten by one on a 'duck feeding' expedition when she was very young. The alternative, as Meadows suggests, is chaos: 'Without concepts we could not predict, could not remember, could not communicate at all exactly, could not act appropriately with other people. The world which flows by us has to be organised if we are to survive' (Meadows 2006: 149).

Children's conceptual development is part of their general cognitive development, and throughout this chapter you may find it useful to think back to many of the ideas looked at in Chapters 2 and 3. Piaget's idea of schema, looked at both in Chapter 2 and in Chapter 6 in discussion of Chris Athey's work, for example, is particularly relevant to any discussion of conceptual development. Chapter 5 considered young children's concepts about their own and other people's thoughts, ideas and feelings. It is also impossible to look at concept development independent of language. For example, Vygotsky's (1986) views about the interdependence of language and thought, discussed in Chapter 7, are relevant in this context. Concepts, as 'public phenomena' (White 2002: 53) are expressed in language, and some aspects of language, such as naming, may contribute to the development of concepts by supporting the process of categorization (Goswami 2008). However, as Pinker suggests: 'If you learned that *wapiti* was another name for an elk, you could take all the facts connected to the word *elk* and instantly transfer them to the *wapiti*' (1997: 86), suggesting that we have a level of representation which is specific to the concepts behind the words themselves.

Concepts involve grouping things together in categories on the basis of their characteristics. There are two major views to account for types of category representation. The 'classical' view assumes that concepts have defining features that act as criteria for defining category membership. Siegler and Alibali (2005) liken these defining features to dictionary definitions, because they focus on the necessary and sufficient conditions to strictly determine whether or not something is an example of a particular category. This classical view assumes rigid boundaries, whereby an example either does or does not meet the definition (Medin *et al.* 2005). Since the 1930s, however, this classical view has been increasingly challenged (Woolfolk *et al.* 2008). Some concepts have clear, defining attributes – for example, a square – but most concepts do not. A defining feature of 'chair' would probably be about sitting on it, but, as Meadows (2006) points out, we would not tend to call a bicycle saddle a chair, nor would we describe a patch of grass we sat down on as a chair. More current views of concept representation suggest that we have a prototype in our minds when we think of a concept. This view is also sometimes called the probabilistic view, because it argues that it is only probable that a category member has the properties of the concept, and different members of the category may share some, but not all, of the same characteristics. It is helpful to bear these two views in mind, because they have influenced ideas about whether, and at what ages, young children are capable of forming concepts.

## How do children's concepts develop?

Both Piaget (Inhelder and Piaget 1964) and Vygotsky (1978, 1986) believe that young children are not skilled at forming and using concepts, in particular that they cannot form stable representations based on defining features. Piaget found that, at the preoperational stage, children could not categorize objects according to taxonomic principles, for example grouping all of the 'red' things together, or making a set of 'vehicles'. Instead, he found that children grouped things according to thematic principles, such as a cake and a table, because you put a cake on a table. Piaget suggests that children's conceptual development follows a path similar to their general cognitive development, and is largely a move from the concrete to the abstract. For Piaget, children's thinking is qualitatively different to that of adults, and their knowledge structures are different at each stage of development. Cognitive conflict, which arises as children try to resolve anomalies in their understanding as a result of their experiences, results in wholesale, global restructuring of knowledge, and stage change.

Vygotsky hypothesizes that children pass through three stages of conceptual development. In the first stage they form thematic concepts, as described above, then chain concepts, in which the basis for classification seems to change during the process of sorting. So, for example, a young child might group a few red things together, then a few circles of red and blue, then a few blue things, and so on. This behaviour, he suggests, is the functional equivalence of concepts, but the third stage, where children form true concepts based on stable, salient criteria, does not become fixed until adolescence. On the basis of evidence such as this, it was concluded that children's ability to form and make use of concepts was very limited until around school age (Meadows 2006). Thus, for both Vygotsky and Piaget, young children's conceptual understanding is fundamentally different from that of older children and adults.

The past 30 years have seen these ideas come under increasing scrutiny, and current thinking suggests that the idea that children structure knowledge differently at different stages may be an over-simplification (Meadows 2006), and that even very young children are capable of representing concepts using both defining and probabilistic features. Siegler and Alibali (2005), for example, point to research which suggests that children as young as one year old can form taxonomic concepts, an ability Piaget and Vygotsky suggest is not present in 4 and 5 year olds. They conclude that the reasons that they did not seem to do so in Piaget and Vygotsky's experimental situations were that, first, children might find the thematic relationships more interesting than the taxonomic one: 'Young children might put dogs and frisbees together, rather than dogs and bears, because they find the relationship between dogs and frisbees more interesting' (Siegler and Alibali 2005: 273). Second, they suggest Piaget and Vygotsky both underestimate the role of specific content knowledge in conceptual understanding. Quite simply, young children may not always have the necessary knowledge and experience to know what the defining features are that enable categories to be formed. This latter reason seems to be at the heart of any difference between young children's conceptual understanding and that of older children and adults. Developmental changes may be more about differentiation and elaboration rather than fundamental changes in the whole basis of conceptualization. What are central to this process are children's knowledge, for example, their event knowledge, and experience. A good example of this is Arnold's (1999) description of the scientific concepts that Georgia is most concerned with from the ages of 2 to 5 years. The three listed are food allergy, childbirth and changes of state. Of these, two have particular significance in Georgia's life: she experiences the impact of childbirth when her brother, Harry, is born when she is 2, and he has potentially life-threatening food allergies.

Knowledge and experience, then, and the information gained from them, play a central part in shaping how we reason and form concepts (Thornton 2002). Siegler et al. (2011) suggest that this is the main reason why a characteristic form of young children's thinking touched on in Chapter 1, magical thinking, dies away with age, as young children increase their knowledge about the world, and as they have experiences that challenge their beliefs, for example, about the existence of the tooth fairy.

## Categorization

The tendency to form concepts seems to be a basic part of what it is to be human, a kind of 'explanatory drive' (Gopnik *et al.* 1999: 85). Babies form them from their earliest days. Karmiloff-Smith (1994: 42) suggests that babies have a 'very simple template' of the human face from birth, which quickly develops into a general concept of a face, before recognition of individual faces. She also suggests that babies know a lot about concepts such as size, space and depth from the very beginning. After about five days, she recounts, babies will only reach for things like mobiles that are within their grasp.

It is primarily through the use of their senses that babies first begin to explore, and develop concepts about, the world around them. Gopnik *et al.* suggest that humans have 'a special kind of knowledge that enables us to translate the information at our senses into representations of objects' (1999: 62). The brain 'systematically transforms' (1999: 62) the wealth of sensory information it receives and, in so doing, organizes that information into a complex, but coherent network. Catherwood (1999) suggests that babies can see categorical similarities at the age of about three to four months, notably of what are generally referred to as 'basic' categories, for example 'car', and possibly even at a higher level, for example 'vehicles'. These perceptual categorizations arise from the 'heuristic inferences' (Thornton 2002: 108) babies and young children make as a result of their experience of the world. Meadows (2006) believes that what may be central to this process is children's representation of meaningful events in their lives, as scripts or 'General Event Representation' (GER). Many of the 'events' of children's lives are highly routinized: getting up, going to the shops, having a drink, playing 'Peekaboo' games, for example. Children's representations of these routines, she argues, help them to attach meaning to them, and also support comparisons with other routines. She cites Nelson, in her suggestion that GERs could be the 'basic building blocks' (Meadows 2006: 161) of cognitive development, and particularly of aspects such as categorization, patterning, making inferences and cause–effect relations, so important in conceptual development.

General Event Representations may play an important part in the development of children's ability to categorize, in particular in moving from basic categories to the development of hierarchies of category. As they develop beyond babyhood, children show an increased understanding of both category hierarchies and causal connections (Siegler *et al.* 2011). Looking at category hierarchies, Rosch (cited in Goswami 2008) suggests that such categorization comprises three levels, and that young children generally learn these three levels of categorization in a similar order. First, children form 'basic' level categories, as in, for example, 'car', then 'superordinate' level categories, as in 'vehicle', the class to which all cars belong. The third level of category formation is known as 'subordinate', and deals with finer discrimination of the basic level, for example, type of car. Another example of the relationship between the three levels would be animal (superordinate), cat (basic) and Siamese (subordinate). Children generally tend to form basic level categories first because these usually have a number of consistent characteristics. In cats, for example, these include fur, whiskers, size and 'meow'. The characteristics of the superordinate level, animal, are less consistent. Subordinate category characteristics are consistent, as in the basic level, but require children to make finer discriminations: differences in fur length and colour in cats, for example. Recent research, however, challenges Rosch's assumption of developmental order (Goswami 2008). In particular, Goswami cites a range of research which shows young children's conceptual development proceeding from a global to basic-level sequence, with sensitivity to superordinate level categories preceding basic-level categories in young children. This direction of travel in young children's conceptual understanding seems to make sense when looked at alongside the idea discussed earlier, that it is prototypical representation which is most significant in categorization. To take the example above, in the superordinate category of animals, only some features will be shared by all animals (for example, motion), whilst many others will not. Goswami (2008) suggests that advances in cognitive neuroscience may be particularly valuable for our understanding of concept representation in babies and young children.

### Causal relationships and categorization

Much of what has been considered thus far focuses strongly (though not exclusively) on the perceptual, that is, grouping on the basis of observable physical characteristics. This is very useful in everyday contexts, but cannot account for all of the 'events' of children's lives. What is needed, and what tends to develop later in infancy, is children's conceptual understanding of causal relationships, although Gopnik et al. (1999) provides evidence of babies making causal connections from as early as three months of age. Thornton (2002) suggests that Carey's (1985) study of the concept of animacy, that is, whether things are alive or dead, is an example of how children's reasoning changes from perceptual to conceptual or 'principled' inference, based upon being able to make causal category definitions. For Thornton, this development represents a radical change, which 'provides the child with a new and more powerful basis for reasoning, better suited to formal, analytical thinking' (2002: 117). In addition, she suggests that it illustrates the difference between Piaget's perspective that new knowledge arises out of a change in the 'mental tools' available to children, and the more current view that increased knowledge supports the development of new ways of thinking. Put simply, 'what you know determines how you reason' (Thornton 2002: 118). As Thornton points out, this may explain why children's reasoning can be so different from one context to another. It is useful to refer back to Chapter 7, and Tizard and Hughes's (2002) ideas of intellectual search: young children's insistent questioning very often relates to questioning of causal relationships.

Elsewhere here we have looked at the idea of novicehood, and noted that children are initially novices at everything, but develop expertise in particular areas, or domains, as a result of their experiences, which will, of course, differ from child to child. This domain-specific knowledge may be particularly important in the development of key aspects of conceptual understanding such as inferential and analogical reasoning, and the identification and use of problem-solving strategies (Thornton 2002). The accumulation of knowledge and expertise means that the expert can recognize a problem as familiar, and is also able to call upon previous experience in solving that problem more quickly and effectively. What the expert does not have to do is to run through the whole of a procedure in order to arrive at the best solution, she already knows that a particular approach will 'work'. Children's early knowledge tends to be heavily procedural (knowing how to do things). Over time, children generally get better at accessing their knowledge without having to use this procedural knowledge, and come to rely more on 'declarative' (knowing that) knowledge (Meadows 2006).

Thus, it seems likely that young children's approaches to forming and using concepts may not be qualitatively different to those of older children and adults. We have seen that young children are capable, for example, of categorizing objects on taxonomic grounds, contrary to Piaget's and Vygotsky's beliefs. In addition, there is evidence to suggest that use of thematic grouping does not die with age, and that adults, too, use such grouping (Meadows 2006). Knowledge seems to be key to the development of young children's concepts, and 'where children are knowledgeable and encouraged to discuss their knowledge they seem to have concepts very like those of adults' (Meadows 2006: 163). It is worth looking back now at the episode in Box 7.11, which shows young children using category-based reasoning to support their conceptual understanding.

## Some implications for practice in supporting the development of children's concepts: experience and adult roles

All of this suggests that the provision of rich experiences which support the acquisition of knowledge and understanding will be key to children's conceptual development, from their earliest days. Goldschmied and Jackson (2004) believe that the provision of 'treasure baskets' and heuristic play provides babies and toddlers with opportunities to make connections in their knowledge and understanding. In playing with a treasure basket, babies are able to explore objects through all of their senses: touching, smelling, mouthing, looking at and listening to a broad variety of natural materials. The role of experience is also borne out in Hatano and Inagaki's (1992) studies of young children's care for goldfish. They concluded that those children who had experience of caring for goldfish tended to be able to make use of this knowledge and experience in analogous situations, such as in thinking about the characteristics of frogs, for example. In this, they were able to make conceptual inferences more advanced than those of their classmates who had no direct experience but who had merely observed their teachers caring for animals in the kindergarten. That is, they had developed conceptual knowledge which they were able to transfer to a new situation. This supports Watson's view that children should be given opportunities 'to develop expertise (domain specific knowledge) in areas that interest them' (1997: 15). A key context for supporting the development of such interconnections is children's play (Claxton 1999b).

One final element of Vygotsky's ideas may be important to consider here. Vygotsky suggests that there are two types of conceptual development, the 'formal' or 'scientific' ones learned as part of the process of schooling, and the 'everyday' ones, acquired in context (1986: 194). In his view, both types interact in children's development, and complement one another, with home concepts being built on by scientific ones, and those, in turn, modifying the home concepts. The implication here may be that 'educational practices have to build on the child's everyday concepts but also to reach into the future where experiences can be created in school and combined with other subject matter concepts (scientific concepts)' (Hedegaard 2005: 14). As Smidt (2009) points out, these are mediated through language, and, in a more general sense, the role of language in conceptual development is critical.

The role of the adult, White (2002) suggests, is to explain, give examples and monitor children's understanding, because, in his view, children will not just pick concepts up. The implication of Navarra's (1955) observations of his son is that careful, sensitive observation is important if adults are to notice, and support, conceptual change. Such observation may reveal children showing their understanding of concepts in many ways, through action as much as through language.

Willig (1990: 13) suggests that five strategies, in particular, are important in extending children's conceptual development, all of which can be seen to have a relationship to the models of cognitive development outlined in Chapter 2:

- matching teaching material to the ability of the learner;
- disturbing the learner's existing ideas;
- teaching by telling;
- learning from observing;
- learning by thinking about thinking.

Willig's suggestion that 'teaching by telling' (1990: 18) is an important strategy in extending children's conceptual development emphasizes 'meaningful reception learning' (1990: 18), rather than any kind of rote learning. It is useful to look at the discussion below on children's conceptions of the Earth and the value of 'telling' there. At the same time, it may seem somewhat at odds with Duckworth's assertion that 'Simply telling children the truth about something could not make them understand it' (1987: 32). Box 1.1, in Chapter 1, illustrates this dilemma, and suggests that repeated opportunities which explore and challenge children's thinking will be necessary in order to support the development of concepts, and, even then, when faced with the novel, or when they feel overloaded or confused by information (Hannust and Kikas 2010), children will often revert back to earlier intuitions (Driver 1983). Paley describes a similar episode, in which the children, faced with a very large, heavy bag of sand in the middle of the kindergarten, 'invent' pulleys and levers in order to move the bag. She later tells them a story in which a man needs to move a heavy rock in front of the entrance to his cave, and asks the children what advice they could have given him. Their responses include no reference to the kinds of strategies they devised when faced with a similar predicament. As she reflects: 'The adult should not underestimate the young child's tendency to revert to earlier thinking; new concepts have not been "learned" but are only in temporary custody. They are glimpsed and tried out but are not permanent possessions' (Paley 1981: 101).

Further general implications for practice in supporting young children's conceptual development are set out at the end of this chapter. The remainder of the chapter focuses on some specific areas of conceptual development, in particular ones such as number, space and time that are 'so important, so pervasive, that they merit special attention' (Siegler and Alibali 2005: 283), using examples here to draw general implications. Although these are considered in 'subject' areas, there is, of course, considerable overlap between these domains, and emphasis is on the holistic way in which children themselves think about things. In addition, there is no suggestion that these are the only aspects of young children's conceptual development of value to consider, merely that there is not sufficient space here to look at everything.

## Thinking about scientific concepts

A good example of young children's holistic thinking is their understanding of 'living' and 'non-living' things. There are many accounts of children's concepts in this area (see, in particular, Carey 1985), and the ways in which they attempt to resolve conflicts in their understanding of life and death: if you bury a dead rabbit it will grow again (see Box 6.1), trees are not alive because they do not move, and so on, and this categorization of things as animate or inanimate is the basis of the later-acquired concept of living and non-living. As early as three months of age, babies distinguish between animate creatures and inanimate objects, on the basis of movement (Goswami 2008). As we saw in Chapter 4, mirror neurons in the brain respond to biological motion, for example a human arm rather than a mechanical robot arm. By the age of 5, most children are able to make 'adult-type' judgements if the objects are well known to them (Meadows 2006). It is not until around the age of 10 that children will have the 'received model' (Selley 1999) of the concept of 'living' and 'non-living' (Carey 1985). Willig (1990) cites research showing confusion in young children's minds about whether dolls are inanimate objects, at least until the age of 6 years (for example, 46 per cent of 3 year olds made errors about this). Children may also have considerable uncertainty about the status of other groups, such as fish, insects and dead animals. As Thornton (2002) suggests, in the early years children will tend to make their inferences about concepts, in this case about animacy, on perceptual grounds: the more a thing 'looks' like the prototypical animate creature, the more likely it is to be assessed as alive. On this basis, dolls look like a better proposition than, say, trees, for a young child. In addition, children's experiences of stories, television programmes and films, where dolls can be just as animate and 'alive' as humans, may have an impact on their thinking.

Children's confusion about death and its permanency is reflected in questions such as 'Is Mrs Z still dead? (Navarra 1955: 96), and in their play, where people often die and come alive again. Lofdahl relates a 'funeral' play episode between two girls, aged 3½ and 4 years, who scatter flowers over a body in a grave in order to make it come alive again. The comment of Maja, one of the girls, also illustrates how children form concepts as a result of the language they hear around them, and try out this language in order to negotiate understanding. Her comment: 'You can just wake up when you feel the flowers on your body' (Lofdahl 2005: 13) may come from hearing people talk about dead people 'going to sleep', alongside a propensity in young children for 'magical thinking' (Paley 1981; Siegler et al. 2011) noted above. What children lack, Carey (1985) suggests, is sufficient biological knowledge to enable them to create unified categories of 'living' and 'non-living' things. Siegler et al. (2011) suggest that some of this knowledge comes through being told it, as Willig (1990) suggests. Young children often do not classify plants as 'alive' because they do not perceive them as moving. Telling 5 year olds that plants move towards sunlight, and that their roots move towards water, can lead them to conclude that plants are living things (Siegler et al. 2011). In addition, more experience of death may influence young children's understanding, and those young children who have experienced the death of someone close to them are more likely to both understand what this means and to express emotions similar to adults (Meadows 2006).

## 'Knowing' and ways of thinking

The accumulation of such knowledge will take time. Also, it may not be enough by itself. Nunes suggests that scientific knowledge is about particular 'ways of thinking' (1995: 194), and is much more than the accumulation of 'facts'. The two girls in Lofdahl's (2005) study might, in some sense, 'know' that one does not come alive again, but still think that one does. For Nunes, the facts are meaningless unless the concepts to which they relate become part of our thinking. In describing the development of the scientific concepts of one boy ('L.B.') over a period of two years, Navarra similarly concludes that development was not just a matter of 'knowing' more:

> Individual experiences and items of information that grew out of L.B.'s activity were continually related and integrated into ever larger, interlocking conceptual patterns. L.B.'s conceptual growth was not merely an additive process in which new information was accumulated. It was, rather, an evaluative process in which the integration of new information could bring about a basic reconstruction in the conceptual framework.
>
> (Navarra 1955: 121)

Navarra's (1955) work is set within the dominant perspective of its time, that of Piaget, with his emphasis on new knowledge arising out of a change in the 'mental tools' available to children. However, it is also possible to read Navarra's observations as a demonstration of the view that enhanced experience and knowledge supports the development of new ways of thinking. A good example of this process is the development of L.B.'s increasingly differentiated concepts of smoke and steam. A very brief selection is shown in Box 8.1, and illustrates L.B.'s active search for meaning, and his increasing use of stable characteristics to denote a concept.

Recent research about young children's understanding of the Earth provides much valuable food for thought here. Knowing about astronomical ideas is problematic for young children because of the inconsistencies between what they experience and what they are taught (Hannust and Kikas 2010). So, for example, children may perceive and experience the sun moving across the sky during the day, but are then taught that it is, in fact, the Earth's daily rotation that produces this effect. The conclusion of a range of studies has tended to be that children's concepts about the Earth proceed through a series of stages. Initially, children form naïve, theory-like mental models (Panagiotaki et al. 2009), for example, that the Earth is flat, based upon their experiences. This initial model is superseded by a 'synthetic' model, which combines children's intuitive beliefs and counterintuitive scientific facts to which children are exposed as part of their culture, for example that the Earth is a sphere, and not flat. Only in late childhood, it is argued, are these synthetic models replaced by the scientific view (Panagiotaki et al. 2009). Recent research (Hannust and Kikas 2010; Panagiotaki et al. 2009; Siegal et al. 2004; and others) has challenged this theory-based view, suggesting instead that 'the majority of young children possess knowledge of the Earth that consists of loosely related fragments that may be accurate, but do not need to be accurate, and that information is stored as individual fragments until a coherent cultural theory is acquired' (Hannust and Kikas 2010: 166). Hannust and Kikas's work, in particular, is interesting because of the young age of the children in

---

*Box 8.1:* L.B., aged 3.2–4.8

| | |
|---|---|
| AUGUST 1951 | (Watching his aunt dusting a rosebush with a spraygun) Is that smoke? |
| AUGUST 1951 | (Looking at haze and fog on the sea) Where's the smoke coming from? |
| OCTOBER 1951 | (Watching his mother iron clothes) What's that – smoke? Where is that coming from? Is there something that makes it smoke? |
| OCTOBER 1951 | (Watching a car being steam cleaned) What's he doing to the car? Is the car burning on fire? (His father replies: No, he's using steam to clean the car.) |
| FEBRUARY 1952 | (Watching boiling water being poured) Hey! Look at all that steam! Are you going to drink that? Where is all that smoke going to? |
| APRIL 1952 | (In a steam-filled bathroom) Look at all the smoke. |
| APRIL 1952 | (In a steam-filled bathroom) Hey, mommy, where does all this steam come from – from the water? ... This is steamy. (Mother says: What do you mean – steamy?) L.B.: It's all wet. |
| AUGUST 1952 | (Smoke is coming out of the chimney of the house next door) Where's that coming from? Is that happening because they want to take a bath? How come no smoke isn't coming out of ours? Isn't our heat on? |
| FEBRUARY 1953 | (L.B. has a hot cup of bouillon for his lunch. His mother tells him to 'wait until it cools off'. He eats the rest of his lunch first) Is it cool now? (Mother says: I don't know) L.B.: Yes, it's cool now 'cause there's no steam. (Mother: Does that mean it's cool?) L.B.: Yes. (Mother: Doesn't steam come from cool things?) L.B.: No, only when it's hot. |

(Adapted from Navarra 1955: 39–44)

---

their study. Starting with children aged between 2 and 3 years, they looked over four years at the children's acquisition of knowledge about astronomy, in particular their knowledge of the Earth. They concluded that, rather than constructing a synthetic model of the Earth, most children's knowledge was fragmented, with accurate knowledge often expressed alongside inaccurate ideas. In a study of 6 and 7 year olds, Panagiotaki *et al.* (2009) also refute the idea of a naïve, theory-like model, and conclude instead that children have substantially more scientific understanding than the naïve model theorists propose, but that this is essentially 'theory free' before the acquisition of a scientific model of the Earth. Both Hannust and Kikas (2010) and Panagiotaki *et al.* (2009) suggest that their contradictory research findings relate partly to different methods used for assessing children's knowledge, and this aspect is looked at below in the discussion on supporting the development of young children's scientific concepts. They also draw attention, along with Siegal *et al.* (2004) to the role of culture here, with young children's experiences as part of their cultural context affecting what is thought about, and how young children's scientific understanding is shaped.

---

Box 8.2:  Charlotte, aged 5.9, in conversation at home with her father

C:                Dad, I've been thinking about it and I think there must be two suns.
                  One goes round the world and makes days and nights. The other always
                  stays in front of Africa, because it's always hot in Africa.

*Charlotte lives in England, but her uncle lives in Africa, and he has told her that it
is hot there all the time. Her father is also a physicist, and has shown her books about
astronomy, so on one level she 'knows' that there is only one sun. How, then, can she make
sense of this when she knows that the sun gives heat, and her uncle has told her it is hot
all the time in Africa? Charlotte attempts to resolve this cognitive conflict by inventing
a second sun, an alternative framework which provides, for her, a consistent model for
explaining the situation. Her knowledge that it is the Earth which goes around the
sun, and not vice versa, as is the case for many children, also supports the idea that
telling children scientific facts may be important for their conceptual understanding, as
suggested by Panagiotaki et al. (2009). What is also interesting here is that the remark
was generated spontaneously by Charlotte herself, and her metacognitive opening
statement 'I've been thinking about it' suggests her understanding about what it means
to think.*

---

### Alternative frameworks

What is clear from the examples we have looked at is that young children's experiences
can result in them developing concepts which may look different to those of older
children and adults (although adults, too, may have concepts which do not match
the received models). As we have noted, this is more the result of lack of knowledge
and experience than of qualitatively different ways of thinking. In Box 7.9 we saw
Abe's hypothesis that 'ladies have their hearts in their boobies'. This is a reasonable
conclusion for Abe to draw on the basis of his knowledge that our hearts are in our
chests, women's breasts are on their chests and so he invents a reality where hearts
are inside them. Such ideas have often been referred to as 'misconceptions' in young
children's scientific thinking. However, a more useful way of considering them is as
'alternative frameworks' (Driver 1983), which are perfectly logical conclusions on the
basis of individual children's understanding and experience. Arguably, this is often what
'real' scientists do, when they invent ad hoc hypotheses to make sense of the world.
Adult attempts to 'correct' a child's thinking may be misplaced, and prevent them from
developing their own ideas, and extending their current working theories (Peters and
Davis 2011). Box 8.2 illustrates one such alternative framework.

### Supporting the development of young children's scientific concepts

In seeking to support the development of young children's scientific concepts, as with
other areas of conceptual development, attention to both process and content will
be valuable. Careful observation and exploration of children's current understanding
(Valanides *et al.* 2000), and sensitive intervention by those working with young
children will be important starting points. Wadsworth (1997) suggests that awareness

of the different kinds of ideas children hold will be important for adults in supporting the development of young children's scientific understanding:

- anthropomorphic views: 'don't cry, little worm';
- egocentric views: 'we've got to go to bed, we can't sleep when it is light';
- ideas based on colloquial use of language: Maja's understanding of 'waking' from the dead;
- ideas based on limited experience and observations: as with Abe in Box 7.9;
- stylized representations: children often draw the sun with lines radiating out, but this does not mean that they understand light travels in straight lines.

Gura (1992) also remarks on the positive impact on children's thinking as a result of watching other children engaged in similar activities, for example blockplay, and on the ways in which adults can help to structure children's enquiry and exploration.

It is worth returning here to Vygotsky's (1986) idea of 'everyday' and 'scientific' or 'formal' concepts. He suggests that young children's concepts arise out of their everyday experiences and, as a result of particular experiences, children generalize to wider concepts. He sees the learning of scientific, or formal, concepts proceeding in the other direction, from the general to the particular. This may be useful in looking at some potential difficulties that children may experience in developing concepts in the area of science itself. Nunes (1995) suggests that they fall into four categories. First, scientific concepts involve us in making distinctions we might not ordinarily make in life, for example between temperature and heat. Second, many scientific concepts represent intensive rather than extensive quantities. Extensive quantities are derived from units of measurement, for example, the centimetre. Intensive measurements involve ratios, for example density is measured as a ratio of mass to volume. Third, scientific concepts often require reasoning about non-perceptible aspects of the physical world, for example, molecules and atoms. Finally, children have already developed some knowledge about the physical world which differs from the established scientific concept, and may have alternative frameworks, as outlined above. Vyogtsky's notion of instruction (see Chapter 2) may be important here. A range of studies cited here (Hannust and Kikas 2010; Panagiotaki *et al.* 2009; Siegler *et al.* 2011) have suggested that *telling* children scientific facts and using more closely focused, closed questions is valuable, both for supporting children's understanding of scientific phenomena and for adults in eliciting that understanding. Panagiotaki *et al.* (2009) suggest that the acquisition of scientific knowledge, in the domain of astronomy at least, derives in part from instruction which provides even young children with scientific information. Furthermore, clearer, less ambiguous (less 'open') questions can support clearer interpretation by children of the adults' meaning, enabling children to display their scientific knowledge more visibly. Hannust and Kikas conclude that 'open questions that provide hardly any clues about what perspective respondents should take are indeed hard for young children to understand' (2010: 175), leading to potentially inaccurate assessments of their understanding.

## Children thinking mathematically

In looking at children's mathematical thinking, the chief focus here is on number, for two reasons. First, number underpins all other aspects of mathematics, including shape, space and measurement, and second, it is in this area that some of the questions about young children's mathematical understanding are best, and most easily, explored. The following section, on young children's geographical thinking, looks at spatial cognition, which is also highly relevant here.

## Understanding number

Young children's understanding of number and the structure of the number system develops gradually, and demands repeated experience over time (Munn 1997). It is also influenced by a number of factors, including socio-economic status (Sarama and Clements 2009). In order to look at what develops, it is useful to begin by clarifying the two basic types of number knowledge, as these will be referred to below. The first is cardinality, or the absolute numerical size of any set or group. Thus, the last number reached when counting stands for the total number of things counted. The second is ordinality, which refers to the relational properties of numbers. Numbers are always said in the same order, and always stand in the same relationship to one another in the sense of being greater or less. You are reading the eighth chapter of this book, perhaps drinking a second cup of coffee, and the number five will always be bigger than the number three.

Given Piaget's interest in the development of children's logical thinking, it should come as no surprise that he devoted considerable time and effort to exploring children's understanding of number, although much of it looks in more detail at older children. This is because, for Piaget, young children, whilst they might be able to use number words and sequences, and even to apply these to objects and actions, do so without real understanding (Bryant 1997). Piaget suggests that children need to have an understanding of both the cardinal and ordinal properties of numbers, and the key operations of classification (putting a set of things together) and seriation (putting the set in order), that accompany them, full understanding of which is not achieved until 7 or 8 (Piaget 1952). Research since Piaget, particularly that involving naturalistic observation, suggests much earlier competence (Donaldson 1978; Gelman and Gallistel 1978; Hughes 1986). This leads Blakemore and Frith to conclude that Piaget was 'simply wrong' (2005: 50) in his views about young children's number concepts. Look back now at Box 1.3, for an example of a girl of 4 years, 3 months who shows clear ability to seriate appropriately.

## What develops?

From the very earliest days, babies demonstrate an interest in pattern ('a fundamental aspect of our intelligence': Fisher 2005: 70), showing, for example, an early ability to distinguish between the faces they see around them. Research evidence suggests that babies of only a few months (Karmiloff-Smith 1994; Siegler and Alibali 2005), or even neonates (Pound 2010), have some sense of cardinality, and can discriminate one object from two, and two from three. Babies as young as five months may also have some understanding of adding and subtracting (Pinker 1997; Karmiloff-Smith 1994; Wynn 1992). Wynn's (1992) conclusion that this means that babies understand simple arithmetic is the subject of much discussion (Siegler *et al.* 2011). A more common conclusion is that they are making use of a perceptual process called subitizing, in which we recognize the quantity of a small set of objects, and apply a number to it without actually counting them.

By the age of 2, children make frequent reference to number words, although this is often idiosyncratic, and may show little reference to the corresponding objects (Meadows 2006). However, just knowing number names is important for later counting and arithmetic. Fuson (cited in Munn 1997) outlines a developmental sequence for counting, suggesting that children initially imitate a string of words when saying a number word sequence, alongside some understanding of appropriate contexts for counting. This is followed by a stage where children begin to count things as an activity in itself, coordinating pointing, naming and object. The third stage is where children integrate counting and cardinality, including considering 'how many?' type questions. This highlights an important point, that number concepts are acquired as part of a process of cultural transmission. Young children both hear and see adults and older children around them using numbers, and are very often inducted into naming and counting by them. Munn sees this sequence of development as essentially Vygotskian:

> First, counting appears on the social plane, between people, with children's activity supported by language and goals. After considerable experience of this joint action, children internalize the cultural practice of counting. It then appears on the psychological plane, at which point children are able to direct their counting according to adult principles.
>
> (Munn 1997: 18)

Gelman and Gallistel suggest that the development of counting marks involves understanding of a number of counting principles, which will, in general, mean that by the age of 3 the majority of children can count up to ten objects reliably (Siegler *et al.* 2011), and, by 5 years old, up to twenty (Meadows 2006). The first three of these principles are 'how to count' ones: the one-to-one principle (you can assign one and only one number word to each object), the stable order principle (numbers are always assigned in the same order) and the cardinal principle (the last number counted represents the value of the set). The fourth principle is the order irrelevance principle, requiring an understanding that the order in which things are counted is irrelevant. The fifth principle, the abstraction principle, means that any set of objects can be counted (Gelman and Gallistel 1978). Their conclusion that young children understand these principles, and therefore know what it means to count, is very different from that of Piaget.

The second type of number knowledge children will need is ordinal knowledge, concerning the relative values or positions of numbers. This knowledge, of which the most basic concepts are 'more' and 'less', develops a little later than cardinality, at around ten months (Sielger and Alibali 2005). Again, as with cardinality, evidence of development seems to be displayed partly as skill in handling larger numbers, and in being able to make sense of questions such as 'Which is more? Four apples or six?' Comparison of numbers closer together in value seems to be much harder, even when children have begun to count (Coltman and Gifford 2008).

### Language in mathematics

The relationship of ordinal knowledge to an understanding of ideas such as more and less highlights a wider issue here that is concerned with language in mathematics. Understanding of mathematics is mediated through language, and children's

---

Box 8.3: Vivian Paley at snack time

Of the eight children at my snack table, six ask for peanut butter and jelly on their crackers, one wants plain peanut butter, and one, plain jelly. My question: What did I make more of, peanut butter and jelly or plain peanut butter? The children stare at me blankly and no one answers.

'What I mean is, did more people ask for peanut butter and jelly or did more want plain peanut butter?' Silence. 'I'll count the children who are eating peanut butter and jelly.' I count to six. 'And only Barney has peanut butter.'

'Because Barney likes peanut butter,' Mollie explains.

'Yes, but why did I make more sandwiches that have both peanut butter and jelly?'

'Because we like peanut butter and jelly,' Frederick responds patiently.

(Paley 1986: 131)

---

understanding of 'mathematical' problems, both contextual ones such as 'how many forks do I need to put on the table if everyone needs to have one?' and abstract number problems such as 'what is 2 and 1 more?' can only be understood if you know what these words mean, and understand that, in a mathematical context, they have a very precise meaning. Words like 'more' and 'less' are used much more ambiguously in everyday speech – we even have an expression 'more or less' to mean 'approximate' or 'roughly equal'! How is a child to reliably know in which context these words are being used? A practitioner working in a London nursery told the children that, as part of their celebration of Chinese New Year that they would be having 'Chinese take away', at which point one boy burst into tears, saying 'Oh no, I can't do adding yet!' (Esther Whalley, personal communication). Box 8.3 provides a good example of this. Reflecting later, Paley says that, had she put her inquiries in dramatic form, the children would have understood. However, it may also be that the children were unclear of the language she used, and even that, for them, the questions had little point.

Fuson and Hall (1983, cited in Anning and Edwards 2006: 116 and abridged here) identify six different contexts in which young children meet number words, each of which serves a slightly different purpose:

1  In the sequence context;
2  In the counting context;
3  In the cardinal context;
4  In the measure context;
5  In the ordinal context;
6  In the non-numerical context.

Young children will need to understand both the context in which the number words are appearing, and the interlocutor's meaning in using them. Gura (1992) suggests that adults need to support the development of children's mathematical understanding and the language needed to go with it, as a simultaneous process:

Rather than seeing the development of mathematical ideas as a two-step process, with action and abstraction preceding language, they should be viewed as an integrated process. The adult role then becomes one of helping the child to develop both the understandings and the corresponding language through shared activity.

(Gura 1992: 93)

This shared activity may be between adults and children but it may also be between the children themselves. Coltman (2006) identifies the value of putting children in the role of instructor, teaching one another how to perform a mathematical operation, or demonstrating to an adult, as a means of encouraging the articulation of methods and strategies.

### 'Everyday' and 'formal' mathematics

Thus far, the focus has been largely on children's acquisition of conceptual understanding in mathematics as part of their daily lives, that is, 'everyday' understanding. Rogoff (2003) and Nunes (1995) both illustrate how competent children of all ages can show themselves to be in contexts which are familiar to them, often using informal, mental strategies. Carr (1992: 4–5, abridged here) describes a framework of the social purposes for which children use mathematics in their everyday lives:

- To indicate comparative status: 'I'm four, you're big';
- To rehearse a culturally significant sequence: in songs, games etc.;
- To recognize culturally significant symbols: in the home, indicating measures (e.g. on heaters), indicating 'how many';
- To solve interesting problems: making and fixing things, checking and timing.

What is not altogether clear is how this everyday expertise translates to the more formal (Vygotsky's 'scientific' understanding) conceptual understanding which is increasingly emphasized as children get older. Both Rogoff (2003) and Nunes (2005), in fact, show how the competence children show in their everyday mathematics can often evaporate in school contexts, where different ways of thinking and different procedures are emphasized. This, in keeping with the general conclusions drawn by, amongst others, Donaldson (1978), has led to a belief in the importance of setting children's mathematical learning in embedded contexts which have meaning for them. Hughes (1986) suggests that children show greater competence in number activities embedded in everyday contexts, and where they are able to handle or see the objects, rather than when tasks are set in more abstract, formal codes.

As a result, many early childhood settings emphasize everyday activities, such as cooking, as contexts for mathematical activities. Whilst this may be valuable in many ways, Gifford (2004a) also points out that many distractions, not the least of which will be an interest in eating the food cooked, may militate against developing the mathematical aspects of the activity. In addition, everyday contexts will tend to make use of very different units: one orange at snack time, and 150g of flour for the cakes (Gifford 2004a). Gifford (2005) further extends her argument to contexts such as role play and scenarios such as shop play which, she suggests, often function better for developing young children's literacy skills, or playing out affective themes, than developing their numeracy. She also cites Walkerdine's argument that 'everyday life' is both culturally bound and often gendered (Walkerdine 1988 cited in Gifford 2005). Whilst not arguing against the value of connecting with children's home lives, Gifford makes the important point that this will require practitioners to have some understanding of what the children's individual home lives are actually like, and also knowledge of the kinds of number experiences children have had.

The kinds of activities Gifford records the 3 and 4 year old children in her study engaging in cognitively with numbers were not always set in everyday contexts. The cognitive activities were noted as (Gifford 2004a: 96: emphasis in original):

- Making connections – pleasure in discovery;
- Predicting – *'cognitive thrill'* of risk-taking and problem-solving;
- Rehearsal – satisfaction in achievement;
- Representation – creativity and satisfaction;
- Spotting mistakes and incongruities – humour in *'number jokes'* and playfulness, both enhancing and protecting self-esteem.

They were each often accompanied by clear indications of positive emotions like excitement, leading her to conclude that these cognitive-emotional aspects combined to form 'hooks' (2004a, 2004b, 2005) which engaged the children. She identifies a number of key mathematics teaching strategies for the early years, including helping children make connections, challenging misconceptions, providing opportunities for representation and discussion, instructing and demonstrating, thinking aloud, providing immersion and apprenticeship opportunities, sharing and scaffolding problem-solving, and giving feedback (Gifford 2004b: 104). This has much in common with Pinker's (1997) view that the passage from 'intuitive' to 'school' mathematics is one which requires attention to, and induction into, specific mathematical concepts.

All of this will have implications for practitioners in supporting the move to formal mathematics. Gifford, for example, stresses the importance of an emphasis on activities related to number, rather than a focus on sorting and matching, which Clements (1984) found had no effect on the number understanding of 4 year olds. Worthington (2007) shows the richness of young children's invented number systems and marks and drawings to represent their mathematical thinking, and suggests the value of these for children in making sense of the formal symbolic language of mathematics. Anning and Edwards (2006) conclude that guiding the participation of young children as mathematical thinkers requires practitioners to have good knowledge of what children already understand about mathematics, to be clear about the mathematics that is available in the experiences they provide and to know how to pace their support for the children's mathematical learning.

## Children's geographical thinking

Young children's geographical thinking is about the way in which they locate themselves, and then others, physically in space, but, just as importantly, it is about their social and cultural location, and their sense of belonging. This will include their view of themselves in relation to others, both their immediate family and community, and the wider world.

## Spatial orientation

Known as primary space use, spatial orientation and knowing the shape of our environment 'represents a domain of early cognitive strength for young children' (Clements 2004: 278). It can can be seen from early babyhood onwards, although developing spatial orientation competencies is a long process, and place learning continues well into the school years (Bullens *et al.* 2010). In charting this development, Siegler and Alibali (2005: 287, adapted here) document three ways in which we represent spatial location:

* egocentric representation: in relation to ourselves, and our own position;
* landmark representation: in relation to landmarks in the environment;
* allocentric representation: by use of an abstract frame of reference, including use of maps, or co-ordinates.

In the earliest stages, babies' understanding of space is 'egocentric', in that it is tied to their own position within it. However, even then there is evidence that, by about three to four months of age, babies have some understanding of concepts of above, below, left and right (Quinn *et al.* 2011). By about six to seven months they have also acquired an understanding of the concept of 'between' (Quinn *et al.* 2011). At about ten months there is evidence that babies are able to generalize these ideas, beyond the immediate situation, indicating the beginnings of an ability to move from the concrete to the abstract (Quinn *et al.* 2011). In so doing, the ability to move – to shuffle, crawl and eventually walk – marks (literally!) a huge step forward. In moving, babies are able to engage all of their senses, and can take more perceptual notice of their surroundings, and the significant landmarks they encounter. The active process of cognitive mapping, that is, the mental maps of the spatial environment we all carry around with us, gathers pace. Karmiloff-Smith (1994: 79) quotes an example from a parent's diary, describing her fourteen-month-old daughter:

> She's become a real explorer. Took her the other day to my friend's house and though she'd never been there before, she went all over the place, opening cupboards – really nosey – and going in and out of different rooms. She'd occasionally pop her head around the door, though, to see if we were still there, and then off she'd go again. Once she got her fingers caught, so then she bawled. Otherwise she seemed really happy.

Exploration, Karmiloff-Smith says, fuels the desire for more exploration. At first, children's mental maps are fragmented, and not linked together, but gradually they connect, to form a much bigger picture, in which landmarks and boundaries are highlighted, and which give each child a growing sense of their place in the world. By eighteen months children are able to use this landmark and boundary information in conjunction to reorient themselves (Bullens *et al.* 2010).

What of the third category of representation, the allocentric? This requires more complex orchestration of spatial information, from multiple perspectives. Siegler and Alibali (2005) suggests that children of one year old can be shown to have a basic allocentric sense, and are able to make use of information in situations where they have no specific landmarks available to help them. By the age of 4 children are able to negotiate their way around a simple maze using a map (Willig 1990), can interpret a range of symbols, such as those for roads, rivers and parks, on a map, and have begun to be able to use co-ordinates, for example on a simple grid (Palmer 1993). A number of factors may be important in the development of this environmental cognition. These include experience (Palmer 1993, for example, cites research pointing to enhanced route learning in children who had the opportunity to walk the route rather than just look at a slide presentation or video), greater familiarity with a wider range of environments and exposure to the particular ideas and social conventions of mapmaking and map-reading (Clements 2004; Haste 1987; Heal and Cook 1998).

In all of this the roles of experience and culture are central. Learning about place is intimately bound up with one's own place in the physical, cultural and social spaces we inhabit. Kearins (cited in Siegler and Alibali 2005) points to the need for highly developed spatial thinking in Australian aboriginal children as an example. Knowing the location of widely spaced wells and creeks may be the difference between life and death for aboriginals who spend much of their time on the move, in desert areas. Comparing the performance of Australian aboriginal children with white Australian children raised in the city, Kearins found that not only did the aboriginal children show superior memory for spatial location, they also used different strategies from the urban children for remembering. The aboriginal children tended to be silent, and concentrated on the look of things, whilst urban children rehearsed the names of the objects. Siegler and Alibali (2005) suggest that both types of strategy fit the children's predominant needs: one for surviving in the bush, the other for verbal efficacy. The wider role of the language we use to represent spatial cognition is a central part of our cultural context. Majid *et al.* (2004) look at a sample of 21 languages across the world, and show that, in those languages representing more industrialized, urban societies (in this sample that includes English, Dutch and Japanese) use of egocentric, relative spatial referencing, for example, 'the boy is to the right of the door' is much more common than allocentric, absolute referencing such as 'the boy is to the north of the door'. The latter type of construction is more often found in the languages of the more rural, small-scale societies in their sample. As Meadows (2006) highlights, the spatial language we all use is associated with whatever that language allows, and this ultimately affects our cognition. More generally, it is also useful to think about ideas on the relationship of language to thought, discussed in Chapter 7.

## Children and maps

Children's symbolic representation of an environment by construction of a 'map' signifies what Meadows (2006) calls 'secondary' spatial use. It is also referred to by geographers as 'graphicacy'. It depends, as she points out, on primary experience, and requires competence in aspects such as mental rotation and perspective taking. Children's early personal recorded maps are generated as part of their graphic representations of the world, and often incorporate marks which may stand for a number of ideas and concepts, and which change meaning as they are being made. Box 8.4 illustrates this well, as Sarah's map moves from being a map of the journey to Sunderland, to a treasure map and back again.

*Box 8.4*: Sarah, aged 3.11, at nursery, sitting with two friends at the graphics table

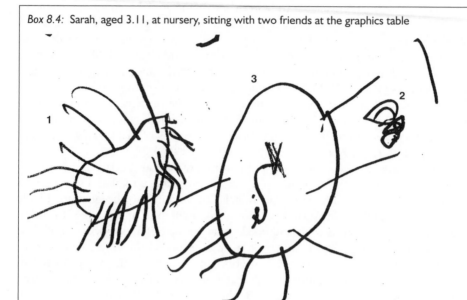

SARAH:    I'm going to make a treasure map (reaches for a sheet of paper and draws a circle – see 1 on drawing). This is the way to Sunderland (starts pulling lines from the edge of the circle out, and continues until lines are radiating out all way round the circle). This is my treasure map too; it's my treasure map and my Sunderland map! These are the traffic lights (adds three circular marks – see 2 on drawing, then another large circle – see 3 on drawing). And then you go over a path to Sunderland, and then you go over another path, then you go over another path, then you go over another path, then another path, then another path, then another path, then another path, then another path (each time she says this she adds another line radiating out from the second circle). And that's the way to Sunderland! (smiles and pats paper).

*In her mark-making Sarah shows a core and radial schema as she represents her understanding not only of maps but also the movement she associates with going to Sunderland. Each radial line added is directly accompanied by her vocalization that 'you go over another path', an example of what Matthews (2003) sees as the child's interest in representing not only figures but movement too. His observations support Athey's research, which found children verbalizing about both objects and action when involved in graphical representation.*

Reproduced with permission of Lisa Guy

The landmarks that children depict will tend to express the personal meanings that these things have for them. In this, they may not differ significantly from adults. Haste (1987) describes research showing adults' representations of their home towns. Like children, they tend to incorporate features that are meaningful for them on a personal level, such as particular buildings and landmarks. Haste (1987) stresses that such representations are not, though, purely idiosyncratic, but serve as shared representations, that the rest of the social group could understand. An account of a project in Reggio Emilia illustrates these ideas well (Piazza and Barozzi 2001). In this project, two groups of 5 and 6 year olds (a group of three girls and a group of three boys) develop their own maps of the city. As Piazza and Barozzi note, the end results look very different, although this difference is more in the kinds of ideas represented than in the form each map takes. The girls' map depicts 'a city full of relationships and life' (2001: 234), and seems to reflect an interest in the places in which they live, go shopping, play and go to school. The boys' map is 'full of functions and connections' (2001: 241), in which topological landmarks like the station, the sewers and the electricity system seem to reflect their interest in an 'urban network'. Piazza and Barozzi also note the different behaviours of the groups in developing their maps. The girls engage in informative and negotiating talk with one another. For the boys, they say, 'dialogue seems to be identified more in the silences, in the shared looks' (2001: 244). Whilst it would be invidious to draw conclusions from one episode, a consideration of gender may nevertheless be important here.

Fisher (2005) outlines a developmental path in children's mapmaking, from simple schematic drawings, where features are generally represented in elevation, that is, seen from the side rather than from above, through the mixing of both plan and elevation in the same map, and finally to a more complex plan view, which includes abstract representations of objects, and in which the relationship of one place to another is set out clearly. As with map-reading, this kind of mapmaking requires considerable skills of abstraction. To use maps, children will need to understand two very important things. First, that a map is a symbol, or representation, and second how the spatial layout of the map corresponds to the physical, real space (Fernyhough 2008). Rogoff suggests that Western 'schooling seems to foster perceptual skills in analysis of two-dimensional patterns and in the use of graphic conventions to represent depth in two dimensions' (2003: 242). As such, this kind of skill may be more valued, and more explicitly developed, in some cultural contexts than others. However, overall, there is evidence to suggest that in this respect, as with many others, young children's competence may have been underestimated in the past (Meadows 2006). Clements (2004) shows 4-year-old children able to learn a route from a map and use simple co-ordinates, for example.

## Children's understanding of history

Much of the accepted thinking about children's historical concepts, often based upon Piaget's conclusions, has, until relatively recently, tended to focus on children's imperfect understanding of temporal relationships, and difficulties in having a sense of the passage of time. Many of the core concepts of history – order, duration, change, continuity, past and present – are, in many respects, abstract and challenging ideas, full understanding of which may only be achieved in late childhood (Lee and Das Gupta 1995). In addition, an understanding of the 'complex interacting concepts' of speed, space and number, necessary for the measurement of time, emerges slowly (Cooper 2002: 9). However, as Hoodless points out, 'a failure to understand the accurate quantification of time is not the same thing as failing to have any concept of time' (1996a: 101), and there is much evidence to suggest that even very young children have a sense of the order of events (Siegler and Alibali 2005).

## Experiencing and understanding order and sequence

From their earliest days babies are developing a sense of past and present. Their recognition of the familiar face of a carer rests upon their ability to connect the past, via memory (I've seen that face before!), to the present. At about three months there is evidence of their ability to detect a repetitive sequence, and by about a year they are able to put in sequence a pair of actions that they have seen only once. By about 20 months, they can reproduce a sequence of three events, indicating that they are able to form a mental representation of first, next and last (Siegler *et al.* 2011). Over time, they develop the ability to do this with an increasing number of events, although there may be an interesting parallel here with the idea of thematic categorization, discussed earlier. Cooper cites research with 4- and 5-year-old children in which, asked to sequence photographs of themselves, they chose what were often seen as idiosyncratic criteria rather than temporal ones, for example, the most recent picture next to a baby one (Cooper 2002). Is this perhaps just a more interesting way of looking at the activity than a conventional timeline, in much the same way that Siegler and Alibali (2005) suggest in their discussion of children's general conceptual development? Fraisse (cited in Hoodless 1996b) seems also to link this with the development of expertise and declarative knowledge, also considered earlier, in his suggestion that, over time, children's increased experience and knowledge facilitates the processing of the perceptual information in front of them.

Up to this point, much of children's understanding of time will be concerned with personal experience. A wider understanding of 'historical' time, and the passage of time, will require some understanding of personal, clock and calendar time (Cooper 2002). This understanding becomes increasingly apparent in children's language, with references to the past, for example, evident in children's talk from about the age of 2 onwards (Lee and Das Gupta 1995). At the age of 2 years 8 months my daughter talked about 'bedtime o'clock', and Hoodless (1996a) records the 3 and 4 year olds she observed spontaneously referring to clock times, as well as words such as 'morning' and 'daytime'.

## Estimating and 'telling' the time

Estimating the duration of events is harder than remembering the order in which they occur. As a consequence, such capability tends to develop later, although, even babies as young as four months can discriminate event durations, particularly those of around one to two seconds. Sensitivity to time increases throughout childhood, reaching adult levels at around 8–10 years. In particular, children show an increased capacity to process longer durations more accurately, partly as a result of the development of attention and working memory capacities (Zélanti and Droit-Volet 2011). Initially, young children's thinking is most evident in their understanding of durations about the past. The future presents a bigger challenge, and it is not until the later primary school years that children can accurately judge how far away future events such as Christmas and birthdays are. (Siegler and Alibali 2005)

Hoodless records the 7-year-old children in her study speculating and hypothesizing about how long an event took. As she suggests, though, duration can seem to vary considerably, depending upon the type of experience. As one child says 'like in assembly,

---

*Box 8.5:* Emma, aged 4.1, at home with her mother, sitting colouring

EMMA:     Mummy, when it's night time how do clocks go faster?

MUM:      What do you mean?

EMMA:     Well, when it's night time and you go to sleep its 7 o'clock and then you fall asleep and it's morning really quickly.

MUM:      Oh, I see. You mean time seems to go quicker when you're asleep.

EMMA:     Yeah … is there a man inside the clocks pushing the … the handles round quicker when you fall to sleep?

MUM:      Do you mean the hands on the clock?

EMMA:     Yeah the hands. It makes it go faster.

MUM:      Well, when you're asleep, the clocks don't really go faster. It just seems to because when you're asleep you're so busy having dreams that time feels like it goes really quickly.

EMMA:     So when I'm busy having dreaming the time goes faster?

MUM:      Well, it's like when Nanny goes on holiday. You always think that a week is a long time but when you're busy with school and things, time seems to go really fast and she's back before you know it!

EMMA:     The clocks don't really go fast then do they? Just at night time when you can't see them. And when Daddy wakes up for work, the clock goes slower because he's stopped dreaming.

MUM:      That's an interesting idea Emma.

*It seems that Emma thinks that the clock, a representational tool of time, is time itself – it is something you can see – and because time appears to pass more quickly when she is asleep, something must happen to make it go faster. In her final comment Emma appears to have grasped the concept that her mother tries to explain to her, but then she reverts back to the idea that clocks do go faster 'at night time when you can't see them' and links this to dreams as a cause, i.e. when you dream time goes faster, when you stop dreaming time goes back to normal.*

Reproduced with permission of KirstyMcLelland

---

it feels like a long time' (Hoodless 1996a: 105). In Box 8.5, Emma, a much younger child, is clearly grappling with this issue of the variability of perceived time.

Hoodless suggest several strategies which children use in order to support their developing concept of historical time. They carry with them implications for practice. She describes the children doing the following (1996a: 109–15, adapted):

- Using sequencing strategies: evident in narratives as well as on other occasions.
- Noticing differences and similarities: involving concepts of classification.
- Referring to location and the process of historical inquiry: an awareness of people living in the same place at different times.
- Imagining and speculating about the past: through exploring possibilities, and thinking about 'what could have happened'.

Whilst Hoodless is looking at professional practice, as we noted in Chapter 7, parents may be particularly significant in this, in talking about past family events, and helping children to 'connect up all those different *nows*', as Fernyhough (2008: 192) poetically puts it.

## Some implications for practice in supporting the development of children's concepts: narrative and play

Narrative, both the children's own narratives and oral and written stories, as well as play, are central to how young children both develop and display their conceptual understanding. The idea that children's own narratives are ways in which they make sense of the world was considered in Chapter 7. These narratives contain many elements of children's conceptual understanding. For example, children's narratives will show their historical and geographical understanding of chronology, sequencing, the use of devices such as the past tense and of the vocabulary of time and place, including that 'borrowed' from story: 'once upon a time', 'a long time ago', 'far, far away' so on. They are rooted in a child's social and cultural experiences.

In the same way, published narratives are sequential, embody the idea of the passage of time, and also often explicitly use the language of time, place and mathematics. Consider, for example, the idea of the passage of time in *Once There Were Giants*, by Martin Waddell, *Kipper's Birthday* by Mick Inkpen, or a traditional tale such as *Sleeping Beauty*, and stories such as *We're Going on a Bear Hunt* by Michael Rosen and Helen Oxenbury for positional vocabulary. Likewise, stories such as *Titch*, by Pat Hutchins, 'provide a venue for reflecting on number in common social purposes' (Carr 1992: 9) such as comparing status, an activity which has great personal meaning for young children. At the same time, whilst they 'are not "true" in the same way that conceptual understanding purports to be true' (Claxton 1999b: 136–7), stories provide opportunities for children to use inferential cues from text and illustration, to hypothesize and to consider alternative pasts, futures, places and identities. Wells suggests that stories provide 'a richer mental model of the world and a vocabulary with which to talk about it' (1987: 151–2). For children, this richer mental model can give them opportunities to explore ideas and situations both within and outside their personal experience, and help them to make sense of these. Such opportunities have clear links with the development of abstract thinking, and may be used, amongst other things, to support children's schemas and nourish their thinking (Nutbrown 2011).

The centrality of play, and a playful approach, as a vehicle for developing young children's thinking and understanding is a theme which runs throughout this book. In Chapter 5 it was considered in relation to understanding other minds, and in Chapter 7 in the context of language. Here, it may be useful to distinguish between spontaneous pretend play, and that which occurs in themed 'role play' areas. I have already noted the importance of children's spontaneous pretence, and of resources which allow children to create 'whatever you want it to be' places (Broadhead 2004: 73). At the same time, many early childhood professionals, theorists and researchers suggest the cognitive value of themed areas (Cooper 2004; Hall and Abbott 1991; Hall and Robinson 2003; Wood and Attfield 2005). Cooper (2002) suggests that pretend play of all kinds allows children to explore the boundaries between imagination and

---

*Box 8.6:* Charlie, 3.3, and Harry, 4.6, are in the garden with Charlie's mother

CHARLIE:    (To Harry) Hey, look, the plane! (grabs mum's arm) Look, mum, plane!

MUM:    Oh, yes, I wonder what nice places they've been to.

CHARLIE:    Been to grandma's!

MUM:    Yeah, they might have been to Oz (Australia).

HARRY:    I'm going to my grandma's for tea.

CHARLIE:    On the plane?

HARRY:    No, in the car.

CHARLIE:    But you can't go in daddy's car cos it's long and the sea.

MUM:    (Laughing) Oh no, Charlie, Harry's grandma doesn't live in Australia.

HARRY:    No, she lives near the park.

CHARLIE:    Oh.

HARRY:    Another one (pointing to another plane) They might be going on holiday.

CHARLIE:    Not all to grandma's then?

HARRY:    No, maybe to Spain.

CHARLIE:    Cos holiday's long?

HARRY:    Yeah, too far to drive.

Reproduced with permission of Joanna Johnson

---

reality, important, for example, in history which is concerned with a past reality which no longer exists, and in geography where places may be geographically distant. At the same time, children have opportunities to explore both their own cultural and social identities, and those of others. Cooper (2004) looks at how this can be supported both indoors and, importantly, outside too. Glauert *et al.* (2007) note that young children's often reduced opportunities for outdoor activity in their home lives may influence the development of their spatial cognition, making it even more important that such opportunities are a strong aspect of early childhood practice.

## Further reflection

Look at Box 8.6, which brings together many of the ideas and concepts considered in this chapter. How might you describe and explain both Charlie's and Harry's conceptual understanding?

## Further reading

Carey (1985)
Cooper (2002)
Gelman and Gallistel (1978)
Gifford (2005)
Gopnik *et al.* (1999: ch. 3)
Goswami (2008: ch. 4)

Hannust and Kikas (2010)
Hoodless (1996a and 1996b)
Karmiloff-Smith (1994: ch. 1 in particular, but see throughout)
Meadows, S. (2006: 67–84, 142–200)
Munn (1997)
Navarra (1955)
Nutbrown (2011)
Palmer (1993)
Siegler and Alibali (2005: ch. 8)
Siegler *et al.* (2011: ch. 7)
Thornton (2002: ch. 5)
White (2002: ch. 2)

# Chapter 9

# Young children's visual thinking

This chapter looks at aspects of the relationship between visual representation and thinking. In other parts of this book young children's visual thinking and representation have been seen to be integral, vital parts of their developing thinking. Bruner's (1966) iconic mode of representation, and Gardner's (1983) category of spatial intelligence, considered in Chapter 2, are underpinning aspects of their theories of cognitive development. For Athey (2007), children's schemas (see Chapter 6) are very often represented in graphic modes. For practitioners in Reggio Emilia, visual representation encompasses some of the 'hundred languages' that children use to represent their experiences and their ideas.

Children's mark-making, drawing, painting and two- and three-dimensional representations are sometimes considered as aspects of 'creative development' in, for example, the English *Early Years Foundation Stage* (DfES 2007). The focus in this chapter is on the ways in which children use visual representation both as a tool for making sense and meaning, and as a way of communicating. Young children's creativity is a very important part of this, but it is also a part of every other aspect of their lives, not confined to 'the arts'. In keeping with this, creativity and creative thinking is looked at in more detail in Chapter 11.

## The relationship of visual representation to young children's thinking

Arnheim (1969) suggests that our perceptual response to the world is at the heart of all of our thinking. In visual representation, the perceptual and the conceptual come together, and 'there is no basic difference in this respect between what happens when a person looks at the world directly and when he sits with his eyes closed and "thinks"' (Arnheim 1969: 13). Hall draws on the work of Adams (2006, cited in Hall 2009) to identify four functions of drawing, all of which relate to thinking. These are drawing as perception, communication, invention and action. Vecchi suggests that each person's thinking and visual representation may be different, but their 'journeys' always combine the perceptive, affective, cognitive and social (Vecchi 2010). For Vygotsky (1978) visual thinking is a vital cognitive process, in which visual images, graphic symbols and models are important tools for mediating cognition.

Children's own visual representations support the creation of personal meaning, and are as vital a narrative form as speech and movement for young children (Anning and Ring 2004; Wright 2010). They are important aspects of the development of metacognitive thinking, and perspective taking (Brooks 2004; Lambert 2007; Reggio Children 1996). Our perception of shape, an interest evident from the earliest days of life, marks the beginnings of concept formation (Arnheim 1969).

Visual representation acts also as an important means of communication for young children, in which they can express ideas, thoughts and theories visually. These may be for themselves, part of what Vygotsky (1978) would regard as thinking aloud, as well as a way of constructing and negotiating meanings in a social context (Cox 2005). In so doing, they are developing shared, collaborative meanings, and creating a forum for reflection, as the 5- and 6-year-old children quoted below demonstrate. The discussion centres on the children's drawings, which illustrate their personal theories of how a fax gets from their centre in Reggio Emilia, to another in Washington DC (Project Zero and Reggio Children 2001: 224):

> Roberta: *See? In Alioscia's drawing you can see how a fax gets to America. It goes inside a pipe, so it doesn't get lost on the way.*
> Alioscia: *It's a long pipe that goes around the things that it runs into on the trip.*
> Matteo: *But you can't tell where it starts and where it goes to. You can't tell which way it goes.*
> Alessandra: *You can tell in Roberta's drawing. You can see that the fax goes over the sea. America is on the other side of the world, on the other side of the ocean.*
> Roberta: *In Lucia's drawing you can tell that America is on the other side of the world – it's real far away.*

As Perkins suggests, this kind of reflection can also be on 'public' works of art, and may be especially supportive in the development of some underpinning thinking dispositions, including personal engagement and connection making. He suggests that looking at art 'recruits many kinds and styles of cognition – visual processing, analytical thinking, posing questions, testing hypotheses, verbal reasoning and more' (1994: 5).

## Views on the development of visual representation

At a physiological level, much is known about the development of the visual system and visual perception (Pinker 1997; Siegler *et al.* 2011). Pinker (1997) emphasizes mental imagery as an important aspect of cognition, and Geake outlines a range of fMRI studies which, he believes, provide 'neuroscientific support for the common maxim in art education that drawing is thinking' (2009: 173).

In developing their thinking, babies and very young children use movement to explore their world, and show interest in shape, form, movement and all types of patterning. Matthews (2003) suggests that young children develop their mark-making skills initially using whatever comes to hand, for example food and drink, as a natural consequence of their physical movement. He identifies three types of movement that are particularly important for all later mark-making, whether it is with porridge or a pencil: vertical arcs (downward swiping), horizontal arcs (wiping or fanning – see Box 9.1), and push-pull (reaching and grasping) movements. These, he suggests, develop early in life, and make their appearance in the order shown here, from about two weeks old to the fourth month (Matthews 2003). What feeds this development is interaction with others, and this supports babies in developing strategies for exploring

*Box 9.1:* Isabella, aged 2.7, at home

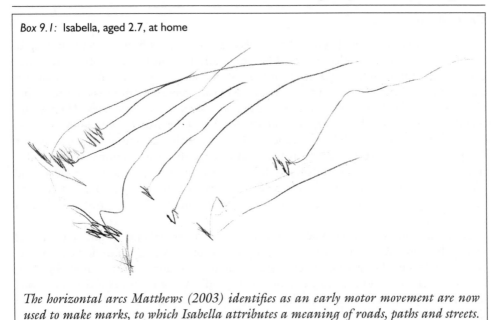

*The horizontal arcs Matthews (2003) identifies as an early motor movement are now used to make marks, to which Isabella attributes a meaning of roads, paths and streets.*

and investigating their world. An understanding that these exploratory movements with whatever comes to hand cause a mark to be made is, for Matthews, 'the most basic principle of drawing' (2003: 54).

## Models of developmental stages in visual representation

One influential account of how children's visual representation develops comes from the work of Piaget (1952). He, in turn, drew on the work of Luquet (Jolley 2009). Put briefly, Piaget's model identifies a first, meaningless (for Piaget) scribbling stage. This is followed by a stage of 'fortuitous realism', in which there is no initial intention to represent an object, but children fortuitously see a likeness to something in the marks that they make. Kellogg (1969) concurs with Piaget here, suggesting that such marks are more to do with movement than representation. In Piaget's third stage, 'intellectual realism', children represent what they know, or intellectually understand, about an object or scene, rather than what they actually see in front of them. For example, children know that people have two eyes, and will draw both of these on a figure, even when that figure is being drawn from a side view. The final stage of visual realism reverses this, and children then draw what they see even if it conflicts with what they know.

Researchers after Piaget further developed this idea of stages. Lowenfeld and Brittain (1982) outline six, whilst Kellogg (1969) attempts to describe universal stages of drawing, with children's representational ability developing as a result of increased skill. Lambert (2005) identifies another stream of work, which again focuses on representation, but emphasizes visual representation as a conscious motivation to reinterpret cognitive perceptions of the world in graphic form. As Anning and Ring (2004) point out, the focus is on cognition in these approaches, with less emphasis being placed on the relationship of affective, aesthetic and psycho-motor aspects to children's visual thinking.

## Chris Athey

The work of Chris Athey (2007), first looked at in Chapter 6, is particularly helpful in describing young children's visual representation. Whilst she is concerned with exploring commonalities and continuities in all aspects of children's spontaneous thought and behaviour, the evidence from their visual representations is integral to her conclusions. Like Piaget, she outlines a series of developmental sequences of behaviour. She differs from him, however, in emphasizing that these are not sequential steps on a path to visual realism. Athey classifies children's activity as a range of schemas (see Chapter 6), which are expressed in four ways: through motor actions; symbolically; functional dependency relationships (children showing understanding of cause and effect); and thought. Whilst these coexist, each is also more closely associated with particular ages. In Athey's research symbolic representations were present in largest numbers at age 4.1.

Athey distinguishes the graphic representations she recorded into 24 different types of mark, which are then further subdivided into two groups of straight lines and curves. She also subdivides marks into a number of space orders, for example the proximity between marks, or representation of 'in front of' or 'behind'. Athey identifies a developmental sequence in young children's drawings, using these three groups of lines, curves and space orders. She stresses that the ages at which schemas appear cannot be generalized, because experience and context will influence this. In documenting a continuum for the development of lines, Athey suggests:

> Given the opportunity, young children draw *lines*, make *lines* with and objects that can be aligned and run in *linear directions*. They construct *circular enclosures* and run in *circular directions*. They construct and draw *zig-zag configurations* and they run in *zig-zag directions*.
>
> (2007: 77; emphasis in original)

A developmental sequence for curves begins with circular scribble, followed by circular enclosure, or core and radial, ovals, semi-circles (closed and open), helix, spirals, concentric circles and multiple loops (Athey 2007). Box 8.6 in Chapter 8 illustrates one girl's use of a core and radial schema.

## Revising stage theories

The influential models of developmental stages outlined by Piaget (1952) and Lowenfeld and Brittain (1982) have, in recent years, been subject to examination and revision. Emphasis on a goal of visual realism may represent a deficit view of young children's drawing (Anning and Ring 2004), and for Cox (2005) 'visual realism' does not represent a more advanced form of thinking than 'intellectual realism', rather it is a different form of depiction, serving different purposes. Duffy (1998) believes that young children's visual representations are much more purposeful and less a matter of unintentional scribbling than either Piaget (1952) or Kellogg (1969) would suggest. She cites young children's awareness of composition, shown, for example, in the careful, deliberate ways in which they place new marks with reference to existing ones.

A strong critic of Piaget's model is Matthews, who suggests that the reason that children do not produce visually realistic pictures is not because they cannot do so, but more because of their desire to represent what, for them, is 'the truth about the structure and characteristics of the object' (Matthews 2003: 97). He includes examples of young children depicting objects and scenes in visually realistic ways at a much younger age than Piaget proposes, and suggests that children do not pass neatly from one stage to another, but develop along a continuum which draws on information from 'different perceptual channels, including touch and movement and also involving language and concepts' (2003: 97). For Arnheim (1969), like Matthews, this perceptual process is a very active one, a matter of both thinking and seeing. As the artist Paul Klee says: 'art does not reproduce what can be seen: it makes things visible' (Marnat 1974), an idea echoed in the collaborative project *Making Learning Visible* (Project Zero and Reggio Children 2001).

As with other aspects of Piagetian theory, criticism of Piaget's model has also focused on the cultural specificity of his ideas about children's visual representation. Lambert (2005) highlights how such stage theories tend to float free of context, downplaying children's cultural and social experience as important in influencing their visual representations. Siegal *et al.* (2004) illustrate key differences between depictions of the Earth amongst young children in Australia and England, attributable, they suggest, to differences in exposure to ideas about geography and astronomy between the two countries. Such data suggest the potential danger of using children's drawings as indicators of their intellectual development.

A useful example of this is the commonly used 'draw a person' test, developed by Goodenough and later revised by Harris (Kellogg 1969). In this test, children are asked to draw the very best picture that they can of a man or woman. The result is scored, with points earned for inclusion of basic elements and features, for example, arms and legs attached to trunk, or inclusion of eyebrows. This score is then regarded as indicative of cognitive maturity. Like all so-called intelligence tests (see Chapter 6), the Goodenough test is standardized on a particular population (in this case North American children), and thus inapplicable to all populations indiscriminately. Just as fundamentally, however, both Matthews (2003) and Kellogg (1969) suggest that children do not learn to draw as a result of observation from life, but as a result of their own mark-making efforts, a phenomenon not acknowledged in such a test, which relies on perceptual information being used to support conceptual understanding. What children choose to include in their picture of a man or woman may reflect their interest at that time, rather than a particular level of ability. Box 9.2 shows the response of one girl to the 'draw a person' test at the age of 3.7. Whilst it would not score very highly on this test, it is, nevertheless, a very sophisticated response, which shows just what Charlotte was noticing about people at that time.

### Mark-making and literacy

The relationship of young children's developing literacy to their visual representation, in particular their mark-making, is complex and disputed. Brooks points out that for young children drawing may, at least initially, be a much more powerful tool, in that 'it is immediately holistic and interactive in ways that writing is not' (2004: 49). Anning and Ring warn of the danger of positioning drawing as somehow less valuable than writing, and as 'only a "temporary" holding form of symbolic representation leading to mastery of the "higher level" ability to form letters and numbers' (2004: 118).

Box 9.2: Charlotte, aged 3.7, at home, asked to 'draw a person'

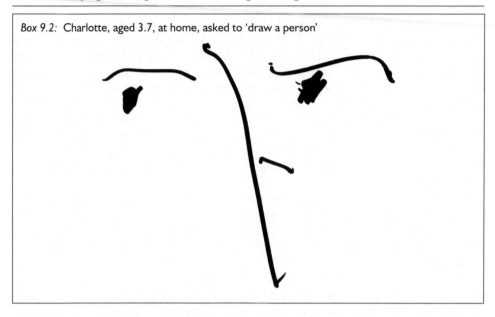

Children's early mark-making is, however, often seen as a precursor to later literacy learning (Matthews 2003), and Wright (2010) suggests that the act of representing thought and action through drawing is beneficial for children's later understanding of literacy and numeracy. However, McBride-Chang *et al.* (2011) suggest that the relationship may, in some ways at least, be in the opposite direction. They found that young children's experiences of literacy had an impact on their spatial skills development. Significantly, this was affected by the writing systems of the children concerned, with the Chinese and Korean children in their study displaying more enhanced visual skill development than those from Spain and Israel. They speculate that the 'denser' visual nature of Chinese and Korean orthographies may force young children to focus more on their visual features, hence facilitating their visual skills. As in other aspects of children's cognition, it may be that cultural context impacts upon development in sometimes very different ways.

Notwithstanding the validity of Anning and Ring's (2004) warning, studying young children's representations which include letter and letter-like shapes can be useful for supporting insights into children's understanding of the language sign system. Box 9.3 shows the combination of image and letterforms in Charlotte's drawing. It reveals much about this 4-year-old girl's understanding, including directionality, the use of a horizontal axis and space. The repeated use of 'H' and 'P' are her early attempts at writing the word 'happy'.

## What (and how) do children represent?

The answer to this question is, of course, everything, but, at an individual level, it will be personal to them (Duffy 1998), and reflect what matters to them (Arnheim 1969; Cox 2005; Matthews 2003). Anning and Ring demonstrate how strongly this is influenced by their experiences, both at home and in early childhood settings. They suggest three particular aspects of this cultural influence. First, expectations of what

Box 9.3:  Charlotte, aged 4.7, spontaneous mark-making at home

it means to be male and female, modelled by members of their communities; second, the impact of the media on the children's choices of what and how to represent; and third, cultural expectations of friendship (Anning and Ring 2004). They document how, at home, the drawing (and play) themes of the girls in their study often revolved around domestic doll play, whilst the boys often engaged in dynamic themes involving action, movement and speed. When they then went to nursery and school, the girls often found more continuity, with their depiction of figures in their drawings being encouraged more than the boys' action representations. This may have important consequences for boys' thinking and understanding, if the themes which are significant for them are not amongst those that seem to be validated by the adults around them.

Young children's representations, then, will include objects, people and scenes, but also ideas such as movement and action (Anning and Ring 2004; Athey 2007). Duffy (1998: 6) identifies four categories, and suggests that children's representations may include one, or a combination, of them:

- configurative aspects – to do with space,
- dynamic aspects – to do with action,
- specific viewpoints – drawn from a particular viewpoint,
- object specific – to do with the main features of an object.

Box 8.6, in Chapter 8, and Box 9.4 both illustrate aspects of this combination. Box 9.4 features both configurative and dynamic aspects, and also illustrates young children's integration of different ways of representing their experience, and the importance of a narrative framework. Here, Nathan is drawing his story, whilst relating it in words. Interestingly, he also refers to his drawing as 'writing' here.

This practice of talking whilst engaged in visual representation may take a number of forms, with different potential benefits. Children's 'thinking aloud' as they draw and paint may support them in reasoning in more abstract, sophisticated ways (Lambert 2005). For Wright (2010), the symbiotic relationship of children's visual and oral narratives, often accompanied by action as embodied narrative, is mutually informing and enriching, and evidence of thinking in action. Talk and drawing represent multi-modal, mutually transformative ways of making meaning, with that meaning often being fluid, represented in changes as the drawing progresses (Cox 2005). Social talk, either *about* the activity, or occurring *during* the activity, may not only be a part of this transformative process, as children take ideas and inspiration from one another, it may also provide adults with valuable insights into children's thinking about many aspects of their lives (Coates and Coates 2006).

The examples illustrated so far have focused on mark-making and drawing, but the many other ways of representing their worlds visually are equally important, both by themselves, but also in multi-modal ways, combining drawing, painting, found materials, model making and construction. Children's visual representations in paint support exploration of light and colour, their use of textiles and other materials give them opportunities to explore texture, touch and feel. Increasingly, the value of children using video cameras, still cameras and computers to play with their thoughts is recognized: 'the computer produces phenomena that put their systems of perceiving the world, of gathering information and constructing thought and behavior, "off-balance"' (Reggio Children 1996: 102). Box 9.5 shows one boy's use of the interactive whiteboard to represent his ideas.

Children's three-dimensional representations give them opportunities to develop representations in ways unavailable to them in two dimensions (Duffy 1998). Gura suggests that blockplay, for example, 'can be used to say certain kinds of things more powerfully than words or words alone can say' (1992: 27). Models and constructions have insides, outsides, tops, bottoms, sides, fronts and backs. They can often be walked around, looked at from different viewpoints, and perhaps entered. They may also more readily lend themselves to collaborative activity. Matthews (2003) stresses the value of supporting children in using materials in their three-dimensional representations in novel, multi-modal ways, which 'transgress' their functional categories. He uses the example of his son who, having looked at a picture in a book of a rocket taking off with flames shooting from its combustion chamber, then builds a three-dimensional representation of the flames out of blocks, laying them on top of the open book. Such a view has much in common with both Trawick-Smith's (1998) emphasis on the use of non-representational materials in the development of metaplay, and Hutt *et al.*'s (1989) views on the cognitive value of supporting children's own associations between materials.

Look back now at the observation recorded in Further Reflection 2 in Chapter 5. This episode of blockplay features the 'heaping' (Matthews 2003: 118) of objects in three-dimensional representation, often the first way in which children classify objects (Athey 2007).

*Box 9.4:* Nathan, aged 4.6, in the nursery

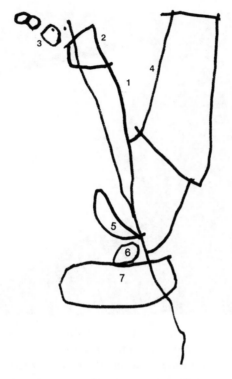

Nathan has just dictated a story to his teacher, when he says:

Now I'm going to write a story. (He starts with the circular shapes at 3)
Once upon a time and he went down the path a long, long (at this point he trails the pen down the page at 1).
Then he crossed the path (drawing the loop at 2).
Then he walked up the steps (holding his pen over 3, then drawing the box shape at 4). That's him, walking around.
(He draws the smaller enclosures at 5, 6 and 7 without commenting, then the sequence of dots at 3.) Then he went up the lane. Then he took 2 steps, 4 steps, 6 steps.

Nathan grins hugely, put his pen down and goes off to play with Ethan.

*Nathan is attributing representational meaning to his marks, although they do not yet resemble the meaning he is attributing to them. For Athey (2007), thinking is what happens when considering the changes between two states. In mature thinking, this happens symbolically without the two end states necessarily being available to the thinker, whilst children play out these changes in state by manipulating the concrete objects. Nathan's verbalization of changes in states can be seen as the precursor to symbolic thinking.*

Reproduced with permission of John Griffiths

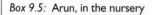

Box 9.5: Arun, in the nursery

Arun rarely uses traditional media to represent. He was keen to access the smartboard and subsequently spent some time depicting his favourite Superhero Spiderman, during his adventures. The smartboard afforded Arun with an avenue for his drawing that was acceptable to, and valid for, him. Through physical, direct experience with the smartboard, Arun's creativity was supported as his body senses gathered 'evidence' (Prentice 1994: 127), and allowed him to express his ideas and make 'powerful intelligent hypotheses' (Matthews 2003: 101).

Reproduced with permission of Lynn Bartlett

## Some implications for practice in developing children's visual thinking

- The importance of experience: Athey (2007) and Brooks (2004) emphasize the value of experience gained through visits in feeding young children's thinking, and in providing opportunities for visual representation.
- Children need time, to interact with materials, with adults, and with each other (Escobedo 1999), in order to develop their visual thinking and representation.
- It may be through their observations of shapes in their own representations that children start to notice shapes in the environment, not, as is generally thought, the other way around (Matthews 2003).
- Matthews suggests that 'premature instruction in drawing from observation damages development' (2003: 109), and that 'sometimes, interaction means doing *nothing*' (2003: 110; emphasis in original).

- Playful, open-ended interactions with children as they develop their visual narratives in verbal, graphic and embodied ways supports both children's meaning making and adults' understanding (Wright 2010).
- There is value for children in interactions with other drawing 'users', more experienced than themselves, who can comment on the processes children are using, developing the vocabulary of mark-making. Anning and Ring (2004) suggest the value of adults drawing alongside children, Matthews (2003) stresses the need for adults to go beyond the 'very nice' response to a child's drawing, and to comment in ways which not only communicate an interest in what a child has done, but also provide a vocabulary for talking about it.
- It is valuable to support the development of children's personal reflections, both on their own representations (Brooks 2004) and on those of others (Project Zero and Reggio Children 2001). Brooks positions this within a Vygotskian framework, suggesting that children's representations operate at both an interpersonal level, where 'drawing is the mediator for an interpersonal dialogic exchange' (Brooks 2004: 47) and an intrapersonal level, where drawing can help children integrate new knowledge with previous ideas and experiences, and where discussion focuses on the construction of representation.

## Further reflection

1  Do you think that there is a universal sequence in the development of drawing?
2  How, for you, does culture influence young children's visual thinking?
3  What is the role of adults in supporting young children's visual thinking?

## Further reading

Athey (2007)
Brooks (2004)
Cox (2005)
Duffy (1998)
Gardner (1983, 1993)
Lambert (2005)
Matthews (2003)
Meadows (2006: 139–49)
Wright (2010)

# Chapter 10

# Young children's thinking in music

*Victoria Rowe*

The social roles of music are richly varied: a young child may encounter live music at home – in lullabies, games, story-telling, ceremonies and dancing – and recorded music through an ever-increasing range of technology. Music can create or regulate mood, encourage group identity and aid memory and communication (Pound and Harrison 2003). For all of these reasons, early pioneers in the education of young children recognized music's potential, not least as a way of easing the transition between home and nursery class. Comenius, Rousseau, Pestalozzi, Froebel and Montessori all advocated the use of musical activities (Greata 2006) and group music continues to be an integral part of the day in most early years settings.

Musical activity in early years settings may often be adult-led, with welcome songs, counting and movement games all providing opportunities for group and individual involvement. However there are other occasions on which children may explore their own original musical ideas: observation of these can reveal evidence of musical creative thinking, ranging from playful vocal experimentation with nonsense sounds and chants to exploration of percussion and other instruments, and to attempts to represent musical sounds with invented notation. This chapter begins with an account of some authors' attempts to model and classify musical development and cognition. Having outlined the kinds of musical activity and behaviour that may be observed and studied, two research methods are discussed which seem to show evidence of children's musical thinking: (1) the analysis and discussion of children's invented notations and (2) observation in which the researcher can take a participant role.

## The development of musical thought

Piaget's central tenet (see Chapter 2) is that the child passes through a process of assimilation, accommodation and equilibration as his or her cognitive development proceeds towards more logical thinking. While this theory has attracted criticism from more recent theorists such as Gardner (1979), it can still be discerned in the structure of educational curricula.

Several writers have sought to discover parallels between phases of child development and musical development. Hargreaves discusses a possible musical aspect of Piaget's 'pre-operational' stage. He describes the work of Pflederer and Sechrest (1968, cited in Hargreaves 1986) in which children were given a small group of 'musical conservation' tasks: tests of repeated melodies with alterations that, for example, preserve the melody but double or halve the note values. They discovered that children aged 5 were not able to understand melodic conservation, whereas children aged 8 could understand it, as with Piaget's number and quantity conservation tests. However, as Hargreaves notes, these tests differed substantially from those of Piaget in that the child was not able to watch the transformation taking place, since music takes place across time. Furthermore, informal musical experiences in naturalistic settings may reveal a richer picture of a child's musical thinking than is possible in laboratory-style testing.

Swanwick and Tillman (1986) attempted to construct a model of musical development based on a progression through stages, as in Piaget's approach. However they added a Vygotskian perspective by taking into account the more social aspects of children's interaction with peers and with their musical culture. This 'Spiral of Musical Development' was based on their analysis of compositions of children aged 3–15. They propose four different focuses of attention as children develop musical thinking: Materials, expression, form and value. On the 'Materials' level, the child aged 0–4 is typically seen as exploring the material, physical attributes and sensory, sonic effects of the instrument (or voice), playing with the possibilities of music and mastering the basic technique of sound production. In later stages the focus moves through imitation and imaginative play to metacognition. While providing an account of necessary ingredients for musical development, this model raises some questions about the stage structure: some children might move through the various levels much faster than others; some might barely develop at all, depending on interest, encouragement and opportunity. And, in suggesting that children's compositions begin to show imitation in ages 4–9 and imaginative play in 10–15, Swanwick and Tillman (1986) may be underestimating the creative powers of younger children.

The Gordon Institute for Music Learning (www.giml.org) categorizes musical growth as a series of developments along three overlapping pathways of what Gordon calls 'preparatory audiation': the ability to 'think' music in the mind with understanding, which provides the foundations of musicianship. The first is 'Acculturation' in which children move from simple absorption of musical sounds, through random response to purposeful response; second is 'Imitation' during which children notice that their movements and sounds do not match those of people round them and then finally 'break the code' as they begin to imitate sounds more precisely; and third, 'Assimilation' in which children realize the need for coordination and can work to develop it. The Gordon Institute likens this process to that of language acquisition: the violin teaching method of Suzuki (1969) is founded on similar precepts.

Cognitive and social developments, however, are not the whole story where music is concerned. Gardner (1979), in a critique of Piaget, pointed out that the single goal of logical-rational thinking makes no allowance for other kinds of mature cognition, such as the thought processes of artists, musicians, athletes, writers, or for the processes of intuition or creativity. Gardner suggests that children are able to acquire and use the symbols and systems necessary to become participants in the artistic process before reaching Piaget's levels of concrete and formal operations.

Despite the wide variation in approaches of these authors, it is clear that in all of them music making in the early years is characterized by experimentation and play with sounds and a focus on process rather than on product, just as children explore all the other materials in their worlds.

## Children's representations of music

In the years since the UNICEF convention on the Rights of the Child (United Nations 1989) there has been a change in the way children are viewed in terms of their rights, capabilities and the importance of play. Children's thinking is now valued in its own right for its imaginative potential, rather than being seen as an inferior or defective precursor to adult thinking (Wright 2010). Wright goes on to explain that artefacts such as drawings can be used as a 'naturalistic way to witness children's creative meaning making, because the source of the content emerges from the child's own thoughts, feelings and imagination'(2010: 26).

In the musical field, Barrett, in several studies (e.g. 1997, 2001, 2005) has investigated children's representations of their musical compositions. While emphasizing (along with Bamberger 2005; Patterson 2009) that too early a focus on the rigours of traditional musical notation might deprive children of the freedom of improvisation and making their own pathways in music, Barrett views the process of inventing representations of music as showing us evidence of the construction of knowledge (see Bruner 1996, cited in Barrett 2005), an externalization of children's musical thinking. In Barrett's 1997 study, children aged between 4 and 6 in a nursery classroom were given free access to an 'instrument corner' where the researcher initially modelled ways of making the instruments play: demonstrating the elements of dynamics, pitch, duration and timbre, but avoiding playing in specific metres or phrase lengths. After time to explore, children were asked to make up a pattern of sounds. They were then asked to find a way of writing down their pattern so that they could remember it (Barrett 1997).

Barrett (2001) categorized the children's drawings in different ways, but she has since stressed that there is not necessarily a progression from one stage to the next: sometimes children make different choices about their representations depending on the type of piece they want to notate. Her categories are summarized below:

- Exploration: little discernible connection between the sounds and the drawing
- Representation of instrument: the instrument is simply drawn
- Representation of instrument with modification: a series of drawings which may focus on a particular feature of the composition, for example varying the size of the pictured instruments to represent different dynamics or durations
- Representation of gesture: a reflection on paper of the movements used to play the composition – perhaps using long lines for long sounds or sweeping movements and small dots for short ones
- Symbolic representation: a series of symbols – dots, lines, circles, etc., in which each symbol corresponds to one sound in the composition. This type of notation is sometimes modified with the use of colours or different sized symbols to reflect musical features such as dynamics.

Other symbolic possibilities noted by researchers include the use of numbers and other mathematical signs, using differently coloured beads or bricks to represent the pattern, written instructions, using the pitch letters that are often marked on the keys of tuned percussion and, if the tune has words, a pictorial representation of the story (Young and Glover 1998).

Barrett talked informally with the children while they were drawing and also asked them to play their compositions again from the drawing they had done. In her case study of 5-year-old Max (Barrett 2001), she found that he used several different strategies. One picture he drew was of three differently sized drum sticks, which he explained as follows:

> So I do one loud tap because that's big, and I do a middle-sized tap, that's the smallest so I do a tiny little tap [Max points to the three symbols in descending order on the page].
>
> (Barrett 2001: 38)

Barrett categorizes this as Representation of Instrument with Modification, with changes in size reflecting the different dynamic levels. On another occasion, however, Max chose first to 'translate' his composition into an onomatopoeic vocalization, and then to notate this with a separate sign for each vocal sound – bold lines for 'boom' and dots for 'scratch'. This was an example of Symbolic Representation: a systematic invented notation which he could explain and reproduce. On yet another occasion, Max drew a picture of the characters in 'Hey Diddle Diddle', using different parts of the page for the two sections of the song, high and low. Max's verbal accounts suggested that he was 'building a repertoire of strategies by which he records his musical experience and meaning-making' (Barrett 2001: 42). Barrett compares this diversity of approaches with similar findings in the visual arts in which children create a variety of visual symbols and combine these freely over time (see also Chapter 9).

The children in Barrett's studies were responding to a task given to them by an adult. Each child interpreted the task in their own individual way, but there was nevertheless an expectation that some kind of 'product', some marks on a page or some kind of musical construction, would result, and that the researchers would then be able to form some kind of interpretation of these products, with the children's help. Young (1995) advocates using a different approach to discover the musical creative process. The adult 'playfully participates with the child', interacting in musical exchanges that involve not just the aural sense, but also movement and facial expressions: the participants are actively making and receiving the musical ideas and talk is kept to the minimum. This is live music-making – a musical conversation that is not expected to be recorded for posterity. While such interchanges can obviously be video-recorded for later analysis, the interaction is the key event. The adult enters into the child's musical world as an equal partner.

## Young children making music

Very young children may have had little experience of playing musical instruments. Vocally, however, they have acquired more expertise, typically beginning with preverbal 'babbling' in the first few months of life, moving on to playing with nonsense syllables and chants and gradually joining in songs with family and friends. The level of control they have over their voices is thus considerably ahead of the fine motor skills that may be needed to play an instrument. Pound and Harrison (2003) suggest that, because of their mastery of the vocal medium, children's made-up songs can show more evidence of musical awareness than their instrumental compositions which can sound rudimentary by comparison. Box 10.1 is a description of a vocal improvisation by a 3 year old. In this extract, Roxana is sometimes talking to herself, and sometimes to me, the researcher behind the camera, but I take no active part in the music-making. In contrast, in Box 10.2, I take a more active role in Antony's improvisation.

---

*Box 10.1  Roxana, aged 3, at the clay table in the children's centre*

Roxana has added some water to the clay and made it wet and sticky. She seems to enjoy the feeling of rubbing her hands in the wet clay. Suddenly she stops: 'Oh look!' and shows me her hands which are covered in brown sticky clay. 'Chocolate. Chocolate cake. That is my chocolate cake. Cake.' She rubs her hands in the clay, faster and faster, making a rising pitched squeaking noise, rather like a whistling kettle. 'I'll do a cake.' She chants to herself:

          cake ↓        cake ↓

'Make a ↑       in a ↑      in a ↓

                       cake'

and repeats this four times. Her voice rises and falls in the same places each time and the rhythm is identical on each repetition – this chanting is very close to a song.

*This is an example of musical invention arising out of an activity. Many musical moments like this can occur as children play with words and sounds. The rhythm of Roxana's song accompanies her hand movements in the sticky clay, much in the manner of traditional work-songs. The shape of the phrase, with its falling ending, is similar to nursery songs she may know: Pound and Harrison (2003) describe a similar awareness of basic musical structure in a boy aged 4.*

---

*Box 10.2: Antony, aged 4, at the keyboard in the children's centre*

Antony is playing alone on a large portable keyboard. He has invented a pattern which involves hopping his finger from the lowest up to the highest notes of the keyboard and then sliding his hand down the keys to the bottom in order to start again. He seems to be dreaming as he repeats this pattern over and over again, at least 30 times, for around five minutes. After a while I decide to see what happens if I join in. I play a high trill and he is startled: 'No!' he says, putting out his hand to stop me with a grin. Immediately after this he drums rapidly on the lowest keys with his two hands. I try another trill and he again responds with fast notes. His playing changes to a more dramatic chordal style and I continue to play small contributions. Eventually Antony returns to his original pattern but with more animation and variety together with some excited vocalizations.

*In this exchange, Antony has a plan in mind, despite his trance-like demeanour. Stepping quite a long way outside the 'neutral observer' role, and taking a more therapeutic view, I decide that he is ready to move on. When I disturb Antony's pattern, he reacts strongly, albeit with a smile. His next action is to try to imitate my fast playing using his two hands to do his own versions of trills and we have several musical exchanges of ideas. When he returns to his original pattern he seems more alert and active, as though the exchanges have changed the mood.*

On some occasions it is possible to observe children interacting together musically. While Benjamin and Malik (Box 10.3) are apparently approaching their keyboard improvisations with different agendas, there are some moments when their minds meet and there is synchronicity in their musical ideas, accompanied by great delight.

---

*Box 10.3:* Benjamin and Malik, aged 4, at the keyboard in the children's centre

Benjamin and Malik are playing on a large portable keyboard. Their activity is being recorded on a camcorder.

Benjamin plays individual notes using alternate hands. The pattern consists of first a low left-hand note, followed by a leap to a higher right-hand note. Then the left hand moves up next to the right hand and the pattern is repeated. The pattern is thus a rising sequence, characterized by alternately large and small musical intervals. Malik is dreaming, drooping with his chin on the keyboard. Benjamin continues to pick out his notes, smiling and watching carefully as he replicates the note pattern. Malik notices the camera and starts playing in a lively 'bangy' style. Benjamin picks up on the style and they play together with enjoyment for several beats. Benjamin returns to his original idea, while Malik looks hard at the camera and slides his chair to make sure he is in shot. Malik makes a screwed-up face, perhaps imitating a pop star and plays in a lively style again. Benjamin continues with his single notes for a few beats and then joins Malik's pop-style, looking at him and smiling.

Benjamin picks out one black note and firmly says 'This one', repeating it several times. He plays other repeated notes. Malik tries some clusters and again Benjamin picks up Malik's idea and plays some of his own. Malik's head has drooped down to the keyboard again. Benjamin continues to pick out single notes and clusters with alternate hands. Malik again plays in a lively random way, wiggling his shoulders, but Benjamin tries to stop him, putting his hand in the way. Malik eyes the camera again. Benjamin presses a rhythm button: Malik tries to turn it off. Benjamin tries a different button and they find a new sound they both like, and play together, smiling. Benjamin is still not satisfied however and leans across to control the volume button: 'Too loud'. Malik comments: 'I can't hear' and tries to turn it back up, but Benjamin leans in front, takes his hand away, and says 'No, like that', looking round at Malik. Benjamin holds Malik's hand tightly to stop him changing the volume and Malik repeats, 'I can't hear it'. Then Benjamin discovers a pre-programmed rhythm that they both like and they both play single notes along with this, smiling at each other.

*In this extract, Benjamin seems to have discovered a pattern that he enjoys. He returns to it, or to something very like it, at least four times. He is also able to respond to Malik's ideas and to enjoy improvising with him, perhaps pretending to be pop stars. However Benjamin has his own plan for the music and he tries to convey this to Malik with his instructions: 'This one', 'Too loud' and even by physically obstructing or preventing him from playing: 'No, like that'. This interaction may be partly about control, but it also shows the discovery and retention of a musical idea despite interruptions. Malik's part in this exchange appears to be more related to role-play – being a pop star for the camera – than about the musical content: his wish for the music to be louder is probably related to the role play.*

Interactions between children, such as the one in Box 10.3, can be fleeting and easily missed in a busy nursery setting. Young (1995) points out that music only really *becomes* music through active listening, and she advocates that practitioners devote as much time to interacting with children in music as they do in mark-making or number activities. She adopts an ethnomusicological approach in which the adult listener becomes a participant in the child's musical experience, contributing either musically or with other physical responses in order to scaffold the child's musical thinking. In order to do this, adults may need to revise their ideas of what constitutes 'music', recognizing 'the qualities of spontaneous and playful impulse, of that creative space between certainty and chaos' (1995: 57).

Young noted (2003) that children engaged with xylophones for the shortest time when they played alone, for longer when playing with an unfamiliar, trained musician and for longest with a familiar adult with no formal training. This seems to suggest that the interpersonal element is an important part of the young child's musical scaffolding. Young proposes that a child's musical creativity derives partly from the context of play – moving with and playing with the instrument, discovering what can be done with it and then interacting socially to share and develop these discoveries with a reciprocating adult. She set up a procedure protocol and listed appropriate types of response for her 'partnering adult'. The purpose of this was to empower the child to take the initiative in response to supportive and non-intrusive contributions. The child would invite the adult to contribute, typically by looking up at them, or by a 'hand-over' gesture with the xylophone beaters, and the adult would wait for such an invitation to make a contribution. Young found that when adults met the children's musical contributions 'on the children's terms' with sympathetic responses in these musical games, the children's music-making showed structural and emotional strength. This kind of playful turn-taking is related to that noted by Trevarthen (2000) in his study of very young babies interacting musically with their carers.

## Music and technology

Recent technological developments have provided opportunities for children to use computers to make their own compositions, using some basic musical units which they can combine and play back to hear the effect. Use of this kind of technology gives children the power to create interesting and impressive sounding music, without being restricted by any lack of instrumental dexterity. Interactive games such as Guitar Hero, Singstar and Rock Band, while targeted at an older age group, also provide young children with an opportunity to become involved in musical activity. Another, arguably more creative, approach is being developed in a new generation of computer programs which provide a player with an improvised 'answer' to their musical input. The way in which the program responds to the player can be varied to produce anything from an exact copy, through increasingly free variations to a completely different kind of response. The MIROR IMPRO program was originally destined for professional jazz players, but has found success in early childhood settings as well (Pachet and Addessi 2004; Addessi and Pachet 2005). Children can become very involved with their interactions with the machine and in hearing how their thoughts are reflected back to them, changing and developing over time. They use similar 'hand-over' gestures to those noted by Young (2003), treating the machine as a musical partner. An advantage of using technology in this way is that it is easy to create a recording for children to take away and show to family and friends, thus contributing to feelings of self-efficacy and pride in achievement.

## Some implications for practice

Singing songs, rhymes and games in the nursery can be very valuable in encouraging bonding, memory, language development and communication. Hearing and participating in these activities provides models on which children can base or develop their own musical ideas. It can also help to reflect ethnic identities and variety. Group activities alone may not, however, offer the child sufficient opportunity for independent creative exploration of musical ideas. Barrett's (1997) research demonstrates that children as young as 4 are capable of composing and recording their own musical ideas with careful attention to detail, providing there is support and encouragement for the process.

There is, among some early-years practitioners, a reluctance to engage with informal musical activities, or even to provide opportunities for children to play freely with instruments. The inevitable 'noise factor' is not the only consideration: the preconception which many people hold of formal 'expert' Western music-making, such as is heard in concerts or recordings, can lead practitioners to believe that they are not sufficiently skilled musically to undertake this kind of activity with the children. The use of technology is one way to encourage musical exploration in settings where practitioners lack musical confidence. However, as Young's (1995, 2003) research suggests, treating music as a play activity, with plenty of enjoyment and communication between adult and child, and meeting children at their own level can result in meaningful, expressive and well-structured musical interactions which can scaffold the child's understanding of music. Young's finding that children remained engaged in musical play for the longest times with a person who was known to them, but was not a skilled musician should provide reassurance that children are happy to explore and play with music alongside an interested, non-expert adult.

## Further reflection

1 How might children's development of motor skills and intellectual capacity influence their musical creativity?
2 How important is it for children to be able to put their musical thinking into words or pictures? What can we learn from these activities and could there be circumstances under which words are superfluous?
3 How might the practitioner's role change between working with music in formal sessions and in informal play activities?

## Further reading

Pound and Harrison (2003: particularly chs 2 and 4)
Swanwick and Tillman (1986)
Young (1995)
Young and Glover (1998)

# Chapter 11

# Approaches to developing young children's thinking and understanding

In this chapter the focus is on ways in which young children's thinking may be developed and supported. A range of approaches aimed at developing thinking is considered, including those informed by ideas of philosophy for children. More generally, young children's creative and critical thinking and problem-solving are considered. These terms are often explicitly stated as aims in many programmes, and problem-solving, in particular, is often conflated with thinking skills (Johnson 2001). It is valuable to consider what each might mean, and what potential benefits they might have for young children's cognitive development. The starting point here is the possible practical implementation of the ideas, theory and research of the preceding chapters.

## Developing 'good' thinkers

The rationale for developing young children's thinking is underpinned by ideas arising from the different theories of cognition considered in Chapter 2, alongside other aspects such as metacognitive development and self-regulation in Chapter 5. McGuinness (1999), like others, suggests that a focus on the development of 'thinking skills' is valuable because it supports active cognitive processes which make for better learning. A fundamental question, however, is what we might mean by 'better' here, and what 'good' thinking looks like. Fisher suggests that an important role for those supporting young children's thinking is to focus attention on 'knowing how' (procedural knowledge) rather than 'knowing that' (declarative knowledge). He also makes the following point:

> If it is by thinking that we learn, then improving pupils' thinking skills will help them make more sense of their learning and their lives.
>
> (Fisher 2005: 209)

Costello (2000) takes this argument further, and suggests that the teaching of thinking skills is an essential element in the avoidance of indoctrination in school.

Initiatives and ideas for supporting young children's thinking are often referred to as 'teaching thinking', 'teaching thinking skills', or even 'teaching children to think', as if, somehow, they were not doing so already. None of these terms seems entirely appropriate as a way of looking at the area. The problem with a term like 'teaching thinking' is that it tends to imply a narrow range of functions for those *doing* the 'teaching', rather than focusing on what it might mean to learn to be a good thinker. The 'catchall phrase' (Lipman 2003: 162) of 'thinking skills' is ambiguous and used very broadly to apply to anything from very specific to very general abilities, and thus can be taken to mean a very wide range of processes and actions. In addition, the word 'skill' suggests that it is a matter, on the learner's part, of applying procedures for thinking, in much the same way that one might have acquired the skill of riding a bike, or using scissors. Whilst it may be possible to suggest that thinking can be characterized as a skill because it can be improved by practice (White 2002), the development of young children's thinking and understanding will be much more than this, and include supporting positive dispositions to use such skills in appropriate situations, and attitudes of 'delight' in so doing (Coles and Robinson 1991b: 14). Johnson (2001) points out that, in many aspects of activity, to have mastered a skill is often taken to mean that one can exercise it *without* thinking!

Traditionally, this idea of skill and cognitive ability has been the defining principle of 'good' thinking (Project Zero Patterns of Thinking). In recent years, however, greater emphasis has been placed upon a wider view. The *Patterns of Thinking* project, led by David Perkins and Shari Tishman, reflects a more current view that it is much more than this:

> Certainly, good thinkers have skills. But they also have more. Passions, attitudes, values and habits of mind all play key roles in thinking, and, in large part, it is these elements that determine whether learners use their thinking skills when it counts. In short, good thinkers have the right 'thinking dispositions'.
>
> (http://pzweb.harvard.edu./Research/PatThk.htm)

These 'thinking dispositions' are underpinned by an enculturation model, based upon building a culture of thinking in a setting.

'Good' thinkers may have a repertoire of strategies for thinking, be able to think reflectively about their own thinking, be confident in their attitude to thinking, and willing to take risks in their thinking and learn from mistakes. Meadows suggests that 'In short they will be people who enjoy thinking' (2006: 410).This may seem to be at odds with the premise outlined in the subtitle to Claxton's *Hare Brain Tortoise Mind* (1998): 'why intelligence increases when you think less'. However, what Claxton is arguing for is less reliance on one particular form of thinking, which he calls 'd-mode' ('deliberate-mode') thinking. This form of thinking is characterized by logic, precision, clarity, generalizations and explicit language. Although, of course, this way of thinking is important, Claxton suggests that it should not be the only way of thinking that we develop and value. As described in Chapter 1, he believes that the mind has three 'processing speeds', including one which is more playful and contemplative. He argues that too much emphasis on the 'deliberate' or 'd-mode' of thinking can prevent us from looking at problems and ideas in different ways, and warns:

> If we see d-mode as the only form of intelligence, we must suppose, when it fails, that we are not 'bright' enough, or did not think 'hard' enough, or have not got enough 'data'. The lesson we learn from such failures is that we must develop better models, collect more data, and ponder more carefully. What we do not learn is that we may have been thinking *in the wrong way*.
>
> (Claxton 1998: 12; emphasis in original)

He suggests that the slower ways of thinking and knowing are just as important because they make use of sensations, images, feelings and hunches as well as clear, conscious thoughts, which can help us to connect different inputs in new ways, and because confusion and uncertainty (allowed in these slower ways) may precede the development of a good idea. One practitioner in our research emphasized the value of children having the opportunity 'just to "be" really', saying that this required time and space. She suggested that outdoor activity provides a particularly good context here, possibly allowing children more time to stand back, watch, take their time and reflect (Robson and Hargreaves 2005).

## Models for teaching thinking

In recent years there has been considerable interest in the explicit development of children's thinking. Two Department for Education and Skills Research Reports in England, for example, have both had as part of their brief to investigate ways of developing young children's thinking (Moyles *et al.* 2002; Siraj-Blatchford *et al.* 2002). Globally, a wide range of programmes has been developed with, McGuinness (1999) suggests, a common aim of developing thinking to a qualitatively higher level. The Thinking Skills Review Group review led by Higgins propose as a working definition (Higgins *et al.* 2004: 1) that such initiatives are:

> Approaches or programmes which identify for learners translatable, mental processes and/or which require learners to plan, describe and evaluate their thinking and learning. These can therefore be characterized as approaches or programmes which:
> - require learners to articulate and evaluate specific learning approaches;
> - and/or
> - identify specific cognitive and related affective or conative processes that are amenable to instruction.

Put more succinctly, these are programmes which specify both what is to be taught and how it is to be taught. Whilst both the majority of programmes and the bulk of research and evaluation about them has tended to focus on work with older children (Higgins *et al.* 2004; Taggart *et al.* 2005), it is worth looking at findings about these, as well as those programmes which have involved younger children. McGuinness categorizes approaches into three 'models for delivering thinking skills' (1999):

- interventions that can be directed towards enhancing thinking skills through structured programmes which are additional to the normal curriculum: for example Feuerstein's *Instrumental Enrichment* programme (1980) or *The Somerset Thinking Skills Course* (Blagg *et al.* 1988);
- approaches that target subject-specific learning such as science, mathematics, geography: for example *Cognitive Acceleration through Science Education (CASE)* (Adey and Shayer 1994);
- infusion across the curriculum through systematic identification of opportunities within the normal curriculum for thinking skills development: for example *Activating Children's Thinking Skills (ACTS)* (McGuinness 2006).

Trickey and Topping (2004) also identify a fourth category of 'Multi-method' programmes. This includes approaches such as Dawes *et al.*'s *Thinking Together* (2000), and *Philosophy for Children* (Lipman *et al.* 1980; Lipman 2003).

There are a number of problems associated with assessing the efficacy of such programmes, including whether any gains are long term (McGuinness 1999), how soon they are evident (Adey and Shayer 1994), and the possibility of the so-called Hawthorne effect, where separating out the impact of a programme over and above that of any novel, enthusiastically applied intervention may be difficult. Methodologically, the evaluations of some of these programmes have also been criticized (Claxton 1999b). All of these factors lead Trickey and Topping (2004) and Wilson (2000) to urge caution in interpreting the available data.

## Are some models more effective than others?

Taking these caveats into account, and the fact that evidence is sometimes contradictory (Wilson 2000), some general conclusions may still be drawn. Looking at the first model in McGuinness's categorization, Claxton (2006) is critical of what he sees as a 'bolt on' approach which, in his view, ghettoizes thinking. It has also been criticized as reductionist and fragmentary, with limited transfer of skills learnt to new contexts (Coles and Robinson 1991b). This idea of transferability, what Woolfolk *et al.* (2008) described as 'mindful abstraction', is seen as the key goal (Leat 1999). It has proved to be a major challenge, with big claims sometimes being made for particular programmes, not always substantiated by evaluation (Claxton 1999b). McGuinness's second category of approaches which focus on discrete subject areas may also be less valuable, given the holistic nature of young children's learning.

McGuinness (1999) suggests that the more successful approaches, including those most likely to support transfer, tend to have strong theoretical underpinnings, well-designed and contextualized materials, explicit pedagogies and good teacher support. In keeping with the accepted views on the value of embedding children's learning in meaningful contexts (Donaldson 1978), the most successful interventions seem to be those which take an embedded approach (Whitebread 2000). In particular, they are ones directed at 'cognitive apprenticeship', which includes scaffolding techniques and metacognitive and self-regulatory approaches (Higgins *et al.* 2004; McGuinness 2006; McGregor 2007; Whitebread 2000), similar to those referred to as infusion approaches (see Swartz on http://www.nctt.net/index.php), the third category in McGuinness's typology. Characteristically, these approaches emphasize classroom talk, interaction and relationships (Higgins *et al.* 2004; Wegerif 2010), where adult interventions such as scaffolding, modelling and questioning make their own thinking explicit to the children, and where the children themselves are required to articulate their thinking, and can enjoy 'playing around with ideas' (Whitebread 2000b: 155). An example of such an approach, Whitebread suggests, is Lipman's *Philosophy for Children* (see below). He also commends ideas such as the *Thinking Books* (Swan and White 1994) referred to in Chapter 5. Dialogic Teaching, commended by Wegerif (2010), is looked at in Chapter 7.

In a similar vein, Taggart *et al.* (2005), in focusing explicitly on data from the early years, identify infusion approaches as most popular. They conclude that 'pedagogical approaches to the promotion of thinking skills in young children are developmentally

204 Developing Thinking and Understanding in Young Children

appropriate in helping children to construct rules for solving problems, hypothesise about possible eventualities, suggest alternatives or reason from given information' (Taggart *et al.* 2005: 37). They highlight three key features that they see as relevant to the development of young children's thinking skills: questioning/dialogue, story and play.

Higgins *et al.*'s systematic review (2004) of the area concludes that a majority of the programmes they looked at demonstrate a positive impact as a result of the programme, and none show a negative impact. Of these, the most impressive at age 16, in terms of transferability of learning and thinking to new contexts, is CASE (Adey and Shayer 1994). This Piagetian approach has been adapted for younger age groups, with one programme targeted at children aged 5 and 6 years, called *Let's Think!* (Robertson 2004). Robertson suggests that, as a result of the programme, children both developed their thinking ability and learned more effectively across the curriculum. Critical success factors she identifies are that the programme is valued by the school as a whole, that collaborative work is supported and developed by the teachers, and that teachers are prepared to respond positively to challenges about any preconceptions they have of children (Robertson 2004). Coles and Robinson (1991b) and McGuinness (1999) suggest that Lipman's work, and Feuerstein's *Instrumental Enrichment* programme have both been rigorously tested and evaluated, and shown to work in a number of settings. Lipman's ideas, in particular, McGuinness (1999) suggests, may have an impact on the quality of discussion, on children's abilities in forming questions and on their self-esteem. Dewey and Bento (2009) also point to affective gains, with positive effects on children's social and emotional development alongside cognitive gains as a result of the ACTS approach of McGuinness (2006).

Finally, Higgins *et al.* caution that the impact of thinking skills approaches may not be the same for all children. Their review suggests greater impact on 'low attaining pupils, particularly when using metacognitive strategies' (2004: 39). However, they do cite one study which shows the opposite, finding the greatest impact on higher attaining children. Overall, they suggest that a long-term view needs to be taken, and that more general emphasis by adults working with young children on making aspects of teaching and learning, particularly reasoning, more explicit may be as beneficial as any particular programme. Similarly, McGuinness (1999) emphasizes the benefits of creating and supporting dispositions for good thinking, and an atmosphere where talking about thinking is actively pursued. In Chapter 6 Carr's ideas about positive dispositions as being the inclination to be 'ready, willing and able' (Carr 2001: 21) were discussed. Perkins and Tishman (http://pzweb.harvard.edu./Research/PatThk.htm) emphasize the key importance of children being ready, willing and able to think. In addition, it is useful to go back to some of the work discussed in Chapter 5, on metacognition, identified as included in, or the basis of, many thinking skills programmes (Larkin 2010). In particular, look back at Pramling (1988) and Robson (2010).

## Philosophy for children

### What is philosophy for children?

Philosophy for Children (P4C), sometimes referred to as 'Philosophy with Children' (PWC), is one of the most widely known types of intervention to support children's thinking. Philosophy for Children was the idea of Matthew Lipman in the United States (Lipman *et al.* 1980; Lipman 1991, 2003). Concerned at what he saw as the low levels of thinking skills of college students, in contrast to the questioning, enquiring minds of young children, he felt that action was necessary to tackle the issue from early in life. The aim of Philosophy for Children is 'to promote excellent thinking: thinking that is creative as well as logical, inventive as well as analytical' (Lipman 1991: 35). He further describes excellent thinking as 'multidimensional', combining critical thinking, creative thinking and 'caring thinking', a mode he suggests is usually seen as 'falling in the affective rather than the cognitive camp' (Lipman 2003: 201), but which he sees as of equal importance to the other two modes. Similar aims underpin the work of others who have developed ideas of philosophical thinking with children. In the United Kingdom, one of the best known advocates is Robert Fisher, who suggests that it exposes children to 'the skills and habits of higher order thinking' (Fisher 2001: 67). Fisher (2008) and Wegerif (2010) both link philosophy for children with dialogic teaching, discussed in Chapter 7, suggesting that they share a rationale that is concerned with using talk to think, and the development of 'me-cognition' (Fisher 2008), which Fisher sees as the foundation of metacognition.

Looked at in relation to the categorization of interventions above, Lipman suggests that philosophy for children steers a middle path between the two very different models that thinking is either best taught through specific subjects, or best approached through an autonomous course in thinking. He suggests that this middle path involves directing the skills learned in the independent course to the 'basic' skills of reading and writing. He believes that, in so doing, children will then transfer the added critical reflectiveness of their reading and writing to other subjects and areas of learning (Lipman 2003). Other advocates, including Costello (2000), Fisher (1998) and Haynes (2002), all emphasize the potential transferability of thinking as a result of a philosophical approach. The principal vehicle for the development of this critical reflection is discussion, drawing on ideas of Socratic dialogue. It is seen as closely related to Vygotskian principles (Fisher 2005; Lewis and Rowley 2002), and to sociocultural concepts such as Rogoff's (2003) idea of guided participation (Lipman 2003).

### The practice of philosophy with children

Lipman's approach to supporting children's thinking was to develop a series of stories, for use with children of different ages. Each story features characters who are depicted discussing ideas. For example, when turn-taking comes up as part of the story, characters are shown discussing underlying principles of sharing and reciprocity. The stories intended for young children focus on the practice of reasoning and inquiry skills, those for older children move on to underlying principles and broader application (Lipman 1991). A typical session devoted to children's thinking begins with the reading of such a story, or part of it. Lipman suggests that this story reading is shared, with children being allowed to 'pass' if they do not wish to read aloud. Costello (2000) suggests that the practice of 'passing', which may tend to be done by less confident readers, can serve to make these children feel less participant, and alienate them from the activity. With younger children, this may be particularly the case. In Costello's view, the reading is best done by the adult. The adult then asks the children for their comments, what they would like to discuss about the story, and the questions they want to ask, using open-ended questions and prompts, such as 'What puzzles you? What interests you? What do you like about this passage?' (Costello 2000: 41–2). As a result of this, a particular topic is selected for exploration by the group, facilitated by the adult. The aim is to create a community of enquiry, or 'habitat' (Lipman 2003: 157) for thinking, in which there is a readiness to reason, mutual respect and an absence of indoctrination (Lipman *et al.* 1980). Rules for discussion are developed, including listening, turn-taking and not interrupting (Fisher 2005), showing respect for others, and the avoidance of ridicule (Haynes 2002). Key to these discussions is supporting children's disposition to be curious: 'more important than knowledge because it is needed to generate knowledge' (Fisher 2008: 51). Chak (2007) suggests that introducing conceptual conflict and supporting children's questions, two central elements of a philosophy for children approach, are key to fostering 'epistemic' curiosity.

Lipman and others such as Fisher (1998, 2001, 2005) have focused the discussions in the community of enquiry around specially written stories, from which moral and philosophical points are drawn and debated. Costello (2000) suggests the value of video material with young children. Haynes broadens the possible range of stimuli, emphasizing the value of 'carefully structured exploration of a variety of narratives found in story, myth, poetry, news, drama, music, painting, photography' (2002: 45). Adult choices from these stimuli are made on the basis of their power 'to express ambiguity, to produce puzzlement, or to evoke a deep response' (Haynes 2002: 22). This includes the use of picture books, for example, of the kinds suggested in Chapters 5 and 8, which may include multilayered, parallel and ambiguous narratives. Haynes (2002: 29–30) summarizes the process of such philosophical enquiry, pointing out that it should be seen as a flexible process, admitting diversions, and discussion over often long periods of time:

- Getting started: this may involve discussion of rules, meditation or silence as preparation.
- Sharing a stimulus to prompt enquiry.
- Pause for thought: children may think alone, in groups, and they may draw or write notes.
- Questioning: questions are recorded for everyone to see.
- Connections: links are made between questions, in the process of which children draw distinctions.
- Choosing a question to begin enquiry: the adult needs to ensure that this is a fair, inclusive process.
- Building on each other's ideas: discussion.
- Recording discussion: notes, webs, concept maps, for all to see.
- Closure and review: summarizing what has been discussed. 'Resolution is rare – new questions are more common' (Haynes 2002: 30). This aspect includes reflection on the process.

Haynes's discussions use the children's own generated questions as starting points, a factor which Papaleontiou-Louca (2003) suggests involves a high degree of metacognitive involvement. Haynes concurs, believing that 'Philosophical enquiry addresses the ground of metacognition as part of the ground of philosophy' (2002: 45). The role of the adult in managing the discussion is to both listen responsively and intervene tactfully, to treat all children's contributions as legitimate, to encourage risk-taking and speculation and to avoid pursuing their own interests (Haynes 2003).

---

*Box 11.1: You can't say you can't play*

Paley introduces a rule into the kindergarten that stipulates 'You can't say you can't play' to any child who wants to join in your game. The following is a very brief extract from one of her discussions with the children about this rule.

ANGELO:    Let anybody play if someone asks.
LISA:         But then what's the whole point of playing?
NELSON:    You just want Cynthia.
LISA:         I could play alone. Why can't Clara play alone?
ANGELO:    I think that's pretty sad. People that is alone they has water in their eyes.
LISA:         I'm more sad if someone comes that I don't want to play with.
PALEY:       Who is sadder? The one who isn't allowed to play or the one who has to play with someone he or she doesn't want to play with?
CLARA:      It's more sadder if you can't play.
LISA:         The other one is the same sadder.

(Paley 1993: 19–20)

---

Fisher emphasizes the importance of good feedback to the children, in ways which demonstrate that adults are not looking for 'right' answers (2005).

Discussions will, in Fisher's view, often revolve around some key themes: fairness, freedom, friendship, truth, knowledge, judgement (2005). This has obvious similarities with the three themes of friendship, fairness and fantasy which Paley (1986) identifies as so important to children. As MacNaughton and Williams (2009) suggest, such philosophical discussions often have moral and ethical dimensions. Paley's work often seems to implicitly combine such issues. A good example is her initiative of presenting the children with a new classroom rule: 'You can't say you can't play' (1993), to avoid the exclusion of some children from play. A brief extract of the children's discussion is shown in Box 11.1. Costello (2000) also emphasizes the relationship of philosophical thinking to the development of citizenship in children.

### Is it philosophy?

Whilst this is not the place for protracted discussion about whether or not young children can engage in philosophy, it is worth highlighting that there are differing views about this issue. White (2002) points out that encouraging children's questions is undoubtedly valuable, but that not all questions are philosophical ones, and that merely asking questions does not make a child into a philosopher. Haynes, reflecting on this idea of the philosophical potential of questions, asks whether questions such as 'How do cats kiss?, Why do men have nipples?, How are rivers made?' (Haynes 2002: 82), all asked by 4 and 5 year olds, belong in philosophy. Costello (2000) relates the arguments of, amongst others, Mary Warnock and Roger Scruton, that philosophy is not an appropriate subject for study by children, and best left until adulthood. Lipman agrees that merely talking, or asking questions, does not constitute philosophy, and suggests that these need to be converted into particular forms of discussion and dialogue, incorporating reasoning, drawing inferences, testing for consistency and comprehensiveness, and learning to think independently (Lipman 2003). He, along with others such as Fisher (2001, 2005, 2008), Haynes (2002, 2003) and Murris (2000), emphasizes that these are all things that children can do. Costello (2000) argues against the idea that these types of discussion in young children are 'pre-philosophical', for the same reasons that we would no longer talk of children's understanding in mathematics as 'pre-mathematical'.

## Critiques and evaluations of philosophy with children

As shown earlier, Coles and Robinson (1991b) and McGuinness (1999) both provide favourable reports on Lipman's work. Wilson (2000) also reports evidence of improvement in intellectual performance and on creativity measures, although this is in children aged 10–13 years. Fisher reports evidence that his programme, *Stories for Thinking* (Fisher 1996), has a positive effect on 'children's self-esteem and self-concept as thinkers and learners, the fluency and quality of children's questioning, the quality of their thinking, their ability to listen to others and engage effectively in class discussion' (Fisher 2001: 71), amongst others. More widely, Trickey and Topping (2004) report positive findings from ten studies, although they do emphasize the difficulty of collecting reliable data. They conclude: 'given certain conditions, children can gain significantly in measurable terms both academically and socially through this type of interactive process' (2004: 375). Looking particularly at evidence from settings which have introduced philosophy with young children, Haynes suggests that the children are more able to generate alternative explanations for hypothetical situations, and to make links between thoughts and feelings in different hypothetical situations (2003: 6), whilst MacNaughton and Williams (2009) cite studies showing enhanced empathy and pro-social behaviour in young children.

Specific criticisms of philosophy for children include Fisher's (1998) suggestion that the specially written novels may lack literary style, and that the absence of pictures, seen by Lipman as important for avoiding prescriptive imagery, means that 'dimensions of meaning to a story' (Fisher 1998: 117) may be lacking. Whalley (1991) points to the potential drawback, if only Lipman's original stories are used, of cultural and linguistic bias, given that they were written for an American market. He also highlights a wider potential criticism, that only one philosophical viewpoint is represented in Lipman's work. Lewis and Rowley suggest that philosophy for children approaches have tended to overemphasize 'question raising', above 'question understanding and question focusing' (2002: 55), and that more attention may need to be paid to ensuring that children understand the question under discussion. This may be particularly important in the early years.

## Creative and critical thinking

Initially, it is worth looking at these aspects of young children's thinking together. Not because critical and creative thinking are one and the same thing, but because they are interdependent, can work together in complementary ways (Lipman 2003) and are often considered, along with problem-solving (below) as 'higher level' mental activities (Wilson 2000). In addition, they are key to problem-solving capability.

How can critical and creative thinking be distinguished? A major problem here is the variety of definitions and attributes suggested by the literature. White, for example, comments on the 'confusedness' (2002: 129) of much writing about creativity and creative thinking. Critical thinking is frequently referred to as convergent, and concerned with deductive reasoning, whilst creative thinking is often described as lateral thinking (de Bono 1991), or divergent thinking, and concerned with inductive reasoning and exploring ideas. De Boo refers to creative thinking as 'hypothetical', or 'intuitive' (1999: 60), and critical thinking as 'reflective' (1999: 64). For McGregor (2007), the difference lies between critiquing the known (critical thinking) and generating the new (creative thinking).

Whilst Sternberg suggests that creative thinking is 'relatively distinct from analytical or practical thinking' (2003: 335) as sets of skills, choices and critical evaluations are made by both participants and observers as part of any creative thinking process. The National Advisory Committee on Creative and Cultural Education (NACCCE) talks of 'generative and evaluative thinking' (1999: 31), and asserts that 'creative thinking always involves some critical thinking' (1999: 31). Rodd suggests creative and critical thinking can be described in the following ways (1999: 351):

Creative thinking –   the ability to produce original and divergent solutions problems.

   *Involves:*   fluency – the ability to propose many solutions;
                 flexibility – the ability to see a problem, issue or
                               incident from different perspectives;
                 originality – the ability to produce novel ideas.

Critical thinking –

   *Involves:*   observation
                 comparison
                 explanation
                 prediction

Problem-solving, looked at later, is for Fisher (2005) where both creative thinking and critical thinking come together. He suggests that creative thinking is good for generating new ideas, many of which may ultimately not be useful (as with Noam's thinking, in Box 11.2). He believes that it is then the role of critical thinking to help children to learn to identify their most powerful ideas. Whilst de Boo (1999) agrees that problem-solving is about application, he differs somewhat from Fisher in suggesting that critical thinking is primarily about metacognitive strategies.

However, the labelling of thinking as either 'creative' or 'critical' may be an oversimplification, and have its roots in our ideas about the functions of the left and right hemispheres of the brain (Fisher 2005). In recent years there has been more emphasis on the commonalities and areas of overlap between creative and critical thinking, as we shall see below. Box 11.2, for example, shows the interdependence of the two, as both Noam and Richard Feynman each consider their different problems.

## Creative thinking

An important starting point here is to look at the relationship of creative thinking to creativity, and also to the idea of creative learning (Craft *et al.* 2008a). Creative thinking is not interchangeable with creativity (Jones and Wyse 2004). What the two share, however, is their applicability to the widest range of human activity. Too often 'creativity' is located within the arts (NACCCE 1999). This is unsatisfactory in that it suggests that aspects such as science and maths are not 'creative', and thus do not involve creative thinking, and Box 11.2 clearly shows this not to be the case! Instead, it may be more helpful to see creative thinking as part of everyday life for young children (Richards 2006), expressed in all aspects of their activity. This is usually referred to as 'little c creativity' (Craft 2003; Kaufmann 2003). In our research we found that it was often in areas not traditionally seen as 'the arts' that young children's creative thinking was most evident (Robson 2012).

---

*Box 11.2:* Noam, aged 5, and Richard Feynman

The first extract features Noam, and the second is an episode from the life of Richard Feynman, the nuclear physicist. Are there similarities in the thinking of Noam and Feynman? What is the relationship of knowledge and interest to their creative (and critical) thinking?

A 5 year old is being interviewed on the subject of heat, using pictures and objects as stimuli.

TEACHER:    What will happen if we put this (pan of milk) on the cooker?
NOAM:        It will go all bubbly.
TEACHER:    Why will it go all bubbly?
NOAM:        Because the hot of the cooker …
TEACHER:    But how does the hotness get into the milk?
NOAM:        It goes all over bottom and it makes a little gap and it squeezes through the  hole and gets into the milk.
TEACHER:    So the heat makes a hole in the saucepan?
NOAM:        You can't see it, it's too really … sort of … (indicates sliding around with his hands).
TEACHER:    Anything else?
NOAM:        (thinks) No. Oh, if it had holes the milk would fall through (shrugs).
(De Boo 1999: 53

I was in the cafeteria and some guy, fooling around, throws a plate in the air. As the plate went up in the air I saw it wobble, and I noticed the red medallion of Cornell on the plate going around. It was pretty obvious to me that the medallion went around faster than the wobbling. I had nothing to do so I started to figure out the motion of the rotating plate.

I discover that when the angle is very slight, the medallion rotates twice as fast as the wobble rate – two to one. It came out of a complicated equation! Then I thought, 'Is there some way I can see in a more fundamental way, by looking at the forces or the dynamics, why it's two to one?' …

The diagrams and the whole business that I got the Nobel Prize for came from that piddling around with the wobbling plate.
(Feynman 1986: 173–4)

## Defining creative thinking

Looking back at some of the terms identified above, creative thinking is often described as 'divergent' thinking, and classically measured by tests such as asking participants how many uses they can think of for an object such as a brick. The greater the number of uses, the higher the score. As Cohen points out, however, not all suggested uses are necessarily evidence of creative thinking: 'If someone said one use of a brick was as a snack, they would be loopy, poking fun, or just wrong' (2002: 143). In addition, he asks whether coming up with fifteen uses for a brick is necessarily more creative than coming up with three good ones. What is clear is that, whilst divergent thinking is a valuable element of creative thinking, creative thinking is not limited to ideas of divergence, and can also be the product of convergent thinking (Dietrich 2007). In addition, divergent thinking does not, of itself, necessarily lead to creative thought.

The NACCCE defines *creativity* as 'imaginative activity fashioned so as to produce outcomes that are both original and of value' (1999: 29). Sternberg defines *creative thinking* as 'thinking that is novel and that produces ideas that are of value' (2003: 325–6). Sternberg's use of 'novelty' is significant in emphasizing that, to count as creative, someone's idea does not have to embody thinking that has never been done before by anyone. Rather, creative thinking is thinking which is new for *that individual*, a point of particular significance when looking at young children's creative thinking. Whilst the NACCCE implicitly focuses on something tangible, Sternberg identifies ideas as the outcome of creative thinking. This has some similarities with Craft *et al.*'s definition of *creative learning* as 'significant imaginative achievement as evidenced in the creation of new knowledge' (Craft *et al.* 2006, cited in Craft *et al.* 2008a: p. xxi). White (2002) suggests that it is these outcomes – whether they are tangible things or ideas – which are the outward evidence of creative thinking. The other key idea common to the definitions of both Sternberg (2003) and the NACCCE (1999) is the notion of value. This has two implications. First, it views creative thinking as inherently social; and second, it highlights the connections between creative thinking and critical thinking and problem-solving, because it involves value judgements made by both ourselves and others.

The idea of imagination as part of creative thinking is discussed by a number of writers. Claxton suggests that imagination, fantasy and entering into 'imaginative scenario(s)' (1999b: 96) are related to creative thinking.

To sum up, it is valuable to look at Sternberg's 'key decisions' that, in his view, underlie creative thinking (abridged from Sternberg 2003: 333–5):

1   Redefine problems
2   Analyse your own ideas
3   Sell your ideas
4   Knowledge is a double-edged sword
5   Surmount obstacles
6   Take sensible risks
7   Willingness to grow
8   Believe in yourself
9   Tolerance of ambiguity
10   Find what you love to do and do it
11   Allowing time
12   Allowing mistakes

## Are there characteristic stages in creative thinking?

The term 'stages' here does not imply a developmental path of progress over time. Rather, it is concerned with possible stages in the exercise of creative thinking. Meadows (2006) and Claxton (1998, 1999b) outline a series of stages which they suggest are characteristic although, as Meadows emphasizes, we do not have enough data to confirm or refute their significance as a possibly cyclic process of creative thinking. These are:

1 Familiarization (Meadows) or preparation (Claxton): information gathering, acquiring expertise – 'Some of this activity is highly purposeful and analytical. Some of it might be much more leisurely and receptive' (Claxton 1999b: 163).
2 Incubation (Claxton) or 'letting it "lie fallow"' (Meadows 2006: 258): an intuitive process that works best when an impasse in understanding has been reached (Claxton 1999b).
3 Insight (Meadows) or illumination (Claxton): a moment or reaction which suggests an answer. This might be abrupt, but may also be slow and subtle (Claxton 1999b).
4 Verification (Claxton) or working out and testing the solution (Meadows).

Claxton believes that different elements of this process may be facilitated by different types of interactions and contexts. He suggests that the first, preparation, stage is often highly social, and even collaborative. Ideas are tested out with others, and discussed, with members of the group bringing different thoughts and experiences to the situation. The second, incubation, stage may be more solitary, allowing individuals the chance to introspect, reflect and develop their own viewpoints. He suggests that this can help to avoid too swift a convergence on a solution. Lloyd and Howe's (2003) research with children of 4 and 5 years of age shows a positive association between solitary active play (solitary pretence and functional play with objects) and divergent thinking. They speculate that the time to think things over and replay experiences, and possibly generate further possibilities, in privacy, may be important in supporting divergent thinking skills. Claxton suggests that time, 'soft thinking' (1998, 1999b) and even boredom are key elements in creative thinking.

## Supporting creative thinking: some implications for practice

Sternberg suggests that, to a great extent, creative thinking is attitudinal: 'creative people are creative, in large part, because they have *decided* to be creative' (2003: 333; emphasis in original), suggesting a key role for motivation, particularly intrinsic motivation (Amabile 1996), although extrinsic factors may sometimes assist creativity (Runco *et al.* 2011). Meadows (2006) identifies a number of attitudes that may be common to creative thinkers, including choosing challenges rather than avoiding them, valuing appropriateness, tolerance of risk, and the ability to both confront uncertainty and enjoy complexity. Claxton (1999b) suggests that the ability to tolerate and manage uncertainty is an important feature of creative thinking. This implies a significant role for the kinds of emotional qualities, such as self-efficacy, self-esteem and mastery, discussed in Chapter 3. Hypothesizing and making leaps of the imagination require confidence on the thinker's part, and a willingness to take risks. The links between emotion and creative thinking are clearly important. Hobson (2002) argues that children learn to think creatively as a result of being part of a loving relationship from which, in infancy, they begin to see things from two perspectives: their own, and that of a primary caregiver. Craft *et al.* (2008b) extend this to the classroom, highlighting the importance of providing a loving, supportive and secure environment in which children's self-determination, involvement and risk-taking is encouraged. Where this is not the case the effects of stress and pressure to perform may contribute to a narrowing of focus, and more interest in 'getting it right' rather than in taking risks and coming up with novel ideas (Claxton 1999b).

This emotional aspect also implies that creative thinking may not be general – none of us is emotionally committed to everything, and most of us have particular interests which motivate us more. Meadows (2006) illustrates this task- or domain-specificity in creative thinking. Only some people, she suggests, are creative thinkers in a range of fields – da Vinci, Freud or Piaget, for example. This is worth remembering alongside Whitebread's (2000b) conclusion that interventions for supporting children's thinking seem to be most successful when they are embedded in contexts meaningful to the children – those contexts may be very different for individual children, and an important implication for practice will be to provide opportunities for the development of creative thinking in a wide range of contexts. Singer (1973) views pretend play and make-believe of all kinds as facilitatory for creative and flexible thinking, and Woolfolk *et al.* (2008) cite research which shows that children score better in creativity tests when they have been engaged in play beforehand. Box 11.2 features contexts that may be important for the protagonists in both parts. Noam, at 5, is hypothesizing on the basis of both previous knowledge and immediate stimuli. His thinking is original but, as de Boo (1999) points out, he also rejects the theory he comes up with, continuing perhaps then to search for a more appropriate idea. The deep interest, and outcome, of Feynman's thinking in the second part of Box 11.2 is clear.

In our research we came to the following conclusions for practitioners interested in supporting young children's creative thinking (Robson 2012):

- Adults play a particularly important role in supporting children's initial engagement in activities.
- The highest levels of children's involvement in activities, and the most frequent expressions of creative thinking, occur in child-initiated activities.
- Playing in a group, or in a friendship pair, may be particularly valuable in promoting children's creative involvement in activities.
- Adult scaffolding, using open-ended questions, speculation and modelling enquiry, may be especially valuable for supporting children in acquiring new knowledge, developing new skills, and making use of these in support of their creative thinking.
- Dialogue between adults and children may be especially valuable for supporting children's analysis of their ideas and activities, and for their reflections on themselves as thinkers.
- Pretend play is particularly valuable for supporting creative thinking.
- Children's opportunities to explore materials and ideas, and to use resources in novel, unexpected ways, supports the development of their creative thinking.
- Outdoors is a powerful context for supporting young children's creative thinking.

## Critical thinking

### Defining critical thinking

As with creative thinking, the concept of critical thinking can prove to be a rather fuzzy one. Lipman observes that 'it has come to denote *any* thinking that, when applied to an instance of thinking, could make it more efficient and reliable' (2003: 56; emphasis in original). He describes 31 different characterizations (see 2003: 56–8) before concluding that a number of key terms, including 'impartial, accurate, careful, clear, truthful, abstract, coherent and practical' (2003: 58) summarize the majority of these positions. For Lipman, the idea of practicality is an important one. Critical thinking is practical in that it can be applied to both abstract and concrete issues. De Boo (1999) positions critical thinking as a metacognitive process, suggesting that it is concerned with our ability to assess the effectiveness of our thinking. It differs, he believes, from problem-solving in this respect, in that the latter he suggests is more to do with evaluating our methods of investigating or our conclusions. Popularly, as noted earlier, critical thinking is often equated with convergent thinking, in which the principle is convergence on one right answer. As Cohen (2002) points out, this principle underpins much testing, particularly of the IQ variety. As such, convergent thinking can only be a part of a wider category of critical thinking.

What might be some of the key critical skills? McGregor (2007) identifies inferring, explaining or reasoning, analysing, synthesizing, generalizing, summarizing and evaluating or judging, and the potential development of these has implications for practice, as discussed below. The last of these skills in her list, evaluation, is also the highest, and most demanding, level in Bloom's influential taxonomy of cognitive skills (Bloom *et al.* 1956). For Bloom, evaluation *is* critical thinking.

## Supporting critical thinking: some implications for practice

Fisher (2005: 53) suggests that the two most important processes in critical thinking are:

- learning how to question, when to question, and what questions to ask;
- learning how to reason, when to use reasoning, and what reasoning methods to use.

Looking at Fisher's first point, in Chapter 7 children's own efforts to make sense of the world, their questions and 'intellectual search' (Tizard and Hughes 2002) were seen as significant in supporting their thinking. De Boo (1999) suggests the value of adults posing open-ended questions which encourage speculation and investigation. Like de Boo, Fisher (2005) also emphasizes the value of adult modelling of such questions, suggesting that, through them, the vocabulary of analysis can be introduced to children. To use some of Lipman's (2003) definitional words, questions can highlight what it might mean to be clear, accurate or careful in one's thinking. Adult modelling may support their use by children in their own questions. In a similar way, the use of metacognitive prompts, and reference to the language of thinking, for example, 'was that a good way for you to decide?', or 'what do you need to think about next?' will be valuable (Robson and Hargreaves 2005; Robson 2010). Box 11.3 illustrates this at one nursery school, where staff decided to focus on using particular words *about* thinking and learning in their interactions with the children, and encouraged the children to

---

*Box 11.3: In the nursery, recounted by a member of staff*

While playing a game with Archie which involved throwing a ball into a tube I said 'I'm going to have to practise because I'm useless at this.'

ARCHIE:      You'll have to practise and practise or you won't be able to do it.

This followed an earlier comment from Carl:

CARL:       You have to practise to learn or you wouldn't know how to do it then.

*'Practise' was one of the 'thinking skills' words staff had been using, these comments show Archie and Carl's use of it in appropriate contexts.*

Reproduced with permission of Pat Gura and Ann Bridges, in collaboration with the staff, children and parents of Vanessa Nursery School

---

use them themselves. Bruner (1987) emphasizes that these kinds of metacognitive processes and critical thinking can be successfully 'taught' to young children.

Most important, though, will be the provision of opportunities for children to question and explore their own ideas, to think aloud, as Vygotsky (1986) proposes, in an environment which supports this process. Forman suggests that the way to help children to ask good questions is to help them to reflect on the facts as they know them, until they discover something new to question (1989). He suggests that this supports the formulation of questions that really arise from the child's own current understanding. He recommends the value of symbolic representation such as children's drawing, as a way of representing their understanding, and as the basis of this kind of reflection, supported by other people. As Richetti and Sheerin (1999) suggest, the ultimate aim is for the questioning to reside with the children, not the adults.

Fisher's second point, that critical thinking requires learning how to reason, is emphasized by Wegerif (2010). Both are underpinned by the practice of hypothesizing. Children's early hypotheses tend to be inductive, that is, they rely on single ideas, which may or may not conform to the 'received model' (Selley 1999), as we saw in Chapter 8. As their experience grows, children tend to begin to have some general principles or hypotheses that support them in thinking deductively (de Boo 1999). Young children's abilities in this area will depend, to some extent, on a number of factors, including first-hand experience, their confidence in the language of discussion, the attitudes and support of those around them, and the kinds of stimuli in their environment (de Boo 1999). We are familiar with the idea of deduction as a feature in detective stories featuring Sherlock Holmes-type figures, but, as Box 11.4 shows, even very young children can question and reason deductively.

As with young children's creative thinking, the part played by emotion may be significant. Just as taking risks in one's thinking may require a sense of self-worth, so challenging one's own thinking, and thinking critically about the ideas and beliefs one has, may also be potentially damaging to one's self-esteem. An environment that supports children's confidence in being self-critical will be important, alongside the development of appropriate ways of challenging the ideas of others. We looked in Chapter 3 at

Box 11.4: David, aged 2.6, at a parent and toddler group

David joins the worker, Helen, at a table, and starts to colour in a picture of a car using a blue crayon.

DAVID:     My dad's got a blue car.
HELEN:     Has he, so has mine.
DAVID:     You got a dad?
HELEN:     Yes.
DAVID:     But you're too big for a dad. (At this point David's mother comes and sits next to him. He looks up at her.) This lady's got a dad.
MUM:       Has she? That's nice, most people do have dads.
DAVID:     But she's too big.
MUM:       But I'm bigger than her and I've got a dad.
DAVID:     Have you? Who's that?
MUM:       Grandad.
DAVID:     But he's grandad, not dad.
MUM:       He's your grandad, but he's my dad.
DAVID:     Oh. (He does not say anything for a while.)
DAVID:     So even big people have dads.

the value of children's experiences in managing negotiation and conflict, and at how practitioners in Reggio Emilia provide children with models of negotiation, discussion and argument as a way of supporting their emotional and cognitive development. These ideas are central to the development of critical thinking skills too. Claxton (1999b) suggests that the development of dispositions to engage in what may often be hard thinking can help children not only to persevere when the going gets tough, but also to recognize the kinds of issues and situations that may, or may not, warrant such thinking.

It was suggested that creative thinking will often be task- or domain-specific (Meadows 2006). Gardner (1993) emphasizes that critical thinking will be no different in this respect. McKendree et al., looking particularly at the role of representation in critical thinking, suggest that children's 'native abilities' (2002: 65) in reasoning will be context-dependent. As before, then, starting from contexts which are within children's experience, and which have meaning for them, will be valuable. Play contexts may be valuable here, both cooperative and solitary.

## Creative and critical thinking and play

Whilst play is seen as central to young children's development, learning and thinking throughout this book, it is worth highlighting the relationship between play and critical and creative thinking here. Prentice (2000), for example, draws attention to the close relationship between young children's play and imaginative activity, and for Vygotsky (2004), children's play is the creative reworking of their impressions, not merely a reproduction of their experiences. It is useful to look at the ideas discussed above in relation to the taxonomy of children's play outlined by Hutt (1979) and Hutt et al.

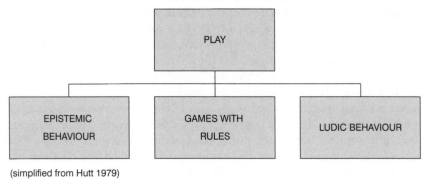

(simplified from Hutt 1979)

*Figure 11.1* A taxonomy of children's play

(1989). A very simplified version of this Piagetian-influenced categorization, showing only the three main subdivisions, is shown in Figure 11.1. Of these three, the subdivision of games with rules 'occupies a special intermediate position' (Hutt *et al.* 1989: 225), with games often having their own conventions, usually socially constrained and highly ritualized. It is worth considering in the context of children's thinking the parts played by the two chief subdivisions of ludic and epistemic behaviour.

What are the features of epistemic behaviour? First of all, it is concerned with the acquisition of knowledge, information and skills, and is relatively independent of mood state (Hutt *et al.* 1989). It may involve exploration, the acquisition of skills and problem-solving, and is particularly characteristic of playing with something new, and exploring ideas of 'what can it do?' Ludic behaviour, by contrast, is 'essentially diversive, that is, concerned with self-amusement' (Hutt *et al.* 1989: 222), and is much more mood-dependent, related to playing for the fun of it. The two major categories of ludic behaviour are symbolic, or fantasy play, involving representation and pretence, and repetitive play, involving the rehearsal of skills and concepts already acquired. It is characterized by more of a sense of mastery and exploring ideas of 'what can I do with it?'. Craft identifies this process of a move from 'what can it do?' to 'what can I do with it?' as at the heart of what she describes as 'possibility thinking' (2001).

It would seem straightforward to identify aspects of epistemic behaviour with critical thinking, and ludic behaviour with creative thinking. However, this may, as I have suggested, inaccurately reflect the ways in which they operate together and are interdependent. In their play children will move in and out of these two types of behaviour. Presented with a new idea, or novel material, for example, children's first actions may be to explore it, to find out what it can do, to investigate and 'problem-solve' with it. Having explored its properties, children may feel more at ease, and more confident about trying out new, divergent ideas for the material – in many ways engaging in more advanced problem-solving! Sylva *et al.* (1976) demonstrated that, in a problem-solving activity, in contexts where children were given opportunities to play with materials, they subsequently outperformed another group 'taught' how to use the materials in ways which would help them to solve the given problem. Not only that, but the group that had the experience of play were both more inventive in the strategies they used, and more persistent in their attempts to solve the problem.

Think of children faced with clay, for the first time, for example. Initially, they may explore its properties, and what it can do – can you squeeze it, roll it into a ball, stretch it, does it break, what happens when you sit on it? This exploratory phase is often then followed by the creation of artefacts – figures, pots, tiles, animals, model buildings, and so on – divergent creations that attempt to address the question 'what can I do with it?'. As a result, children often then develop a deeper understanding of the material, developing critical judgement about what, for them, are the 'best' ways of solving problems about how to join pieces of clay together, how to stop it crumbling, how to make a good pot.

As Tyler (1991) suggests, both ludic and epistemic behaviour are important, and work together, in complementary ways, much like creative and critical thinking. Too much emphasis on epistemic behaviour may ensure much new learning, but may not help children to use their knowledge and understanding in novel and creative ways, and to transfer that learning to new situations. Overemphasis on the ludic aspects of behaviour may not support children in acquiring fresh knowledge. Similarly, creative thinking can help children to think of many ways to solve a problem, in novel ways, but thinking critically may be what is needed to support them in deciding which of these is the best 'fit' for a particular problem.

## Problem-solving

### What is problem-solving and why does it matter?

Problem-solving is a goal-directed activity. The goal may be chosen by ourselves, or we may be set it by someone else. For Meadows (2006), problem-solving is what you do when you work towards that goal, but either do not have a routine way of getting there, or an obstacle like lack of skill or knowledge means that a previously possible solution does not work. For Fisher (2005) and de Boo (1999), this involves the application of both critical and creative thinking. Problem-solving for them is the point where critical thinking and creative thinking are applied in a process which culminates in a product of some kind. That product may be a tangible object or design, or it may be a mental solution.

Problems come in many forms, ranging from 'life-threatening' to 'minor irritant' (Fisher 2005: 83). They may be physical, requiring a baby to work out the best way of retrieving the teddy that is just beyond their reach. Other types of problem are inherently more social. These may involve both positive and negative strategies, for example the use of aggression to solve conflict (Siegler et al. 2011), negotiation in sharing toys or role taking in pretend play. The episode in Box 11.5 illustrates just such a social problem as the children negotiate their way through the rules of their classroom. Other types of problem are more symbolic, requiring the manipulation of signs and symbols in areas such as mathematics. Much of this activity may be unconscious, not reserved for special 'problem-solving' occasions. Bailey and Farrow suggest that 'The significant point is that organisms are always *actively* (though not necessarily consciously) involved in exploring their environment, seeking information from it in species-typical ways, and attempting to solve the problems it throws up' (1998: 270). Bereiter and Scardamalia (1989) link the idea that all learning can be seen as a kind of problem-solving to information processing theorists (see Chapter 2). The problem with this position, they suggest, is that learning varies considerably in the extent to which it poses problems for people. Much everyday learning is relatively *un*problematic. Can this still be seen as problem-solving?

Box 11.5 Nandeep, aged 5.7, Kai, aged 4.10, and Ryan, aged 5.3, problem-solving in play

Nandeep, Kai and Ryan are playing with construction materials with which they have constructed long sticks. They are pointing them at one another and making gun-type noises, when adult A comes by.

KAI:          (to adult A) This is a gun.
RYAN:         We're not allowed to have guns at school.
NANDEEP:     (to adult A, waving his stick) This is a firework!

Whilst much problem-solving does occur in everyday, real-life situations, problem-solving is also used as a learning tool in early years education and care. Crucial features of real-life problems are that they are often ill-defined and multi-faceted, amenable to no single or final solution (Fisher 2005). In this, they are often (but not necessarily) different to the types of problems 'set' for children to solve in nurseries and schools. As discussed below, this may be important for children's interest and motivation in tackling the problem as defined.

Why does problem-solving matter? What benefits might it have for young children? Given the context of this book, do children become better thinkers as a result of engaging in problem-solving? Meadows (2006) sees problem-solving as a microcosm of cognition, because it involves such a wide range of cognitive processes, and the view that children are problem-solvers is a central tenet of a number of theorists, including Piaget and Bruner (see Chapter 2). Problem-solving is linked by Bronson (2000a), DeLoache and Brown (1987) and Wood (1998), amongst others, to the development of aspects such as self-regulation (see Chapter 5). Fisher (2005) suggests a reciprocal relationship between problem-solving and thinking, viewing problem-solving as helping to develop children's thinking, at the same time that it is also supported by it. Hope also relates this to learning, asserting that 'when we solve a problem we learn something new' (2002: 265). MacNaughton and Williams (2009) propose that problem-solving is, though, more than cognition, citing research that it supports the development of young children's social competence, resilience and confidence in working things out for themselves, including resolving conflict, alongside helping to develop initiative, creativity and mathematical thinking.

### How do children's problem-solving skills develop?

Children are, in many important respects, engaged in solving problems from early in life, in self-initiated and self-directed ways, 'in situations where there is no external pressure to improve or change, no obvious guidance, and no feedback other than their own satisfaction' (DeLoache and Brown 1987: 111). They are constantly puzzling about how the world around them works, and about how they themselves can make things happen. At three months they know that their own actions can influence events (Gopnik et al. 1999), and from about six months onwards, they engage in 'sophisticated voluntary actions' (Karmiloff-Smith 1994: 186) which imply goal-directed behaviour, already suggested as a defining feature of problem-solving.

A critical part of this process will be the formulation of plans to reach whatever goal is identified. In Chapter 2, the roles of planning and expertise are considered,

---

*Box 11.6:* Thomas, aged 3.8, in the nursery garden

Thomas is in the garden. He has a plant pot tray, a 'stompalong' (child's plastic stilt) and a short piece of plastic pipe. He experiments with the three items, piling them on top of one another, trying out different combinations in an attempt to find in which order the three things will balance. Eventually, he places the plant pot tray first, then the plastic stilt, and finally he places the pipe into the upturned, open end of the stilt.

THOMAS:    There! That's a perfect fit.

---

along with suggested reasons why young children do not always make use of plans, and it is useful to look back at the discussion there. Here it is worth noting that for young children, planning and action will often occur simultaneously (Gura 1992), but, gradually, the ability to plan in advance of action will develop. As children get older, they are able to create more complex plans, which take a greater number of factors into account, and which have more steps (Thornton 2002).

The simplest planning strategy, used by adults, children and species such as chimpanzees (Karmiloff-Smith 1994), is that of trial and error. Whilst it is very characteristic of the approach of young children to problem-solving, Thornton (2002) points out that it is by no means a primitive strategy that we develop away from, but one which we continue to use throughout life. What may change over time are the ways in which the strategy is employed. Young children, for example, 2 and 3 year olds, may try out different solutions to a problem, but in no particular order, and may often repeat themselves. Adults and older children tend to approach trial and error as a problem-solving strategy more systematically, and may also try a broader range of possibilities. Both of these characteristics mean that older children are more likely to be successful than younger ones, even in trial and error strategies (Thornton 2002). Box 11.6 shows a boy engaged in this trial and error process in his experimentations with shape, size and balance.

Meadows (2006) identifies a number of ways in which more expert problem-solvers may have more sophisticated planning strategies than novices. Note here, as before, that the emphasis is not on this necessarily being a function of age alone, but the extent of the expert's knowledge and experience in the particular domain involved. She suggests that expert problem-solvers are more skilled at means–end analysis, that is, in selecting actions which lead to the achievement of the goal. For anything but the simplest of problems, this may include setting up sub-goals. For example, in painting a picture my first sub-goal might be to collect together paints, paper and brushes, before I can begin to paint. As Meadows (2006) points out, in many instances young children do not always need to put such sub-goals into effect, because an adult does this preliminary work, in this case putting out materials (and sometimes even supplying the picture to be painted, but that is another matter!). This suggests the value of developing practical approaches which increasingly give the responsibility for such activity to the children themselves, in order for them to have opportunities to develop skill in structuring their plans. Given such opportunities, it is evident that even young children have developed considerable expertise in this type of planning. For example, at the age of 3 years, children can solve a problem that requires two moves to progress from start to attaining the goal, by the age of 4 they can solve four-move problems, and by the age of 5 or 6 the length of problem may be five or six moves (Siegler and Alibali 2005).

Other aspects that Meadows (2006) suggests may be different between experts and novices include the extent of their knowledge of the subject of the problem, their ability to interpret how that knowledge needs to be used, how flexible their plans are, memory capacity and their experience in potentially helpful metacognitive activities. Thornton (2002) emphasizes that this skill in identifying which factors are (or are not) relevant to a problem, and which strategies may be most effective, is only possible in situations where we have knowledge and expertise. To sum up here, the development of children's knowledge about a specific problem context will play an important part in determining whether they can plan in a systematic way, or whether they will need to rely on trial and error. It is useful to refer back here to the discussion in Chapter 8 on the role of experience and expertise in conceptual development.

### Different models to explain the development of problem-solving in young children

Whilst there is much consensus about aspects such as the role of trial and error, planning, and knowledge in children's problem-solving skills, there are some key differences in the models used to describe its development. DeLoache and Brown suggest a 'general acquisition mechanism' (1987: 115) or sequence of stages which may be common when children approach a problem. Describing both the behaviour of children aged 1½ to 3½ years in nesting a set of cups, and children aged 4 to 7 years in train track play, they suggest that there is a progressive sequence over time in the strategies children use to correct their errors in construction. This sequence has some similarities to Piaget's stage model of cognition. Children progress from trying to correct their errors in construction by:

a  exerting physical force without changing any of the elements: for example, brute force in trying to make a larger cup fit into a smaller one;
b  making limited changes in a part of the problem set: local correction, for example, taking out one piece of the track and trying to make it fit, whilst ignoring the rest;
c  considering and operating on the problem as a whole: for example, a consideration of the whole set of cups, and multiple relationships.

The first stage was characteristic of the youngest children in each group, with the final stage of more 'advanced correction strategies' (DeLoache and Brown 1987: 112) only being used by the older children in each group. Both age groups displayed similar approaches in that they spontaneously monitored the success of their own goal-directed efforts, and attempted to correct their errors.

Thornton suggests that the 'traditional model' (2002: 135) that new and powerful strategies replace older ones as children develop may be fundamentally wrong. The use of microgenetic study (study of the same children repeatedly over short periods of time), she suggests, reveals that older and weaker strategies are not replaced, but continue to be used alongside newer, more sophisticated strategies, often for considerable lengths of time. These newer, more powerful strategies do not necessarily grow out of the older ones, and may be unconnected with them (Thornton 2002). Siegler and Alibali

(2005) also note that children generally think about problems in multiple ways at any one time, and that innovations in problem-solving technique follow success as well as failure. Thornton (2002) suggests that Siegler's overlapping waves theory (see Chapter 2, and Siegler *et al.* 2011) provides a useful model here, with children using different strategies at the same time, and even for the same problem. In a particular situation, a young child's choice of strategy will depend on its history in the child's experience. Each experience provides more feedback, with particular strategies gradually becoming more closely associated with success in particular contexts. Smith *et al.* (2011) suggest that a key factor here is the environment, and the ways in which this creates a context in which children realize the importance of particular strategies. They also suggest that this model may be most likely in contexts where children have a moderate amount of experience at a task. When children (and adults) are very familiar with a task, they suggest, they will have established, and will consistently use, the most appropriate strategy they have. In very novel situations, similarly, strategy use will tend to be more restricted, as people do not yet have enough knowledge of the context. When people are at the stage of developing their understanding of a situation, they may try out a number of different problem-solving strategies at the same time.

Look now at the episode described in Box 11.7, which shows Mark using a range of problem-solving strategies, including hypothesizing, trial and error, metacognitive knowledge and even physical force, in his own, self-initiated and self-directed activity.

## Some implications for practice in supporting young children's problem-solving

### Strategies and processes

There is considerable debate about whether there are general problem-solving strategies which can be taught, or whether much critical and creative thinking and problem-solving is task- or domain-specific (Meadows 2006). Woolfolk *et al.* (2008) suggest that there is evidence for both, with children and adults moving between general and specific skills depending on the situation and their level of expertise. Whitebread nevertheless identifies some processes which he believes are 'involved in solving any problem' (2000a: 156). These are:

- understanding and representing the problem (including identifying what kinds of information are relevant to its solution);
- gathering and organizing relevant information;
- constructing and managing a plan of action;
- reasoning, hypothesis testing and decision-making;
- using various problem-solving tools (drawings, maps and other representations).

(Whitebread 2000a:156–7)

Fisher (2005) and MacNaughton and Williams (2009) also add to these the importance of children reviewing and evaluating what has been done. However, whilst such general processes may be identifiable, they do not form a 'recipe' for problem-solving, and attempts to teach procedures at the expense of understanding 'do not foster (and may inhibit) the development of strategies for regulating one's own problem solving' (Wood 1998: 294).

Box 11.7:  Mark, aged 3.8, at the water tray in a community preschool

Mark is playing alone at a transparent water tray. He slots a length of thin flexible tubing inside the neck of a bottle, fits a funnel into the tubing and takes a deep breath. Holding the neck of the bottle he uses a large jug to pour water slowly down the funnel and tubing into the bottle. He repeats this several times with varying degrees of accuracy, shaking the bottle each time. He pauses and stares blankly at the water. He then lifts the bottle higher and tries the same activity. This time the water spills before reaching the funnel.

MARK:      Oh no. (He looks puzzled, and continues pouring the water, readjusting his position.)

Removing the tubing, he pours the water out of the bottle. He reaches for a wider piece of black tubing and tries to slot it into the neck of the bottle. He tries banging the tubing over the neck, and then twisting it in a screwing motion. With a frown he gives up.

   He picks up a thin rigid tube and a different jug. Holding it at the top, he rests the end of the tube on the base of the water tray. He watches the top of the tube intently as he pours water accurately down it. He then lifts the tube above the water and watches it flowing out of the bottom. He repeats this sequence several times. He pauses, and looks puzzled. He suddenly crouches down and looks underneath the water tray, seeming confused. He reaches out to touch the base in several places. He then stands back up, and looks closely down one end of the tubing, placing it near to his eye. As he does this some water drips from the tube. He then puts the opposite end of the tube to his eye.

*Mark develops 'a complex interaction between strategy and declarative knowledge' (Meadows 2006: 127). Metacognitive strategies are apparent, first, as Mark constructs a theory, based on previous experience, that objects can be screwed or banged to make them fit; second, in his search for an explanation as to why he did not see the water coming out of the tube again. He knows the water has not just disappeared, so it is logical that he would see it come out again. Finally, Mark concludes that the water must be either under the trough or alternatively still in the tube. Mark's observations lead to conflicting ideas about how water behaves when changing the height of the tube. He searches for clues to extend and test his hypotheses.*

Abridged and reproduced with permission of Janet Roberts

### Knowledge and experience in meaningful contexts

Whilst concurring with Whitebread that there are problem-solving strategies which can be applied in many different situations, Meadows (2006) emphasizes the crucial importance of these being set in meaningful contexts. These experiences provide children with opportunities for developing knowledge, both declarative (knowing that) and procedural (knowing how), and expertise, and a bigger repertoire of problems on which to draw (Whitebread 2000b). This emphasis on the value of knowledge and experience links to Tizard and Hughes (2002) in Chapter 8, as well as to all of the theoretical positions outlined in Chapter 2. Gura suggests that, in relation to blockplay, experience and developing expertise go hand in hand, leading to more complex representation and problem-solving:

> Our own study shows a direct link between exploratory activity with blocks, ie materials-mastery play, and the ability to use them with increasing fluency and *flair* in creating representations covering a wide range of content. This involves a great deal of problem-solving as children work out which aspects of the object or experience they want to represent can be done with blocks, and how.
>
> (Gura 1992: 118; emphasis in original)

Play of all kinds provides valuable contexts for the development of problem-solving. Sociodramatic pretend play, in particular, may have a reciprocal relationship with problem-solving (Bergen 2002), and provide opportunities for meaning-making, role-taking and negotiation, supportive of problem-solving (Hope 2002).

Looked at more widely, the sociocultural context will also play a part here. The problems that young children spontaneously want to solve in their lives arise as part of their cultural context, and may even determine what is seen as a 'problem' (Hope 2002).

### Whose problem is it? Choice and direction in problem-solving

The relationship between child- and adult-initiated activity in early childhood settings is a subject of considerable debate, much of which is outside the scope of this book. In the context of children's thinking, Siraj-Blatchford *et al.* (2002) and Sylva *et al.* (2010) found that the 'excellent' and 'good' settings in their study tended to have an equal balance between adult-led and child-initiated activity. In our research, those working with children aged 3 and 4 tended to suggest a balance which placed more emphasis on activities that were mostly child chosen, whilst those practitioners working with 4 and 5 year olds were more likely to favour an equal division between child-chosen and adult-led activities (Robson and Hargreaves 2005). Siraj-Blatchford *et al.* (2002) also found that the percentage of adult-initiated activities also increased, as a function of the age of the children. This may be attributable to a number of factors, but the tendency for increasing formalization of the curriculum, and of children's activities, and the requirement to move 'children through a predetermined series of narrowly defined goals and targets' (Hendy and Whitebread 2000: 251) as they go through school will play a part here in determining what is seen as appropriate. As Hendy and Whitebread (2000) observe, this may not be conducive to a classroom atmosphere in which initiative and the ability to think for oneself as a child is likely to flourish.

Is there a relationship between choice and 'ownership' and children's problem-solving and thinking skills? De Boo cites research which suggests that, when children are presented with a problem to solve, they give fewer and less varied responses than when they identify and solve their own problems (Tuma and Reif 1980, cited in de Boo 1999). Looking at children's play activities as contexts for thinking, Sylva *et al.* suggest that 'freely chosen play activities often provided the best opportunities for adults to extend children's thinking' (2010: 158), and Wright (2010) highlights the ways in which adults can either inhibit or encourage children's creative thinking and problem-solving depending upon their openness to the children's own ideas and choices. Segar (2004) studied groups of children aged 3–5 years in English nursery and reception classes. She found similar levels of persistence at tasks in individual children, whether they were child- or adult-initiated, suggesting that the children were prepared, in most instances, to 'go along with' whatever was asked of them. What differed were the levels of involvement of the children, with child-initiated tasks consistently associated with higher levels of involvement than those initiated by adults. Laevers (1999) suggests that involvement is an outward sign of intense mental activity in a child. The episode in Box 11.8 provides an example of an adult-initiated activity which seemed to have little meaning for the children, and in which nevertheless a potentially rich opportunity for understanding and extending the children's thinking was missed.

Fisher (2005) suggests that it is the child's experience and environment which should provide the catalyst for problem-solving. Such a statement, however, can be interpreted in a number of ways. In Reggio Emilia, for example, long-term projects arise out of the children's expressed interests and concerns. A similar approach is outlined in Katz and Chard (2000). See, for example, the inspiration for *The Crowd*, a project undertaken by children and adults in Reggio Emilia, which is briefly outlined in Box 11.9.

A common approach in many early childhood settings is to use familiar contexts for young children as vehicles for the development of problem-solving skills, often linking this with wider learning intentions and planning. Belle Wallace outlines a model known as TASC: Thinking Actively in a Social Context, which 'sets out a framework for the development of a problem-solving and thinking skills curriculum' (2002: 8). This approach is intended to develop such skills in an integrated way across all activities and areas of the curriculum, using a number of skills, conceptualized as a cyclic 'wheel', which are designed to guide the actions of practitioners in their work with children:

- gather/organize: find out what children know, show how ideas link, stimulate children's questions, focus on questions to explore;
- identify: explain/demonstrate the task, discuss what is needed;
- generate: ask for learners' ideas, add ideas, discuss ways of finding out and recording;
- decide: look at feasibility of ideas, share tasks amongst group;
- implement: use variety of activities and finding out and recording skills;
- evaluate: check if goal was achieved, think about improvements, discuss group cooperation;
- communicate: share with others and encourage communication;
- learn from experience: reflect on process, state what has been learned, look for uses in other lessons.

(Adapted from Wallace 2002: 18–19)

Chandler (2004), noting the use of TASC in one school, records a teacher's comment that the TASC wheel gave the children a structure for their thinking, which can nevertheless be used flexibly, either in whole or in part. The examples provided by Wallace (2002) include ideas for work in classes for children between 3 and 7 years, around topics such as 'Our Teddy Bears Picnic' and 'What do we know about buildings?', linked to the class's medium-term planning, and involving a number of areas of the curriculum.

Lambert (2000) suggests that such an approach, which starts from curriculum intentions identified by the adults in the setting, may be problematic for young

Box 11.8: Boy A aged 3.3, Boy B aged 3.1 and Practitioner P, in an adult-directed activity of a 'treasure hunt'

Each child has been given a map of the environment.

PRACTITIONER:  Do you know where you are on the map?

A:  No. (Looks at his map.)

PRACTITIONER:  If you stand this way and look at the map can you see where the book corner is?

A:  Yes, there (pointing to the actual book corner).

PRACTITIONER:  Yes, but can you show me on the map?

A:  (Looks at map and turns it around in his hands.) I think you should put the treasure there (points to the window sill).

PRACTITIONER:  If I did that you wouldn't need your map because you would know where it was.

A:  But I can't find the treasure.

PRACTITIONER:  Why don't you and B hunt for the treasure together?

A TO B:  Let's go and look in the role play (they run to the role play, look and run to the creative area, look, and A finds the treasure (coloured stones in a bottle.)

A TO B:  We found it. (They both smile and approach the practitioner.)

A TO P:  I found it under the table, it's funny treasure, my book at my house has coins.

PRACTITIONER:  There are lots of different sorts of treasure, shall we hide the treasure again?

A TO B:  This is like hide and seek, we don't need a map.

*Wells (1987) cautions against adults' providing activities children are unable to relate to their own understanding and as a result have no purpose for them. For Child A it could be argued that his responses to the practitioner's comments show that the activity had no purpose or meaning for him. He stresses the importance of 'collaborative construction of meaning' (1987: 101). For Child A it could be argued that this was not apparent.*

*It could be further argued that A's comment, 'I found it under the table, it's funny treasure, my book at my house has coins', provided an opportunity for sustained shared thinking (Sylva et al. 2010) which I would suggest was not evident in the practitioner's response. Longitudinal studies such as the Effective Provision of Pre-School Education (Sylva et al. 2010) and Researching Effective Pedagogy in Early Years (Siraj-Blatchford et al. 2002) indicate sustained shared thinking as one of the most effective elements of practice.*

Abridged and reproduced with permission of Katie Brendon

children precisely because the focus is on problems prescribed by the curriculum, rather than on ones that the children spontaneously want to solve, arising from their real-life experiences. The procedures involved may often be divorced from real-world procedures. She emphasizes that the kinds of problems children are often interested

---

*Box 11.9: The Crowd, Reggio Emilia*

Just back from the summer vacation, talking with his friends and a teacher, Gabriele commented on a summer evening he remembers:

GABRIELE:   In the evening, it was full of people, people walking up and people walking down. You couldn't see anything, just people, legs, arms and heads.

Staff decided to explore other children's images of crowds:

- When there's a lot of people, they make a lot of noise.
- It's a carpet of people that walks and moves.
- Everybody passes by with their shoulders all squeezed together.
- I was right in the middle. When there's lots and lots of people, it's a real big problem because you can get lost.
- Crowds at night are real dangerous because it's dark.

One girl drew people all going in the same direction. To explore this, and other ideas, staff thought of as many different ways and situations in which the children could test out their thinking. The children went out into the town square, projected images of crowds onto a wall at the centre, drew each other from multiple perspectives, made paper and card models of themselves and put them together as 'crowds', and explored spaces of different sizes, being part of a crowd. Two final representations, one in clay, and one graphic, resulted from the children's self-directed, collaborative activity.

(Adapted from Reggio Children 1996: 142–55)

---

in solving differ in many respects from those 'given' to them as exercises in settings. Box 11.10 summarizes the differences as she sees them.

Whilst the differences that she proposes may not apply to all 'problem-solving' approaches, including TASC, her comparisons are useful, in pointing to possible ways in which there may be differences between the reasoning and problem-solving strategies that children use in adult-initiated and child-initiated activities. She suggests that an approach which starts from the child's interests is 'aligned with how children in the first years of school simply prefer to think' (Lambert 2000: 37).

### Time and space

Giving sufficient, uninterrupted, time to children's problem-solving, and fostering an atmosphere of trial and error, supports them in developing deeper understandings and more complex knowledge about the problems they are addressing (Lambert 2000). In addition, children will need to know that this time is available. Gura (1992), looking at children's blockplay, for example, comments on the way in which a 'hit and run' attitude seemed to develop amongst children where lack of time prevented them from embarking on sustained play which develops over a period of time. Practitioners in our research suggested that this was one of the biggest challenges they faced, but

*Box 11.10:* Lambert (2000): adult- versus child-initiated problems

| Adult-initiated problems | Child-initiated problems |
|---|---|
| Predetermined goal | Spontaneous discovery or selection of own goals |
| Information needed to solve the problem may be given | Information may be diverse and not yet known |
| One solution or answer | Solutions may be diverse |
| Not 'real-life' problems | 'Real-life' problems |

they emphasized the importance they placed upon both time for activity, and time for children to talk about their thinking, and Claxton (2006) suggests that adults should make time for 'reverie' in children, where they have opportunities to spend time reflecting on what they are learning.

### Relationships, attitudes and dispositions

Children's attitudes and dispositions, including their interest, motivation and confidence, will be crucial to their success in problem-solving (Fisher 2005). The impact of stress and pressure may be to lessen children's creativity in problem-solving (Claxton 1998).

This suggests a number of key aspects of the role of adults in their interactions with young children. Most importantly, relationships between adults and children which are 'responsive and reciprocal' (Carr 2001) seem to promote greater persistence at activities and cooperation with others (Claxton 1999b), and greater receptivity to new ideas (Robson 2012). Other benefits to children's problem-solving seem to be related to adult modelling of language and problem-solving (Bronson 2000a; Gura 1992; Mercer 2000; Siraj-Blatchford 2007), adult suggestions of problem-solving strategies (Bronson 2000a) and joint adult–child participation in problem-solving activities (Bronson 2000a; Gura 1992). Discussions between adults and children in problem-solving activities provide opportunities for adult examples of strategy use that children can then use in their private speech, in the way Vygotsky describes (1986), as well as providing a forum that supports the making of meaningful connections between ideas (Craft *et al.* 2008b) and discussion about how children are thinking about, and trying to solve, problems (Wood 1998; Mercer 2000). Wegerif's emphasis on the value of playful talk is similar to an important aspect of Craft's (2001) ideas of possibility thinking, and the posing of 'what if?' questions that encourage playful, imaginative dialogue between adults and children.

Adult diagnosis of children's problem-solving processes is facilitated by direct involvement with activities, allowing for both discussion and direct observation. The pitfalls of adult questions were looked at in Chapter 7, and Wegerif (2010) emphasizes the importance of open-ended questioning and reasoning, whilst Gura (1992) suggests the value of non-evaluative comments, rather than questions, for finding out about children's problem-solving.

*Box 11.11:* 6 children, including Angelina, aged 3.9, Jake, aged 3.3, and Hollie, aged 3.5, making peppermint creams in the nursery, with Cathy, a practitioner

Each child has their own bowl and spoon, and, before the point at which we join the activity, the children, working with Cathy, have explored the ingredients, and measured out icing sugar into their bowls. Jo, another staff member, is nearby.

CATHY:     When we make icing to ice our biscuits we add water but today we are making peppermint creams so we have different ingredients. Look and see what else we can add to bind the icing sugar and make it stick together.

ANGELINA AND JAKE:     Cream!

JAKE:     Yukky cream. (He makes a face and others laugh. They take it in turns to pour the cream. Jake puts too much cream in his bowl.)

CATHY:     Jake, it's a bit too runny, what do you think you should do to make it thicker?

JAKE:     More cream.

CATHY:     Are you sure?

JAKE:     Yes. (He pours more cream in. He then turns tearfully to another member of staff.) It's still runny Jo.

JO:     That happened to me once but when I put more icing sugar in it made it thicker.

JAKE:     Oh. (He adds three more spoonfuls of sugar.)

HOLLIE:     Well done, Jake, that's nicer, it's smooth now. Clever Jake, aren't you Jake.

(Jake nods and smiles, and adds two more spoonfuls of sugar.)

JAKE:     It's getting thicker (whispered).

*What could have been a negative learning experience became for him a positive experience of collaborative adult/child problem-solving, and can be seen as part of a process of developing a positive disposition towards learning. Jake's self-esteem was raised by Hollie's praise of his accomplishment and provided him with the confidence to proceed.*

Abridged and reproduced with permission of Jo Short

Box 11.11 shows the importance of joint adult–child participation and discussion, whilst also highlighting the importance of supporting children's interactions with one another.

### Playing together and alone

Children's interactions with one another will have an important impact upon their problem-solving skills. In Chapter 7 the value of cooperative and collaborative activity, particularly in pairs, was discussed. In the context of developing problem-solving skills, peer collaboration has much potential (Fawcett and Garton 2005; Robson 2012), with the potential for playful interaction between collaborators being particularly significant

(Siraj-Blatchford 2007). Children who are friends are more successful in problem-solving activities than non-friends (Garton 2004), a phenomenon which seems to be related to their willingness to coordinate what they do and resolve conflicts. Even where they are not friends, children in novice–expert pairs who are prepared to exchange and resolve differences of opinion show significant improvements in their performance in problem-solving tasks. Katz and Chard (2000) suggest that this improvement even carries over into other tasks. In larger groups, the thinking of both children and adults contributes to 'a larger, more meaningful whole' (Project Zero and Reggio Children 2001: 247). Developing children's ability to both take feedback from others, and to give constructive, in-depth feedback of their own, can help children to think about problems and solutions in new ways (Gura 1992).

Children's solitary play may also support problem-solving, by allowing children time and space to reflect privately (Lloyd and Howe 2003). Lloyd and Howe believe that such solitary play is not necessarily a more immature form of play, as has often been asserted. They suggest the importance of creating opportunities and spaces for children to play together, or alone, as they choose, whilst emphasizing the importance of helping 'reticent' children to engage with their physical and social environment.

## Implications for practice: a final summary

The points set out here provide an overall summary and conclusion for the chapter, and, in many ways, for the book as a whole:

- The importance of a loving, supportive and secure environment (Craft *et al.* 2008b) where questioning and risk-taking in thinking are encouraged (Claxton 1999b; De Boo 1999).
- Provision of a physical environment of which the children feel a sense of ownership (Walsh *et al.* 2007), and in which they have opportunities to explore materials and ideas and use resources in novel, unexpected ways (Robson 2012).
- The importance of experience for feeding young children's thinking (Fisher 2005).
- Interventions aimed at supporting children's thinking are most effective when they are set in contexts which are meaningful for children. Such contexts will be different for individual children (Whitebread 2000a; McKendree *et al.* 2002).
- The importance of narrative, dialogue and play for developing children's thinking (Taggart *et al.* 2005).
- Pretence and make-believe may be particularly valuable for problem-solving, developing creative thinking, negotiation and talk about mental states (Bergen 2002; Singer 1973; Robson 2012).
- Children may show their highest levels of involvement in self-initiated activities, and these often provide the best contexts for problem-solving and extending their thinking (Lambert 2000; Siraj-Blatchford *et al.* 2002; Robson 2012).
- Giving sufficient, uninterrupted time to children's problem-solving supports the development of deeper understanding and more complex knowledge (Lambert 2000).
- The value of supporting the development of children's personal reflections, both on their own ideas and representations and on those of others.

- The value of adult use and modelling of metacognitive strategies, including identifying what you don't know, speculating, generating questions, thinking aloud and problem-solving (Fisher 2005; Mercer 2000; Robson 2012; Wegerif 2010).
- Adults play a particularly important role in supporting children's initial engagement in activities (Robson 2012; Sylva *et al.* 2010).
- Adult–child joint problem-solving may be valuable for supporting metacognition and problem-solving (Bronson 2000a). However, when adults get involved children may sometimes be more likely to say that they cannot do something. When working with other children, they may be less likely to question their ability, and often gain confidence through mimicking another child (Whitebread *et al.* 2005).
- The most effective response from an adult to a child asking for help may be to direct them to another child who has competence or expertise in the area. Often just watching another child supports metacognitive development (Whitebread *et al.* 2005).
- Opportunities for children to collaborate, particularly amongst friends, may be especially helpful in the development of thinking (Garton 2004).
- Children's solitary play may support problem-solving, by allowing children time and space to reflect privately (Lloyd and Howe 2003).
- Adult diagnosis of children's thinking may be facilitated by their direct involvement in children's activities, their discussions with children and their use of non-evaluative comments to probe understanding (Gura 1992).
- Talk between adults and children may be especially valuable for supporting children's self-assessment and reflections on themselves as thinkers (Robson 2010).
- 'To ensure effective development in children's thinking, the next step for the early years practitioner is to: foster creativity, offer alternatives, make links with previous learning, promote reflection, provide challenge, and introduce a degree of ambiguity and reflective thinking on the part of the children' (Walsh *et al.* 2007: 59).

## Further reflection

1 In your view, are thinking skills transferable and generalizable? Can children be supported in developing such transferable thinking skills? If so, how, in your view, can this be done?

2 Costello (2000: 3) clearly sets out the arguments 'for' and 'against' the teaching of philosophical thinking to young children. The chief arguments against the teaching of philosophy to young children are that it is not 'real' or 'serious' philosophy, and that children will not be able to understand it. What is your response to this? If you disagree, what arguments would you offer in favour of philosophy for young children?

3 What problems have you solved this week? How did you tackle them? Are there similarities, or do you approach different kinds of problems in different ways?

## Further reading

*Developing 'good' thinking, and models for teaching thinking:*

Claxton (1998, 1999b)
Costello (2000)
Fisher (2001, 2005)
Haynes (2002)
Higgins *et al.* (2004)
Lipman (2003)
Meadows (2006: ch. 6)
McGregor (2007)
McGuinness (1999)
Walsh *et al.* (2007)

*Creative thinking, critical thinking and problem-solving*

De Boo (1999: chs 3 and 6)
Claxton (1998, 1999b)
Craft *et al.* (2008a)
DeLoache and Brown (1987)
Fisher (2005: chs 2, 3 and 4)
Fumoto *et al.* (2012)
Karmiloff-Smith (1994: 121–5, 186–93)
Lambert (2000)
Meadows (2006: 127–32, 253–60)
Project Zero and Reggio Children (2001)
Siegler and Alibali (2005)
Sternberg (2003)
Thornton (2002: ch. 6)
Wallace (2002)
Wegerif (2010)

# A brief selection of useful websites

21st Century Learning Initiative: http://www.21learn.org
Cambridgeshire INDependent LEarning in the Foundation Stage: www.educ.cam.ac.uk/cindle
Childrenthinking: www.childrenthinking.co.uk
Creative Partnerships: http://www.creative-partnerships.com
Institute for the Advancement of Philosophy for Children (IAPC): http://cehs.montclair.edu/
    academic/iapc
Institute for Habits of Mind: http://www.instituteforhabitsofmind.com/
International Mind, Brain and Education Society http://www.imbes.org/
DialogueWorks: www.dialogueworks.co.uk
Making Learning Visible: http://pzweb.harvard.edu/mlv
Ministry of Education, New Zealand: www.educate.ece.govt.nz/learning/
    curriculumAndLearning/Assessmentforlearning/
KeiTuaotePae/National Center for Teaching Thinking (USA): www.nctt.net
Project Zero: http://pzweb.harvard.edu
Reggio Children: www.reggiochildren.it
Rich Learning Opportunities http://www.richlearningopportunities.co.uk/
Sightlines Initiative: www.sightlines-initiative.com
Society for the Advancement of Philosophical Enquiry and Reflection in Education
(SAPERE): http://www.sapere.org.uk/
Teaching Thinking (Robert Fisher): www.teachingthinking.net
Thinking Together http://thinkingtogether.educ.cam.ac.uk/

# Bibliography

Addessi, A. R., and Pachet, F. (2005) 'Experiments with a musical machine: musical style replication in 3 to 5 year old children', *British Journal of Music Education*, 22(1): 21–46.

Adey, P., and Shayer. M. (1994) *Really Raising Standards: Cognitive Intervention and Academic Achievement*, London: Routledge.

Ainsworth, M. D. S., Blehar, M. C., Waters, E., and Wall, S. (1978) *Patterns of Attachment*, Hillsdale, NJ: Erlbaum.

Albon, D. (2011) 'Postmodern and post-structuralist perspectives on early childhood education', in L. Miller and L. Pound (eds), *Theories and Approaches to Learning in the Early Years*, London: Sage, pp. 38–52.

Alderson, P. (2005) 'Children's rights: a new approach to studying childhood', in H. Penn, *Understanding Early Childhood*, Maidenhead: Open University Press.

Alderson, P., and Morrow, V. (2011) *The Ethics of Research with Children and Young People*, London: Sage.

Alexander, R. (2006) (3rd edn) *Towards Dialogic Teaching*, Cambridge: Cambridge University Press/ Dialogos.

Amabile, T. M. (1996) *Creativity in Context*. Boulder, CO: Westview Press.

Anning, A., and Edwards, A. (2006) (2nd edn) *Promoting Children's Learning from Birth to Five*, Buckingham: Open University.

Anning, A., and Ring, K. (2004) *Making Sense of Children's Drawings*, Maidenhead: Open University Press.

Anning, A., Cullen, J., and Fleer, M. (eds) (2009) *Early Childhood Education: Society and Culture*, London: Sage.

Armstrong, M. (2006) *Children Writing Stories*, Maidenhead: Open University Press.

Arnheim, R. (1969) *Visual Thinking*, Berkeley, CA: University of California Press.

Arnold, C. (1999) *Child Development and Learning 2–5 Years*, London: Hodder & Stoughton.

Arnold, C., and the Pen Green Team (2010) *Understanding Schemas and Emotion in Early Childhood*, London: Sage.

Astington, J. (1994) *The Child's Discovery of the Mind*, London: Fontana.

Astington, J. (1998) 'Theory of mind goes to school', *Educational Leadership*, 56(3): 46–9.

Astington, J. W., and Baird, J. A. (2004) 'Why language matters for theory of mind', *International Journal of Behavioral Development*, 28(3), Supplement Newsletter, 1/45: 7–9.

Astington, J. W., and Baird, J. A. (2005a) *Why Language Matters for Theory of Mind*, Oxford: Oxford University Press.

Astington, J. W., and Baird, J. A. (2005b) 'Representational Development and False-Belief Understanding', in J. W. Astington and J. A. Baird (eds), *Why Language Matters for Theory of Mind*, Oxford: Oxford University Press, pp. 163–85.

Athey, C. (2007) *Extending Thought in Young Children: A Parent Teacher Partnership*, London: Paul Chapman.

Bailey, D. R., Jnr (2002) 'Are critical periods critical for early childhood education? The role of timing in early childhood pedagogy', *Early Childhood Research Quarterly*, 17: 281–94.

Bailey, R. (2002) 'Playing social chess: children's play and social intelligence', *Early Years*, 22(2): 163–73.

Bailey, R., and Farrow, S. (1998) 'Play and problem-solving in a new light', *International Journal of Early Years Education*, 6(3): 265–75.

Bamberger, J. (2005) 'How the conventions of notation shape musical perception and performance', in D. Miell, R. MacDonald, and D. J. Hargreaves (eds), *Musical Communication*, Oxford: Oxford University Press, pp. 143–65.

Baron-Cohen, S. (1995) *Mind Blindness*, Cambridge, MA: MIT Press.

Baron-Cohen, S. (2004) *The Essential Difference: Men, Women and the Extreme Male Brain*, London: Penguin.

Barratt-Pugh, C., and Rohl, M. (2000) *Literacy Learning in the Early Years*, Buckingham: Open University Press.

Barrett, M. (1997) 'Invented notations: a view of young children's musical thinking', *Research Studies in Music Education*, 8(1): 2–14.

Barrett, M. (2001)'Constructing a view of children's meaning -making as notators: a case study of a five-year-old's descriptions and explanations of invented notations', *Research Studies in Music Education*, 16(1): 33–45.

Barrett, M. (2005) 'Representation, cognition and communication: invented notation in children's musical communication', in D. Miell, R. MacDonald, and D. J. Hargreaves (eds), *Musical Communication*, Oxford: Oxford University Press, pp. 117–42.

Bartholomew, L., and Bruce, T. (1993) *Getting to Know You*, London: Hodder & Stoughton.

Bartsch, K., and Wellman, H. M. (1995) *Children Talk about the Mind*, Oxford: Oxford University Press.

Bauer, P. J., and Souci, P. S. (2010) 'Going beyond the facts: young children extend knowledge by integrating episodes', *Journal of Experimental Child Psychology*, 107: 452–65.

Baumeister, R. F., Campbell, J. D., Krueger, J. I., and Vohs, K. D. (2005) 'Exploding the self-esteem myth', *Scientific American*, 292(1): 70–7.

Bayley, R. (2002) 'Learning Styles', *Early Years Educator*, 4(5), suppl.

Bell, M. A., and Wolfe, C. D. (2004) 'Emotion and cognition: an intricately bound developmental process', *Child Development*, 75(2): 366–70.

Bennett, N., and Dunne, E. (1992) *Managing Classroom Groups*, London: Simon & Schuster.

Bereiter, C., and Scardamalia, M. (1989) 'Intentional learning as a goal of instruction', in L. B. Resnick (ed.), *Knowing, Learning and Instruction*, Hillsdale, NJ: Lawrence Erlbaum Associates.

Bergen, D. (2002) 'The role of pretend play in children's cognitive development', *Early Childhood Research and Practice*, 4(1), online. <http://ecrp.uiuc.edu/v4n1/bergen.html> (accessed Feb. 2005).

Bergin, C., and Bergin, D. (2009) 'Attachment in the classroom', *Educational Psychology Review* 21: 141–70.

Bidell, T. R., and Fischer, K. W. (1992) 'Cognitive development in educational contexts: implications of skill theory', in A. Demetriou, M. Shayer and A. Efklides (eds), *Neo-Piagetian Theories of Cognitive Development*, London: Routledge, pp. 11–30.

Bingham, S., and Whitebread, D. (2009) 'Teachers supporting children's self-regulation in conflict situations within an early years setting', in T. Papatheodorou and J. Moyles (eds), *Learning Together in the Early Years*, London: Routledge.

Blackburn, S. (2003) 'State of mind', review of *The Blank Slate*, in *New Scientist* (24 May): 24.

Blagg, N., Ballinger, M., and Gardner, R. (1988) *Somerset Thinking Skills Course*, Oxford: Basil Blackwell.

Blakemore, S-J. (2005) 'Life before three: play or hot-housing?', *RSA Journal* (Feb.): 36–9.

Blakemore, S-J., and Frith, U. (2005) *The Learning Brain*, Oxford: Blackwell.

Bloom, B. S., Krathwohl, D. R., and Masia, B. B. (1956) *Taxonomy of Educational Objectives: Cognitive Domain*, New York: McKay.

Bodrova, E., and Leong, D. J. (2011) 'Revisiting Vygotskian perspectives on play and pedagogy', in S. Rogers (ed.), *Rethinking Play and Pedagogy in Early Childhood Education*, London: Routledge, pp. 60–72.

Boekaerts, M., and Cascallar E. (2006) 'How far have we moved toward the integration of theory and practice in self-regulation?', *Educational Psychology Review*, 18: 199–210.

Boekaerts, M., Pintrich, P. R., and Zeidner, M. (eds) (2000) *Handbook of Self-Regulation*, San Diego, CA: Academic Press.

Bowlby, J. (1969) *Attachment and Loss*, vol. 1, *Attachment*, London: Hogarth Press.

Bredekamp, S. (1987) *Developmentally Appropriate Practice in Early Childhood Education Programs Serving Children from Birth through Age 8*, Washington, DC: National Association for the Education of Young Children.

Bretherton, I. (ed.) (1984) *Symbolic Play: The Development of Social Understanding*, New York: Academic Press.

Broadhead, P. (1997) 'Promoting Sociability and Cooperation in Nursery Settings', *British Educational Research Journal*, 23(4): 513–31.

Broadhead, P. (2004) *Early Years Play and Learning: Developing Social Skills and Cooperation*, London: RoutledgeFalmer.

Bronfenbrenner, U. (1979) *The Ecology of Human Development*, Cambridge, MA: Harvard University Press.

Bronfenbrenner, U., and Ceci, S. J. (1994) 'Nature–nurture reconceptualized in developmental perspective: a bioecological model', *Psychological Review*, 101(4): 568–86.

Bronson, M. (2000a) *Self-Regulation in Early Childhood: Nature and Nurture*, New York: Guilford Press.

Bronson, M. (2000b) 'Recognizing and supporting the development of self-regulation in young children', *Young Children*, 55(2): 32–7.

Brooker, L. (2002) *Starting School: Young Children Learning Cultures*, Buckingham: Open University.

Brooks, M. (2004) 'Drawing: the social construction of knowledge', *Australian Journal of Early Childhood*, 29(2): 41–9.

Brown, A., and DeLoache, J. S. (1983) 'Metacognitive skills', in M. Donaldson, R. Grieve and C. Pratt (eds), *Early Childhood Development and Education*, Oxford: Blackwell, pp. 280–9.

Browne, E. (1994) *Handa's Surprise*, London: Walker Books.

Browne, N. (2010) 'Children's social and emotional development', in L. Miller, C. Cable, and G. Goodliff (eds), *Supporting Children's Learning in the Early Years*, London: Routledge in association with the Open University, pp. 86–98.

Bruer, J. T. (1997) 'Education and the brain: a bridge too far', *Educational Researcher*, 26(8): 4–16.

Bruer, J. T. (1998) 'Brain science, brain fiction', *Educational Leadership* (Nov.): 14–18.

Bruer, J. T. (1999) *The Myth of the First Three Years: A New Understanding of Early Brain Development and Lifelong Learning*, New York: Free Press.

Bruner, J. (1960) *The Process of Education*, Cambridge, MA: Harvard University Press.

Bruner, J. (1966) *Towards a Theory of Instruction*, Cambridge, MA: Harvard University Press.

Bruner, J. (1986) *Actual Minds, Possible Worlds*, Cambridge, MA: Harvard University Press.

Bruner, J. (1987) 'The transactional self', in J. Bruner and H. Haste (eds), *Making Sense*, London: Methuen, pp. 81–96.

Bruner, J. (1988) 'Vygotsky: a historical and conceptual perspective' in N. Mercer (ed.), *Language and Literacy from an Educational Perspective*, vol. 1, *Language Studies*, Milton Keynes: Open University Press.

Bruner, J., and Haste, H. (eds) (1987) *Making Sense*, London: Methuen.

Bruner J. S., Jolly, A., and Sylva, K. (eds) (1976) *Play*, Harmondsworth: Penguin.

Bryant, P. (1997) 'Mathematical understanding in the nursery school years', in T. Nunes and P. Bryant (eds), *Learning and Teaching Mathematics: An International Perspective*, Hove: Psychology Press, pp. 53–67.

Bullens, J., Nardini, M., Doeller, C. F., Braddick, O., Postma, A., and Burgess, N. (2010) 'The role of landmarks and boundaries in development of spatial memory', *Developmental Science*, 13(1): 170–80.

Butterworth, G. (1987) 'Some benefits of egocentrism', in J. Bruner and H. Haste (eds), *Making Sense*, London: Methuen.

Cahill, L. (2005) 'His brain, her brain', *Scientific American*, 292(5): 22–9.

Carey, S. (1985) *Conceptual Change in Childhood*, Cambridge, MA: MIT Press.

Carlson, S. M. (2011) 'Editorial: introduction to the special issue: executive function', *Journal of Experimental Child Psychology*, 108: 411–13.

Carpendale, J., and Lewis, C. (2006) *How Children Develop Social Understanding*, Oxford: Blackwell.

Carr, M. (1992) *Maths for Meaning: Tracing a Path for Early Mathematics Development, SAME papers 1992*, Hamilton, NZ: University of Waikato Centre for Science and Mathematics Research and Longman Paul.

Carr, M. (1998) *Assessing Children's Learning in Early Childhood Settings*, Wellington, NZ: New Zealand Council for Educational Research.

Carr, M. (2001) *Assessment in Early Childhood Settings*, London: Paul Chapman.

Case, R. (1992) 'The role of central conceptual structures in the development of children's scientific and mathematical thought', in A. Demetriou, M. Shayer and A. Efklides (eds), *Neo-Piagetian Theories of Cognitive Development*, London: Routledge, pp. 52–64.

Catherwood, D. (1999) 'New views on the young brain: offerings from developmental psychology to early childhood education', *Contemporary Issues in Early Childhood*, 1(1): 23–35.

Cattell, R. B. (1971) *Abilities: Their Structure, Growth and Action*, Boston, MA: Houghton-Mifflin.

Central Advisory Council for Education (CACE) (1967) *Children and their Primary Schools* (The Plowden Report), London: HMSO.

Chak, A. (2001) 'Adult sensitivity to children's learning in the zone of proximal development', *Journal for the Theory of Social Behaviour*, 31(4): 383–95.

Chak, A. (2007) 'Teachers' and parents' conceptions of children's curiosity and exploration', *International Journal of Early Years Education*, 15(2): 141–59.

Chandler, S. (2004) 'How TASC (Thinking Actively in a Social Context) helped to ensure rapid school improvement', paper presented at National Teacher Research Panel Second Conference, March, online: <http://www.tascwheel.com/files/chandler-wallace.pdf> (accessed June 2011).

Chomsky, N. (1957) *Syntactic Structures*, The Hague: Mouton.

Chukovsky, K. (1963) *From Two to Five*, Berkeley, CA: University of California Press.

Cimpian, A., Arce, H-M. C. Markman, E. M., and Dweck, C. S. (2007) 'Subtle linguistic cues affect children's motivation', *Psychological Science*, 18(4): 314–16.

Clark, A. (2010) *Transforming Children's Spaces*, London: Routledge.

Clark, A., and Moss, P. (2001) *Listening to Young Children: The Mosaic Approach*, London: National Children's Bureau and Joseph Rowntree Foundation.

Clark, A., Kjorholt, A. T., and Moss, P. (2005) *Beyond Listening*, Bristol: Policy Press.

Claxton, G. (1998) *Hare Brain, Tortoise Mind*, London: Fourth Estate.

Claxton, G. (1999a) 'Sure Start – brighter future', British Association for Early Childhood Education Conference Lecture, Westminster, London, June.

Claxton, G. (1999b) *Wise Up: The Challenge of Life Long Learning*, London: Bloomsbury.

Claxton, G. (2006) 'Thinking at the edge: developing soft creativity', *Cambridge Journal of Education*, 36(3): 351–62.

Claxton, G., and Carr, M. (2004) 'A framework for teaching learning: the dynamics of disposition', *Early Years*, 24(1): 87–97.

Clements, D. H. (1984) 'Training effects on the development and generalisation of Piagetian logical operations and knowledge of number', *Journal of Educational Psychology*, 76(5): 766–76.

Clements, D. H. (2004) 'Geometric and Spatial Thinking in Early Childhood Education', in D. H. Clements and J. Sarama (eds), *Engaging Young Children in Mathematics: Standards for Early Childhood Mathematics Education*, London: Lawrence Erlbaum, pp. 267–97.

Clements, D. H., and Sarama, J. (eds) (2004) *Engaging Young Children in Mathematics: Standards for Early Childhood Mathematics Education*, London: Lawrence Erlbaum.

Coates, E., and Coates, A. (2006) 'Young children talking and drawing', *International Journal of Early Years Education*, 14(3): 221–41.

Cohen, D. (2002) *How the Child's Mind Develops*, London: Routledge.

Cohen, L. (2009) 'The heteroglossic world of preschoolers' pretend Play', *Contemporary Issues in Early Childhood*, 10(4): 331–42.

Cole, M. (1996) *Cultural Psychology: A Once and Future Discipline*, Cambridge, MA: Belknap Press.

Cole, M. (2005) 'Cultural-historical activity theory in the family of socio-cultural approaches', *International Journal of Behavioral Development*, 29(3), Supplement Newsletter, 1/47: 1–4.

Cole, M., and Scribner, S. (1978) 'Introduction', in L. Vygotsky (ed.), *Mind in Society*, Cambridge, MA: Harvard University Press.

Cole, M., Gay, J., Glick, J. A., and Sharp, D. W. (1971) *The Cultural Context of Learning and Thinking*, London: Methuen.

Cole, P. M., Martin, S. E., and Dennis, T. A. (2004) 'Emotion regulation as a scientific construct: methodological challenges and directions for child development research', *Child Development*, 75(2): 317–33.

Coles, M. (1996) 'The magicfying glass: what we know of classroom talk in the early years', in N. Hall and J. Martello (eds), *Listening to Children Think: Exploring Talk in the Early Years*, London: Hodder & Stoughton, pp. 1–17.

Coles, M. J., and Robinson, W. D. (1991a) *Teaching Thinking: A Survey of Programmes in Education*, London: Bristol Classical Press.

Coles, M. J., and Robinson, W. D. (1991b) 'Teaching thinking: what is it? Is it possible?', in M. J. Coles and W. D. Robinson (eds), *Teaching Thinking: A Survey of Programmes in Education*, London: Bristol Classical Press, pp. 9–24.

Coltman, P. (2006) 'Talk of a number: self-regulated use of mathematical metalanguage by children in the foundation stage', *Early Years*, 26(1): 31–48.

Coltman, P., and Gifford, S. (2008) ' "How many shapey ones have you got?" Number and shape in the early years', in D. Whitebread and P. Coltman (eds), *Teaching and Learning in the Early Years*, London: Routledge.

Cooper, H. (2002) *History in the Early Years*, London: RoutledgeFalmer.

Cooper, H. (ed.) (2004) *Exploring Time and Place through Play*, London: David Fulton.

Corrie, L. (2000) 'Neuroscience and early childhood? A dangerous liaison', *Australian Journal of Early Childhood*, 25(2): 34–40.

Cortazar, A., and Herreros, F. (2010) 'Early attachment relationships and the early childhood curriculum', *Contemporary Issues in Early Childhood*, 11(2): 192–202.

Costa, A. L. (ed.) (1991) *Developing Minds*, Alexandria, VA: Association for Supervision and Curriculum Development.

Costello, P. J. M. (2000) *Thinking Skills and Early Childhood Education*, London: David Fulton.

Cox, S. (2005) 'Intention and meaning in young children's drawing', *International Journal of Art and Design Education*, 24(2): 115–25.

Craft, A. (2001) 'Little c creativity', in A. Craft, B. Jeffrey and M. Liebling (eds), *Creativity in Education*, London: Continuum, pp. 45–61.

Craft, A. (2003) 'Creative thinking in the early years of education', *Early Years*, 23(2): 143–54.

Craft, A., and Jeffrey, B. (2010) 'Creative practice and practice which fosters creativity', in L. Miller, C. Cable and G. Goodliff (eds), *Supporting Children's Learning in the Early Years*, London: Routledge in association with the Open University, pp. 133–40.

Craft, A., Jeffrey, B., and Liebling, M. (eds) (2001) *Creativity in Education*. London: Continuum, pp. 45–61.

Craft, A., Cremin, T., and Burnard, P. (eds) (2008a) *Creative Learning 3–11 and How we Document it*, Stoke on Trent: Trentham.

Craft, A., Cremin, T., Burnard, P., and Chappell, K. (2008b) 'Possibility thinking with children in England aged 3–7', in A. Craft, T. Cremin and P. Burnard (eds), *Creative Learning 3-11 and How we Document it*, Stoke on Trent: Trentham, pp. 65–73.

Crystal, D. (1998) *Language Play*, London: Penguin.

Csikszentmihalyi, M. (1979) 'The concept of flow', in B. Sutton-Smith (ed.), *Play and Learning*, New York: Gardner Press, pp. 257–74.

Cutting, A. L., and Dunn, J. (1999) 'Theory of mind, emotion understanding, language, and family background: individual differences and interrelations', *Child Development*, 70(4): 853–65.

Dahlberg, G., Moss, P., and Pence, A. (2007) *Beyond Quality in Early Childhood Education and Care: Postmodern Perspectives*, London: Routledge.

Dawes, L., and Sams, C. (2004) *Talk Box: Speaking and Listening Activities for Learning at Key Stage 1*, London: David Fulton.

Dawes, L., Mercer, N., and Wegerif, R. (2000) *Thinking Together*, Birmingham: Questions Publishing Co.

de Bono, E. (1991) 'The CoRT thinking program', A. L. Costa (ed.), in *Developing Minds*, Alexandria, VA: Association for Supervision and Curriculum Development, pp. 27–32.

de Boo, M. (1999) *Enquiring Children, Challenging Teaching*, Buckingham: Open University.

de Boo, M. (ed.) (2000a) *Science 3–6: Laying the Foundations in the Early Years*, Hatfield: Association for Science Education.

de Boo, M. (2000b) 'Why early years science?', in M. de Boo (ed.), *Science 3–6: Laying the Foundations in the Early Years*, Hatfield: Association for Science Education, pp. 1–6.

DeLoache, J. S., and Brown, A. L. (1987) 'The early emergence of planning skills in children', in J. Bruner and H. Haste (eds), *Making Sense*, London: Methuen, pp. 108–30.

DeLoache, J. S., Sugarman, S., and Brown, A. L. (1985) 'The development of error correction strategies in young children's manipulative play', *Child Development*, 56: 928–39.

Demetriou, A., Shayer, M., and Efklides, A. (eds) (1992) *Neo-Piagetian Theories of Cognitive Development*, London: Routledge.

Dennison, P. E., and Dennison, G. (1994) *Brain Gym: Teacher's Edition Revised*, Ventura: Edu-Kinesthetics Inc.

Department for Children, Schools and Families (DCSF) (England) (2009) *Every Child a Talker: Guidance for Early Language Lead Practitioners, Second Instalment Spring 2009*, London: DCSF.

Department for Education and Employment (DfEE) (2000) *Curriculum Guidance for the Foundation Stage*, London: HMSO.

Department for Education and Skills (DfES) (2005) *Excellence and Enjoyment: Social and Emotional Aspects of Learning*, London: DfES.

Department for Education and Skills (DfES) (2007) *Statutory Framework for the Early Years Foundation Stage*, Nottingham: DfES publications.

Desautel, D. (2009) 'Becoming a thinking thinker: metacognition, self-regulation, and classroom practice', *Teachers College Record*, 111(8): 1997–2020. Online: <http://www.tcrecord.org>, ID number 15504, accessed May 2011.

Dewey, J., and Bento, J. (2009) 'Activating children's thinking skills (ACTS): the effects of an infusion approach to teaching thinking in primary schools', *British Journal of Educational Psychology*, 79: 329–51.

Diamond, A., and Amso, D. (2008) 'Contributions of neuroscience to our understanding of cognitive development', *Current Directions in Psychological Science* 17(2): 136–41.

Dietrich, A. (2007) 'Who's afraid of a cognitive neuroscience of creativity?', *Methods*, 42: 22–7.

Dockett, S. (1998) 'Constructing understandings through play in the early years', *International Journal of Early Years Education*, 6(1): 105–16.

Doherty, J., and Hughes, M. (2009) *Child Development, Theory and Practice 0–11*, Harlow: Pearson.

Doherty, M.J. (2009) *Theory of Mind*, Hove, East Sussex: Psychology Press.

Donaldson, M. (1978) *Children's Minds*, Glasgow: Fontana/Collins.

Donaldson, M. (1992) *Human Minds*, London: Penguin.

Dowling, M. (2002) 'How young children learn', *Early Education* (Summer).

Dowling, M. (2005) *Supporting Young Children's Sustained Shared Thinking: An Exploration* (DVD and supporting materials), London: British Association for Early Childhood Education.

Dowling, M. (2010) (3rd edn) *Young Children's Personal, Social and Emotional Development*, London: Sage.

Drayton, S., Turley-Ames, K. J., and Guajardo, N. R. (2011) 'Counterfactual thinking and false belief: the role of executive function', *Journal of Experimental Child Psychology*, 108: 532–48.

Driver, R. (1983) *The Pupil as Scientist?*, Milton Keynes: Open University Press.

Duckworth, E. (1987) *'The Having of Wonderful Ideas' and Other Essays on Teaching and Learning*, New York: Teachers College Press.

Duffy, B. (1998) *Supporting Creativity and Imagination in the Early Years*, Buckingham: Open University Press.

Dunn, J. (1987) 'Understanding feelings: the early stages', in J. Bruner and H. Haste (eds), *Making Sense,* London: Methuen, pp. 26–40.

Dunn, J. (1988) *The Beginnings of Social Understanding,* Oxford: Blackwell.

Dunn, J. (1993) *Young Children's Close Relationships: Beyond Attachment,* London: Sage.

Dunn, J. (2004a) *Children's Friendships,* Oxford: Blackwell Publishing.

Dunn, J. (2004b) 'Commentary: broadening the framework of theory-of-mind research', *International Journal of Behavioral Development,* 28(3), *Supplement Newsletter,* 1/45: 13–14.

Dunn, J. (2005) 'Relationships and children's discovery of the mind', British Academy/British Psychological Society Annual Lecture, London, 5 April.

Dunn, J., Cutting, A. L., and Fisher, N. (2002) 'Old friends, new friends: predictors of children's perspective on their friends at school', *Child Development,* 73(2): 621–35.

Dunn, J., Brown, J., Slomkowski, C., Tesla, C., and Youngblade, L. (1991) 'Young children's understanding of other people's feelings and beliefs: individual differences and their antecedents', *Child Development,* 62: 1352–66.

Durden, T., and Dangel, J. R. (2008) 'Teacher-involved conversations with young children during small group activity', *Early Years,* 28(3): 251–66.

Dweck, C. S. (2000) *Self-Theories: Their Role in Motivation, Personality and Development,* Hove: Psychology Press.

Dweck, C. S. (2007) 'The perils and promises of praise', *Educational Leadership,* 65(2): 34–9.

Edwards, C., Gandini, L., and Forman, G. (1998) (2nd edn) *The Hundred Languages of Children,* Westport, CT: Ablex.

Edwards, S. (2003) 'New directions: charting the paths for the role of sociocultural theory in early childhood education and curriculum', *Contemporary Issues in Early Childhood,* 4(3): 251–66.

Elfer, P. (2006) 'Exploring children's expressions of attachment in nursery', *European Early Childhood Education Research Journal,* 14(2): 81–95.

Elias, C. L., and Berk, L. E. (2002) 'Self-regulation in young children: is there a role for sociodramatic play?', *Early Childhood Research Quarterly,* 17: 216–38.

Ellis, S., and Kleinberg, S. (2000) 'Exploration and enquiry', in M. de Boo (ed.), *Science 3–6: Laying the Foundations in the Early Years,* Hatfield: Association for Science Education, pp. 15–27.

Elman, J. L. (2005) 'Connectionist models of cognitive development: where next?', *TRENDS in Cognitive Sciences,* 9(3): 111–17.

Escobedo, T. H. (1999) 'The canvas of play: a study of children's play behaviors while drawing', in S. Reifel (ed.), *Play and Culture Studies,* vol. 2, Stanford CA: Ablex Publishing, pp. 101–22.

Evans, R., and Jones, D. (eds) (2008) *Metacognitive Approaches to Developing Oracy,* London: Routledge.

Fabricus, W. V., Boyer, T. W., Weimer, A. A., and Carroll, K. (2010) 'True or false: do 5-year-olds understand belief?', *Developmental Psychology,* 46(6): 1402–16.

Farver, J. A., and Shin, Y. L. (1997) 'Social pretend play in Korean- and Anglo-American preschoolers', *Child Development,* 68(3): 544–56.

Fawcett, L. M., and Garton, A. F. (2005) 'The effect of peer collaboration on children's problem-solving ability', *British Journal of Educational Psychology,* 75: 157–69.

Fernyhough, C. (2008) *The Baby in the Mirror,* London: Granta.

Feynman, R. (1986) *'Surely You're Joking, Mr Feynman!',* London: Counterpoint.

Filippova, E., and Astington, J. W. (2008) 'Further development in social reasoning revealed in discourse irony understanding', *Child Development,* 79(1): 126–38.

Fischer, K. W. (2009) 'Mind, brain and education: building a scientific groundwork for learning and teaching', *Mind, Brain and Education* 3(1): 3–16.

Fisher, J. (ed.) (2002) *The Foundations of Learning,* Buckingham: Open University Press.

Fisher, R. (1996) *Stories for Thinking,* Oxford: Nash Pollock.

Fisher, R. (1998) *Teaching Thinking: Philosophical Enquiry in the Classroom,* London: Cassell.

Fisher, R. (2001) 'Philosophy in primary schools: fostering thinking skills and literacy', *Reading,* 35(2): 67–73.

Fisher, R. (2005) (2nd edn) *Teaching Children to Think,* Oxford: Basil Blackwell.

Fisher, R. (2008) 'Dialogic teaching: developing thinking and metacognition through philosophical discussion', in R. Evans and D. Jones (eds), *Metacognitive Approaches to Developing Oracy*, London: Routledge.

Flavell, J. H. (1977) *Cognitive Development*, Englewood Cliffs, NJ: Prentice Hall.

Flavell, J. H. (1979) 'Metacognition and cognitive monitoring', *American Psychologist* 34(10): 906–11.

Flavell, J. H., and Hartman, B. M. (2004) 'What children know about mental experiences', *Young Children*, 59(2): 102–8.

Flavell, J. H., Flavell, E. R., and Green, F. L. (2001) 'Development of children's understanding of connections between thinking and feeling', *Psychological Science*, 12(5): 430–2.

Fleer, M. (2006) 'The cultural construction of child development: creating institutional and cultural subjectivity', *International Journal of Early Years Education*, 14(2): 127–40.

Foote, R. C., and Holmes-Lonergan, H. A. (2003) 'Sibling conflict and theory of mind', *British Journal of Developmental Psychology*, 21: 45–58.

Forman, G. E. (1989) 'Helping children ask good questions', in B. Neugebauer (ed.), *The Wonder of It: Exploring How the World Works*, Redmond, WA: Exchange Press, pp. 21–4.

Forman, G. E. (1999) 'Instant video revisiting: the video camera as a "tool of the mind" for young children', *Early Childhood research and Practice*, 1(2). Online: <http: //ecrp.uiuc.edu/v1n2/forman.html> (accessed Feb. 2005).

Frampton, K. L., Perlman, M., and Jenkins, J. M. (2009) 'Caregivers' use of metacognitive language in child care centers: prevalence and predictors', *Early Childhood Research Quarterly*, 24: 248–62.

Frost, R. (1915) 'The death of the hired man', *North of Boston*, New York: Henry Holt.

Fumoto, H., Robson, S., Greenfield, S., and Hargreaves, D. J. (2012) *Young Children's Creative Thinking*, London: Sage.

Gardner, H. (1979) 'Developmental psychology after Piaget: an approach in terms of symbolization', *Human Development*, 22: 73–88.

Gardner, H. (1983) *Frames of Mind*, London: Heinemann.

Gardner, H. (1991) *The Unschooled Mind*, London: Fontana.

Gardner, H. (1993) *Multiple Intelligences: The Theory in Practice*, New York: Basic Books.

Gardner, H. (1999) *The Disciplined Mind*, New York: Simon & Schuster.

Gardner, H. (2007) *Five Minds for the Future*, Boston MA: Harvard Business School Press.

Garton, A. (2004) *Exploring Cognitive Development: The Child as Problem-Solver*, Oxford: Blackwell.

Garvey, C. (1977) *Play*, Glasgow: Fontana.

Geake, J. G. (2009) *The Brain at School*, Maidenhead: Open University Press.

Gelman, R., and Gallistel, C. R. (1978) *The Child's Understanding of Number*, Cambridge, MA: Harvard University Press.

Gerhardt, S. (2004) *Why Love Matters*, London: Routledge.

Giffin, H. (1984) 'The coordination of meaning in the creation of a shared make-believe reality', in I. Bretherton (ed.), *Symbolic Play: The Development of Social Understanding*, New York: Academic Press.

Gifford, S. (2004a) 'Between the secret garden and the hothouse: children's responses to number focused activities in the nursery', *European Early Childhood Education Research Journal*, 12(2): 87–100.

Gifford, S. (2004b) 'A new mathematics pedagogy for the early years: in search of principles for practice', *International Journal of Early Years Education*, 12(2): 99–115.

Gifford, S. (2005) *Teaching Mathematics 3–5*, Maidenhead: Open University Press.

Glauert, E., Heal, C., and Cook, J. (2007) 'Knowledge and understanding of the world', in J. Riley (ed.), *Learning in the Early Years*, London: Sage.

Gold, K. (2002) 'Pick a brain', *Times Educational Supplement: Friday Section* (20 Sept.).

Goldschmied, E., and Jackson, S. (2004) (2nd edn) *People under Three*, London: Routledge.

Goleman, D. (1996) *Emotional Intelligence*, London: Bloomsbury.

Goleman, D. (1999) *Working with Emotional Intelligence*, London: Bloomsbury.

Gopnik, A., Meltzoff, A., and Kuhl, P. (1999) *How Babies Think*, London: Weidenfeld & Nicolson.

Gordon Institute for Music Learning: Early Childhood. (n.d.) Online: <http://www.giml.org/mlt_earlychildhood.php> (accessed Dec. 2010).

Goswami, U. (2004) 'Neuroscience, education and special education', *British Journal of Special Education*, 31(4): 175–81.

Goswami, U. (2008) *Cognitive Development: The Learning Brain,* Hove: Psychology Press.

Grammer, J. K., Purtell, K. M., Coffman, J. L., and Ornstein, P. A. (2011) 'Relations between children's metamemory and strategic performance: time-varying covariates in early elementary school', *Journal of Experimental Child Psychology*, 108: 139–55.

Greata, J. (2006) *An Introduction to Music in Early Childhood Education,* New York: Thomson Delmar Learning.

Gregory, R. L. (1977) 'Psychology: towards a science of fiction', in M. Meek, A. Warlow, and G. Barton (eds), *The Cool Web: The Pattern of Children's Reading,* London: Bodley Head.

Grieshaber, S., and McArdle, F. (2010) *The Trouble with Play,* Maidenhead: Open University Press.

Gura, P. (ed.) (1992) *Exploring Learning: Young Children and Blockplay,* London: Paul Chapman.

Gutstein, S. E., and Whitney, T. (2002) 'Asperger Syndrome and the development of social competence', *Focus on Autism and Other Developmental Disabilities,* 17(3): 161–71.

Hadwin, A., and Järvelä, S. (2011) 'Introduction to a special issue on social aspects of self-regulated learning: where social and self meet in strategic regulation of learning', *Teachers College Record,* 113(2): 235–9.

Hall, E. (2009) 'Mixed Messages: the role and value of drawing in early education', *International Journal of Early Years Education,* 17(3): 179–90.

Hall, N., and Abbott, L. (eds) (1991) *Play in the Primary Curriculum,* London: Hodder & Stoughton.

Hall, N., and Martello, J. (eds) (1996) *Listening to Children Think,* London: Hodder & Stoughton.

Hall, N., and Robinson, A. (2nd edn) (2003) *Exploring Writing and Play in the Early Years,* London: David Fulton.

Halliday, M. A. K. (1985) *An Introduction to Functional Grammar,* London: Edward Arnold.

Hannust, T., and Kikas, E. (2010) 'Young children's acquisition of knowledge about the Earth: a longitudinal study', *Journal of Experimental Child Psychology,* 107: 164–80.

Harcourt, D., Perry, B., and Waller, T. (eds) (2011) *Researching Young Children's Perspectives,* London: Routledge.

Hargreaves, D. J. (1986) *The Developmental Psychology of Music,* Cambridge: Cambridge University Press.

Harris, P. L. (1989) *Children and Emotion,* Oxford: Blackwell.

Haste, H. (1987) 'Growing into rules', in J. Bruner and H. Haste (eds), *Making Sense,* London: Methuen, pp. 163–95.

Hatano, G. (2004) 'Commentary: Socializing and Relativizing ToM', *International Journal of Behavioral Development,* 28(3), Supplement Newsletter, 1/45: 15–16.

Hatano, G., and Inagaki, K. (1992) 'Desituating cognition through the construction of conceptual knowledge', in P. Light and G. Butterworth (eds), *Context and Cognition,* London: Harvester, pp. 115–33.

Haynes, J. (2002) *Children as Philosophers,* London: RoutledgeFalmer.

Haynes, J. (2003) 'Philosophising with young children', *Early Education* (Summer): 5–6.

Heal, C., and Cook, J. (1998) 'Humanities: developing a sense of place and time in the early years', in I. Siraj-Blatchford (ed.), *A Curriculum Development Handbook for Early Childhood Educators,* Stoke on Trent: Trentham, pp. 121–36.

Heath, S. B. (1983) *Ways with Words,* Cambridge: Cambridge University Press.

Hedegaard, M. (2005) 'A cultural-historical perspective on children's cognitive development', *International Journal of Behavioural Development,* 29(3), Supplement Newsletter, 1/47: 12–15.

Hendy, L., and Whitebread, D. (2000) 'Interpretations of independent learning in the early years', *International Journal of Early Years Education,* 8(3): 243–52.

Henning, A., Spinath, F. M., and Aschersleben, G. (2011) 'The link between preschoolers' executive function and theory of mind and the role of epistemic states', *Journal of Experimental Child Psychology,* 108: 513–31.

Hester, P. P., Hendrickson, J. M., and Gable, R. A. (2009) 'Forty years later: the value of praise, ignoring and rules for pre-schoolers at risk for behavior disorders', *Education and Treatment of Children*, 32(4): 513–35.

Higgins, S., Baumfield, V., Lin, M., Moseley, D., Butterworth, M., Downey, G., Gregson, G., Oberski, I., Rockett, M., and Thacker, D. (2004) *Thinking Skills Approaches to Effective Teaching and Learning: What is the Evidence for Impact on Learners?* (Research Evidence in Education Library), London: EPPI Centre, Social Science Research Unit, Institute of Education.

Hindle, D., and Smith, M. C. (1999) *Personality Development: A Psychoanalytic Perspective*, London: Routledge.

Hobson, P. (2002) *The Cradle of Thought: Exploring the Origins of Thinking*, London: Macmillan.

Hohmann, M., and Weikart, D. (1995) *Educating Young Children: Active Learning Practices for Preschool and Childcare Programs*, Ypsilanti, MI: High/Scope Education Research Foundation.

Holland, P. (2003) *We Don't Play with Guns Here*, Maidenhead: Open University Press.

Hoodless, P. (1996a) 'Children talking about the past', in N. Hall and J. Martello (eds), *Listening to Children Think*, London: Hodder & Stoughton, pp. 100–16.

Hoodless, P. (1996b) *Teaching of History in the Primary School 69: Time and Timelines in the Primary School*, London: Historical Association.

Hope, G. (2002) 'Solving problems: young children exploring the rules of the game', *Curriculum Journal*, 13(3): 265–78.

Howard-Jones, P. (2007) *Neuroscience and Education: Issues and Opportunities. A Commentary by the Teaching and Learning Research Programme*, London: Economic and Social Research Council.

Howe, C., and Mercer, N. (2007) *Children's Development, Peer Interaction and Classroom Learning: Research Survey 2/1b for The Primary Review*, Cambridge: Faculty of Education, University of Cambridge.

Hughes, C., Deater-Deckard, K., and Cutting, A. L. (1999) '"Speak roughly to your little boy"? Sex differences in the relations between parenting and preschoolers' understanding of the mind, *Social Development*, 8(2): 143–60.

Hughes, C., Jaffee, S. R., Happé, F., Taylor, A., Caspi, A., and Moffitt, T. E. (2005) 'Origins of individual differences in theory of mind: from nature to nurture?', *Child Development*, 76(2): 356–70.

Hughes, M. (1986) *Children and Number*, Oxford: Basil Blackwell.

Hughes, M., and Westgate, D. (1988) 'Re-appraising talk in nursery and reception classes', *Education 3–13*, 16(2): 9–15.

Hutchins, P. (1997) *Titch*, London: Red Fox.

Hutt, C. (1979) 'Exploration and play (#2)', in B. Sutton-Smith (ed.), *Play and Learning*, New York: Gardner Press, pp. 175–94.

Hutt, J., Tyler, S., Hutt, C., and Christopherson, H. (1989) *Play, Exploration and Learning: A Natural History of the Preschool*, London: Routledge.

Immordino-Yang, M.H. (2011). Implications of affective and social neuroscience for educational theory. *Educational Philosophy and Theory*, 43(1), 98–103.

Immordino-Yang, M.H., & Damasio, A.R. (2007). We feel, therefore we learn: The relevance of affective and social neuroscience to education. *Mind, Brain and Education*, 1(1): 3–10.

Inhelder, B., and Piaget, J. (1964) *The Early Growth of Logic in the Child*, London: Routledge.

Inkpen, M. (1993) *Kipper's Birthday*, London: Hodder Children's Books.

Isaacs, S. (1930) *Intellectual Growth in Young Children*, London: Routledge & Kegan Paul.

James, A., and Prout, A. (eds) (1997) *Constructing and Reconstructing Childhood: Contemporary Issues in the Sociological Study of Childhood*, London: Falmer Press.

Johnson, S. (2001) *Teaching Thinking Skills*, Impact No. 8, London: Philosophy of Education Society of Great Britain.

Johnson, S.C., Dweck, C.S., and Chen, F.S. (2007) 'Evidence for Infants' Internal Working Models of Attachment'. *Psychological Science*, 18(6):501-2.

Jolley, R. (2009) *Children and Pictures: Drawing and Understanding*, Chichester: Wiley-Blackwell.

Jordan, B. (2009) 'Scaffolding learning and co-constructing understandings', in A. Anning, J. Cullen, and M. Fleer (eds), *Early Childhood Education: Society and Culture*, London: Sage, pp. 39–52.

Jones, R., and Wyse, D. (2004) *Creativity in the Primary Curriculum*, London: David Fulton.

Karlsdóttir, K., and Garðarsdóttir, B. (2010) 'Exploring children's learning stories as an assessment method for research and practice', *Early Years*, 30(3): 255–66.

Karmiloff-Smith, A. (1994) *Baby it's you*, London: Ebury Press.

Karpov, Y. V. (2006) *The Neo-Vygotskian Approach to Child Development*, Cambridge: Cambridge University Press.

Katz, L., and Chard, S. (2000) (2nd edn) *Engaging Children's Minds*, Norwood, NJ: Ablex.

Kaufmann, G. (2003) 'What to measure? A new look at the concept of creativity', *Scandinavian Journal of Educational Research*, 47(3): 235–51.

Kehily, M. J. (ed.) (2009) (2nd edn) *An Introduction to Childhood Studies*, Maidenhead: Open University Press.

Kellogg, R. (1969) *Analyzing Children's Art*, Palo Alto, CA: Mayfield Publishing Co.

Kenner, C., Wells, K., and Williams, H. (1996) 'Assessing a bilingual child's talk in different classroom contexts', in N. Hall and J. Martello (eds), *Listening to Children Think: exploring talk in the early years*, London: Hodder & Stoughton, pp. 117–30.

Krafft, K. C., and Berk, L. E. (1998) 'Private speech in two preschools: significance of open-ended activities and make-believe play for verbal self-regulation', *Early Childhood Research Quarterly*, 13(4): 637–58.

Kuhn, D. (2000) 'Does memory development belong on an endangered topic list?', *Child Development*, 71(1): 21–5.

Laevers, F. (ed.) (1994) *The Leuven Involvement Scale for Young Children* (manual and video), Experiential Education Series, 1, Leuven: Centre for Experiential Education.

Laevers, F. (1999) 'The Project Experiential Education: well-being and involvement make the difference', *Early Education* (Spring).

Laevers, F. (2000) 'Forward to Basics! Deep-Level-Learning and the Experiential Approach', *Early Years*, 20(2): 20–9.

Lagattuta, K. H., Wellman, H. M., and Flavell, J. H. (1997) 'Preschoolers' understanding of the link between thinking and feeling: cognitive cuing and emotional change', *Child Development*, 68(6): 1081–1104.

Lambert, B. (2000) 'Problem-solving in the first years of school', *Australian Journal of Early Childhood*, 25(3): 32–8.

Lambert, B. (2005) 'Children's drawing and painting from a cognitive perspective: a longitudinal study', *Early Years*, 25(3): 249–69.

Lambert, B. (2007) 'Diagrammatic representation and event memory in preschoolers', *Early Years*, 27(1): 65–75.

Larkin, S. (2010) *Metacognition in Young Children*, London: Routledge.

Lave, J., and Wenger, E. (1992) *Situated Learning: Legitimate Peripheral Participation*, Cambridge: Cambridge University Press.

Layard, R., and Dunn, J. (2009) *A Good Childhood*, London: Penguin.

Learning and Skills Research Centre (LSRC) (2004) *Should we be Using Learning Styles? What Research has to Say to Practice*, London: Learning and Skills Development Agency.

Leat, D. (1999) 'Rolling the stone uphill: teacher development and the implementation of thinking skills programmes', *Oxford Review of Education*, 25(3): 387–403.

LeDoux, J. (1998) *The Emotional Brain*, London: Phoenix.

LeDoux, J. (2003) *Synaptic Self*, London: Penguin.

Lee, V. L., and Das Gupta, P. (1995) *Children's Cognitive and Language Development*, Milton Keynes: Open University in Association with Blackwell Publishers.

Leslie, A. M. (1987) 'Pretense and representation: the origins of "theory of mind"', *Psychological Review*, 94: 412–26.

Lever, R., and Sénéchal, M. (2011) 'Discussing stories: on how dialogic reading intervention improves kindergartners' oral narrative construction', *Journal of Experimental Child Psychology*, 108: 1–24.

LeVine, R. A., and New, R. S. (eds) (2008) *Anthropology and Child Development*, Oxford: Blackwell.

LeVine, R. A. and Norman, K. (2008) 'Attachment in Anthropological Perspective', in *Anthropology and Child Development*, (eds) R.A. LeVine and R.S. New, Oxford: Blackwell, pp.127-42.

Lewis, L., and Rowley, C. (2002) 'Issues arising in the use of philosophical enquiry with children to develop thinking skills', *Education 3–13* (June): 52–5.

Licht, B., Simoni, H., and Perrig-Chiello, P. (2008) 'Conflict between peers in infancy and toddler age: what do they fight about?', *Early Years*, 28(3): 235–49.

Light, P., and Butterworth, G. (1992) *Context and Cognition*, London: Harvester.

Lipman, M. (1991) 'Philosophy for children', in A. L. Costa (ed.), *Developing Minds*, Alexandria, VA: Association for Supervision and Curriculum Development, pp. 35–8.

Lipman, M. (2003) *Thinking in Education*, Cambridge: Cambridge University Press.

Lipman, M., Sharp, A. M., and Oscanyan, F. S. (1980) *Philosophy in the Classroom*, Philadelphia: Temple University Press.

Lloyd, B. and Howe, N. (2003) 'Solitary play and convergent and divergent thinking skills in preschool children', *Early Childhood Research Quarterly*, 18: 22-41.

Lofdahl, A. (2005) '"The funeral": a study of children's shared meaning-making and its developmental significance', *Early Years*, 25(1): 5–16.

Lowenfeld, V., and Brittain, W. (1982) (7th edn) *Creative and Mental Growth*, New York: Macmillan.

Luwel, K., Foustana, A., Papadatos, Y., and Verschaffel, L. (2011) 'The role of intelligence and feedback in children's strategy competence', *Journal of Experimental Child Psychology*, 108: 61–76.

McBride-Chang, C., Zhou, Y., Cho, J-R., Aram, D. Levin, I., and Tolchinsky, L. (2011) 'Visual spatial skill: a consequence of learning to read?', *Journal of Experimental Child Psychology*, 109: 256–62.

McGregor, D. (2007) *Developing Thinking Developing Learning*, Maidenhead: Open University Press.

McGuinness, C. (1999) *From Thinking Skills to Thinking Classrooms* (Research Report 115), London: DfEE.

McGuinness, C. (2006) *Building Thinking Skills in Thinking Classrooms, ACTS (Activating Children's Thinking Skills) in Northern Ireland, Teaching and Learning Research Briefing*, 18, for Teaching and Learning Research Programme, online: <www.tlrp.org> (accessed March 2009).

McKendree, J., Small, C., Stenning, K., and Conlon, T. (2002) 'The role of representation in teaching and learning critical thinking', *Educational Review*, 54(1): 57–67.

MacNaughton, G. (2003) *Shaping Early Childhood*, Maidenhead: Open University Press.

MacNaughton, G., and Williams, G. (2009) *Teaching Young Children*, Maidenhead: Open University Press.

Majid, A., Bowerman, M., Kita, S., Haun, D. B. M., and Levinson, S. C. (2004) 'Can language restructure cognition? The case for space', *Trends in Cognitive Science*, 8(3): 108–14.

Marchant, J. (2008) 'A way with words', *New Scientist* (5 July): 44–5.

Marsh, J. (2005) 'Digikids: young children, popular culture and media', in N. Yelland (ed.), *Critical Issues in Early Childhood Education*, Maidenhead: Open University Press, pp. 181–96.

Marnat, M. (1974) *Klee*, London: Spurbooks.

Matthews, J. (2003) *Drawing and Painting: Children and Visual Representation*, London: Paul Chapman Publishing.

Mayr, T., and Ulich, M. (2009) 'Social-emotional well-being and the resilience of children in early childhood settings – PERIK: an empirically based observation scale for practitioners', *Early Years*, 29(1): 45–57.

Meade, A., and Cubey, P. (2008) *Thinking Children*, Maidenhead: Open University      Press.

Meadows, S. (2006) *The Child as Thinker*, London: Routledge.

Meadows, S. (2010) *The Child as Social Person*, London: Routledge.

Medcalf Davenport, N. A. (2003) 'Questions, answers and wait-time: implications for assessment of young children', *International Journal of Early Years Education*, 11(3): 245–53.

Medin, D. L., Ross, B. H., and Markman, A. B. (2005) *Cognitive Psychology*, Hoboken, NJ: John Wiley.

Meins, E. (1997) *Security of Attachment and the Social Development of Cognition*, Hove: Psychology Press.

Meins, E. (1999) 'Sensitivity, security and internal working models: bridging the transmission gap'. *Attachment and Human Development*, 1: 325–42.

Mercer, N. (2000) *Words and Minds*, London: Routledge.

Mercer, N. (2011) 'Dialogue for the development of self-regulation in the classroom', BJEP Psychological Aspects of Education Current Trends Conference: Self-Regulation and Dialogue in Primary Classrooms, University of Cambridge, 2 and 3 June.

Mercer, N., and Littleton, K. (2007) *Dialogue and the Development of Children's Thinking*, London: Routledge.

Midgley, M. (2002) 'It's all in the mind', review of *The Blank Slate*, *Guardian Review* (21 Sept.): 10.

Miller, L. (1999) 'Babyhood: becoming a person in the family', in D. Hindle and M.V. Smith (eds), *Personality Development: A Psychoanalytic Perspective*, London: Routledge, pp. 33–47.

Miller, L., and Pound, L. (2011) *Theories and Approaches to Learning in the Early Years*, London: Sage.

Miller, L., Cable, C., and Goodliff, G. (2010) (2nd edn) *Supporting Children's Learning in the Early Years*, London: Routledge in association with the Open University.

Milligan, K., Astington, J.W. and Dack, L.A. (2007) 'Language and theory of Mind: Meta-Analysis of the Relation Between Language Ability and False-belief Understanding. *Child Development*, 78(2): 622-46.

Ministry of Education, New Zealand (1996) *Te Whariki; Early Childhood Curriculum*, Auckland, NZ: New Zealand Learning Media Ltd.

Monette, S., Bigras, M., and Guay, M-C. (2011) 'The role of the executive functions in school achievement at the end of Grade 1', *Journal of Experimental Child Psychology*, 109: 158–73.

Moore, C. (2004) *George and Sam*, London: Penguin Viking.

Motluk, A. (2002) 'You are what you speak', *New Scientist* (30 Nov.): 34–8.

Moyles, J., Adams, S., and Musgrove, A. (2002) *SPEEL Study of Pedagogical Effectiveness in Early Learning* (Research Report 363), London: DfES.

Munn, P. (1997) 'Children's beliefs about counting', in I. Thompson (ed.), *Teaching and Learning Early Number*, Buckingham: Open University Press, pp. 9–19.

Murphy, P. (ed.) (1997) *Making Sense of Science Study Guide*, Buckingham: SPE/Open University.

Murris, K. (2000) 'Can children do philosophy?', *Journal of Philosophy of Education*, 34(2): 261–79.

Naito, M. (2004) 'Is theory of mind a universal and unitary construct?', *International Journal of Behavioral Development*, 28(3), Supplement Newsletter, 1/45: 9–11.

National Advisory Committee on Creative and Cultural Education (NACCCE) (1999) *All Our Futures*, Sudbury: Department for Education and Employment.

National Oracy Project (1990) *Teaching, Talking and Learning in Key Stage 1*, York: National Curriculum Council.

Navarra, J. (1955) *The Development of Scientific Concepts in a Young Child*, Westport, CT: Greenwood.

Nelson, K. (2004) 'Commentary: the future of ToM lies in CoM', *International Journal of Behavioral Development*, 28(3), Supplement Newsletter, 1/45: 16–17.

Nunes, T. (1995) 'Mathematical and scientific thinking', in V. Lee and P. Das Gupta (eds), *Children's Cognitive and Language Development*, Milton Keynes: Open University in association with Blackwell Publishers, pp. 189–229.

Nunes, T. (2005) 'What we learn in school: the socialization of cognition', *International Journal of Behavioral Development*, 29(3), Supplement Newsletter, 1/47: 10–12.

Nunes, T., and Bryant, P. (eds) (1997) *Learning and Teaching Mathematics: An International Perspective*, Hove: Psychology Press.

Nutbrown, C. (2011) (4th edn) *Threads of Thinking: Young Children Learning*, London: Sage.

Olson, K. R., and Dweck, C. S. (2008) 'A blueprint for social cognitive development', *Perspectives on Psychological Science*, 3(3): 193–202.

Pachet, F., and Addessi, A. R. (2004) 'When children reflect on their playing style: experiments with the Continuator and children', *ACM Computers in Entertainment*, 2(2) (Jan.).

Paley, V. G. (1981) *Wally's Stories*, Cambridge, MA: Harvard University Press.

Paley, V. G. (1986) 'On listening to what the children say', *Harvard Educational Review*, 56(2): 122–31.

Paley, V. G. (1993) *You Can't Say You Can't Play*, Cambridge, MA: Harvard University Press.

Paley, V. G. (2004) *A Child's Work*, Chicago: University of Chicago Press.

Palmer, J. (1993) *Geography in the Early Years*, London: Routledge.

Panagiotaki, G., Nobes, G., and Potton, A. (2009) 'Mental models and other misconceptions in children's understanding of the earth', *Journal of Experimental Child Psychology*, 104: 52–67.

Papaleontiou-Louca, E. (2003) 'The concept and instruction of metacognition', *Teacher Development*, 7(1): 9–30.

Papatheodorou, T., and Moyles, J. (eds) (2009) *Learning Together in the Early Years*, London: Routledge.

Pascal, C., and Bertram, T. (2002) 'Assessing what matters in the early years', in J. Fisher (ed.), *The Foundations of Learning*, Buckingham: Open University Press, pp. 87–101.

Patterson, K. (2009) 'Improvisation: children making their own music', in F. Griffiths (ed.), *Supporting Children's Creativity through Music, Dance, Drama and Art*, London: Routledge.

Pellicano, E., and Rhodes, G. (2003) 'The role of eye-gaze in understanding other minds', *British Journal of Developmental Psychology*, 21: 33–43.

Penn, H. (2005) *Understanding Early Childhood*, Maidenhead: Open University Press.

Perels, F., Merget-Kullmann, M., Wende, M., Schmitz, B., and Buchbinder, C. (2009) 'Improving self-regulated learning of preschool children: evaluation of training for kindergarten teachers', *British Journal of Educational Psychology*, 79: 311–27.

Perkins, D. N. (1992) *Smart Schools*, New York: Free Press.

Perkins, D. N. (1994) *The Intelligent Eye: Learning to Think by Looking at Art*, Occasional Paper 4, Santa Monica, CA: Getty Center for Education in the Arts.

Perkins, D., Tishman, S., Ritchhart, R., Donis, K., and Andrade, A. (2000) 'Intelligence in the wild: a dispositional view of intellectual traits', *Educational Psychology Review*, 12(3): 269–93.

Perlman, S. B., and Pelphrey, K. A. (2011) 'Developing connections for affective regulation: age-related changes in emotional brain connectivity', *Journal of Experimental Child Psychology*, 108: 611–20.

Perner, J. (2004) 'Tracking the essential mind', *International Journal of Behavioral Development*, 28(3), *Supplement Newsletter*, 1/45: 4–7.

Perry, N. E. (2011) 'Understanding classroom processes that support children's regulation of learning', BJEP Psychological Aspects of Education Current Trends Conference: Self-Regulation and Dialogue in Primary Classrooms, University of Cambridge, 2 and 3 June.

Perry, N. E., VandeKamp, K. O., Mercer, L. K., and Nordby, C. J. (2002) 'Investigating teacher-student interactions that foster self-regulated learning', *Educational Psychologist*, 37(1): 5–15.

Peters, S., and Davis, K. (2011) 'Fostering children's working theories: pedagogic issues and dilemmas in New Zealand', *Early Years*, 31(1): 5–17.

Peterson, C. C. (2004) 'Journeys of mind: ToM development in children with autism, sensory or motor disabilities', *International Journal of Behavioral Development*, 28(3), *Supplement Newsletter*, 1/45: 11–13.

Peterson, C. (2011) 'Children's memory reports over time: getting both better and worse', *Journal of Experimental Child Psychology*, 109: 275–93.

Phillips, H. (2008) 'Beautiful minds', *New Scientist* (4 Oct.): 28–33.

Piaget, J. (1950) *The Psychology of Intelligence*, London: Routledge & Kegan Paul.

Piaget, J. (1952) *The Child's Conception of Number*, London: Routledge & Kegan Paul.

Piaget, J. (1959) *The Language and Thought of the Child*, London: Routledge & Kegan Paul.

Piaget, J. (1962) *Play, Dreams and Imitation in Childhood*, London: Routledge & Kegan Paul.

Piazza, G., and Barozzi, A. (2001) 'The City of Reggio Emilia', in *Making Learning Visible: Children as Individual and Group Learners*, Project Zero and Reggio Children, Reggio Emilia, Italy: Reggio Children, pp. 228–45.

Pickering, S. J., and Howard-Jones, P. A. (2007) 'Educators' views on the role of neuroscience in education: a study of UK and international perspectives', *Mind, Brain and Education*, 1(3): 109–13.

Pinker, S. (1994) *The Language Instinct*, London: Penguin.

Pinker, S. (1997) *How The Mind Works*, London: Penguin.

Pinker, S. (2002) *The Blank Slate*, London: Penguin.

Pinker, S. (2007) *The Stuff of Thought*, London: Allen Lane.

Pintrich, P. R. (2000) 'The role of goal orientation in self-regulated learning', in M. Boekaerts, P. R. Pintrich, and M. Zeidner (eds), *Handbook of Self-Regulation*, San Diego, CA: Academic Press, pp. 451–502.

Pound, L. (2006) *Supporting Mathematical Development in the Early Years*, Maidenhead: Open University Press

Pound, L. (2010) 'Born mathematical?', in L. Miller, C. Cable, and G. Goodliff (ed.), *Supporting Children's Learning in the Early Years*, London: Routledge in association with the Open University, pp. 151–7.

Pound, L., and Harrison, C. (2003) *Supporting Musical Development in the Early Years*, Buckingham: Open University Press.

Powers, N., and Trevarthen, C. (2009) 'Voices of shared emotion and meaning: young infants and their mothers in Scotland and Japan', in S. Malloch and C. Trevarthen (eds), *Communicative Musicality: Exploring the Basis of Human Companionship*, Oxford: Oxford University Press, pp. 209–40.

Pramling, I. (1988) 'Developing children's thinking about their own thinking', *British Journal of Educational Psychology*, 58: 266–78.

Pramling Samuelson, I. (2004) 'How do children tell us about their childhoods?', *Early Childhood Research and Practice*, 6(1). Online: <http://ecrp.uiuc.edu/v6n1/pramling.html> (accessed Feb. 2005).

Prentice, R. (1994) 'Experiential Learning in Play and Art', in J. Moyles (ed.), *The Excellence of Play*, Buckingham: Open University Press.

Prentice, R. (2000) 'Creativity: a reaffirmation of its place in early childhood education', *Curriculum Journal*, 11(2): 145–58.

Project Zero and Reggio Children (2001) *Making Learning Visible: Children as Individual and Group Learners*, Reggio Emilia, Italy: Reggio Children.

Qu, L. (2011) 'Two is better than one, but mine is better than ours: pre-schoolers' executive function during co-play', *Journal of Experimental Child Psychology*, 108: 549–66.

Quinn, P. C., Doran, M. M., and Papafragou, A. (2011) 'Does changing the reference frame affect infant categorization of the spatial relation BETWEEN?', *Journal of Experimental Child Psychology*, 109: 109–22.

Raban, B., Ure, C., and Waniganayake, M. (2003) 'Multiple perspectives: acknowledging the virtue of complexity in measuring quality', *Early Years*, 23(1): 67–77.

Rees, G., Bradshaw, J., Goswami, H., and Keung, A. (2010) *Understanding Children's Well-Being: A National Survey of Young People's Well-Being*. London: Children's Society.

Reggio Children (1996) *The Hundred Languages of Children* (exhibition catalogue), Reggio Emilia, Italy: Reggio Children.

Reifel, S. (ed.) (1999) *Play and Culture Studies*, vol. 2, Stanford, CA: Ablex Publishing.

Resnick, L. B. (ed.) (1989) *Knowing, Learning and Instruction*, Hillsdale, NJ: Lawrence Erlbaum Associates.

Revell, P. (2005) 'Each to their own', *Education Guardian* (31 May): 6–7.

Richards, R. (2006) 'Frank Barron and the Study of Creativity: A Voice That Lives on'. *Journal of Humanistic Psychology*, 46(3): 352-70.

Richetti, C., and Sheerin, J. (1999) 'Helping students ask the right questions', *Educational Leadership*, 57(3): 58–62.

Rinaldi, C. (1998) 'Projected curriculum constructed through documentation – Progettazione: an interview with Lella Gandini', in C. Edwards, L. Gandini, and G. Forman (eds), *The Hundred Languages of Children*, Westport, CT: Ablex, pp. 113–25.

Rizzolatti, G., and Craighero, L. (2004) 'The mirror-neuron system', *Annual Review of Neuroscience*, 2004(27): 169–92.

Roberts, R. (2010) *Wellbeing from Birth*, London: Sage.

Robertson. A. (2004) 'Let's think! Two years on', *Primary Science Review*, 82: 4–7.

Robson, S. (2010) 'Self-regulation and metacognition in young children's self-initiated play and reflective dialogue', *International Journal of Early Years Education*, 18(3): 227–41.

Robson, S. (2011) 'Producing and using video data with young children: a case study of ethical questions and practical consequences', in D. Harcourt, B. Perry and T. Waller (eds), *Researching Young Children's Perspectives*, London: Routledge, pp. 178–92.

Robson, S. (2012) 'Children's experiences of creative thinking', in H. Fumoto, S. Robson, S. Greenfield, and D. J. Hargreaves (eds), *Young Children's Creative Thinking*, London: Sage.

Robson, S., and Fumoto, H. (2009) 'Practitioners' experiences of personal ownership and autonomy in their support for young children's thinking', *Contemporary Issues in Early Childhood*, 10(1): 43–54.

Robson, S., and Hargreaves, D. J. (2005) 'What do early childhood practitioners think about young children's thinking?', *European Early Childhood Education Research Journal*, 13(1): 81–96.

Rodd, J. (1999) 'Encouraging young children's critical and creative thinking skills', *Childhood Education*, 75(6): 350–5.

Rogers, S. (ed.) (2011) *Rethinking Play and Pedagogy in Early Childhood Education*, London: Routledge.

Rogers, S., and Evans, J. (2008) *Inside Role-Play in Early Childhood Education*, London: Routledge.

Rogoff, B. (1990) *Apprenticeship in Thinking: Cognitive Development in a Social Context*, Oxford: Oxford University Press.

Rogoff, B. (2003) *The Cultural Nature of Human Development*, Oxford: Oxford University Press.

Romaine, S. (2004) 'Bilingual Language Development', in K. Trott, S. Dobbinson and P. Griffiths (eds), *The Child Language Reader*, London: Routledge, 287–303.

Rosen, M., and Oxenbury, H. (1997) *We're Going on a Bear Hunt*, London: Walker Books.

Runco, M. A., Çayirdağ, N., and Acar, S. (2011) 'Quantitative research on creativity', in P. Thomson and J. Sefton-Green (eds), *Researching Creative Learning*, London: Routledge, pp. 153–71.

Salovey, P., and Mayer, J. D. (1990) 'Emotional intelligence', *Imagination, Cognition and Personality*, 9(3): 185–211.

Samuels, B.M. (2009) 'Can the differences between education and neuroscience be overcome by mind, brain and education?', *Mind, Brain and Education* 3(1): 45–55.

Sansone, A. (2004) *Mothers, Babies and their Body Language*, London: Karnac Books.

Sarama, J., and Clements, D. H. (2009) *Early Childhood Mathematics Education Research: Learning Trajectories for Young Children*, London: Routledge.

Schneider, W. (2008) 'The development of metacognitive knowledge in children and adolescents: major trends and implications for education', *Mind, Brain and Education*, 2(3): 114–21.

Schutte, N. S., Malouff, J. M., Simunek, M., McKenley, J., and Hollander, S. (2002) 'Characteristic emotional intelligence and emotional well-being', *Cognition and Emotion*, 16(6): 769–85.

Scoffham, S. (2003) 'Teaching, learning and the brain', *Education 3–13* (Oct.): 49–58.

Segar, S. (2004) 'If we want deep level learning we cannot do without involvement', unpublished thesis, University of Surrey Roehampton.

Selley, N. (1999) *The Art of Constructivist Teaching in the Primary School*, London: David Fulton.

Sharp, J. (ed.) (2002) *Primary Science: Teaching Theory and Practice*, Exeter: Learning Matters.

Sharp, J. (2004) 'Children's ideas' in J. Sharp (ed.), *Primary Science: Teaching Theory and Practice*, Exeter: Learning Matters, pp. 25–37.

Siegal, M., Butterworth, G., and Newcombe, P. A. (2004) 'Culture and children's cosmology', *Developmental Science*, 7(3): 308–24.

Siegler, R. S. (2000) 'The rebirth of children's learning', *Child Development*, 71(1): 26–35.

Siegler, R. S., and Alibali, M. W. (2005) (4th edn) *Children's Thinking*, Upper Saddle River, NJ: Prentice Hall.

Siegler, R., DeLoache, J., and Eisenberg, N. (2011) *How Children Develop*, New York: Worth.

Singer, J. L. (1973) *The Child's World of Make-Believe: Experimental Studies of Imaginative Play*, New York: Academic Press.

Siraj-Blatchford, I. (ed.) (1998) *A Curriculum Development Handbook for Early Childhood Educators*, Stoke on Trent: Trentham.

Siraj-Blatchford, I. (2007) 'Creativity, communication and collaboration: the identification of pedagogic progression in sustained shared thinking', *Asia-Pacific Journal of Research in Early Childhood Education*, 1(2): 3–23.

Siraj-Blatchford, I., and Manni, L. (2008) '"Would you like to tidy up now?" An analysis of adult questioning in the English Foundation Stage', *Early Years* 28(1): 5–22.

Siraj-Blatchford, I., Sylva, K., Muttock, S., Gilden, R., and Bell, D. (2002) *Researching Effective Pedagogy in the Early Years* (Research Report 356), London: DfES.

Smidt, S. (2009) *Introducing Vygotsky*, London: Routledge.

Smilansky, S., and Shefatya, L. (1990) *Facilitating Play*, Silver Spring, MD: Psychosocial and Educational Publications.

Smith, A. (1998) *Accelerated Learning in Practice*, Stafford: Network Educational Press.

Smith, A., and Call, N. (1999) *The ALPS Approach: Accelerated Learning in Practice,* Stafford: Network Educational Press.

Smith, P. K., Cowie, H., and Blades, M. (2011) (5th edn) *Understanding Children's Development,* Oxford: Blackwell.

Snow, C., De Blauw, A., and Van Roosmalen, G. (2008) 'Talking and playing with babies: ideologies of child-rearing', in R. A. LeVine and R. S. New (eds), *Anthropology and Child Development,* Oxford: Blackwell, pp. 115–26.

Sperling, R. A., Walls, R. T., and Hill, L. A. (2000) 'Early relationships among self-regulatory constructs: theory of mind and pre-school children's problem solving', *Child Study Journal,* 30(4): 233–53.

Spinney, L. (2010) 'Who's the oddball?', *New Scientist* (13 Nov.): 42–5.

Statham, J., and Chase, E. (2010) *Childhood Wellbeing: A Brief Overview,* London: Childhood Wellbeing Research Centre.

Sternberg, R. J. (1985) *Beyond IQ: A Triarchic Theory of Human Intelligence,* Cambridge: Cambridge University Press.

Sternberg, R. J. (1986) *Intelligence Applied: Understanding and Increasing your Intellectual Skills,* Orlando, FL: Harcourt Brace Jovanovich.

Sternberg, R. J. (2003) 'Creative thinking in the classroom', *Scandinavian Journal of Educational Research,* 47(3): 325–38.

Sutton-Smith, B. (ed.) (1979) *Play and Learning,* New York: Gardner Press.

Suzuki, S. (1969) *Nurtured by Love: A New Approach to Education,* New York: Exposition Press.

Swan, S., and White, R. (1994) *The Thinking Books,* London: Falmer Press.

Swanwick, K., and Tillman, J. (1986) 'The sequence of musical development', *British Journal of Music Education,* 3: 305–39.

Sylva, K., Bruner, J. S., and Genova, P. (1976) 'The role of play in the problem-solving of young children 3- to 5-years-of-age', in J. S. Bruner, A. Jolly and K. Sylva (eds), *Play, its Role in Development and Evolution,* Harmondsworth: Penguin, pp. 244–57.

Sylva, K., Roy, C., and Painter, M. (1980) *Childwatching at Playgroup and Nursery School,* London: Grant McIntyre.

Sylva, K., Melhuish, E., Sammons, P., Siraj-Blatchford, I., and Taggart, B. (2010) *Early Childhood Matters,* London: Routledge.

Sylwester, R. (2010) *A Child's Brain: The Need for Nurture,* Thousand Oaks, CA: Corwin.

Szarkowicz, D. L. (2000) 'When they wash him they'll know he'll be Harry: young children's thinking about thinking within a story context', *International Journal of Early Years Education,* 8(1): 71–82.

Taggart, G., Ridley, K., Rudd, P., and Benefield, P. (2005) *Thinking Skills in the Early Years: A Literature Review,* Slough: NFER.

Talay-Ongan, A. (2000) 'Neuroscience and early childhood: a necessary partnership', *Australian Journal of Early Childhood,* 25(2): 28–33.

Tavistock Clinic Foundation (2002) *Observation Observed Video 1: Fundamental Aspects of the Observation Approach,* London: Tavistock Clinic Foundation.

Thompson, I. (ed.) (1997) *Teaching and Learning Early Number,* Buckingham: Open University Press.

Thompson, R., and Nelson, C. A. (2001) 'Developmental science and the media: early brain development', *American Psychologist,* 56(1): 5–15.

Thomson, P., and Sefton-Green, J. (eds) (2011) *Researching Creative Learning,* London: Routledge.

Thornton, S. (2002) *Growing Minds,* Basingstoke: Palgrave Macmillan.

Tickell, C. (2011) *The Early Years: Foundations for Life, Health and Learning,* London: Department for Education.

Tizard, B., and Hughes, M. (2002) (2nd edn) *Young Children Learning: Talking and Thinking at Home and at School,* London: Fontana.

Trawick-Smith, J. (1998) 'A qualitative analysis of metaplay in the preschool years', *Early Childhood Research Quarterly,* 13(3): 433–52.

Trevarthen, C. (1995) 'The child's need to learn a culture', *Children and Society,* 9(1): 5–19.

Trevarthen, C. (2000) 'Musicality and the intrinsic motive pulse: evidence from human psychobiology and infant communication', *Musicae Scientiae*: special issue 1999–2000: 155–215.

Trickey, S., and Topping, K. J. (2004) ' "Philosophy for children": a systematic review', *Research Papers in Education*, 19(3): 365–80.

Trott, K., Dobbinson, S., and Griffiths, P. (eds) (2004) *The Child Language Reader*, London: Routledge.

Tyler, S. (1991) 'Play in relation to the National Curriculum', in N. Hall and L. Abbott (eds), *Play in the Primary Curriculum*, London: Hodder & Stoughton, pp. 10–28.

Umek, L. M., and Musek, P. L. (2001) 'Symbolic play: opportunities for cognitive and language development in preschool settings', *Early Years*, 21(1): 55–64.

United Nations (1989) *Convention on the Rights of the Child*. Online: <http://www.unicef.org/crc> (accessed Jan. 2008).

Valanides, N., Gritsi, F., Kampez, M., and Ravanis, K. (2000) 'Changing pre-school children's conceptions of the day/night cycle', *International Journal of Early Years Education*, 8(1): 27–39.

Vecchi, V. (2010) *Art and Creativity in Reggio Emilia*, London: Routledge.

Veenman, M. J., and Spaans, M. A. (2005) 'Relation between intellectual and metacognitive skills: age and task difference', *Learning and Individual Differences* 15(2): 159–76.

Veenman, M. V. J., Van Hout-Walters, B. H. A. M., and Afflerbach, P. (2006) 'Metacognition and learning: conceptual and methodological considerations', *Metacognition and Learning*, 1: 3–14.

Vygotsky, L. (1976) 'Play and its role in the mental development of the child', in J. S. Bruner, A. Jolly and K. Sylva (eds), *Play, its Role in Development and Evolution* (eds), Harmondsworth: Penguin, 537-54.

Vygotsky, L. (1978) *Mind in Society*, Cambridge, MA: Harvard University Press.

Vygotsky, L. (1986) *Thought and Language*, Cambridge, MA: MIT Press.

Vygotsky, L. (2004) 'Imagination and creativity in childhood', *Journal of Russian and East European Psychology*, 42(1): 7–97.

Waddell, M. (1989) *Once there were Giants*, London: Walker Books.

Wadsworth, P. (1997) 'Document 9: children's ideas in science', in P. Murphy (ed.), *Making Sense of Science Study Guide*, Buckingham: SPE/Open University.

Walkerdine, V. (2009) 'Developmental psychology and the study of childhood', in M. J. Kehily (ed.), *An Introduction to Childhood Studies* (2nd edn), Maidenhead: Open University Press, pp. 112–23.

Wall, K. (2004) *Autism and Early Years Practice*, London: Paul Chapman.

Wall, K. (2008) 'Understanding metacognition through the use of pupil views templates: pupil views of learning to learn', *Thinking Skills and Creativity*, 3: 23–33.

Wall, K., and Higgins, S. (2006) 'Facilitating metacognitive talk: a research and learning tool', *International Journal of Research and Method in Education*, 29(1): 39–53.

Wallace, B. (2002) *Teaching Thinking Skills across the Early Years*, London: David Fulton.

Waller, T. (ed) (2009) *An Introduction to Early Childhood*. (2nd ed.) London: Sage.

Walsh, G., Murphy, P., and Dunbar, C. (2007) *Thinking Skills in the Early Years: A Guide for Practitioners*, Belfast: Stranmillis University College. Online: <http://www.nicurriculum.org.uk/docs/skills_and_capabilities/foundation/ThinkingSkillsintheEarlyYears_Report.pdf> (accessed May 2011).

Waters, J. (2009) 'Well-being', in T. Waller (ed.) *An Introduction to Early Childhood* (2nd ed) London: Sage, pp. 16-30.

Watson, L. (1997) 'Children's misconceptions and conceptual change', *Australian Journal of Early Childhood*, 22(2): 12–16.

Wegerif, R. (2010) *Mind Expanding: Teaching for Thinking and Creativity in primary Education*, Maidenhead: Open University Press.

Weikum, W. M., Vouloumanos, A., Navarra, J., Soto-Faraco, S., Sebastián-Gallés, N., and Werker, J. F. (2007) 'Visual language discrimination in infancy', *Science*, 316(5828): 1159.

Wellman, H. M. (2004) 'Theory of mind: developing core human cognitions', *International Journal of Behavioral Development*, 28(3), *Supplement Newsletter*, 1/45: 1–4.

Wellman, H. M., and Liu, D. (2004) 'Scaling of theory-of-mind tasks', *Child Development*, 75(2): 523–41.

Wellman, H. M., Cross, D., and Watson, J. (2001) 'Meta-analysis of theory-of-mind development: the truth about false belief', *Child Development*, 72(3): 655–84.Social attention and prschool social cognition

Wellman, H. M., Phillips, A. T., Dunphy-Lelii, S., and LaLonde, N. (2004) 'Infant social attention predicts preschool social cognition', *Developmental Science* 7(3): 283–8.

Wells, G. (1987) *The Meaning Makers*, Sevenoaks: Hodder & Stoughton.

Whalley, M. J. (1991) 'Philosophy for children', in M. J. Coles and W. D. Robinson (eds), *Teaching Thinking: A Survey of Programmes in Education*, London: Bristol Classical Press, pp. 66–76.

White, J. (2002) *The Child's Mind*, London: Routledge Falmer.

Whitebread, D. (ed.) (2000a) *The Psychology of Teaching and Learning in the Primary School*, London: Routledge Falmer.

Whitebread, D. (2000b) 'Teaching children to think, reason, solve problems and be creative', in D. Whitebread (ed.), *The Psychology of Teaching and Learning in the Primary School*, London: Routledge Falmer, 140–64.

Whitebread, D. (2011) 'The characteristics, identification and assessment of self-regulation in young children', BJEP Psychological Aspects of Education Current Trends Conference: Self-Regulation and Dialogue in Primary Classrooms, University of Cambridge, 2 and 3 June.

Whitebread, D., and Coltman, P. (eds) (2008) (3rd edn) *Teaching and Learning in the Early Years*, London: Routledge.

Whitebread, D., Anderson, H., Coltman, P., Page, C., Pasternak, D. P., and Mehta, S. (2005) 'Developing independent learning in the early years', *Education 3–13*, 33(1).

Whitebread, D., Bingham, S., Grau, V., Pasternak, D. P., and Sangster, C. (2007) 'The development of metacognition and self-regulated learning in young children: the role of collaborative and peer-assisted learning', *Journal of Cognitive Education and Psychology* 6(3): 433–55.

Whitebread, D., Coltman, P., Pasternak, D. P., Sangster C., Grau, V., Bingham, S., Almeqdad, Q., and. Demetriou, D. (2009) 'The development of two observational tools for assessing metacognition and self-regulated learning in young children', *Metacognition and Learning* 4: 63–85.

Whitehead, M. (2002) (2nd edn) *Developing Language and Literacy with Young Children*, London: Paul Chapman.

Whitehead, M. (2010) (4th edn) *Language and Literacy in the Early Years*, London:Sage.

Wigfield, A., Klauda, S. L., and Cambria, J. (2011) 'Influences on the development of academic self-regulatory processes', in B. J. Zimmerman and D. H. Schunk (eds), *Handbook of Self-Regulation of Learning and Performance*, London: Routledge, pp. 33–48.

Willig, J. (1990) *Children's Concepts and the Primary Curriculum*, London: Paul Chapman.

Wilson, V. (2000) *Education Forum on Teaching Thinking Skills*, Report. Online: <http://www.scie-socialcareonline.org.uk/repository/fulltext/educthinking.pdf> (accessed June 2005).

Wolfe, P., and Brandt, R. (1998) 'What do we know from brain research?', *Educational Leadership* (Nov.): 8–13.

Wood, D. (1998) (2nd edn) *How Children Think and Learn*, Oxford: Blackwell.

Wood, D., and Wood, H. (1996) 'Vygotsky, tutoring and learning', *Oxford Review of Education*, 22(1): 5–16.

Wood, D. J., Bruner, J. S., and Ross, G. (1976) 'The role of tutoring in problem-solving', *Journal of Child Psychology and Psychiatry*, 17: 89–100.

Wood, E., and Attfield, J. (2005) *Play, Learning and the Early Childhood Curriculum*, London: Paul Chapman.

Woolfolk, A., Hughes, M., and Walkup, V. (2008) *Psychology in Education*, Harlow: Pearson.

Woolley, J. D. (1997) 'Thinking about fantasy: are children fundamentally different thinkers and believers?', *Child Development*, 68(6): 991–1011.

Worthington, M. (2007) 'Exceptional children: researching the young child's mathematics', *Maths Coordinator's File*, 25. Online: <http://www.childrens-mathematics.net/articles_exceptional_children.pdf> (accessed Feb. 2011).

Wright, S. (2010) *Understanding Creativity in Early Childhood*, London: Sage.

Wynn, K. (1992) 'Addition and subtraction by human infants', *Nature*, 358: 749–50.

Yamaguchi, M., Kuhlmeier, V. A., Wynn, K., and vanMarle, K. (2009) 'Continuity in social cognition from infancy to childhood', *Developmental Science*, 12(5): 746–52.

Young, S. (1995) 'Listening to the music of early childhood', *British Journal of Music Education*, 12(1): 51–8.

Young, S. (2003) 'The interpersonal dimension: a potential source of musical creativity for young children', *Musicae Scientiae*, special 10th anniversary conference issue 2003–4: 175–91.

Young, S., and Glover, J. (1998) *Music in the Early Years*, Abingdon: RoutledgeFalmer.

Zélanti, P. S., and Droit-Volet, S. (2011) 'Cognitive abilities explaining age-related changes in time perception of short and long durations', *Journal of Experimental Child Psychology*, 109: 143–57.

Zelazo, P. D., Müller, U., Frye, D., and Marcovitch, S. (2003) *The Development of Executive Function in Early Childhood*, Monographs of the Society for Research in Child Development, 68(3), serial no. 274.

Zentall, S. R., and Morris, B. J. (2010) '"Good job, you're so smart": the effects of inconsistency of praise type on young children's motivation', *Journal of Experimental Child Psychology*, 107: 155–63.

Zimmerman, B. J., and Schunk, D. H. (eds) (2011a) *Handbook of Self-Regulation of Learning and Performance*, London: Routledge.

Zimmerman, B. J., and Schunk, D. H. (2011b) 'Self-regulated learning and performance: an introduction and an overview', in B. J. Zimmerman and D. H. Schunk (eds), *Handbook of Self-Regulation of Learning and Performance*, London: Routledge, pp. 1–12.

# Index